HARVARD EAST ASIAN SERIES 36

The Rhetoric of Empire: American China Policy, 1895–1901

The East Asian Research Center at Harvard
University administers research projects
designed to further scholarly understanding
of China, Korea, Japan, and adjacent areas.

MARILYN BLATT YOUNG

The Rhetoric
of Empire

AMERICAN
CHINA
POLICY
1895–1901

Harvard University Press, Cambridge, Massachusetts, 1968

© Copyright 1968 by the President and Fellows of Harvard College
All rights reserved

Distributed in Great Britain by Oxford University Press, London

Preparation of this volume has been aided
by a grant from the Ford Foundation.

Library of Congress Catalog Card Number 68–54028
Printed in the United States of America

**This book is dedicated,
with love, to my parents,
Aaron and Mollie Blatt.**

Acknowledgments

I began this book as a doctoral dissertation at Harvard University, supported by the Committee on American Far Eastern Policy Studies. Most directly, I worked under Professors John King Fairbank and Ernest R. May, both of whom have had the fortitude to read my manuscript in its various transformations. To them I owe a debt of gratitude impossible to measure or repay.

Various librarians have made the task of collecting data so smooth that one is merely left with the job of reading. In particular, I should like to thank the librarians of the National Archives and Library of Congress in Washington, D.C., Houghton and Widener libraries at Harvard, and the Toyo Bunko in Tokyo. A number of friends have read drafts of this book in whole or part and to them I extend now formal thanks: Dorothy Borg, Howard Zinn, and Sara Ruddick. I have been fortunate in having the skilled editorial help of Mrs. Olive Holmes of the Harvard Center for East Asian Studies, who miraculously managed to work with me by air mail over a distance of 10,000 miles for a period of many months.

Finally, though in truth preceding all others, I want to thank my husband, Ernest P. Young, for his constant support and merciful criticism.

MARILYN BLATT YOUNG

Hanover, New Hampshire
Spring, 1968

Contents

Introduction   1

One   Official Neutrality, Private Intervention   14

Prelude to the Sino-Japanese War: Korea, 16. America and Korea, 16. Efforts to Intervene, 19. American Reactions to the War, 20. The Spy Case, 23. Plots and Plans, 27. Treaty Making, 30.

Two   Early Investment Schemes   34

American Concession Hunting: The Background, *1884–1895,* 34, Increase in American Interest, 52.

Three   Investment and Speculation   56

The Competing Efforts of Bash and Wilson, 56. The Return of Wharton Barker, 62. The Failure of the Bash-Brice Group, 64. Wilson's Ministerial Scheme, 68. America and Russia, 69.

Four   Threat of a Closing Door   74

Missionaries and Sino-American Conflicts, *1895–1897,* 76. American Reaction to the Seizure of Kiaochow, 87. Railroad Activity, *1898,* 88.

Five   Preparation for Action   93

Rise of Popular Expansionism, 95. The Possibility of a Base in China, 98. Changes in China, 106. Activation of American Public Opinion, 109. Continued Tribulations of the American China Development Company, 110.

Six   The Open Door   115

Development of the Open Door Concept, 115. Writing of
the Open Door Note, 123.

Seven The Long Hot Summer   137

Conger, Rockhill, and "Integrity," 138. The Mission Societies' Recovery, 142. The Boxers, 143. United States
Action and Reaction, 149. Intervention, 158. The Siege
and the July 3 Note, 160.

Eight The Problems of Peace   172

Relief, 173. Amoy, 175. The Russian Proposal, 179.
Missionaries, 187.

Nine Temporary Solutions   198

A Base for the Navy, 204. The Protocol, 213.

Ten   Conclusion   219

Notes   235

Bibliography   287

Index   295

The Rhetoric of Empire: American China Policy, 1895–1901

Introduction

The focus of this book is the formation of United States policy toward China in the key years of transition from 1895 to 1901. It would be dramatically satisfying to be able to write of a real confrontation between China and America, between East and West. What occurred, however, was quite different. The two countries peered cautiously at each other, only half understanding, only half wanting to understand.

China, in the last years of the Ch'ing dynasty, was not an easy country to understand. The ruling bureaucracy, in the main, stood firmly on thousands of years of triumphant civilization and seemed oblivious to fifty years of almost constant humiliation. The mass of people, peasants and laborers, suffered and were silent. Occasionally, their discontent would burst out in traditional forms—a secret society rebellion, a xenophobic riot against intrusive foreigners, a violent protest against those modern devices that would intensify their suffering by disturbing the powerful geomantic forces of *feng-shui*. China's passive resistance to modernization infuriated those Westerners who would love her. Here was a country that would not learn. No matter how many times the superiority of the West was demonstrated, the rulers of China refused to accept the lesson, and the people did not care.

China and America came into direct and significant contact at a turning point in the history of each. In America the severe depression of 1893 shook personal and national confidence in the infinite and inevitable linear progress of the United States. Fear of stagnation, economic and moral, of foreign enemies, real and imagined, internal and external, shaped the thought and behavior of politicians and intellectuals.

For China, overwhelming defeat in the Sino-Japanese War gave the lie to those who believed that the limited mid-century effort at military and industrial reform was sufficient to stave off disaster for country and culture alike. Damage to China was material and palpable: the war saddled the treasury with a crushing burden of debt, the effect of which

1

was incalculable, the infant modern navy was utterly destroyed and foreigners were given new opportunities for exploitation. At the same time it humiliated the Chinese far more than her defeat at the hands of Europeans had done. Japan, seen by China as a passive recipient of her cultural beneficence, had now shown herself to be a successful disciple of the West, strong beyond China's imagining. The pain was material and ideological and it evoked a similarly dual response. Attempts to master the technology of the West were redoubled and the more difficult task of taming Western knowledge and values also began. In a burst of publications, organizations, plots, and rebellions, China responded to the imminency of dismemberment and total collapse.

Many Americans saw in China their national salvation. Only such a vast market could absorb the surplus products of an industrial machine that, they thought, had satiated the domestic market and yet on whose continued full-scale operation the prosperity of the entire society depended. China was an object to be used. She offered America consumers; influence on her destiny signified American power. For this prize, traditional American foreign policy would be radically remolded. To China, America, like England, Germany, France, and to a lesser degree, Russia, was both threat and hope. If only China could distill from the West the essence of its strength she could then use it against the West itself, in self-defense. There was unity in neither society. Opposition to change came, in both China and America, from those who believed the means used to preserve the state would pervert the thing itself; one did not succor a besieged democracy by becoming imperialist, nor a Confucian empire by transforming it into a Westernizing nation.

It is essential to understand the changes that had taken place in American society during the last decade of the century, changes that make comprehensible the mingled notes of fear and triumph that dominate the rhetoric of this period.

Perhaps the major psychological factor operating in the years before the turn of the century was the fact, and the awareness of that fact by most Americans, that the country was no longer (if indeed it ever had been) homogeneous and united. Signs of disorganization, even disintegration, were everywhere. For Americans, no strangers to disunion and fearful of revolution, the years from 1885 to 1897 were anxious ones.

The pace of urbanization had increased tremendously. The disrupting effect of such growth was intensified by the spectacular speed with which some cities grew. For example, Chicago, unlike the older urban centers, did not receive a steady flow of migrants but grew to a city of one million people in what was almost one great rush.[1] And though the service problems (such as sewage disposal, sanitation, and water supply) were no longer as serious as they had been in the cities of the early nineteenth century, the problems of social organization were much greater. It was in the late nineteenth century that cities were first loved and cursed as "jungles."

The changing nature of immigration complicated the urban problem. A flood of impoverished, alien people congregating in loathsome, sickeningly visible slums, threatened and challenged the "native" American city-dwellers. In every social group the city produced near intolerable strains, which each tried to meet in its own way. Everywhere, clearly defined neighborhoods grew up—a geographical expression of self-definition.

People in the middle class began what proved to be a steady migration toward the suburbs where, behind white picket fences and neat lawns, they strove to demonstrate their ties with an older, simpler, native, and rural America. Both upper and middle classes dissociated themselves, occasionally to the point of organized opposition, from the immigrants. Now, to be an immigrant was to belong to the undifferentiated mass of unskilled workers.

The severe depression of 1893 gave actual shape to the anxieties that gripped America in its New World version of a *fin de siècle* pathology. On one level, the depression weakened, perhaps destroyed, an earlier blithe belief in America's infinite material expansion. There was increased talk of economic stagnation, of overproduction, permanent unemployment of large masses of people, of decay and decline. Fear of revolution was encouraged by two developments: the organization of the Populist party with its radical economic program; and the frequency of strikes and actual warfare between capital and labor.[2]

On the psychological level, the depression had an equally destructive impact. The prevailing ideology of Social Darwinism, which in its most simplistic and popular form saw failure as evidence of personal inadequacy, added to the economic distress of being unemployed or bankrupt.[3]

3

Other economic developments contributed to the tension and confusion of life in the nineties. The unorganized middle class found itself caught between two major contending forces: the nascent labor union movement and the increasingly powerful force of big business. Reflecting in relative tranquility some fifteen years later, Henry Adams believed that the years of the great depression ushered in the full capitalistic system, "the whole mechanical consolidation of force which ruthlessly stamped out the life of the class into which Adams was born."[4] The American dream of homogeneity, of an organic, infinitely progressive nation had never before seemed so impossible of achievement.

One expression of the uneasiness that gripped American society at this time was the growth of a new, virulent, and for the first time nationwide, nativist movement. The nativism of the nineties is distinguished from earlier movements by its intensity and by its conscious, extreme nationalism.[5] Nativist nationalism offered two easy verbal solutions to the painful dilemma of a changed and unstable America. By blaming disunity on the evil influence of the new immigrants, it absolved from blame and protected from criticism the more basic contradictions in the economic and social system. If immigrants were the root of the trouble, the solution was comparatively simple: keep them out. Viewed as unassimilable, revolutionary, and inherently inferior, the immigrant could be made a convenient catch-all scapegoat. Second, by indulging in an orgy of fervent nationalism, the reality of American life could be denied, even, for the moment, forgotten. As John Higham points out, the "two anti-foreign movements—one international, the other internal—complemented each other, so that the jingoist atmosphere of the decade helps explain the depth and intensity of its nativism."[6]

It is in these terms that the emotional force of the Spanish-American War becomes comprehensible. The national neurosis described above was acted out in the fantastic fervor that preceded, and perhaps made inevitable, the war. Moreover the pious references to "blue and grey marching together" were not empty bombast. The war was seen as a unifying force, killing Spaniards hand in hand a proof of that unity.

Only in the context of the omnipresent anxiety and frustration of the nineties does the growth of an imperialist spirit in America make sense. To be sure, specific pressure groups, with an emotional appeal to wider

4

groups of the population, played an important part.[7] In addition, there were several writers whose thinking expressed the loose ideology of American imperialism in the years before 1898.

Three important concepts were held in common by the men whose thought is described below.

1. That the United States suffered from overproduction, the domestic market was satiated, and overseas commerce alone could save the country from economic stagnation and death.

2. That America was a great world power with concomitant responsibilities; among these was the duty to play a significant political role in world diplomacy. (A variation of this was—if America was to be, and it should be, a great power, it must play such a political role. After 1898 this formulation disappears—America's great power status was accepted as proved.)

3. That, because of the extension of Social Darwinist concepts from the individual to the international sphere, international relations were seen in a survival-of-the-fittest framework.[8]

To a great extent the ideas, even the phraseology of the imperialist theorists overlapped, the differences between them are those of emphasis. Captain A. T. Mahan, officer, historian, and propagandist, was chief spokesman for one of the most ardent imperialist groups, the Navalists. As early as 1894 Mahan was stressing the importance of America's geographical position. The fact that two mighty oceans lapped our shores took on almost mystical significance for Mahan. In an article discussing the possibilities of an "Anglo-American reunion," Mahan succintly stated his vision of the world. Competition, victory over others, were signs of a living, progressing nation. Mahan saw a revitalized nationalism as the best obstacle to socialism and found in the unlikelihood of "the leading peoples turning their swords into ploughshares" a comfort. The fate of civilization lay not in passive universal harmony but in the ongoing struggle of "each people to provide first for its own."[9]

In keeping with the most common economic theory of the day that an expanding overseas trade was essential to America's economic survival, Mahan argued that an extensive network of foreign markets required a strong merchant marine. In turn a large merchant marine would need an appropriately strong navy to protect it. Such a navy would require coaling stations, which in turn would require naval protection. An additional benefit of a large navy was that it served as a force for peace. "The endurance of civilization," Mahan wrote, "depends ultimately upon due organization of force . . . such force is but the means to an end, which end is durable peace and progress, and therefore beneficence."[10]

Without a large navy, America could never play a significant role in world affairs, nor would she be worthy of one. Mahan's specific interest —the extension of American naval power—was both a means to an end and the end itself. His justification for the navy was the major part it would play in increasing American power in general. To this end he discussed the vital role the navy would play in fulfilling America's two-ocean destiny. At the same time one cannot help feeling that Mahan was devoted to the navy as such. A large navy was itself both the symbol and substance of greatness.

A different line of thought was pursued by those who saw the world in power terms and whose urgent desire was to place America in a leading power position. The most interesting of those who thought and wrote in such terms was Brooks Adams. Grandson of John Quincy Adams, brother of Henry Adams, he felt himself to be the scion of a noble race done to death by the triumph of the economic man. A lawyer and frustrated politician, Adams watched the advance of finance capitalism with both despair and scientific curiosity.[11] A member in good standing of the unorganized, highly educated, upper middle class, Brooks looked at America in the 1890's and was afraid. The Republican party, he felt, was the "party of the capitalists" working successfully and inexorably toward a government that would legislate in the interests of private profit.

Although Adams identified the victory of free silver with socialism and the death of democracy, he believed a strict gold policy would mean the triumph of the plutocrats and the death of democracy by different hands. The panic of 1893 increased Adams' sense of doom. He saw the struggle between plutocrat and productive laborer writ large in the history of civilization. He wandered "over half the earth" examining ancient ruins, puzzling over the seeming chaos of man's history, aching to find the fixed law that would explain it all.[12]

The intricacies of Adams' theories, especially as they are so often opaquely stated and obsessively pursued, need not detain us. Only the broader outlines of his early thought will be described here. In his first book, *The Law of Civilization and Decay,* Adams held that all history

6

was a slow oscillation between barbarism and civilization, or in the physical terms he believed more precise, between dispersion and concentration. Civilization is synonymous with concentration and consolidation —the progressive gathering of the energies of a community to a high point of social use. Rome at the height of her empire, the West in the late nineteenth century are two examples he used. Barbarism, conversely, is the dispersion of energy, the return of a community to a primitive level of existence. In early stages of concentration the mental types that dominate civilization are the religious, the military and the artistic. But as concentration advances, "the Economic organism tends to supersede the emotional and martial."

From this point on, economic competition and wars are inevitable. At last a plateau is reached at which one of two things can happen: either a stationary period, terminated by war or exhaustion, or total disintegration of the society and its return to a primitive form of organism.[13] So it had been at the end of the Roman empire and so it seemed to be in 1894 when, according to Adams, the Lombard Street bankers, the Rothschilds, in short, the Jews, manufactured a panic that threatened all of Western civilization. *The Law of Civilization and Decay* was an apocalyptic book, pointing out with a thin, raised forefinger the doom that awaited the United States should she fail to heed the lessons of past empires. After the Spanish-American War Adams would delineate the way America must go to survive.

Another group of conscious advocates of imperialism can be characterized by the emotional nature of their arguments. The outstanding example of this group is Theodore Roosevelt, though it includes Henry Cabot Lodge, and to a lesser extent, John Hay.

Navalism was an important element in Roosevelt's thinking, but overriding it was his passionate nationalism. His utter scorn for the Chinese was based on their alleged lack of nationalism. Indeed national sentiment seems to distinguish men from beasts for Roosevelt. Though influenced by Brooks Adams, Roosevelt's temperament and basic outlook were radically different from, even antagonistic to, those of the hypersensitive New Englander. To his close friend Cecil Spring Rice, Roosevelt wrote: "I would have written my review of *The Law of Civilization and Decay* very much more brutally than I did, but really I think his trouble is largely that his mind is a little unhinged. All his thoughts show extraordinary intellectual and literary dishonesty but I don't think it is due to moral shortcomings. I think it really is the fact that he isn't quite straight in his head."[14]

Much is sometimes made of the fact that Roosevelt and Adams discussed the possibility of the former's leading a revolt of the "emotional classes."[15] But when Roosevelt's statement on this matter is read in context, it takes on a sarcastic rather than zealous coloring: "Adams, underneath, still looked forward with fiendish satisfaction to the enslavement of everybody by the Jews and other capitalists; but on the surface he allowed his fancy a moment's lurid play as to the possibility of my leading some great outburst of the emotional classes which should at least temporarily crush the Economic Man."[16]

Roosevelt, too, feared economic man but did not personify him as a Jew, nor did he suffer from the Adams brothers' hysterical fears of Jewish conspiracy. He feared economic man for what he would do to the moral fiber of America. He dreaded *softness* in himself or others, and a good deal of his scorn for Brooks Adams must have been a shrinking from the almost effeminate flutterings of fear Brooks was prone to. He saw America's danger in isolation, in being "so immersed in our own mere material prosperity, or lack of prosperity . . . that we shall become genuinely effete."[17]

Roosevelt's vision of the ideal life was one of immense vigor and activity. This attitude is reflected in his review of Charles H. Pearson's book on *National Life and Character*. Roosevelt passionately rejected Pearson's gloomy view of contemporary history. He found instead a wide diffusion of happiness, of excitement, pleasure, and infinite possibility in the world around him. Roosevelt was particularly stirred by the opportunities for empire, fairly won by the sword, that awaited the adventurous nineteenth-century man.[18]

Roosevelt's reaction to the Venezuelan dispute of 1895 was sharp and characteristic. The objective issue excited him hardly more than the reaction to the dispute by the "peace-lovers." He vented his spleen in an angry letter to Henry Cabot Lodge. "Personally," he declared, "I rather hope the fight will come soon. The clamor of the peace faction has convinced me that this country needs war."[19]

Though he found the spirit of the "banker, the broker, the mere manufacturer and mere merchant" to be "unpleasantly prominent" in America,

Roosevelt did not despair of the future. "I believe in the expansion of great nations. India has done an incalculable amount for the British character. If we do our work well in the Philippines and the West Indies, it will do a great deal for our character. In the long run I suppose all nations pass away, and then the great thing is to have left the record of the nation that counts—the record left by the Romans—the record that will be left by the English speaking peoples."[20]

Roosevelt felt a close personal identification between himself and the nation, and he extended his scale of personal values to the nation itself. As he had struggled, prospered, expanded his power, so he urged the nation on to his kind of victory. His devotion to an imperial future for America was at heart romantically emotional, almost sentimental. Though he knew and understood the theories of Brooks Adams and was even more sympathetic to the writing of A. T. Mahan, the motivating force for Roosevelt lay elsewhere—in glory, in a nation molded in his image.

The changes shaping late nineteenth-century America had their roots in industrialization; those that violently disrupted China were a consequence of that industrialization—not simply in America but in Europe and Japan as well. Industrialization at home might be an ugly and frightening process; industrialization as expressed in imperialism had at least as profound an impact on the victim.

Foreigners came to China, not as unskilled workers despised for their hopeless ignorance and poverty, but as conquerors. The conquest was slow and not always military, but everywhere they put Chinese, people, state, and society, on the defensive. The foreigners could be despised for their ignorance, their frequently ludicrous efforts at an elegant literary style, their inability to master the forms and subtleties of Chinese ritual. But these foreigners were hardly hopeless. They were ignorant but powerful, barbarian but strangely and ineluctably seditious. Earlier barbarian invaders had conquered and, at least in the case of the Ch'ing dynasty, had chosen to rule China along Chinese lines. The new barbarians had no need to rule China as Chinese, for their home base was not the hostile wastes of the steppe, but prosperous independent nations far from China. Moreover, they did not really *want* to rule. Unlike the British in India, foreign powers in China chose instead to reap the benefits of special privileges without the burdensome responsibility of governing.

Urbanization in China was thus given a special twist. Chinese coming to the cities were subject not only to the influence of a style of life different from rural areas but to the specific influence of foreigners. The largest, most prosperous cities were the treaty ports, where, protected by Western law, a new style of Chinese businessman emerged. For the first time a social alternative to the ruling bureaucracy appeared. The ports became islands of "personal and commercial security." Western military force pushed the Ch'ing toward its doom, while the political example of the West exposed Chinese to new possibilities undreamed of in their own philosophies.

America and China in the 1890's provide a marked contrast in nationalism. The intense nationalism of the United States turned outward against the world; the nascent, tentative, quantitatively limited nationalism of China turned inward seeking reform and defense. Some intellectuals, like Chang Ping-lin, found in the Manchus the Chinese equivalent of the immigrants despised in America. The pure Han race might well have been able to meet the threat of the West with equanimity, but a China subverted by the alien Manchus was helpless. Only by eliminating the Manchus could China hope to save herself.

In the period just following the Sino-Japanese War, however, relatively few nationalists followed a racist route to salvation. Rather, like K'ang Yu-wei and Liang Ch'i-ch'ao, they attempted to use Confucianism itself as the source of modernization. The goal was rapid change, but change with honor and dignity. If within Confucianism, one could find a sanction for reform, then it was possible to achieve Western power without sacrificing Chinese pride. Psychologically rooted in the traditional culture of China, K'ang made a great effort to demonstrate that the Classics themselves, properly interpreted, sanctioned reforms as varied as national assemblies and Western dress.[21]

In America, a perfervid belief in Social Darwinism created unbearable strains on the individual who found himself, as a result of the depression, jobless and poor. We have already seen to what dire conclusions Brooks Adams, in his own version of the Darwinist struggle, came. The impact of Social Darwinism on China was both profound and varied. As interpreted by Yen Fu, it was preeminently a hopeful dogma. Clearly, China had fallen off the evolutionary path at some point, and that fact was to be deplored. However, that a linear evolutionary line of development existed at all was an exhilarating discovery. By the conscious effort of devoted legislators, China could pick up where, centuries ago, she had left off. By abandoning the ancient ideals of social harmony and treasuring in their stead individual energy, struggle, and a united passion focused on the advancement of the state's wealth and power, China was bound to progress.[22]

To others, like Liang Ch'i-ch'ao, Social Darwinism was a less happy philosophy. Would the West give China time to reform? In the ongoing struggle between fit and unfit would not China be eliminated at once? Though reactionaries like Wo Jen might contemplate the disappearance of the state with Olympian calm, confident that the Chinese "spirit" would live on, nationalists like Liang were obsessed by the fear of partition. In the face of the Western threat, men like Liang lost confidence in the superior virtues and permanency of the Confucian way, and they gained instead an attachment to China *as a nation*.[23] However, except for a few of the more unusual missionaries, most Americans in China were unaware of the tremendous intellectual turmoil that marked the post Sino-Japanese war years.

A study of the postwar period must take account of the unsuccessful but highly ambitious schemes of a few American capitalists, of the wider net of propaganda about China's markets that inspired them and upon which they themselves fed. It must deal with the behavior of the American missionaries in China and their relation to the formation of policy.

The relationship between the two countries was not an equation. Americans treated China as an object, lacking in coherent aims or motives and unable to change American policy except through obstruction. Occasionally, as in the Boxer outbreak, China would turn from its semblance of passivity to frightening independent action that surprised and disturbed American businessmen, missionaries, and diplomats but did not change their attitude.

At every level, Sino-American relations were marked by powerful ambivalences. The missionary, whose commitment to China was total, found himself hating both country and people fully as much as he loved them. The parishioner, convinced of the special love he felt for China each time he dropped a coin in the collection box, was also in whole-hearted agreement with those who kept Chinese from emigrating to America. An able diplomat, like W. W. Rockhill, argued vociferously for a policy that worked for a strong and independent China but, at the same time, demanded from China strict enforcement of treaties that were symbol and instrument of her weakness.

Chinese attitudes toward America were marked by similar contradictions. America was distinguished from other foreign powers as both a special friend and a special enemy. From 1905 on, the immigration policy of the United States aroused waves of furious anti-Americanism; yet neutral observers testified to the sincerity of the frequent "demonstrations of good will and friendship," which were "not due to Government direction, but to individual good feeling."[24]

On both sides, expressions of good will became elements of policy. The Chinese, as one British diplomat put it, recognized the "possibilities afforded by the disinterested friendship of one of the great nations of the world."[25] Lacking a territorial base on the mainland of China, American officials, too, felt that a special emotional tie with China could have real benefits.

On the American side, expectations of future power and interest were often confused with present realities. In relation to no other country did the rhetoric of politicians and businessmen, diplomats and missionaries so quickly become a force, influencing behavior, coloring reality, determining policy. Policy decisions that were firmly rooted in the necessities of a particular situation became, almost at the moment of inception, sacred doctrine, at least partly because of the success of the propaganda of specific interest groups. Arguments intended to spur the interest of the public were accepted as facts and themselves became elements of policy in a dizzying spiral increasingly remote from reality. Thus the notion of a special friendship between China and America, of the riches of the China market, of America's role as balancer of powers in Asia, were all accepted as actual descriptions of the situation and not as mere possibilities.

There was a kind of beauty about the way in which policy pronouncements on China suited the American mood and the American past. Bold departures were made in the language of America's favorite clichés.

A major démarche into Asia became simply a plea for a "fair field and no favor"—a request difficult to protest. And yet withal there was a sense of new initiatives, of the flexing of untried muscles, which fit the nation's sense of itself as powerful in a degree and manner unknown to past decades.

one

Official Neutrality, Private Intervention

The massive breakdown in the traditional international order of East Asia, which reached a climax in the Sino-Japanese War opened China fully to the predatory policies of the West. The upheaval in the East forced the Cleveland administration to find an answer to a question that could no longer be avoided: What was America's real interest in Asia?

The international relations of the Chinese empire had been maintained by a delicate, ritualistic tributary system. This system had begun to deteriorate even before Western nations opened trade with China in the seventeenth and eighteenth centuries.[1] In the early nineteenth century, England in particular strained the logic of the tributary system, pressing its trade but refusing to behave like a tributary state. After the Opium War, China was forced to admit that her relations with Western powers were outside any tributary system. At the same time, China rejected the logic of a Western system of international relations; the situation remained undefined and full of danger for China.

Following the line of its own idealism, the United States played an independent hand in Korean affairs in opposition to both the European powers and China. Impatient with a tributary system that seemed a blatant anachronism and alert to the possible commercial benefits of an independent Korea, the United States became a minor, but significant, factor in the increasingly acrimonious struggle between Japan and China over Korea. Yet, in a manner that became characteristic of American relations with Asia, gains won by individual American diplomats were not supported by the government. Content with verbal victories, with the success of having all parties agree to a proper *statement* of the situation, the government did not go on to insure that the statement was maintained. Thus, diplomats working for the recognition of Korea as a sovereign nation saw the fruit of their efforts accepted by the government but not acted upon. Each gain opened the way for forceful action;

but instead of extending what had been won, the United States rested content with the initial victory and made no move to prevent its dissipation by the actions of other countries.

The Sino-Japanese War caught the interest of the American public. Although the administration of Grover Cleveland sought to maintain strict neutrality, the sympathy of the country went to Japan. A patronizing admiration for the military skill of Japan's "plucky little soldiers" and an increasing scorn for the blundering inefficiency of China turned the public reaction against the temporizing role of the American government. Secretary of State Gresham became the object of violent press attacks for his neutral handling of a case involving alleged Japanese spies in China, and the American public opposed its government's offers to act as mediator between the two combatants because these offers seemed to favor British, not American, interests in Asia.

In 1895 the pattern of earlier Sino-American relations, though beginning to break down, remained dominant. Individual Americans, diplomats, missionaries, adventurers, acted independently of government direction in the belief that personal efforts could have a direct effect on the destiny of nations, even empires. A small group planned a coup d'état in China from their offices in America. Their failure is less significant than the fact that they tried at all. For over a century China had been the embodiment of the goddess of fortune. However, as international rivalries increased, the prerequisite for success became strong government backing, not the heroic efforts of an individual, and bold schemes on the part of restless Americans disappeared. Government initiative replaced that of the individual and, by the end of the first decade of the twentieth century, roles had been so far reversed that the government found itself looking for individual support rather than the other way around.

The period from 1895 to 1901 was transitional. Opportunities for grand schemes of exploitation were rapidly disappearing in America. A sense of impending foreclosure depressed many Americans, who saw in China a new frontier. In some instances they succeeded in involving the American government. More generally, the government was moving on a parallel plane, with different objectives in mind. As the impetus of government activity increased, that for individual enterprises decreased at a rapid rate. Yet the spirit with which they had conducted their schemes was, in part, passed on to the government itself.

15

Prelude to the Sino-Japanese War: Korea

Korea was one of the earliest countries to enter into a tributary relation with China.[2] Its cultural and political ties to China were very strong and the rulers of the Hermit Kingdom were intent on keeping those ties intact. The tributary relationship was an ambiguous one and hard for Westerners, even sympathetic ones, to grasp. At the height of China's power, Korea had been free internally, owing China only the formalistic right to invest the Korean king. But the allegiance of Korea to a Chinese dynasty was essential to the legitimacy of a new Chinese emperor and Korea's lingering loyalty to fallen dynasties sometimes resulted in military pressure.[3] In external affairs, China acted as Korea's protector, coming to her aid when attacked. The curious aspect of Korea's tributary relation to China as it developed in the nineteenth century was that, for both Koreans and Chinese, the relationship persisted despite Chinese avowals of her inability to make foreign or domestic policy for Korea. China's dilemma was her inability either to protect Korea by force of arms from Western incursions, or to force Korea to modernize and sign treaties with the insistent Western powers.[4] Ch'ing policy, then, lay in informally advising Korea to follow China's model by entering into contractual relations with foreigners while, at the same time, trying to manipulate those powers to her own advantage.

America and Korea

It is understandable that Western diplomats found China guilty of the greatest duplicity. Korea referred all Western appeals to China; China denied she had the authority to deal with them; at the same time, China and Korea both affirmed that a "special" relationship between them still existed.

Japan finally broke Korea's isolation. Certain that China would remain neutral, Japan responded to a Korean attack on a ship of war in 1875 by staging a naval demonstration and forcing the Korean king, in January 1876, to sign a treaty of commerce, whose opening clause stated unequivocally that Korea was an independent state.[5]

Treaties with the Western powers followed and by 1886, the United States, England, France, Russia, Italy, and Germany all had treaties with Korea.[6] It is significant that the European powers ignored the independence clause in the Japanese treaty and acknowledged Chinese suzerainty over Korea, or avoided the issue by having their representative to Peking responsible for Korea as well. The United States, however, in accordance with its prejudice in favor of independent states and its extreme distaste for the Ch'ing government, sent a minister to Seoul of equal rank with the minister to China.

Although the European powers, effectively pressuring China for further commercial concessions, saw no need to push her clearly to define Korea's status, an independent Korea was more in accord with American interests than one subordinate to China. For the first time, the aloof cooperation with Europe that satisfied all immediate American needs with reference to China, was inappropriate. England, France, and Russia were predominant in China. If Korea were opened to trade, but still subservient to China, the predominant position of the European powers in China would probably extend to Korea as well. An independent Korea, on the other hand, would be that favorite American situation —"a fair field and no favor." Moreover, the independence of vassal states, especially if the mother country were a corrupt absolute monarchy, suited American ideals as well as interests.

In a conversation in 1883 between the American minister to China, John Russell Young, and Li Hung-chang, then the powerful governor-general of Chihli, Li tried to explain how Korea could be both independent in its internal and external affairs and at the same time tied to China. China's tributaries were self-governing, owing the emperor only an allegiance satisfied by prescribed ceremony. The emperor thereafter refrained from any interference in internal affairs. "At the same time," Li insisted, "their independence concerned China, and he could not be insensible to any attack upon it."[7] Young replied that tributary states were an impossible anachronism. One could have colonies or territories, like Alaska. China must consolidate her empire and declare the exact extent of her territory. The concept of a sphere of influence, later used with such effect on China by the West, was denied to China herself.

That same year, 1883, Li sent Yuan Shih-k'ai as resident to Seoul, and began slowly to reassert Chinese influence in Korea. Nor was the policy deterred by a clash between China and Japan, which resulted in the Tientsin Convention of 1885.[8] In the agreement, the two nations agreed to inform each other if either planned to send troops to Korea to quell any disturbance; each was to withdraw troops that were already in Korea; Korea should be urged to organize her own army, but neither China nor Japan could supply advisers to such a force. The Convention was an implicit demonstration of the equal status of China and Japan in relation to Korea. From the viewpoint of Western international organization, China had forfeited all claims to a special relationship with Korea. But Li Hung-chang had no intention of abandoning Korea.

Although the American government did nothing to support China's claims, individual Americans worked against China. Owen N. Denny, former American consul at Tientsin, was dispatched to Korea at Yuan Shih-k'ai's request to serve as adviser to the Korean government.[9] Denny, however, promptly espoused what he considered to be Korean interests and did his best to strengthen the country and lessen its dependence on China. Yuan Shih-k'ai and Denny worked at cross purposes and it was only a matter of time before Denny overreached himself. The situation came to a head in 1887 when the first Korean mission to the United States left for Washington. The mission had been inspired by Dr. Horace N. Allen, a medical missionary then in Seoul.[10] At the insistence of the Chinese the Korean king instructed Allen, who was to lead the delegation, to follow orders from the Chinese legation in Washington. Having put the Pacific Ocean between himself and his employers, Allen chose to ignore instructions and present his papers directly to the American authorities rather than through the Chinese legation. By so doing Allen felt he had taken a firm stand on the issue of Korean independence.[11]

This significant diplomatic ploy was not lost on the Chinese who worked hard to counter Allen's influence. Although the Chinese could not get at Allen himself, Denny was subject to dismissal and in 1888 he resigned, under a compromise agreement.[12] It was a conditional surrender and Denny's fight was ably carried on by Allen.

Horace N. Allen, missionary, doctor, businessman, diplomat, and intriguer, was a dominant figure on the Korean scene until the final victory of Japan forced his withdrawal. Allen, working for an independent Korea, did his best to destroy Yuan Shih-k'ai's patient policy of building Chinese influence. To fight China, which he saw as the greatest danger in the 1880's, he worked with Japan, and sometimes Russia. When Russia became the greater danger he worked with, and for, Japan, and when the power struggle shifted again he supported Russia.[13] Allen's main hope was to persuade the United States to take a positive interest in protecting Korea. By 1884 he had convinced the Korean king that the United States was the only country that had both the power and the self-restraint to support Korea in a disinterested manner.[14] But Korea's repeated appeals to America were always in vain. The American government would do nothing to compromise Korean independence; indeed it would, until 1905, act as though Korea were independent, whatever the facts. At the same time, no American administration ever acted to ensure even the nominal independence of that country.

Tension between China and Japan over Korea grew steadily in the late 1880's. War was avoided principally because neither country felt ready to fight. By the early 1890's, however, war between the two most important nations of Asia seemed inevitable. Each country feared that the other was preparing to annex Korea; each felt Korea to be an area essential to its national security, a "dagger pointed at the heart." As in most armed conflicts in history, the immediate circumstances that led to war were confused, even trivial events. First a Korean rebellion, successfully quelled, without the help of foreign troops, by the Korean army itself. Next the superfluous request, at Chinese instigation, for Chinese troops to aid in keeping order. To this move Japan responded by sending a large body of troops until finally, at the end of the summer of 1894, two large, hostile armies faced each other in the small country.

Efforts to Intervene

The war went badly for China. Early in the conflict, at the battle of Hai-yang Island, the Chinese navy under Admiral Ting Ju-ch'ang, was severely beaten by a Japanese naval force. Near the end of the war the remainder of Ting's fleet was destroyed as it lay helplessly at anchor in Wei-hai-wei harbor. In ground engagements, too, the Japanese were overwhelmingly victorious. Often Japanese and Chinese forces were evenly matched in men, firepower, and equipment. But the Japanese had learned the lessons of modern strategy well. Their generals were capable of brilliant maneuvers, their forces were well-disciplined, and there was little of the waste and inefficiency that characterized the Chinese forces.[15]

On October 6, 1894, the British, anxious to reduce China's losses but unwilling to take a decisive unilateral stand, invited Russia, Germany,

France, and the United States to join her in intervening between China and Japan. The powers would then try to arbitrate the dispute on the basis of the independence of Korea and a money indemnity paid by China to Japan. The United States, despite its earlier encouragement of Korean independence, refused, as did Germany, and the project never materialized.[16] Secretary of State Gresham was anxious, however, to make it clear to China that America's intentions were of the friendliest. In a conversation with the Chinese ambassador in October, for example, he pointed out that America's rejection of a Chinese request to join England and Russia in an arbitration attempt earlier in the year was based on a mistrust of England and Russia and not on any hostility to China. He pointed out that Europe was interested in capitalizing on China's misery and that, in contrast, America was concerned for China's welfare. Yang Ju was convinced that the United States was sincerely interested in China's fate.[17] But whatever England's motives, her efforts toward early mediation were more relevant to China's desperate situation than were American expressions of disinterest and sympathy. Gresham's earnest talks with Yang Ju were characteristic of American behavior throughout the war—attempts to retain the friendship of both parties without a commitment to positive action on behalf of either. In November the Chinese government appealed to the United States and the other powers to mediate on the basis of Korean independence and an indemnity from China to Japan. The United States indicated its willingness, provided Japan had no objections.

American Reactions to the War

Charles Denby was America's envoy to China in these years before the full engagement of American interests in the Far East. During his last few years as minister, he was dean of the diplomatic corps in Peking. In the small foreign colony Denby was a man of great eminence and power. He thoroughly enjoyed this importance and was conscious of his role as representative of the United States. Indeed, he often behaved as if he were a living personification of his nation.

Denby had little respect for Chinese customs, government, people, and culture. In a report to the State Department he commented on the value of teaching English to the Chinese: "The educated Chinaman, who speaks English, becomes a new man; he commences to think."[18] In another dispatch, this one not included in the published documents for 1894, Denby's attitude toward the Chinese is revealed in his suggestions for dealing with antimissionary riots. He urged that any town in which a riot had occurred should be demolished. "Even when riots occur in the interior," he wrote, "where the offenders cannot be reached by a foreign force, the doctrine of reprisals in other localities might be brought to bear."[19] Apparently the Chinese returned Denby's distaste for them. Li Hung-chang's American secretary, William Pethick, commented to a friend that the "Colonel has not been a success with the Chinese. They do not like his manner—which is too pompous, austere and unbending."[20]

Given the background of the conflict, American attitudes toward China, the success-orientation of American values at the time, and the history of individual American activity in Korea, it is not surprising that most Americans, in or out of office, had little sympathy with China. The *Boston Herald* expressed a popular sentiment when it commented on how the war had changed the American image of Japan. Writing after the news of a great Japanese victory at Ping-yang had reached America, the editorial noted: "This event changes the entire position of Japan . . . with the Western world. Last week the Japanese Empire, although known to be inhabited by a progressive people was rated . . . on a low plane of intelligence and efficiency when compared with the Western nations . . . But in consequence of this victory, won by the utilization of the most approved methods of warfare, the world's estimate of Japan must be recast."[21]

The Japanese minister to the United States, Kurino Shinichiro, claimed that the war was "in some measure a struggle between the forces of modern civilization and the *vis inertiae*" of Chinese conservatism,[22] and the editorial writers of the *New York Tribune* saw the war in precisely the same terms—as a struggle between "progress" and "stagnation." In England, too, general conclusions were drawn from Japanese victories. The *Review of Reviews,* reluctantly giving Japan her due, declared that Japanese success "tells in favour of the party of reform everywhere just as the utter rottenness and decrepitude of China reacts, though to a lesser extent, against Conservatism everywhere."[23]

In September 1894, the *North American Review* published a symposium on the war by Augustine Heard, former American minister to

Korea, D. W. Stevens, counselor to the Japanese legation in Washington, and Howard Martin, ex-secretary of the American legation at Peking.[24] Heard openly complained that anti-Chinese sentiment in America was so strong he felt obliged to set the record straight at the risk of offending Japan. His article branded Japan as the aggressor, but the remaining articles in the symposium supported Japan in the strongest possible terms. Martin, whom one might have expected to be relatively sympathetic to China, praised Japan as the defender of "reform and progress" and saw the best interests of everyone, including China, in a Japanese victory.[25]

The success of the Japanese pleased Americans immensely. For one thing, it confirmed the somewhat shaken belief that the history of civilization was linear and progressive. He who did not reform would not; perfection was open to all who would reach for it. Editorials and articles sympathizing with China for her overwhelming defeat had an unpleasant, almost gloating, tone. Americans played the role of the omniscient big brother, pointing out to China that bad conservative countries get what they deserve. An editorial in the *Missionary Review of the World* rhetorically asked who did not sorrow "with the Celestial Empire in her humiliation?" "Some 300 million bursting with conceit," the editorial noted with relish, "beaten time after time . . . by a puny nation of only 40,000,000." Yet, the editorial concluded, "China has only herself to thank."[26]

Frequently this attitude was linked with the belief that the war had been good for China. The *Missionary Review* saw a "highway . . . opened for the entrance of Christian forces."[27] The State Department's China expert, William W. Rockhill, declared, "A good thrashing will not hurt China in the least . . . It is the only tonic which seems to suit [her]."[28]

Although Secretary of State Gresham responded favorably to the Chinese request for intervention in November 1894, Japan's objections prevented any action and the war continued. Gresham's own attitude toward the war was clear, and he communicated it to American ministers in Japan and China in terms of the utmost lucidity. The war was "deplorable" but endangered no American policy in Asia. Looking only toward the welfare of Japan and China, the United States would follow a path of the strictest neutrality. Gresham was aware, however, that too overwhelming a victory by Japan might well excite the interference of

European powers in a manner "not favorable to Japan's future security." Where America would stand in such an event Gresham did not say; it was clear, however, that Japan should not expect the United States to defend her against the actions of interested powers.[29]

Despite America's declared neutrality, the pro-administration *American Review of Reviews* early in the war urged America to intervene and "minister to the cause of peace and justice."[30] The violently Republican *New York Press,* however, made anti-Cleveland propaganda out of the war whenever it could. Its response to Gresham's cautious offer of good offices in November 1894 is typical of the extreme Republican wing of the press:

> The offer was an impertinence. It was made in the interest of Great Britain, and, in all probability, at British suggestion. [Its only effect would be to] preserve from destruction a dynasty which stands for all that is odious, reactionary, cruel, and detestable in the government of mankind. Defeat will mean the liberation of many millions . . . from the bonds of ignorance, tyranny, and barbarity . . . For an American President and Secretary of State to undertake the rescue of China from the Japanese was an offense against international justice.[31]

Though Japan was admired, it still suffered a certain degree of condescension.[32] A slightly patronizing air toward Japan combined with a scolding one toward China allowed Americans to feel themselves impartial, just, and at the same time, superior to both—a very satisfying feeling and one that would be frequently adopted in United States' relations with Asian countries.

The Spy Case

Any American involvement in the war received a great deal of newspaper coverage and comment. One issue in particular aroused interest— and fury. At the start of the war, the American government had agreed to allow its ministers in China and Japan to safeguard the welfare and property of Japanese residents in China and of Chinese in Japan.[33] On August 18, 1894, Secretary of State Gresham cabled the legation in China about a Chinese complaint that the United States consul-general in Shanghai had been protecting two Japanese spies.[34] Gresham asked for, and received, an immediate reply from Charles Denby, Jr., who was chargé in his father's temporary absence.

Denby, Jr., reported that according to the Tsungli yamen, the prefect of Shanghai had stopped two suspicious Japanese in Chinese dress in the French concession and attempted to arrest them. The French consul, however, refused to allow the Chinese officer to make an arrest. Instead he had taken the two Japanese to the American consul, who in turn, refused to give them up without instructions from Peking. The consul-general, Thomas R. Jernigan, then cabled Denby, Jr., explaining that the suspects were mere "schoolboys" who had been resident in China for over three years. The documents found on them contained "personal information" and nothing more.[35]

Denby, Jr., supported Jernigan as part of a general policy to strengthen the attempt of the International Settlement to seal itself off from Chinese authority. Under the settlement's rule, arrests in the settlement could only be made by order of the consuls. In a report to Gresham, Denby, Jr., requested that the prisoners be examined by consul-general Jernigan in the presence of a Chinese official. If the boys were found guilty China should be prevented from punishing them inhumanly.[36] Gresham's reply was brief and unambiguous. America's role as protector in each country did not confer rights of extraterritoriality on Japanese citizens. Denby should never have received the two Japanese, Gresham stressed, and must not hold them. His suggestion that American consuls act as arbitrators was rejected.[37]

Denby, Jr. was ordered to deliver up the Japanese. He argued the matter in a further cable, but Gresham remained firm. Finally, on September 1, 1894, Denby, Jr., notified the Department that he had ordered Jernigan to surrender the Japanese.[38] He went on to explain why he had ignored Department instructions for several weeks. His unstated premise throughout was that Gresham, comfortable and safe in his Washington office, simply could not understand the special problems of diplomacy in China.

In his report, Denby, Jr., tried to make Gresham understand the nature of the struggle of the International Settlement against the Chinese government. In peacetime, foreigners in Shanghai, whether or not their own government had extraterritorial rights, were tried by the Mixed Court. It was the aim of the settlement to establish this principle in wartime as well, so that the subjects of a belligerent power would be protected. Denby's colleagues in the diplomatic corps had pointed out that if he allowed the Japanese to be handed over to Chinese authorities, he could expect the same treatment of Americans if the United States were ever to go to war with China. His attempt to establish the inviolability of the settlement was based on the neutrality of the settlement and an abhorrence of Chinese law.

Denby, Jr., argued that his second major reason for refusing to hand over the Japanese was that of simple humanity. The two Japanese were boys; they were probably innocent; the Chinese would torture and then execute them; there was reasonable doubt as to their guilt. How could he turn them over to the Chinese? He had not intended to allow the consul-general to protect them permanently.[39] Rather he intended to deliver them on condition that a fair trial would be accorded them—preferably with a foreigner present. Denby, Jr., concluded the dispatch with a plea to Gresham's pity, at the same time indicating that his delaying action had been much praised by the diplomats of other powers in China. "These young men," he wrote, "have the fullest sympathy of all foreigners in China, and the advice of the high officials of all nationalities has been not to give them up without conditions."[40] Later in the year Denby, Sr., discovered that the two boys were indeed spies and that their years of study in China had been spent in the service of Japanese intelligence agencies.[41] But, at the time, he, and with him the entire American colony in China, were convinced that Gresham's legalism had condemned the boys to death and that Gresham was, in this sense, their murderer.

Julian Ralph, Far Eastern correspondent for *Harper's Weekly,* gave the incident national publicity. He told his readers that the Japanese had certainly been tortured (though he had no reliable information on this point). Claiming to represent the feelings of Americans in China, Ralph asserted that Gresham's surrender had been a serious blunder and a dangerous precedent. "A higher influence than law," Ralph declared, "that of common humanity, demanded that a country which we officially characterize as semi-civilized should not be allowed to wreak its anger upon our wards until we were satisfied that they had offended that nation's law."[42] Ralph's report created a tremendous stir in the United States. The *New York Sun* disputed Gresham's argument that, had the

25

situation been reversed, Japan would have demanded precisely what the Chinese did. The *Sun* argued that China, being semi-civilized, was not entitled to the same consideration as Japan, whose display of military might had won her a place in the fully civilized world.[43]

Partisan Republican newspapers took up the cry in a violently exaggerated form. According to the Philadelphia *North American,* "The blood of these tortured and murdered Japanese is on [Gresham's] head, and the honor of the Nation has been stained in a fashion that the American people will neither forget nor forgive." [44] The most sustained attack came from the fiery nationalist, Cushman K. Davis, Republican senator from Minnesota. To Davis, as to Denby and other Americans in China, it was not a legal question at all, nor even simply a humanitarian issue. Rather the delivery of the spies involved a national humiliation. It sullied American pride, independence, and righteousness. Davis quite explicitly labeled Gresham, and Cleveland, un-American.

Senator George Gray, Democrat from Delaware, undertook to defend the administration. He did so legalistically at first but soon got down to the real issue between Davis, and politicians of his kind, and himself. Their debate has an ominously contemporary tone. Gray would not recognize a Democratic or Republican diplomacy, but said:

> I am prepared to admit that I have heard of a spurious diplomacy—sometimes called "thoroughly American"—which its advocates are welcome to the privilege of calling Republican . . . Its conscious advocates are perhaps few, but there is reason to fear that its dupes are many . . . It is meddlesome and aggressive; it is envious and suspicious; it is covetous and not very scrupulous; it exemplifies the evil of power without self-control, and of susceptibility to insult without a due proportion of self-respect. Its spirit is that of conquest; its first reason, as well as its last, is force.[45]

In the spy case and similar incidents, Charles Denby tried to cooperate with the other powers in China in establishing precedents, juridical and administrative, that would govern foreigners in China. Among them was the sanctity of the International Settlement at Shanghai. His effort was defeated by the State Department, which, though it took cognizance of his arguments, preferred to remain as neutral as possible in an area of the world where neutrality was becoming increasingly difficult.

Plots and Plans

In the fall of 1894 there was much speculation in the press as to Japan's next military move. Many articles and editorials looked forward to Japan's marching straight on to Peking, overthrowing the Manchus and establishing a new regime. The editor of the *Outlook* felt that only such a drastic move would force the Chinese to realize the bankruptcy of their civilization. The *New York Tribune* predicted that Japan would capture Peking and then divide China into three states, with Li Hung-chang ruling one portion.[46] What these journalists could not know was that some Americans were actively trying to persuade the Japanese government to fulfill the *Tribune's* prophecy.

A group of intriguers centering around William Pethick, Li Hung-chang's private secretary, and James H. Wilson, a Delaware business-man, urged the Japanese to capture Peking, establish a new Chinese dynasty and put Li Hung-chang in charge of a unified, foreign-controlled, reinvigorated China. Pethick, Li's faithful secretary for over twenty years, kept up an active correspondence with Wilson from 1886 to the end of his life. They had met during Wilson's brief trip to China in 1885 and had become good friends. Wilson sold Chinese *objets d'art* on account for Pethick, and Pethick supplied Wilson with inside information on possible railroad and investment concessions.[47]

Wilson was involved in a large variety of major and minor business operations.[48] From his home base in Delaware, he took an active part in local party politics. He had good lower echelon contacts in Washington and, as in his relationship with Pethick, he exploited these as much as possible. Wilson was not a deep thinker, but he felt strongly on a number of issues. His ambitions for the United States were unbounded. In a letter to William Rockhill he described a conversation he had had with Senator Gray. "I said I was in favor of ultimately annexing everything in sight," Wilson proudly related, "and of taking whatever in the adjacent seas any considerable number of Americans thought we might need, or ought to have, and also of so shaping our national policy as to secure the expulsion of the British flag from the Western Hemisphere."[49]

In the late summer of 1894 Pethick was in the United States on a brief visit.[50] He met sometime in late September with Wilson and they discussed the possibility of Japan's overthrowing the Manchu dynasty and making Li Hung-chang emperor. Li Hung-chang was, as the Chinese

official best known to Americans, a logical choice. They called him Earl
Li and the great viceroy and occasionally translated his titles into mis-
leading Western terms that betrayed their basic misunderstanding of his
position and his powers. From 1870 to 1895, when he bore the burden
for China's defeat (and suffered thereby a radical diminution in power),
Li was perhaps the most powerful bureaucrat in the empire. Holding
several positions at once, Li used each to strengthen the other, adding in
time industrial projects to the power he already derived from the Anhwei
Army. However, among the many things the conspirators failed to
understand was Li's strict loyalty to the empress dowager, who remained
the effective ruler of China from 1870 to her death in 1908. Despite the
reality of his regional power Li's independence was limited not only
politically but ideologically—he was a faithful minister to the throne.[51]
Determined to overthrow the Manchu dynasty and make Li emperor,
Pethick and Wilson decided to seek the aid of a small number of well-
placed people. They got in touch with John W. Foster, former counselor
to the Chinese legation, ex-secretary of state and personal friend of Li
Hung-chang. Next they spoke with D. W. Stevens, counselor to the
Japanese legation, and Charles Denby, American minister to China.

The urgency and secrecy of their dealings is revealed in a letter from
Pethick to Wilson signed "The Man in the Moon" and bearing the postscript, "Burn this." Pethick began the letter by reminding Wilson, in a
sprawling hand, each word underlined in its desperate sincerity, of the
necessity to keep any hint of the plot from the Chinese legation. Fearful
of endangering Li, Pethick urged that no one in China, except Denby,
be let in on the plan until Japanese intentions and capabilities were
clear.[52]

A letter from Wilson to D. W. Stevens contains the clearest account
of what Pethick and Wilson hoped for. Wilson noted that China was
ruled by a small group of aliens wholly lacking in the qualities that had
enabled their ancestors to conquer the empire. Unless Japan acted
quickly to change this situation she would surely lose the fruits of victory, and China would be divided between Russia and England. Wilson
then asked and answered a series of provocative questions. If the Manchus fell, who would succeed to the throne; what country would decide
the fate of an anarchic China? His answers were that Li should be
emperor (or his son, if Li felt himself to be too old) and that Japan

should dictate the new situation. Thus Japan had it in her power to become China's savior by ridding her "of the hopeless Manchus." A grateful China could then join Japan as an ally. Together they would control the future of East Asia. And if China could be so tied to Japan, how much more would Li Hung-chang be tied to Wilson. As Pethick wrote Wilson, "The fate of an Empire is grand work."[53]

Within a week Stevens replied that he had shown Wilson's letter to Kurino, Japanese minister to the United States, and planned to send copies of it to Mutsu Munemitsu, the minister of foreign affairs, and Itō Hirobumi, the prime minister.[54] Pethick had found Foster responsive to the plot and things seemed to be progressing extremely well. The safest policy, Pethick decided, was to urge the plan on the Japanese legation and get Denby to support Li Hung-chang should the Manchu emperor fall. At that moment the American government must become an open advocate of Li as the new ruler of China.[55]

After his conversation with Pethick, Foster wrote to Denby reminding him of the benefits to China, and the world, of a Japanese victory. Avoiding any direct mention of the plot, Foster advised Denby to keep his "eyes and ears open" and seize any opportunity both to secure his future fame and serve China.[56] It was just the sort of appeal to attract a man of Denby's temperament. Wilson's letter to Denby, written on the same day, was more explicit. "I want you," Wilson said, "when the time comes, to play the part of Warwick."[57]

In a few months it became clear that Japan had no intention of marching to Peking. In May 1895 Stevens wrote a post-mortem on their plot to Wilson, in which he explained that Japan could have captured Peking if she had wanted to do so. Fearing a power scramble after the downfall of the dynasty, in which Japan would be robbed of a fair share by the European powers, the Japanese had felt it wiser not to risk their current success for a gamble on the scale Wilson had urged.[58]

The assumptions on which Wilson based his plot are interesting and probably representative of what many Americans involved in the Far East at this time firmly believed. The rationale for the scheme was that the Manchu dynasty alone blocked reform in China, stymied the development of the Chinese market, obstructed railway development, and allowed the European powers to achieve such a hold on China that interested Americans were forced to fight for crumbs of business and influence. Once rid of the Manchus, and guided by Japanese and Americans, China would develop as she was meant to, enriching all who associated with her.

Li Hung-chang was believed to be exceptionally friendly to the United States. A new China, ruled by Li, was the ideal of all Americans whose ambitions lay in profitable Chinese investments and speculation.

The strength of conservatism in China was thus radically underestimated. If the Manchus alone stood in the way, the problem had a single, definitive solution. But this was not the case. Wilson and his fellow intriguers did not wish to take over China. Their ambition was to form a kind of joint American-Japanese co-prosperity sphere for Asia with Europe excluded. As in so much of nineteenth-century thinking about China, that country was taken simply as an object, not as an independent factor. When China did act without benefit of foreign inspiration, as in the Boxer rebellion, Americans long resident in China and supposedly well versed in her ways, were profoundly shocked.

Similarly, though greatly admiring Japan, Wilson and his friends could not see the Japanese as acting independently and for their own ends. None of them saw the possibility that Japan herself might endanger their hopes for a developed, completely opened China. Nor did they feel that the interests of the United States and Japan might come into extreme conflict.

Wilson's project was spectacular. It promised quick returns for a minimum investment. Neither he nor his associates showed any interest in a more modest approach to winning influence in China. A serious, organized group of China-oriented businessmen might have attempted to pressure the government into taking a more active stand on the Sino-Japanese War. Twice China had appealed to America to serve as mediator, and twice she was refused.

Treaty Making

Although Charles Denby had missed, through no fault of his own, the opportunity to play Warwick to a new dynasty, he found another chance for fame in the desperate straits in which China found herself at the close of the Sino-Japanese War. Gresham's offer in November 1894 to give China the benefit of America's "good offices," was understood by the

Chinese to mean just that. The United States would not, in the face of Japanese opposition, act as mediator; nor was America prepared to join other powers in a forced move to end the war. By treating Charles Denby as a mediator, however, the officials of the Tsungli yamen perhaps hoped to force the United States into a more useful, active role.[59] Denby knew, of course, that the Chinese were seeking help from every country that had dealings with China. Indeed he often complained of this very fact.[60] Yet Denby allowed himself to be convinced that he, above all other diplomats in Peking, was needed by the Chinese.

The Chinese method can be deduced from a report Denby made to the State Department complaining, a little, of the deference shown him:

> I beg to say here *confidentially* and not for *publication* that the ignorance and helplessness of these people pass all comprehension . . . They know nothing of such diplomacy as war demands. My position in regard to them is very peculiar. Understanding that my government favors peace my effort has been to bring about that result, but I am always confronted with the assertion of the excessive friendliness of the U.S. and with a piteous and helpless reliance which makes me an adviser when in truth I am only an intermediary between two governments.[61]

What Denby took for piteous helplessness might well have been the familiar policy of the weak toward the strong—to flatter those with power into the position of protector.

Denby tried to use his position for the benefit of anticipated American commercial ventures in China. In December 1894 Denby reported that he had advised the Chinese government to provide for the indemnity Japan would surely demand by disposing "of her valuable franchises which are still untouched." At the same time he was urging American capitalists of his acquaintance to pick up such concessions should the Chinese indeed follow his advice. Denby was convinced that the course of the war had resulted in an enormous increase of American prestige in China. Indeed, the United States now had "an overshadowing influence." Moreover, that influence could undoubtedly be converted into hard cash by securing commercial privileges for American citizens. Denby urged that the United States take an active role in the treaty negotiations, perhaps to the extent of actual supervision.[62]

Gresham consistently rejected Denby's frequent requests that the government take a peace-making role. When Denby transmitted a Chinese request that the United States ask Japan to sign an armistice, Gresham firmly replied that such an action would be inconsistent with America's neutral attitude toward the conflict.[63] A few months later Gresham reminded Denby that he was to be a "neutral channel of communication" only.[64]

By early spring, 1895, China reluctantly recognized the fact that direct intervention by a European power was unlikely and Chinese officials began to sue for peace in earnest. Two envoys were sent to Japan in January, but the "full powers" document that Denby had helped prepare was not used and the Japanese refused to meet the envoys at all. By the time Denby wired the Japanese that he had proper credentials prepared and would cable them immediately, it was too late.[65] Before Chinese and Japanese representatives met again, Wei-hai-wei had fallen, Japan was in a stronger position to dictate the peace, and the Chinese government acted swiftly to open negotiations before further losses occurred.

In March, Li Hung-chang was appointed ambassador extraordinary for the peace negotiations. Before he left for Shimonoseki, Denby had a long interview with him. Ignorant of Li's vulnerable position as the man who must take personal responsibility for the anticipated harshness of the peace terms, Denby urged that the viceroy should arrange in advance to have a controlling voice in internal improvements upon his return. Moreover, Li must undertake this under the supervision of English-speaking people, for the "second language of the Chinese [is] English."[66]

Two Americans accompanied Li Hung-chang to Shimonoseki: his secretary, William Pethick, and John W. Foster, who came at Li's request to advise him during the negotiations. According to Pethick, Foster was of great help in drafting replies to the Japanese notes. However, the easing of terms, which occurred midway through the conference, was due to Li's skill alone.[67] There is a complete transcript of the negotiations in English. They demonstrate Li Hung-chang's clever diplomatic maneuverings: the effective way in which he used the attempt on his life to ease the terms; his tentative proposal for an alliance between China and

Japan against the non-Asian world and his warning that Europe might yet interfere should Japan overreach herself.[68]

Despite the modifications that Li won, the terms were very hard. China was forced to cede the Liaotung Peninsula, Formosa, and the Pescadores Islands; the indemnity was set at $150 million (two hundred million taels); several new ports were opened. A separate commercial treaty signed in July granted explicit permission for foreigners to establish manufacturing businesses in the open ports.[69]

Almost all foreigners in China had hoped Japan would use the victory to press on China the traditional program of commercial demands: abolition of oppressive internal taxation on goods, currency reform, opening of ports on a vast scale.[70] Denby, too, saw Japan's role in this light.[71] In proportion to his hopes, therefore, he found the treaty sadly wanting. Through its vast territorial concessions, Denby complained, it made Japan a "continental power." Posing as the "knight errant of civilization," Japan had not secured key privileges for foreign commerce but had merely pursued her own national advantage, and the Western powers gained little."[72]

Gresham's veiled warning to Japan that her successes might displease the European powers was almost immediately justified. Barely a week after the signing of the Treaty of Shimonoseki, Russia, Germany, and France joined in "recommending" that the Japanese return the Liaotung peninsula to China. With bitter reluctance Japan acquiesced and the external forces working toward the disintegration of the Chinese empire were, ironically, stimulated rather than inhibited.

two   Early Investment
                                                      Schemes

Charles Denby's estimation of his central role in Chinese affairs and of the favored position of Americans in China was not due solely to his overweening egoism. In the decade before the Sino-Japanese War, when it seemed to foreigners that the self-strengthening movement of the 1870's would follow the logic of industrialization and succeed in developing China's railroads and mines, Li Hung-chang, then at the peak of his power, had shown deep interest in specifically American cooperation. A contract for the first Sino-foreign joint-stock company had been granted to an American syndicate; proposals for sweeping bank concessions to the same syndicate had almost succeeded. When both these failed, Li had gone to extraordinary effort to persuade an American businessman to open a bank in China that would have the secret cooperation of key Chinese officials. Nothing concrete resulted from the strenuous attempts of both the Chinese and the Americans because of miscalculations on both sides. Like so many attempts of this kind in Sino-American history, it was a revealing failure.

American Concession Hunting: The Background, 1884–1895

Before the Sino-Japanese War the few Americans interested in the development of Chinese railways, telephone and telegraph systems, or mining faced two major difficulties: the strong opposition of a powerful group within the Chinese government and a general lack of interest among investors in the United States. In this early period, lack of interest on the part of the American government did not necessarily doom a project. After the Sino-Japanese War, investors faced quite different problems. As development projects became involved in international rivalries and the Chinese government attempted to use concessions as political weapons, the indifference or half-hearted support of the American government could be fatal to the success of a project. However, when the government began to show more interest, American capitalists, recovering fully from the depression, gave only sporadic attention to investment opportunities in China.

General James H. Wilson provides a link between the two periods. We have seen him in an earlier chapter plotting a coup d'état against the Manchu dynasty. He was as deeply involved in many of the American attempts to profit from China's undeveloped state. As early as December 1884, Wilson wrote to John W. Foster, then practicing law in Washington and serving as an adviser to the Chinese legation, that China was the only populous country in the world without a railroad system. He asked Foster for advice on how to get the contract for building a few "initial trunk lines." If successful, he noted, he would not only make a fortune for himself but would also advance general American influence and interests in the East.[1]

In the spring of 1885 Wilson traveled to China in an effort to assess the possibilities of railroad construction. He had found the State Department representatives totally incapable of supplying him with accurate information on the real state of affairs in China. During this trip Wilson made contacts that were to serve him in all his future operations in China. He formed a lifelong friendship with William Pethick, won Minister Denby's confidence and aid, and made his name well known to Li Hung-chang. But the journey yielded no positive results.[2]

Li Hung-chang, however, was deeply interested in railway construction, especially in connection with the further development of the Kaiping Mines.[3] In 1882, three years before Wilson's trip to China, he had had seven miles of railroad constructed, running from the mouth of the mines to Hsu-ko-chuang, where the road connected with a series of canals that could bring the coal to a depot nine miles above the Taku forts. He had done this virtually unknown to the court, under the euphemism of a "horse road." By 1886 the road had demonstrated its usefulness to such an extent that Li won the support of the powerful Prince Ch'un, head of the Board of Admiralty. In 1886 and 1887 Li memorialized openly for the extension of this short road as far as Tientsin.[4]

Though opposed to any foreign control of Chinese railroads, Li was not averse to using foreign skills. In the spring of 1886, in connection with his effort to extend the Kaiping railroad, he suggested to Pethick that Wilson send three miles of gift railroad to China. The court would find such a gift difficult to refuse, and it would perhaps win new adherents to Li's cause. Apparently this was done.[5] In April 1887 Li organized the Chinese Railway Company, a *kuan-tu shang-pan* enterprise, that is, a joint-stock company in which, using Li's own definition, "The government will lay down the general principles and keep its eye on the company's merits and demerits, the merchant directors . . . will be permitted to propose their own regulations so that the shareholders will be satisfied."[6]

By 1880 the original Kaiping line had been extended as far as Taku, a distance of eighty-one miles. The company now wished to build the road to T'ung-chou, at the head of barge navigation on the canal, and the closest the company could hope to get to Peking. Li Hung-chang, more interested in extending the railroad north toward Shanhaikwan for military reasons, supported the Tientsin–T'ung-chou line because of its revenue-earning possibilities, which could then be applied to the Shanhaikwan extension.[7] Li memorialized and permission was granted. At this point, however, a storm of opposition put a temporary halt to further progress.

Wilson was kept informed of all these developments by Pethick. Their correspondence does not make clear to what extent, and in precisely what capacity, they were involved in the China Railway Company. According to Pethick, however, denunciations of Li included passing insults directed at both Wilson and Pethick himself. Pethick reported that the opposition, which came to a head in February 1889, was led by the censorate. Memorials by the censors included a firm warning against the intrusion of foreigners into Chinese railroad enterprise.[8]

Another source of opposition was the junk interest, which saw a successful railroad as a great danger to their grain-carrying trade by river to T'ung-chou. Violent rioting by the junkmen at this time was apparently inspired by officials opposed to Li on personal and political grounds.[9]

The opposition was so great that the empress dowager rescinded her prior permission and sought the advice of the Grand Council. In addition she called for memorials from the provincial governors-general and governors commanding them to express an opinion on the general problem of railroad construction.[10] The issue was decided by Chang Chih-tung (then governor-general of the provinces of Kwangtung and Kwangsi), who, while opposing Li's scheme, supported railroads in general and substituted a plan of his own. Chang proposed that instead of adding to the original Kaiping road, China begin a program of rational railroad construction, building key trunk lines as part of a national system. He urged that a line be built from Lu-kou-ch'iao (the "Marco Polo Bridge") to Hankow, as a start in the program. Chang was immediately taken up on his proposal, transferred to the governor-generalship of the provinces of Hunan and Hupei, and put in charge of construction. Funds from the Board of Revenue were authorized, but the project was kept in abeyance because of the opposition of Li Hung-chang and his supporters.[11] A recent Chinese study of early railroad development asserts that more was involved than simple rivalry with Li Hung-chang. Determined to bar foreign participation, more interested in the economic value of railroads than their military usefulness, Chang Chih-tung urged that China undertake the entire burden of development. Railroads must wait until China could produce enough iron, coal, steel, and rolling stock. The author, Li Kuo-ch'i, argues that Chang's plan was a sensible, if over-idealistic, scheme. If China waited for the perfect moment to build railroads, they would never be built.[12] As a start in that direction, however, Chang established the Hanyang Iron Works.[13]

Li Hung-chang's construction plans were based on several considerations. At first the road was simply the most sensible way to expand and exploit the Kaiping Mines. With the organization of the China Railway Company, however, other considerations entered Li's plans. His projected line of development—toward and beyond the Great Wall—was connected with his concern for Manchuria.

Aware of Russian ambitions in Manchuria, Li was anxious to strengthen China's hold on this area. In 1890 he sent his chief engineer, C. W. Kinder, on a survey of southern Manchuria. At this time he discussed his plan for a railroad that would cross south Manchuria from east to west: Shanhaikwan (a branch to this point was authorized in 1891 and completed in 1894) to Chinchow; Chinchow to Hsinmintun; Hsinmintun to Mukden; Mukden to Hunchun on the Tumen River. He also planned a branch south from Mukden to Newchwang.[14] Such a development would also strengthen and expand Li's regional base of operations. Though all projects were ultimately justified in terms of strengthening the nation, they also, by the way, served to strengthen the regional position of the individual involved.[15]

Wilson's early entry into the quicksands of Chinese railway development was a total failure. A failure of a different kind, though, equally illustrative, lies in the adventures of one Count Eugène Stanislaw Kostka de Mitkiewicz. He arrived in Peking in the summer of 1887, carrying letters of introduction from President Cleveland, Chang Yin-huan, the Chinese minister to the United States, Jay Gould, the fabulously successful speculator, Wharton Barker, a Philadelphia broker, and various prominent bankers. Pethick, in a puzzled letter to Wilson, reported that Mitkiewicz claimed to come on behalf of a Philadelphia syndicate seeking concessions for a telephone system, telegraph, railroads, or whatever else the Chinese seemed ready to give him. Unhesitatingly Pethick declared, to Wilson if not to Li, that Mitkiewicz was a fraud.[16]

Pethick was only partially correct. The Count Eugène de Mitkiewicz, though a friend vouched for his authenticity on the Almanac de Gotha, was no Russian aristocrat but a clever confidence man with a prison record in England, a Russian wife, and a manner of dress and discourse that deceived as skillful a businessman as Wharton Barker, as discerning a diplomat as Chang Yin-huan, and as great a statesman as Li Hung-chang.[17] His mission to China was real enough as were the impressive credentials he carried. The story of his near success in securing vast concessions from China for a Philadelphia syndicate led by Barker was the financial sensation of 1887.

In the fall of 1886 Mitkiewicz and a friend, William Paine, had secured the confidence of the Chinese minister to the United States, Chang Yin-huan, and his staff.[18] To understand the motives of a man like Chang Yin-huan would be to begin to understand, in depth, the world of the late Ch'ing empire. Urbane, sensitive, a good administrator, and at times, a bold innovator, Chang was also, like his sometime mentor, Li Hung-chang, ready to take bribes, great and little, when the occasion offered. Perhaps this issue of bribery is a false one, a product of the same cultural parochialism that caused the missionaries to condemn the Chinese for an insufficient sense of sin. Chang's acceptance of money did not seem to bind him to his patrons, and it is impossible to know to what extent his judgment was affected by a handsome reward for his acquiescence in a policy he already favored.

The involvement with Mitkiewicz and Paine began well. Chang agreed to help the two, with introductions to key Chinese officials, in their effort to obtain a concession for the "sole and exclusive right and privilege and power, to build, construct, maintain, use and operate telephonic instruments, telephones . . . and other devices and appliances" in a long-distance telephone system in the open ports for a period of thirty years.[19] Paine, having no financial resources of his own, approached Wharton Barker, head of the then prosperous Philadelphia banking firm of Barker Brothers and Company. Barker had had some experience with foreign business enterprises. In 1878 he was appointed special financial agent by the Russian government and entrusted with having four cruisers built for the government by American shipbuilders. In 1879 he was invited to Russia to advise the government on the development of coal and iron mines and received the Order of St. Stanislaus for his services. A political maverick, Barker had played an important role in the Republican campaigns of 1884 and 1888. Hurt by the depression of 1893, however, he became increasingly interested in bimetallism and in 1896 he supported Bryan. His monetary views became more radical and in 1900 he ran for President as the candidate of moderate Populist groups. Like James Wilson, Barker was interested in Continental Union, suspicious of Great Britain, and intrigued by the idea of American-Russian cooperation in the development of Chinese railroads.[20]

Skillfully playing on Barker's speculative temperament, Paine soon induced him to take a leading role in the scheme. In early February Barker visited Chang Yin-huan in Washington and discussed the business thoroughly. On February 8 he wrote the minister's secretary to confirm his decision to undertake the concession. One hundred thousand dollars would be raised for preliminary expenses with the expectation of an annual profit of $2 million.[21] By May 1887, Barker had assembled an impressive roster of donors each of whom had paid in $5,000 and pledged $10,000 more. Among them were Samuel R. Shipley, a prominent insurance man, Hamilton Disston, wealthy Philadelphia manufacturer, Thomas Potter, the largest oil-cloth manufacturer in Pennsylvania, H. D. Fling, manufacturer of "notions," several bankers, the largest Philadelphia brewer, and several "men of means." The $10,000 they subscribed was pure venture capital. If the concession was not granted the money would be lost and Barker could not be held responsible. Should the enterprise prove successful, their capital would then represent shares in the subsequent joint-stock company.[22] Chang Yin-huan and other helpful legation employees were to receive sizable amounts of certificates convertible into stock should the concession be granted as seemed certain.[23] Meanwhile the legation staff seemed to be occupied with nothing but the preparation of appropriate papers for Mitkiewicz to take to China.

The months of preparation were tense. Barker reluctantly doled out increasingly larger sums of money, quarreled violently with Paine, and worried about the count's reliability.[24] He took the precaution of sending a personal agent, Mr. Simon Stern, along on the trip.

In San Francisco, for a slight fee, Mitkiewicz obtained more letters of commendation from the Chinese consul-general. Stern reported to Barker that the vice-consul assured him that " 'No white man ever went to China with such letters as these.' " After a stop in Tokyo for inconclusive negotiations on a telephone concession there, the delegation finally arrived in Shanghai in June.[25]

They were met by the prominent Ma brothers who became their hosts and boosters. Ma Chien-chung, a protégé of Li Hung-chang, was at that time assistant manager of the China Merchants Steam Navigation Company; his brother held an important job in the Imperial Chinese Post Office. Both were deeply involved in Li's early industrial schemes.[26] From the outset it had been understood that the telephone concession was only one of the possibilities Mitkiewicz planned to explore. Stern was pleased, therefore, when the Ma brothers told him that long-distance telephones were a luxury for China; railroads were vital. The brothers assured Stern that if the group had enough money at its command, nothing stood in the way of obtaining railroad concessions. As an earnest of the group's affluence and interest, each of the brothers received $1,000 with promises of future payments. Stern was a little uneasy but felt he had no choice but to trust the officials to whom Chang Yin-huan had sent them.[27]

By July the telephone part of the deal was closed and Li Hung-chang telegraphed Barker that he approved the proposition and expected a "very favorable conclusion." Li also hinted at a larger enterprise. Barker's response was to cable Mitkiewicz at once the $5,000 the count insisted he needed for this new phase of the operation.[28] A final act of faith was required, however. In order to secure the telephone concession, Barker was asked to cable $20,000 at once for "registration fees." After several protesting cables to Stern, he did so. On July 18 Stern wrote him a long summary of the negotiations thus far. The count was working constantly, seeing a variety of people, traveling furiously between Tientsin and Shanghai, and, in general, making every effort on Barker's behalf. Sheng Hsuan-huai, director-general of the Imperial Telegraph Administration and taotai of Chefoo, was opposing the telephone concession on the grounds that it would interfere with his own concern, the telegraph system. As a result the concession was confined to the treaty ports then open.[29]

Li had proven unwilling to grant a concession for railways or mines, but he was interested in the establishment of a bank modeled on American national banks. Such a Sino-American financial organization would have the power to issue bank bills, mint currency, and furnish government loans for all public improvement projects. Li was ready to be its director. Li saw the bank as the "pivot" on which all of China's subsequent development could turn. It would offer low-interest loans to the government, no-interest loans to himself, finance a vast series of railroads, mines, and manufacturing enterprises. To settle details of the bank's organization, Li would send Ma Chien-chang to America as his "special envoy." In conjunction with Chang Yin-huan, he would negotiate a protocol with Barker; then Barker must himself come to China to negotiate the final details.[30]

Li Hung-chang was as wary of foreign control of Chinese enterprises as Chang Chih-tung. His readiness to grant an American syndicate such immense benefits is puzzling. It can be explained, in part at least, by Li's apparent belief that Americans were less venal than other interested foreigners. More important, however, was the persuasive theory of using barbarians to fight barbarians. From the 1860's on, Li had been badgered by the representatives of France, Germany, and England to grant railroad loans, mine exploitation privileges, and other development concessions. Often the demands verged on outright threats and on several occasions Li had been forced to sign agreements that seemed to grant preferential treatment to one country or another. The most-favored-nation clause in the treaties multiplied the danger of any such grants. The Barker syndicate was a new weapon to hand.

The more parties competing for the privilege of lending China money —in the hope of eventually obtaining full concessions to build rail-roads—the better China's position became. Li was able to use the very rumors of what he had granted one group to force down interest rates on other loans he hoped to get. In mid-July, for example, the rumor that the American syndicate would lend China money at 4 percent re-sulted in a loan of Tls 2,500,000 by the German syndicate at that low rate of interest.[31]

Moreover, Li was vitally interested in the rapid development of a railroad system for purposes of national defense. China simply did not have the capital resources necessary for the task. With the fate of Egypt and Turkey in mind, outright railroad concessions to foreign firms were opposed by all Chinese officials as compromising the nation's sover-eignty. By establishing a bank, whose charter would provide for low-interest loans, Li would at one stroke have the capital he needed and a large degree of control over the loan operation itself. The bank would draw foreign capital and skill into the service of China, under Chinese control. It was hoped that the organization could be sinified as success-fully as the Imperial Maritime Customs had been. Clearly the entire bank scheme was initiated by the Chinese. Mitkiewicz had broached no such idea to Barker at any time in their association, although he had discussed specific railroad concessions.

Although every effort had been made to keep the negotiations secret, it was not long before the small foreign community knew, in great if often inaccurate detail, of Barker's coup. In early August the *North China Herald* ran a long article on "the great Concession." For years, the editor declared, foreigners had hoped China would institute a sys-tem of national banking, but few had thought Li would be so daring as to sanction such vast changes. The article predicted great opposition to the concession on the part of Chinese officials and foreign interests alike. Only a few months before, Li had refused a much smaller concession to

Herr Exner, representative of a German syndicate, on the grounds that China didn't want any foreign debts. Yet now Li, the editorial protested, had approved far more dangerous concessions, which sold China's vital interests to the "highest bidders."[32]

Another article in the same issue of the *Herald* noted that the telephone concession, by allowing foreigners to join Chinese in operating a new enterprise, meant that "the gates of exclusion are thrown open." Logically it meant that foreigners could now ask for concessions in mines and railways, as well as legal partnership status with Chinese merchants for business outside the treaty ports.[33] The American consul in Tientsin, who had put himself at Mitkiewicz's disposal as soon as he knew what was afoot, drew similar conclusions. All earlier efforts to secure joint Sino-foreign stock companies had failed. Now the way was open to similar enterprises in railway development.[34]

If the telephone concession was thus a new precedent, the bank scheme, an anonymous writer for the *North China Herald* proclaimed, was "the most astounding transaction as regards magnitude, that has ever been made since the round world began." This one bank would eclipse all the others; indeed shares in the Hong Kong and Shanghai Bank had already begun to drop.[35]

Meanwhile Charles Denby fretted over his lack of means to help the concessionaires succeed. Mitkiewicz's immense self-confidence had led him to ignore Denby altogether. In August, however, Consul Smithers at Tientsin advised Mitkiewicz that Li was worried by rumors of British and German opposition and urged that Denby be requested to press Barker's suit at the Tsungli yamen.[36] On August 13, 1887, Denby wrote Secretary of State Bayard a worried report. The plans of the syndicate were widely discussed and the English, French, and German ministers were "much exercised" over it. The British-dominated *North China Daily News* published "ponderous leaders against the scheme," calling the concessions rash, disastrous for China, tantamount to an American protectorate over the entire country. There had been rumors that Chang Chih-tung was anti-American as well as anti-Li and would fight the concession at the highest level.[37] A few weeks later Denby informed Bayard that he had unofficially tried to impress the Chinese with the worthiness of American motives and superior skill. He had stressed that the American scheme was completely private, that the government was in no way involved and that, therefore, China need have no fear of complications.[38]

Li conceived of the bank as a private venture on both the Chinese and American side. According to Li Kuo-ch'i, Li had never favored the joint merchant-official operation known as *kuan-tu shang-pan*. Only the lack of sufficient merchant risk capital, and the pressure of official opposition, had led him to this compromise solution. A private company, Li reasoned, would mean less risk for the Chinese government. Foreign demands could be met frankly with the assertion that the company was in no position to grant rights pertaining to the imperial government. Though Li specifically offered his protection to the enterprise, it would yet be private enough to avoid all pitfalls.[39]

Meanwhile, Ma Chien-chang arrived in America in late July as Li's "special envoy." Though ordered by Li to aid in the negotiation of a protocol, Chang Yin-huan was disturbed by the growing criticism reaching him from China, Europe, and even America. The American press had launched a campaign of exposure against the count, and he was a pitifully vulnerable mark. Chang was puzzled when he discovered that the bank capital would be strictly private and that government officials would neither manage it nor supply it with funds. Hoping to escape over-involvement in what now appeared a most controversial enterprise, Chang tried to put all responsibility for signing agreements with Barker on Ma. As Li's envoy, Ma and not Chang had both more information and more authority. Tired by his battles over the immigration problem, worried about the feasibility of the vast scheme that had somehow become partially his responsibility, Chang wrote Ma that he would soon leave for Niagara Falls, "to see the cataract and to wash the dust out of my heart." In a diary notation for September 11, one of the few that mention his role in the negotiations, Chang tersely commented that the bank matter was concluded and that he didn't wish to discuss it with anyone further.[40]

Barker persisted in referring to the documents he, Chang, and Ma signed as a concession granted to him by the emperor.[41] In fact, imperial permission for the bank had not even been requested, much less granted. As proposals, they were as sweeping as all the rumors had supposed. The bank was to be exempt from all taxes on its business or profits; it was to be protected, "in all its rights," by Li Hung-chang; its charter was permanent. Bonds issued by the bank for public works would be guaranteed by the government, and the bank would share equally with the government any profit from railroad construction. The initial railways project discussed was for two trunk lines: one from Peking to Tientsin and one from Shanghai to Canton.[42]

As news of Barker's alleged concessions spread, requests to buy into the syndicate, job applications from railway men, telephone men, old China hands, and miscellaneous relatives and friends began to pour into Barker's office. Almost simultaneously, disparaging articles about both Mitkiewicz and the syndicate itself appeared, with growing frequency and virulence, in American and foreign newspapers.

The attack came from many sources. According to T. G. Morrow, editor of the *Sunday Gazette,* a Washington weekly, the Bell Telephone Company was determined to "balk" Barker because, in an attempt to circumvent their monopoly, Barker's engineer had negotiated with a small electronics firm for the necessary telephonic instruments. Later sallies against the syndicate were laid to the frustrated ambition of Russell and Company, and to the jealous designs of every European country having dealings with China. Jardine, Matheson and Company acted vigorously to kill the enterprise. The firm's agents were instructed to warn Chinese officials against the American plan. The aim was to frighten the Chinese into canceling the agreement. At the same time, Jardine's agent planned to draw up an integrated scheme of his own, to be put before "the proper officials in Peking (but who are they?) to provide money, railways and everything connected with it." A critique of the American plan was translated and sent to a high Manchu official, I-tsung, leader of the conservative faction, in the hope of exciting his determined opposition.[43]

The press campaign against Mitkiewicz was so vigorous that the *North China Herald* commented editorially on how strange it was for American newspapers to discredit a man who had done so much for his adopted countrymen.[44] It is possible that the representatives of both Bell Telephone and Russell and Company were behind the attack, at least to the extent of supplying the papers with exhaustive accounts of Mitkiewicz's early career. Barker's attempt to keep the enterprise as secret as possible added to the confusion. There seemed to be some doubt that as reputable a man as Barker was involved at all. More probably the newspapers simply seized on the story because it was so inherently sensational. The drama of a financial coup in the Middle Kingdom secured by a fake Russian count who possessed the doubtful distinction of a dossier in Scotland Yard was irresistible.

Understandably worried, Barker asked former American minister to China, John Russell Young, how far Li Hung-chang could be trusted. Young assured him that "so long as you are dealing with the Viceroy Li you are dealing with China." But he warned Barker that ultimate power remained in Peking, that Li had enemies and that interested Europeans would do all they could to block the concession. Young reminded Barker that this was China's first move toward opening her resources to a foreign nation. It would require the greatest tact and diplomacy to bring it off. Li himself was subject to the vagaries of Chinese politics and would need all the aid he could get. Young urged Barker to enlist the help of the State Department.[45]

In Peking Denby was doing his best to help the syndicate. He unofficially urged the Chinese to put all their faith in America and Americans because "of our form of government, our fixed determination to acquire no territory . . . and the vast experience we have in the construction of railways." In Washington, however, Bayard was extremely cautious. He reported to Denby that when Mitkiewicz called on him, he was told that the Department would take no action because the matter was purely private in nature.[46] Late in September Denby detailed the considerable opposition to the project that had developed in China. The hostility drew on a variety of anti-American sentiments, and on China's fears of foreign domination. The anti-American sentiment was directly attributable to the extremely harsh anti-Chinese immigration law that Congress had recently passed despite all Chang Yin-huan's efforts to defeat it. Acting without instructions, Denby had called on the Tsungli yamen to counter charges that the concession would be a monopoly in violation of the treaties, that America would try to establish a protectorate over China or interfere in any way with her internal affairs. The Tsungli yamen denied their responsibility in the matter and Denby left the interview convinced that America's great chance was lost.[47]

Hoping to salvage the scheme without unduly endangering his own position, Li Hung-chang answered the Tsungli yamen's suspicious queries about the enterprise with a letter startling in its mixture of fact, fiction, and clever ambiguities. Li protested that the projected bank was private, not official, that the plan was still in its preparatory stage, and that if it should materialize it would benefit China.[48] Li's explanation did not still the opposition. In response to several memorials protesting the establishment of the bank, the Grand Council, on September 28, issued an edict warning Li against the "relentless profit-seeking" of foreigners and ordering him to explain his conduct further. On October 6, the Grand Council noted Li's failure to respond to the earlier edict and, citing public opposition to the project and the defects inherent in the business itself, Li was ordered to cease all discussion of the matter.[49] On the following day, Li reported to the Tsungli yamen, by telegraph, that he had wired the American merchants to drop the plan entirely.[50]

On October 5, Ma Chien-chang informed Barker that, because of opposition in Peking, negotiations were suspended. He told Barker that Li was very anxious to have Barker visit China and establish a purely American bank in one of the ports. This last proposal may have been an attempt, on Li's part, to make Barker's actions coincide with his description of them to the Tsungli yamen.[51]

The newspapers, which had been sniping at Barker and Mitkiewicz for several months, now had a field day.[52] Barker continued to deny all knowledge of the withdrawal but added that if it were true he would request the protection of the State Department.

Barker's hope of government interference was short-lived. Denby was profoundly disappointed by the fiasco and wrote Bayard that he would have helped Mitkiewicz had the latter ever called on him. In reply Bayard warned Denby to remain aloof from concession-seeking Americans until the Department informed him otherwise. Consul Smithers, in Tientsin, had embraced Mitkiewicz without any introduction from the State Department or proof of citizenship. He had given his endorsement to a private project of which the Department was completely ignorant. Although Bayard wanted to forward American interests in China, it was essential that they be responsible interests. In future, Denby was strictly forbidden to further "individual plans and contracts connected with foreign governments" until they had been submitted to and approved by the Department.[53]

John Russell Young, determined to aid Barker in every way he could, wrote to Li, spoke to Bayard and had a long private talk with Chang Yin-huan. The results were discouraging. Bayard expressed a desire to help "within the diplomatic powers of his office," but he conceived these very narrowly indeed. Chang informed him that the anticoncession forces in Peking had won a complete victory. Li, Young wrote Barker, had withdrawn in the face of the storm, leaving Barker in the position "of doing as other foreigners do—namely starting an ordinary bank, and taking the ordinary chances of trade."[54] By January, Barker had at last admitted that the splendid vision of a monopolistic Sino-American Bank managing vast projects all over the empire, was forfeit. He had lost a large sum of money, Mitkiewicz was suing him, and a few unsportsmanlike members of the original syndicate were demanding their money back.

One would have expected Barker, at this point, to wash his hands of China, concentrate on his not inconsiderable domestic railway and banking schemes, and become a minor prophet of doom for anyone who retained illusions of China's unexploited wealth. Instead, he seemed to become obsessed with China. Every few years he put forth new projects, solicited funds, sometimes successfully, and spun out projects equal in scope and ambition to the much mourned bank. But the scheme must be vast. Personal invitations from Li Hung-chang, stated in the most flattering prose, urging Barker to come to China himself and establish a purely American bank, or supply a limited loan, or undertake a small branch railway, were all impatiently rejected. Barker did eventually organize an American Oriental Trust Company, consisting of those members of the original syndicate still interested in picking up some concessions in China. As agent for the trust company he appointed a resident American businessman in Shanghai, John Purdon. At first this was under the assumption, tenaciously held by Barker, that the original concession would be carried out, at least in part. Later Purdon disposed of Barker's store of telephone equipment and kept him in touch with developments in China. To all requests to come to China, Barker replied that he would go only when he was certain of a concession and not on the "chance of finding business" there. He wrote Ma Chien-chang that as soon as Li was ready to ask him to come for the purpose of fulfilling the 1887 contract or any similarly large-scale scheme, he would set out at once. Moreover, he had been in contact with one of the Russian engineers of the Trans-Caspian railroad and was convinced that all three countries, America, China, and Russia, could work through him.[55]

In March 1888 Barker replied to earlier suggestions that he raise a large loan for China. He had been ready, he declared in a long letter to Ma Chien-chang, to undertake vast schemes in China, yet the engagements he had entered into in the autumn of 1887 had never been confirmed or even discussed in their correspondence. Barker rejected any "mere money-lending scheme." He would undertake any railroad anywhere in China, provided it remained in his control; nothing less would bring him across the Pacific. Almost rudely he disabused Ma of any notion that he would leave America without a definite assurance of a contract.[56]

Yet Li Hung-chang, wary as he was of any foreign control of China's railroads, continued to press Barker to come. In May 1888 he wrote Barker apologizing for the necessity of voiding all prior agreements signed by Mitkiewicz. He had done so, Li ingenuously wrote, to preserve Barker's own reputation. Ma Chien-chang had convinced him of Barker's worth and, in the language of the translated letter in Barker's papers, Li was "on the tip-toe of expectation for the day when you will in your goodness come to China." One week later, Ma Chien-chang wrote that the ideal occasion for Barker to demonstrate his integrity to wary high officials in Peking had arrived. Li's own railroad effort, the line extending from the Kaiping Mines to Taku, had a mortgage of one million taels borrowed at 5 percent from a French syndicate and the Hong Kong and Shanghai Bank. The loan was due in three years and Ma suggested that Barker pick it up at a lower rate of interest for a ten year period. In this way Barker would win the regard of the government. The line involved was semi-governmental in nature and one that Prince Ching and Li both wished to see pushed on all the way to Peking.

Ma suggested several other limited projects that would make Barker's position as the key foreign developer of China impregnable. At the same time he made it perfectly clear that Barker could not operate on so large a scale without making small beginnings. Nor could he run things without Chinese control, even if the latter were only nominal. Ma suggested, for example, that Barker establish a bank, which he might name the Americo-Chinese Bank and which would be in his name and under his control. Li and all Ma's friends would help him. All financial matters would be in Barker's hands, but any railroads or mines sponsored by the Bank would, "to satisfy national prejudice," be owned by a Chinese. Barker was assured of all the real power he might want, but titular possession he could not have.[57] There is a distinct similarity between Ma's suggestion and the form later foreign enterprises took in China. Ma's Americo-Chinese Bank is an early version of the Russo-Chinese Bank, founded in 1895 as an instrument of Russian expansion in Manchuria. In 1887 Li could still be confident that ultimate control rested in Chinese hands. But even in 1895 he found this form more congenial than an outright grant to a foreign government. The Russo-Chinese Bank represented a compromise, a face-saving device for the Chinese. It is apparent now that it was also a form familiar to Li and one that he had attempted to use for development purposes almost ten years earlier.

Barker interpreted Ma's letter as a fairly hard offer of a railroad concession and in July he wrote Li that he would come to China the following autumn with a competent engineer. In August he wrote Li that he planned to travel through Europe and then go on to Russia where he would discuss schemes for joint Asian railroad development. In October a rapid telegraphic correspondence between Barker and Ma seemed to approach a firm agreement on a loan from Barker in return for a railroad concession, but the negotiations broke on the twin rocks of Barker's desire for a vast scheme and his insistence on a guarantee before he would go to China. In January Ma firmly told Barker that China was not like Europe; definite advance proposals were impossible. Barker must personally negotiate these with Li in China.[58]

The following month Barker's agent, Purdon, discouraged Barker in more final terms. The loan had been made by the Hong Kong and Shanghai Bank at 5 percent.

For a time Barker ceased his unrelenting effort to derive some profit from his expensive 1887 documents. There was a pause on the Chinese side as well. In November 1889 Ma Chien-chang reported that powerful opposition to all railroad activity had been gaining and it seemed, after so much progress had been made, that China was further away from real railroad development than ever before.[59]

Barker's failure and Li's frustration at being unable to obtain aid from responsible Americans was due to an almost total lack of understanding between the two parties. Li's desire to engage Barker was sincere. Distrusting all foreigners, he yet made distinctions among them. Clearly America was least dangerous. After the failure of the bank scheme Li had every reason to expect Barker to realize the value of the contacts he had made through Mitkiewicz, to come to China on some lesser errand, and to build a base of profitable operations with Li's help. A single failure, as Li's own railroad efforts showed, was hardly a reason for giving up altogether. If Li could build a short railroad and call it a horse road, surely Barker could offer China one low-interest loan in the confident expectation that, in time, he would be in a leading position vis-à-vis Chinese development. Li expected Barker to behave like a Chinese bureaucrat. Through the liberal disbursement of funds and the cultivation of contacts and, above all, through a readiness to wait years for an enterprise to bear fruit, Barker would get all he hoped to out of China.

This was, indeed, the way other foreign concerns in China did operate. Jardine, Matheson and Company had for years been involved in the painstaking work of buying, through low-interest loans and other favors, the influence of important Chinese bureaucrats. The firm tried to work within the traditional Chinese framework rather than against it. From 1885 to 1895, the agents of Jardine, Matheson and Company sought to obtain a position of influence with Li Hung-chang and other officials interested in modernizing projects. Throughout, the realities of bureaucratic power were accepted and the firm displayed a "general willingness to cooperate with this power to their own advantage." With skill and care the agents of the company attempted to gain the very power that Barker so cavalierly rejected—the opportunity to cooperate, on almost any terms, with bureaucrats like Li Hung-chang, in the hope of participating in development projects. In July 1887, for example, Jardine lent Li Tls 150,000 at below the current rate of interest, for the construction of the Taku-Tientsin railroad. James Keswick explained to the London office that profit from the loan would not be very great, but it would establish Jardine as the leading firm in the expected railroad boom.[60] Despite all the encouraging letters from Li Hung-chang and the Ma brothers, Barker could never adopt this long-range perspective. Instead, he tried to force his dealings with the Chinese into an American mold.

In the United States Barker was used to dealing with huge financial schemes of an essentially speculative nature. The collection and free use of a large venture capital fund was not a strange operation to him. He did expect, however, that once a deal was made, even in skeletal form, it could be depended upon. He demanded guarantees from the Chinese that the latter simply could not offer. When he inaccurately called Li the prime minister of China, he was expressing his understanding of Li's position in the Chinese government. It is true that the 1880's represented the peak of Li Hung-chang's power but, as John Russell Young warned Barker, Li's position was by no means unassailable. To succeed in China, Barker would have to move slowly, secretly, patiently, and with utmost circumspection. This he would not, or could not, do. The disappointment was great on both sides.

Meanwhile, Pethick was urgently trying to get more responsible Americans interested in China. In January of 1891 he wrote Wilson that Li Hung-chang was interested in a thirty million tael loan but had so far found no terms attractive to him. He asked if Wilson could not line up sufficient American capital to form a syndicate that would lend money as well as secure railroad concessions. "I can only stand by and wring my hands," Pethick wrote, "because no Americans are in the swim." Pethick reported that Li was seeking to borrow money from foreign bankers in order to build the railroad further and faster into Manchuria.[61] But no Americans were interested and as a flood of his letters to Wilson reveal, Pethick continued to wring his hands at the lost opportunities.

Increase in American Interest

It is clear, from a simple comparison between popular American magazines before and after the Sino-Japanese War, that a tremendous change took place in the extent and kind of general interest in Far Eastern affairs after 1895. In 1891 Pethick might well despair; in 1895 he complained, instead, of the flood of petitioners arriving in Peking. In the earlier period, journals carried fairly regular articles describing the customs, manners, and general oddities of the mysterious Orient. From 1894 on, these capsule culture essays virtually disappear. In their place are political, social, and economic reports and analyses by a new group of amateur and professional Far Eastern experts.

Part of this increasing interest can, of course, be explained by the obvious news value of the events that took place in Asia during this period. The drama and complexity of international rivalry in the Far East were intense, and it would have been most surprising if Americans had *not* shown any interest. But events were more and more being reported from an American viewpoint rather than discussed as items of general interest. There was a widespread acceptance of the fact that what took place in China could and would have direct relevance to the United States.[62]

There was even talk of an Anglo-American alliance. The *Literary Digest* reported American opinion divided on the prospect of such an alliance but noted that few agreed with Senator Chandler, whose personal opinion sheet, the Concord *Monitor,* urged an alliance with Russia against England with the aim of seizing Canada.[63] The division is indicated nicely by the *New York Tribune* and the *New York Sun.* The *Tribune,* a solidly Republican paper that had rarely hesitated to denounce the British, now commented that the United States could never be drawn into a war between Britain and Russia on Russia's side. America realized that its own commercial interests in Asia would only suffer from Russian domination.[64] The jingoistic *Sun,* however, agreed with Senator Chandler, at least insofar as American sympathies were concerned. Why, it asked, should the United States connive to deprive a friendly Russia for the sake of greedy England, "which in all times of trouble has shown herself our enemy?" The *Sun* was confident that Russian dominance in China would not interfere with American interests.[65]

Li Hung-chang's 1896 visit to America provoked much comment and speculation in the American press. Most newspapers devoted a fair amount of space to biographies of Li and injunctions to him. *The Chicago Record,* for example, was confident that Li's journey could not "fail to impress him still further with the need of bringing the Oriental Empire nearer to the plane of civilization."[66]

Although Li was actually on his way back to China from a mission of great importance to Russia, most American newspapers agreed with the British *Contemporary Review* that his trip to Moscow was of secondary importance.[67] The real purpose of the journey was commercial. The New York *Journal of Commerce* called the trip a landmark in the ongoing march of Western commerce and confidently expected large orders for goods to follow Li's trip, giving Americans a fair chance for profitable competition.[68]

At the urging of John J. McCook, Li was given an official presidential reception. The Pennsylvania Railroad put itself at his disposal and, after some initial hesitation, the government went all out to receive Li in state. The only concrete result was the purchase, soon after Li's return, of eight Baldwin locomotives by the Chinese government.

In China, Charles Denby was receiving the first wave of American speculators and businessmen. The myth of a vast China market, born with the first American ship that sailed to China, could rest on real statistical gains in the decade 1890–1900. In dollar value, cotton goods alone increased from $5,331,251 in 1887 to $8,500,802 in 1897. China bought nearly 50 percent of all American cotton exports. Total exports to China rose from $7,385,362 in 1890 to $23,745,000 in 1900.[69] An increase of 220 percent was dazzling to many businessmen, though on reflection they might have noted that China trade still remained a small fraction of general U.S. exports, which from 1890 to 1900 had risen from $875,502,548 to $1,478,050,000.[70] Cotton goods were America's major export to China. Kerosene, wheat flour, and later, iron and steel, were the other important items.[71] But if the Sino-Japanese War seemed, to Americans, to open China anew to possibilities at the very moment when the United States was thought to be closing, this good fortune was also felt to be almost immediately threatened.

In November 1900 Sir Robert Hart spoke to a young American reporter, Wilbur Chamberlin, amid the wreckage of Peking's streets. Chamberlin questioned the old man anxiously about the possibilities of a partition of China. "My son," Hart replied, "I have been in China 47 years, and there has not been a year since I came here that they haven't talked of partitioning the country."[72] Yet in 1895 something very like partition had begun. Perhaps it would be more accurate to call it apportionment. Between the Treaty of Shimonoseki and the Boxer uprising, China's railways, mines, even some of her ports, were distributed among the European countries.

The Dreibund Powers, France, Germany, and Russia, each expected to be rewarded by China for having saved the Liaotung Peninsula from a rapacious Japan, although few even pretended that their action had been altruistically motivated. In July 1895, France demanded and received a highly favorable treaty in which the Yunnan-Annam border was redrawn in France's favor. In addition, France was granted priority rights for the exploitation of mines in Yunnan, Kwangtung, and Kwangsi, as well as a railroad concession, the first granted to a foreign power.

The British, rivals of the French for power, prestige, and profit in southwest China, demanded corresponding privileges on the China-Burma frontier as "compensation." These British gains threw the French into the field again, and in the summer of 1897 the latter received, in "compensation," further railroad and mining concessions in southwest China. The Russians gained handsome concessions for the Trans-Siberian Railroad in exchange for a mutual defense treaty.[73] Chinese diplomats fought hard against each of these gains, trimming them to the core, granting only what it would have taken force of arms to deny. However, there had been no large-scale loss of territory. China's railroad map might have to be drawn in the colors of several nationalities, but an effort was made to balance one nation against the other, and though the whole process was humiliating, nothing irrevocable (all the railroad concessions included redemption clauses) had yet occurred. It was in this ominous atmosphere of a golden gate providentially opened by Japan only to be wickedly shut again by the European powers that the first Americans seriously interested in exploiting China since Barker and Wilson arrived in Peking.

three   Investment and
                                           Speculation

The end of the Sino-Japanese War brought a flood of speculators and advance agents to China from all over the world. Americans were not slow to follow. The major difference between American demands and successes and those of other foreigners is that the United States government remained quite completely in the background, helpful but not instigating. The curious group of Americans that showed up in Peking represented the American government neither officially nor semi-officially. The same cannot be said for any other country, including Britain, who in June of 1895 made a *governmental* demand for a railroad concession to counter one that France had just received.

Accounts of American railroad interests in China thus far have had only one story to tell, a sorry one at that, involving the American China Development Company.[1] In fact there was another group interested in Chinese railways that, failing to obtain a concession for itself, worked to undermine the Development Company.

The plans of both groups are distinguished by their firm belief in Russian predominance in Manchuria and North China. Unlike the majority of political analysts in America, they saw Russian strength as a positive asset to America's future position in Asia. They worked to trade on Russia's position so that their expected concessions would be the result of both Russian and Chinese guarantees. Whereas an alliance with Great Britain would bring the center of American influence down to the Yangtze Valley, a working agreement with Russia would locate it in the heart of actual American economic interests in China, for the great bulk of American exports went to North China and Manchuria.

The Competing Efforts of Bash and Wilson
Just before John W. Foster, who stepped in and out of State Department service throughout his career, left for China to help Li Hung-chang

in the Shimonoseki negotiations, he arranged a private code for communication with General Wilson. Foster's first coded communication to Wilson is dated April 23, 1895, and is the earliest mention of an American syndicate that would build a road from Peking to Canton. Wilson answered immediately, expressing interest and a determination to be in on the ground floor. But he was already too late, for A. W. Bash, accompanied by ex-Senator Dolph of Oregon was busy negotiating in Peking. Bash represented a group of eager Washington state businessmen and politicians whose thoughts paralleled Foster's—to engage to build a trunk line spanning China from north to south with the additional possibility of building northward toward the Trans-Siberian railroad.[2]

Meanwhile, during the summer of 1895, Charles Denby carried on a rather harried correspondence with the State Department, trying to obtain instructions so specific they would protect him against all contingencies. He firmly believed in the importance of American enterprise in China as a lever to greater American prestige in the Far East. At the same time he had no wish to find himself attacked for indiscretions by the Chinese government and unsupported by his own. In May he wrote a long personal letter to Gresham, which the latter was never to answer. Denby found himself beseiged by petitioners anxious to enlist his aid in their quest for concessions.[3]

In the letter, Denby referred to his 1887 instructions from Bayard, which had strictly limited the scope of any effort he might want to make. Bash, the first agent to contact Denby, had been surprised and dismayed at their rigidity. Denby himself wished to do everything possible to advance American interests but felt he could not act as anyone's agent. Without committing himself, and using Bash's displeasure as a prod to action in the direction he wished, Denby concluded by putting the burden on Gresham: "If, however, by any possibility, your Administration could get the glory of greatly increasing and spreading American interests in China, it would be a grand consummation."[4]

On May 12, 1895, only a few days after writing his letter, Denby cabled for advice on how to deal with a request by the American Trading Company to present to the Chinese its proposal for a large loan. He was instructed to limit himself, on his own discretion, to a formal introduction of the eager Americans to the relevant Chinese officials. He must not in any way use his own official status to press their suit.[5]

Although strict, these instructions went considerably beyond Bayard's, which had required prior Department approval before Denby could make any move at all. Indeed, Denby quickly pointed out that mere introductions were just not done in China. To introduce a petitioner to the government implied support and he felt that too much responsibility had been placed on him.[6] This modest appeal was contradicted by Denby's subsequent actions.

Without waiting for an answer to his telegram about the American Trading Company, though one came just two days after his plea for advice, Denby had acted on the Company's request as soon as he heard that it represented an American syndicate supported by J. P. Morgan. He took care, however, to inform the Department of his actions by pouch, a process taking well over a month before he could expect an answer. Believing it dangerous for Russia to assume the entirety of the first indemnity loan, he had felt it prudent to act quickly on behalf of the American Trading Company—though his efforts came to nothing.

It was not until June 22, 1895, that Denby received an answer to his dispatch of May 13, and its author was not Gresham but the new, vigorous secretary of state, Richard Olney. Full responsibility was placed on Denby. He was authorized to introduce Americans to the Chinese government "with such representations as to their character and responsibility as facts known to you warrant, but without using your diplomatic character or influence to further their business enterprise."[7] It was a distinction without a difference, for as Denby pointed out, such neutral introductions were difficult in China, particularly as Denby was being hard pressed by the Americans involved, was himself convinced that their cause was just and larger than individual profit, and was receiving demanding letters from his best friends at home. Moreover Denby's son, Charles, Jr., sometime legation official and pride and joy of his father, was deeply involved in a variety of business schemes, some of dubious legality.[8]

In September 1895, Denby, Jr., reported to Burnham, Williams and Company, a prominent Pennsylvania railroad company, that Bash had spoken to both the Chinese and Russians about American participation in Manchurian railroad construction as well as in the Peking-Canton trunk line. He had been favorably received but nothing had been decided. Wilson's friends in Burnham, Williams and Company sent this letter on to him and Wilson replied that "his syndicate," which at this time was merely a project, was fully prepared to build a railroad from a suitable point on the Trans-Siberian through Kirin to Peking by way of Tientsin. All that was lacking was a concession from the Chinese and a contract with the Russians. Wilson's vision of future power and glory are evident in his confident expectation that his group could secure concessions covering all railroads in Manchuria.[9]

When Bash returned from China in August of 1895 he immediately wrote Wilson an admiring letter asking if he would be interested in joining Bash and his friends to form one large "association" for obtaining concessions. The speculative nature of the arrangement was indicated by Bash's proposal to get a concession *first* and *then* raise money. Bash offered Wilson a leading role in such an association. Wilson, however, turned down Bash's offer and continued to make efforts on his own.[10] A full year passed before Wilson was able to make any progress.

By this time Senator Brice of Ohio had assumed a leading role in Bash's group. Calvin Brice was a prominent figure in Washington.[11] Active in railway promotion schemes and a sharp corporation lawyer, he was an ideal man to head the syndicate. The syndicate, incorporated in New Jersey as the American China Development Company, was generally referred to as the Bash-Brice syndicate. In August 1896, Pethick wrote Wilson a rather penitent letter. He had done what he could to aid the Bash-Brice group in hopes that Wilson would join them. He was bitterly disappointed that Wilson had not done so. On August 24, 1896, Pethick peremptorily cabled Wilson urging him to join Brice as his success seemed imminent. But Wilson had other plans. A few days later Pethick described how far Bash had been able to go. Pethick had introduced him to Sheng Hsuan-huai, recently appointed director-general of the Imperial Railway Administration, and an understanding had been reached on a concession for the Peking-Hankow line. The plan was linked to promised concessions for roads in all of north China and Manchuria.[12]

In late October, Wilson lunched with Clarence Cary, a shrewd New York lawyer who had been retained by the Brice group. He learned that the syndicate had no money and no prospects of raising any until after the coming presidential election. Apparently businessmen were taking no chances on foreign investment until they were certain that McKinley would win and the dreaded Bryan revolution was buried for at least another four years. Wilson's meeting with Cary galvanized him into action. Already in September he had written to his good friend Jacob Schiff, of the powerful Kuhn, Loeb and Company, that quick action must be taken if he and his friends were to gain a concession for Chinese and Manchurian railroad business.[13]

The day after his meeting with Cary, Wilson contacted John J. Mc-Cook, a prominent railroad promoter, and urged him to join Wilson in his effort to exploit railroad opportunities in China. A combination of all interested parties had to be formed to prevent "rivalry" and ensure "successful operations." Such a syndicate should have, as a start, enough money to send a businessman, a lawyer, and a diplomat to St. Petersburg to enlist the aid of the Russian government and the Russian officials and capitalists. No large-scale business could be conducted in China without first securing the approval of the Russians. Once that approval was secured a mission would be sent to China with enough money to stay two years and arrange the necessary contracts, surveys, and so forth. Thus, only $250,000 would be needed in the preliminary stages.

Wilson, whose diplomatic ambitions were great, added another suggestion: "It should not be forgotten that the appointment of proper men as Ambassador to Russia and Minister to China will be essential to the complete success of the syndicate and hence it may be important that our friend Mark Hanna should be a member of the syndicate." Should McKinley win, Wilson and his friends might reasonably expect some patronage reward. As the scheme developed, Wilson hoped to place himself in Russia and William Rockhill in China, thus adding their combined diplomatic powers and pressure to the weight of money and skill he hoped the syndicate would possess. Wilson wrote confidently to Pethick that, although Cary and other members of the Brice group had offered him a leading position in their outfit, they were moving very slowly and he simply could not wait around for their plans to mature.[14]

Wilson's plans for working both the Russian and Chinese end of a projected major railroad did not wait for a government appointment, however. He was already in contact with a Major J. G. Pangborn, President of the World's Transportation Commission of Chicago. Pangborn had arrived in Russia in February 1895 and had spent eighteen months studying the transportation problem in both China and Russia. He was anxious to be of help to anyone interested in the construction of railroads in the Far East.[15] In the spring of 1896 McCook himself went to Russia as an aide to his brother, General A. W. McCook, who was representing the United States at the czar's coronation. While there, McCook became friendly with Prince Hilkoff, the minister of ways and communications. He also met Li Hung-chang, who was in St. Petersburg for the same event, and discussed with him the possibility of American participation in building and supplying a railroad linking north China with the Trans-Siberian road. Both Li and Hilkoff were expected to visit America later in the year. Wilson and McCook had high hopes of arranging an actual concession at that time. As an additional measure, McCook requested Secretary of State Olney to grant the secretary of the American legation in St. Petersburg an extended leave. Prince Hilkoff had invited the secretary, Herbert Peirce, to accompany him on his trip. It was hoped that during the long journey, which would extend to America via Siberia and China, Peirce could convince Hilkoff of the value to Russia of American participation in the building of any railroads connecting the Trans-Siberian with China.[16]

Through November and December 1896, Wilson and McCook met with a varied group of influential businessmen, who expressed interest in the scheme but would commit themselves no further. Frank Thomas of the Pennsylvania Railroad, Flagler of Standard Oil, J. P. Morgan, and others were dined alternately by McCook and Wilson. Flagler pointed out that the completion of the Trans-Siberian Railroad would most likely harm Standard Oil in China, and Wilson's plans for an extension of that road through Manchuria would hurt them even more; but he expressed interest nevertheless. J. P. Morgan refused to consider the project while it was in a preliminary stage.[17] Carnegie expressed no interest whatsoever.

Meanwhile, Wilson did what he could to dynamite the Brice group. In November he wrote Pethick that Cary and ex-Senator Washburn of Minnesota would sail for China early the next month. Washburn, he warned, was bankrupt and "a man with whom the Chinese cannot afford to waste their time."[18] Although he told Pethick his information on Washburn was confidential, the very next day he wrote Minister Denby that "old Washburn, the played-out Senator from Minnesota," was on his way to China. Wilson warned Denby that none of his friends in

America were interested in the Brice group. A few days later he wrote Charles Denby, Jr., on the same theme. The Brice group amounted to "nothing." Though some respectable people were involved, the subscribed capital was very low. If this group were to obtain a concession, Wilson went on, China would need someone to protect her interests; Wilson indicated that he himself would be responsive to a good offer along these lines. Meanwhile, he informed Denby that there was a rival group backed by "the best people—those who will be closest to McKinley's administration," which intended to form a syndicate to control railroads in both China and Siberia. He was whistling in the dark, however, for Wilson's grand syndicate showed no signs of ever becoming organized. Wilson's December correspondence with his contacts in China was wholly occupied with cursing Brice, Bash, and Washburn, the Chinese who trusted them (showing, Wilson declared, "the utter fatuity of the Oriental mind"), and the Americans who aided them.[19]

The Return of Wharton Barker

Wharton Barker, who had suffered bankruptcy in 1890, saw a new chance for profit in China after the Sino-Japanese War. He had maintained a friendly correspondence with Ma Chien-chang for many years and, in January 1895, wrote Ma expressing a profound interest in China's development. Ma's reply was friendly. He asked if Barker was cooperating with Foster and Wilson and assured him that he and his brother Ma Chien-chung would base their attitude toward Foster on this fact alone. In March Ma wrote that Li was once again in position of power. His conservative opponents had been silenced by Japan's success. Now, Ma was confident, reforms would come quickly and China, under Li's guidance, would become "a powerful nation." Ma Chien-chung, his brother wrote, was closely associated with Li and would undoubtedly play an important role in the future. Indeed his brother had asked Ma to urge Barker to be ready to come to China at any time.[20]

In a letter designed to interest subscribers, Barker quoted liberally from Ma's letters and referred as well to his connection with Russian railroad interests. His plan was the old one—to establish a bank that would have all the privileges of the 1887 concession. If he could not get a bank concession, Barker hoped to get contracts for railroads, steamships, mines, iron and steel mills; anything in short. "I expect," Barker concluded, "to bring about . . . undertakings of the greatest magnitude, enterprises as far reaching as those undertaken by the East India Company, and they should be quite as profitable." The fund he collected was to be purely exploitive. No accounting would be offered; he was to stay in China until the money was spent or he had a concession in hand.[21]

Despite the well-known failure of his last China project, Barker was able to raise a venture capital fund of $50,000 by August 1895. The outcome of the Sino-Japanese War had convinced most foreigners, as it had Ma Chien-chang himself, that China now had no choice but to develop, that the Great Awakening, first glimpsed in the abortive railway schemes of the 1880's, was at last at hand. At the end of August, Barker, with an associate named Garland, was in China. He presented lengthy petitions to Li Hung-chang, Chang Chih-tung, and Sheng Hsuan-huai. In each he proposed building 5,000 miles of trunk line, which would put China "in the first rank of nations." The promoters would have the right to buy land, open mines, organize steel and textile factories, and in general exploit all development opportunities. The operation would be in the complete control of the promoters with the expectation that the whole system would revert to China in twenty-five years.[22]

According to Pethick, who was an unfriendly witness, Li had responded to Barker's petition by asking him how he proposed to undertake vast enterprises when his own business had collapsed so totally in 1890. Barker replied that he had recovered his fortunes. Then Garland announced that Barker would probably be the next President of the United States. As Li told the story to Pethick, Barker, upon this statement, "assumed a profound and dignified air." Li assured Pethick that he could hardly contain his laughter at this announcement of Barker's imminent eminence.[23]

Barker's account of the interview was less colorful but more interesting. Li told him that his scheme would hand China over to foreigners and this would not be tolerated. Barker had warned Li that China stood in danger of partition and that his plan would make her independent. Li answered that though Americans enjoyed more trust than Europeans, the time had not yet come when China would offer so much power to any foreigners. Once more Li urged Barker to establish a private bank and

Barker once more refused. Barker expressed pleasure in the widespread interest in railroads he found everywhere in China, and despite the negative tone of the interview felt he had made much progress. He returned to the United States confident that if any concessions were granted he and his friends were in a good position to secure them.[24]

Although Barker was satisfied, his associates weren't, particularly when rumors of the Bash-Brice concession reached them. Garland wrote an angry letter accusing Barker of squandering the $50,000 entrusted to him. He warned Barker that he had better explain what had become of the money.[25] Barker's answer simply pointed out that the money had been given as pure risk capital with no accounting expected by the subscribers.[26] His association with Mitkiewicz had apparently taught Barker much about how to use China to raise money for oneself. In 1891 Mitkiewicz had raised $25,000 by a similar judicious use of his old letters of recommendation and his persuasive tongue.[27] Barker undoubtedly hoped to realize something from his trip to China, but when he found Li unwilling to sponsor his large schemes he characteristically lost interest.

The Failure of the Bash-Brice Group

Under instructions from Olney, Denby had become much more active in pushing private American interests. In December of 1896 Denby received a lengthy instruction from Olney, which radically increased his scope of activity. Though Denby was not to assume any responsibility for American enterprises in the name of the government, he was to use whatever influence he had, personal *and* diplomatic, to secure for Americans "the same facilities as are enjoyed by any other foreign commercial enterprise" in China. Olney refused to define Denby's duties in any strict way; indeed he enjoined the minister not to follow earlier instructions "too literally." He could take as his guideline the "extension of American commercial interests in China." [28] To "secure . . . the same facilities" was, as Olney well knew from Denby's reports, to give Denby a free hand in pressuring the Chinese government to meet American demands. For a secretary of state to instruct a minister not to follow his own instructions strictly was clearly an invitation to Denby to do as he saw fit. The main aim, a new one for the Department of State if not for the legation in Peking, was to extend American interests in China. As Wilson's syndicate had come to nothing, this meant in practice to aid by all means the American China Development Company.

Sheng Hsuan-huai, though officially the director of railroad development in China, in fact became a kind of broker between competing foreign interests. He attempted to use this rivalry to neutralize, if not eliminate, the dangers of foreign control of China's railway system. His method was to try to work out some kind of balance between the powers through railroad concessions. It was an immensely dangerous game and, in the end, unsuccessful. Sheng was interested in the American China Development Company's bid for the Peking-Hankow railroad contract as part of his own balancing scheme. Li Hung-chang, Sheng's early sponsor, was also in favor of Americans running this road, though according to Pethick Li had only limited influence over Sheng.[29]

By the Russo-Chinese treaty of 1896, China had been forced to grant Russia the right to extend the Trans-Siberian railroad across Manchuria, thus forever destroying Li Hung-chang's hope of a Chinese road in this area. The danger of Russian control of the trunk line south from Peking was clear to all concerned. But a Belgian syndicate, allied financially with French interests and by extension with Russia, was attempting to outbid the American company. Because of the strong personal interest King Leopold took in the road, the Belgians were able, indeed were pressured by the king, to offer Sheng a contract so liberal as to be virtually impossible to refuse.[30]

Denby fought against the Belgian concession as hard as he could. On January 9, 1897, he had an angry interview with the Tsungli yamen during which he insisted that Sheng Hsuan-huai be ordered to close with the Development Company. He told Prince Kung he must treat Americans justly and grant them the contract they wanted. With some relish, Denby reminded the yamen that America alone had not asked to be compensated for its aid to China during the war, though "all the gentlemen present well knew that to the Department of State belonged the honor of having made peace for China." But it was not merely a matter of rewarding virtue and showing gratitude. All the world knew that Americans built better railroads than anyone else. Nor was it a matter of skill alone. Everyone agreed "that the work of developing China should be conceded to Americans, because the United States had and could have no ulterior designs on Asiatic territory." Should the yamen withhold this contract it ran the danger of dissipating the fund of friendship Americans at home universally felt for China.[31] Denby's instructions allowed him to go far in persuading the Chinese and he took advantage of them. Although Olney might not have intended that Denby threaten the Chinese nor make extravagant statements as to their debt to America, this was certainly included in "proper means" used by other ambassadors and ministers in China.

Although no objection was made to Denby's actions thus far, he found himself in difficulty because of one rather innocuous statement he had made. Urging the Tsungli yamen to force Sheng to sign with the American China Development Company, Denby informed them that the company had been formed by immensely wealthy men. At this very time Wilson was writing to everyone he knew about the company's actual lack of funds despite the real interest several important New York bankers took in its activities. Their interest waited upon success and was based on no actual investment. In early March Wilson wrote Rockhill, then third assistant secretary of state, suggesting that Denby be repudiated for his endorsement of the "Bash-Brice-Washburn gang." Two days later McKinley's secretary of state, the weak and aged Sherman, sent a sharp cable to Denby ordering him to be cautious in his endorsements. According to Department information, the cable went on, the American China Development Company had limited liability and small capital; the personal affluence of some of the Company's members was irrelevant.[32]

Behind the Belgian company, as it soon appeared, stood the full weight of the Belgian and later the French and Russian governments. Behind the Development Company stood Denby and little else. It would have been politically absurd for McKinley, so freshly installed, to enter into a tangled web of Far Eastern railroad intrigue. The idea never occurred to him. Though the American people had grown more interested in Chinese affairs, the thought of possibly warring with European nations to defend an as yet only incipient American investment interest was clearly ridiculous. Denby himself felt that the American company would be foolish to agree to the liberal terms the Belgians were offering.

Investment without control was foolish. In this area, Denby believed, "the principle of extra-territoriality should be pushed to the utmost limit" for foreign control benefited not only the foreigners but China herself. Denby did not feel Americans would suffer because of their insistence on total control. China, and the world, realized that control by American capitalists could never mean territorial absorption or governmental interference as was usually the case with Europe. The Chinese may well have understood this; but they also understood its corollary: that the American government was not yet ready to defend the interests of its capitalists or, by extension, of China, when American interests coincided with China's attempt to balance another power. This, plus the extraordinarily liberal terms of the Belgian offer, sealed the fate of the Development Company so far as the Peking-Hankow road was concerned.[33]

By May 1897, Denby admitted defeat. In a long, mournful letter to the Department he was no longer so sympathetic to the Development Company's scruples regarding the contract. "Much as it is to be regretted that this first great step in the railroad development of China should have been taken by others, it must be admitted that our fellow citizens failed solely because they were unwilling to accept the terms offered by China and which have been accepted by the Belgians." By placing some of the blame on the Company itself for refusing the contract, Denby cleared himself of any incompetence that others, if not Sherman, might have charged him with. His report to the Department concluded on a depressed, if philosophic, note.

This conclusion of an enterprise which has engaged the attention of American capitalists, assisted by this Legation, for many months past, is exceedingly discouraging. The ominous suspicion that European politics are figuring in commercial concessions . . . is not promising for Americans. If the colonial ambitions of the Great Powers of Europe lead them to support syndicates in doubtful business undertakings here Americans will be greatly handicapped, because commercial matters for them in Asia cannot be mixed up with the schemes of political ambition. Our Government cannot be expected to demand concessions . . . on political grounds . . . As we have no political designs to serve in the Far East we have nothing to offer China in return for concessions. It thus happens that our great boon of being removed from and independent of foreign complications constitutes a correlative weakness.[34]

When Sheng Hsuan-huai signed with the Belgians, he found his balancing scheme more threatened than ever. Ascertaining that the Belgian syndicate had ties with Russia, the British entered a strong protest. More interested in using than destroying the Belgian contract, the British were successful: several pending concessions were quickly granted. The American China Development Company did not lose out completely. It was generally understood that, failing to secure the Peking-Hankow concessions, they would be in line for the next large trunk-line, the Hankow-Canton road.[35] These negotiations will be dealt with in the next chapter.

Wilson's Ministerial Scheme

Although General Wilson's grand plans had come to nothing, he had still another scheme. Returning to his early vision of himself in Moscow and a friendly Rockhill (who would be in part beholden to Wilson for his office) in China, Wilson wrote to McCook early in 1897 discussing this possibility. "With you in Russia and Rockhill in China," McCook replied, "I feel as if the 'plant' had been established and that good ought to come not only to the country, but to the many interests where the business of its people touches those of Russia and China." Rockhill, longing to return to China, was glad of the support Wilson and his friends offered, although he had played no part in their various schemes. Though he had occasionally sent Wilson excerpts from reports about railroad developments in Russia and China, his general attitude toward such efforts was one of extreme skepticism.[36]

With or without Rockhill's enthusiastic consent, Wilson went to work for him. Rockhill had the support of John Hay, Henry Cabot Lodge, Henry Adams, and Theodore Roosevelt as well. Wilson's support was solidly business-oriented. Alba Johnson, of the Baldwin Locomotive Company, met with all the leading Pennsylvania businessmen and successfully elicited their support. At the same time rival candidates were discouraged. McCook spoke long and piteously to a rival for the Russian post of the horrors of Russian winters.[37]

Alba Johnson played a slightly dirtier game. With Wilson's knowledge he wrote to a business associate in Russia giving him certain information on John DeYoung of California, who was rumored to be McKinley's choice for the job. The result was a protest by the Russian minister to Rockhill. The minister declared that he had information that DeYoung was of Jewish descent, if not himself Jewish; if appointed, the Russian government would certainly declare him *persona non grata*. Rockhill, who knew nothing of Johnson's actions, wrote in some distress to Wilson about this incident. Perplexed, Rockhill had asked John W. Foster's advice. Should he report the Russian minister's protest to the President? With some relish Foster told him it was his positive duty to inform the President.[38]

Rockhill encountered some trouble from undercover missionary opposition to his appointment. To counter this, McCook went to see the head of the Presbyterian Mission Board who denied having interfered. Wilson spoke to Bishop Leighton Coleman and wrote Rockhill that this interview would secure the Episcopalians; McCook continued to work on the Baptists. Despite all the efforts, and the dirty work on Wilson's part, neither Rockhill nor Wilson succeeded. Both, coming from the East, failed to fit into McKinley's regional patronage pattern. According to the head of the *Tribune's* Washington bureau, McKinley had remarked to several people that the China post was too important and well paid to waste on a political non-entity like Rockhill, whatever his other merits.[39] Having satisfied the Hay-Lodge group with Roosevelt's appointment as assistant secretary of the navy, McKinley could fob Rockhill off with the ministry to Greece. Wilson did not even rate compensation. In September 1897, Wilson wrote disconsolately to Pethick that the appointment of Conger to China and Hitchcock to Russia had put an end to all his political aspirations.[40] Wilson turned his attention to McCook's own pet project, the Cuban independence movement.

Two years of effort had yielded no returns. From 1897 on, American commercial interests centered around the fate of the American China Development Company and the increase in commodity trade with China.

America and Russia

For a time, American business interest in Russia ran parallel to the growing interest in China. Indeed, in most instances the same people were involved. From Wharton Barker, with his pathetic attempt to play on past honors received from the Russian government, to Wilson and

McCook and their hope of using a personal friendship with Prince Hilkoff, to Bash and Brice, with their straightforward, and equally unsuccessful, bid to share the burdens and profits of the China-Eastern railroad, Americans realized that the ideal form of China investment involved Russia as well. Wilson was convinced that Russian permission would be required for any extensive China projects undertaken by Americans. But beyond this he, and Barker and Bash as well, were interested in milking both ends of a projected railroad scheme. The location of the American China Development Company's concession in south China put a final end to this dream.

Yet very early in the history of the Trans-Siberian railroad, Russia had made it quite clear it wanted no help in the actual construction of any part of the railway. In response to an early inquiry by Secretary of State Olney, Minister Breckenbridge reported that the Russian government firmly intended to construct the Trans-Siberian Railway, allowing no contracts to outside parties. Still, the issue wasn't closed. Breckenbridge was informed that, should any parts of the road be contracted to outside parties, Americans would be given an equal chance to place bids. In concluding his report, the minister urged that reputable railway men come to Russia to consult with him. As we have seen, at least one, J. G. Pangborn, did so, and J. J. McCook, under the pleasant guise of attending the coronation, did so as well.[41] Besides wishing to keep the entire building of the road in Russian control, the Russian government, in the years before the Spanish-American War, had a low opinion of the importance of the United States. The government, Breckenbridge reported, considered America "as a long way off, good enough as a check in her place and way to some of the tendencies of England but quite unable to affect the sentiment of those parts of the world which most concern this Empire."[42] The result was that Russia saw no reason to encourage American government interest through cooperation with her nationals. At a later date, when the Russian government feared the formation of an Anglo-American alliance that would oppose Russian interests in China, the vested interest of such a group might have been useful. By then it was too late.

Although McKinley did not appoint Wilson minister to Russia, his choice of Ethan Allen Hitchcock showed his interest in developing profitable trade links with Russia. Hitchcock had spent twelve years in

China working for the prominent Olyphant and Company. On his return to America he established himself as a prominent businessman in St. Louis, interested in railroads. A close friend of the President's, Hitchcock could be depended upon to forward American commercial interests as vigorously as Wilson might have.[43] Moreover, Hitchcock was apparently given special verbal instructions on his mission by the President regarding Russian American commercial relations.[44]

Hitchcock worked hard to increase American influence in Russia. In January 1898, he urged that the American legation in St. Petersburg be raised to the status of an embassy. One month later this was done and Russia returned the compliment. American businessmen trading with Russia found in Hitchcock a most helpful public servant. In March 1898, he reported that he had used his influence with the ministries of finance and marine on behalf of the Cramp shipbuilding firm. Hitchcock took Cramp's success as another sign of the "confidence and friendship" of Russia for America. In April, Cramp signed a contract for $7 million with the expectation of a supplemental agreement that would make a total order of $15 million. In May, the Baldwin Locomotive Company, Wilson's chief backers on the China project, received an order for 65 locomotives for the Manchurian railroad making a total of 80 "Baldwins" ordered by that railroad over a nine week period and a grand total of 138 sold to the Russians during the spring of 1898. Another company, Westinghouse, had received an air-brake contract worth $2 to $3 million.[45]

As in China, diplomatic pressure was brought to bear when an American company ran into difficulties with the government. In December 1898 the Pennsylvania Steel Company learned that its rails would no longer be acceptable to the director of the Manchurian railroad despite the fact that they had supplied 35,000 tons of the rails in the past. Hay instructed Peirce, acting chargé at the time, to further American commercial interests in every way possible. When the company itself withdrew its protest, Peirce told them that he could not let the matter drop because it involved discrimination against American goods and went beyond the interests of any one company. Peirce's protest was successful and he informed Hay that his policy of authorizing diplomatic officers to use their influence on behalf of American citizens in commercial affairs had been triumphantly justified. The Pennsylvania Steel Company, only two and one half weeks after its original protest, was granted a contract for 80,000 tons of steel rails.[46]

Hitchcock also did his best to combat unfavorable publicity given to Russia's internal affairs. A vigorous editorial in the *New York Tribune* denouncing Russian living conditions was answered, at Hitchcock's direction, by Peirce. Hitchcock called the *Tribune's* article unjust and dangerous to the Russian moves toward closer economic and diplomatic relations. On home leave in Washington, Hitchcock spoke constantly of the value of Russian friendship. In his diary, Whitelaw Reid noted Hitchcock's strong views about the right of Russia to a Chinese port as an outlet for the Trans-Siberian railroad. Hitchcock, Reid recorded, "considered the English claim to being the champions of the open-door singularly unfair, and protested that they exacted it as well as other nations."[47]

Although the McKinley government kept an open mind about Russia during its first year, the growing conflict between American and Russian interests in Asia soon turned the tide. To be sure, the British did their best to convince the United States that Russia opposed American expansion in East Asia. However, objective evidence pointed to the same conclusion. More was involved than the appointment of an admittedly anglophile secretary of state. In November 1898, for example, an extremely hostile article appeared in the St. Petersburg *Exchange Gazette*. An official Russian disclaimer was printed in the semi-official St. Petersburg *Journal,* but the original article, reprinted in the London *Times,* did great damage. Peirce informed Lamsdorff that the American public would find it hard to understand how any article in opposition to government policy could be printed. Lamsdorff replied that censorship was, regrettably, not perfect. The article noted America's "progressive intoxication" with its victories and declared that Europe would not allow American interference in the balance of power in Asia. An article the government could not disclaim appeared in the *Novoe Vremya* later in November and was duly translated by Peirce. Although primarily attacking England, the author spoke ominously of the clouds darkening Russo-American friendship. The article went on to discount the importance of the very issue most exercising the McKinley administration at that time: "It is impossible that the reason [for Russo-American difficulties] could be the empty question of the 'open door' in Corea or

Manchuria. For our opinion, the Americans should be not blinded by such narrow ideas." The author noted that there was more profit for the United States in Alaska, Russia's freely given gift to America, than in either Korea or Manchuria. Asia, surely, was big enough for everyone. Still the article called for "full assurance" that America's recent "extreme" friendship for Great Britain was not aimed at obstructing Russia in Asia. Although Russia was in no sense opposed to American territorial expansion, it did object to seeing America "in tow of England in trade and politics in the Far East. Less than this, we think could not be claimed by a century-old friend and ally." Russia could assure America it would not interfere in Cuba or the Philippines; it expected a reciprocal restraint on the part of America in the Far East.[48]

It was, then, on the issue of China that the McKinley administration began to define its policy in opposition to that of Russia. One of the earliest instructions sent to Hitchcock's successor as ambassador to Russia concerned the petition of prominent American cotton manufacturers to the State Department urging that the government be alert to any threat to American cotton trade in north China and Manchuria. Tower was ordered to keep a close watch on the issue as the recent efforts of European powers "to gain a foothold in China" was of utmost concern to McKinley.[49]

It has been argued that the defeat of Wilson and McCook's plan to have themselves installed in key positions confirmed the drift toward a policy of Anglo-American cooperation. It would seem that the personnel involved was really irrelevant. The division occurred over a conflict of policy in the Far East, one that the appointment of Wilson (who was no more pro-Russian than Hitchcock) could not have affected. As the McKinley administration became more concerned with the scramble for power and trade in China, and as the outline of Russian imperialism in Asia became more clear, the policies of the two countries were bound to conflict.[50]

four   Threat of a Closing Door

four

Germany must bear the full onus of having begun a movement far more dangerous to China than the concession hunting of 1895–1897.[1] What the British had been able to do in the 1840's—detach Hong Kong from China without international repercussions—was no longer possible. The successful German seizure of Kiaochow, in the context of the intense international rivalry of the period, was a severe blow to the stability of the Manchu dynasty.

In 1895 and again in 1897, Germany asked for the lease of Kiaochow Bay in Shantung province as a coaling station. Both times China categorically refused. The timely murder of two German priests in Shantung provided the pretext for force that allowed Germany to send ships and troops into Kiaochow and seize it in November 1897. All attempts on China's part to satisfy German demands in other ways were in vain. On March 6, 1898, a ninety-nine year lease of Kiaochow Bay was signed providing as well for general German priority in assisting the Chinese for unspecified purposes with men, money and material. German troops conducted punitive raids in the countryside fulfilling the kaiser's boast, in a letter to Bülow, of making "hundreds of thousands of Chinese . . . quiver when they feel the iron fist of Germany heavy on their necks."[2]

For two years Russia had unsuccessfully sought the right to build a branch of the Chinese Eastern Railway to a port on the Yellow Sea. Now they took the German action as an opportunity to seize what was needed. Though Russian councils were divided, in March 1898 a demand was made for Talienwan and Port Arthur on a twenty-five year lease basis. Great Britain, to appease an inflamed public opinion, to counter Russia, and with China's acquiescence if not at her request, asked for and received a similar lease on Wei-hai-wei. In William Langer's words, she protested and "joined the criminals." By April 1898, a full circle had been drawn when the French were granted a ninety-nine year lease for Kwangchow-wan on the south coast of China. In addition, France obtained a new railroad concession.[3]

In effect, a series of agreements between the powers and between each power and China were made, which resulted in a fairly neat delineation of spheres of influence. In February 1898, in return for the last of the indemnity loans, China promised Britain never to alienate the Yangtze Valley and further assured the British that, so long as British trade predominated, the head of the Imperial Maritime Customs would be English. In April 1898 France and China signed a nonalienation agreement covering Yunnan, Kwangtung, and Kwangsi. In the same month, China and Japan signed a similar agreement covering the province of Fukien. Interpower agreements included one between France and Britain in 1896 in which each agreed to share privileges either gained in Yunnan and Szechuan; the Anglo-German agreement of 1900 covering Shantung and the Yangtze Valley; and the Russo-British agreement of 1899 in which each agreed not to seek railroad concessions in the other's sphere.[4] Since China obviously had no desire to alienate any territory whatsoever, the nonalienation agreements amounted to a first lien on that area to the power concerned. *If* China should ever be forced to alienate territory in the Yangtze area, Britain would have first choice; or, in slightly different terms, if China should ever break up in earnest, the agreements were a notification to all other powers that this area belonged to Britain. Thus, by the end of 1899, China was crisscrossed by agreements, leases, railroad and mining concessions that tied down portions of territory to particular foreign powers. Both in China and in Europe there was a growing fear that these divisions might become final and the partition of China would occur with incalculable effects on the rest of the world.

It will be important to keep this outline in mind in order to understand the following discussion of United States reactions to the Far Eastern situation. A few dates will also help clarify the sequence of events, and in themselves constitute a kind of comment. On February 15, 1898, the battleship *Maine* exploded and sank in Havana harbor. On March 6, 1898, the Chinese conceded the lease of Kiaochow. On March 15 the Spanish government asked the European powers to mediate between Spain and the United States. On March 28 the Chinese signed the lease for Port Arthur and Talienwan. On April 21 the United States broke relations with Spain. The time of greatest ferment in the Far East coincided with the high point in the United States' dispute with Spain. Even so, space was given, in newspapers across the country, to comment on the latest developments in an area of the world newly interesting to Americans. The American reaction was at least in part conditioned by the presence in China of a large and vocal missionary body.

Missionaries and Sino-American Conflicts, 1895–1897

By 1899 there were 1,037 American missionaries in China. In 1900 over one fifth of the total American investment in China consisted of missionary property. Represented by influential and very well-organized boards in the States and, through the boards, in contact with millions of church-going Americans, China missionaries had an immense potential audience. Between 1895 and 1897, as a result of a series of antimissionary riots in which Americans were, sometimes very peripherally, involved, American missionaries in China were also the subject of angry dealings between China and the United States.

Missionaries in China were subversive in the literal sense. They were devoted to the task of converting the Chinese to a faith that attacked, at every point, the accepted state ideology of Confucianism as well as the eclectic popular religions of Buddhism and Taoism. For a particularistic ethic they wished to substitute a universalistic one. Loyalty, they preached, must be to the Christian God above all, not to one's present parents or past ancestors. Missionaries introduced into China a concept of sin unknown before, and found themselves involved in the peculiar task of convincing innocents of their inherent guilt.[5]

Because American missionaries were both American and religious, along with Christian dogma they preached a wide-ranging set of contemporary beliefs, from the concepts of free enterprise and private property to the ideas of progress and the benefits of a republican form of government. Some, with their unquestioned assumption of Anglo-Saxon or, more generously, white superiority, sought to instill in the Chinese a proper sense of place. Maddened by Chinese attitudes of superiority, they railed at the "stuck-up" people they had to deal with.[6] Missionaries, in part by treaty rights, in part by long accepted practice, spread to all parts of China and brought with them their extensive and sometimes vague extraterritorial rights. They challenged not merely the superstitions of the peasant but the position of the gentry itself, official and unofficial. In small towns they could establish themselves as dispensers of goods, legal protection, and food and seize an intermediary position between the people and their government, which traditionally belonged to the local officials and gentry. What made the ordinary missionary seem so very pernicious to the Chinese was his connection with foreign powers and his willingness to call for government protection. Conversely, as in the German action in Shantung, the need to protect missionaries could serve as a cover for aggression.

The American missionary movement had prospered since its beginnings in the 1830's. But toward the end of the century, interest in missions had begun to flag and the depression of 1893 had hit the foreign mission societies very severely.[7] A prayer week for missions was declared in April 1895, but it raised little interest and less money. Although the rest of the economy was well on the way to full recovery by the end of 1897, mission societies remained heavily in debt and the home churches showed little sign of increasing their contributions. In an editorial in the *Missionary Review of the World* for January 1897, the situation was declared almost hopeless—"At no time during the half century now closing have missions to the heathen been at greater peril of utter collapse."[8]

Retrenchment alone allowed the societies to continue in operation. The American Baptist Missionary Union was forced, by lack of funds, to turn down five out of every seven approved candidates. By March 1897, twelve missionary societies representing five denominations, were in debt $1,013,632 and would have been, they calculated, three quarters of a million dollars further in debt had they not practiced "severe retrenchment." In January 1897, an Interdenominational Rally for Foreign Missions was held at Carnegie Hall as a "sort of climax to a week of prayer, and a starting point in an aggressive missionary movement." Yet despite good weather and careful arrangements, Carnegie Hall was only one third full.[9]

Though the mission press praised the way in which "God through little Japan" had opened China, and cleared a "highway"[10] for Christian forces, these stirring events did not bring about an expected increase in contributions. Then in the late summer of 1895, events in China worked to the advantage of the mission societies. Two antimissionary riots in Szechuan and Fukien provinces created great interest in the domestic press. The

State Department was also interested, Minister Denby was positively fire-breathing, and the missionary journals carried full accounts.

The reaction of the secular press was not wholly satisfying. Although most papers agreed that the Chinese should be severely punished for any damage done or lives lost, some openly doubted the propriety of the missionaries' presence in China at all. In August 1895, the *Literary Digest* divided newspaper opinion into two groups: those who defended the missionaries and proposed a foreign protectorate over China to prevent such incidents in the future and those who felt the missionaries had failed in their conversion attempts and should be withdrawn altogether.[11]

The *Minneapolis Tribune* suggested that America do what Germany was to do later—use the missionary incident as an excuse for assuming a protectorate over an area of China. If England and the United States did not act in this direction, the *Tribune* warned, Russia would.[12] Although extreme and certainly forceful enough, the *Tribune* paid little attention to the specifically missionary aspect of the events and was frank in its political concerns.

The *Washington Post* argued against the very principle of missionary work in China. The Chinese obviously did not want Christianity. It was illogical for the United States to assume the responsibility of protection over missionaries, since it had no established national religion. Or, the *Post* pointedly asked, had the United States "gone into the business of proselytizing for the benefit of some favored creed?"[13]

In November 1895, the *Literary Digest* reported that the desirability of continuing missionary work in China along current lines was widely debated in the press. It noted that the secular press was largely opposed to continued missionary activities without some change in the way they were conducted—either missionaries should confine themselves to easily protected coastal areas, or the United States, in cooperation with Great Britain, should enforce some kind of protectorate over China. The *Christian Advocate* felt public hostility to missionaries was growing and accused the press of slandering the missionary movement rather than merely criticizing it.[14]

In China, missionaries and businessmen sent petitions to the State Department demanding action.[15] For almost a week at the end of May 1895, rioting Chinese in Cheng-tu, the capital of Szechuan province, put fear into the hearts of resident missionaries and destroyed their property.

The main sufferers were Roman Catholic missionaries, but six Americans of the Methodist Episcopal Church were also forced to flee.[16]

Minister Denby, in reporting to the Department, was convinced that official connivance was the basic cause of the riot. His reasoning was not watertight, however, since he refused to believe that after two hundred years of Catholic missionary work in Szechuan any popular anti-Christian sentiment could remain. He had more conclusive evidence in the reputation of the outgoing governor-general, Liu Ping-chang, whose official yamen in Cheng-tu was not far from one of the missions destroyed. This official was known, by the missionaries, to look with disfavor on their activities and both Denby and the missionaries saw the riot as Liu's parting gesture of defiance. In any event he had not acted promptly to quell the disturbance, though soldiers were available, nor had he paid any attention to prior missionary requests for action against antimissionary propagandists, who were busy posting inflammatory placards in the days preceding the riot. The United States had no consul near Cheng-tu and, on the basis of an 1886 precedent, Denby decided to ask the British consul at Chungking, J. W. Tratman, to represent American interests in investigating and assessing damages. To aid Tratman, Denby asked the Reverend Spencer Lewis to join in the investigation.[17]

Before this action could be commented upon by the Department, Denby had changed his mind. In a letter to Secretary of State Olney, written on July 26 but not received in Washington till September 6, Denby explained why he had decided to withdraw from the joint investigating committee arranged with Tratman. Earlier in the day he had received an account of a large meeting of Americans in Shanghai and a copy of their petition. The Americans demanded an independent American investigation led by a consul of high rank, one that would impress upon the Chinese the force and majesty of the United States.[18] Denby wrote that, upon further consideration he too had decided the occasion called for a more impressive commission and one on which Americans would be more fully represented.[19] He therefore notified the British minister of his withdrawal and awaited instructions. Naturally these would be slow in coming since the Department could not possibly receive his message for several weeks.

On August 13 Denby sent a cable that mystified the Department because of its reference to actions as yet unknown to them: "Will you appoint a commission of Americans exclusively to investigate Szechuan riots as asked by Americans in China?" The Assistant Secretary of State, A. A. Adee, cabled back promptly that the Department had received Denby's earlier notification concerning the appointment of the Reverend Mr. Lewis to aid Consul Tratman and had found this plan perfectly acceptable. Adee was therefore somewhat shocked to receive an answering cable from Denby: "I refused to have anything to do with the Szechuan commission three weeks ago." In a long letter written the next day (but not received until September 26) Denby reviewed his actions in the Cheng-tu case. Apparently he had been subject to severe criticism by Americans in China for having agreed to the joint commission in the first place and was at some pains to make clear to everyone that he had withdrawn from it on the first hint of opposition.[20]

The situation was complicated further by a telegram from Adee to Denby on August 20, which instructed him to go ahead with the joint commission "as far as possible notwithstanding previous withdrawal." However, the British commission, headed by Tratman, had by the end of August not even left Chungking. A French inquiry had yielded more evidence of Liu Ping-chang's culpable negligence and, on the basis of this, Denby had entered a strong protest with the Tsungli yamen demanding Liu's instant punishment. This combination of Chinese and British inaction finally moved the State Department to grant Denby's request for an independent commission. On September 4, almost three months after the event, Adee cabled: "Your unsatisfied demand for degradation of viceroy Szechuan and delay in British Cheng-tu investigation makes independent investigation necessary . . . Organize at once an American commission—consul at Tientsin, missionary and naval officer, with Chinese officer of suitable rank."[21]

The Chinese, through their minister in Washington, Yang Ju, immediately protested. Yang noted that American missions had suffered only slight damage; that in recent cases of American anti-Chinese riots where death had resulted no Chinese commission was organized; that a commission, entering the area so long after the riot, would only excite the populace again. Adee replied that Chinese obstructionism would be considered an unfriendly act toward the United States and might lead to America's taking independent action. Denby's response to Chinese objections, unpublished in the otherwise complete section on this issue in

Foreign Relations 1895, was to suggest the bombardment and leveling of some accessible Chinese town, since Cheng-tu itself was out of reach.[22]

Yang Ju, in various communications with Olney, had tried to separate the United States from Great Britain and to play upon America's supposed sense of special sympathy with China. On September 9, Yang had transmitted a message from the Tsungli yamen itself which asked Olney, in the interests of international amity, to prevent Britain and France from offering "more trouble," which they would assuredly do if the United States continued to demand its own investigating commission. In his letter to Denby, Olney showed that he resented these Chinese appeals to an image of America—mediating, gentle, supporting China against the rapacious world—that was increasingly unattractive to Americans. Olney wrote:

> It is the Department's conviction that the apparent policy of the Chinese Government, to separate the United States from the questions raised by the occurrences in Szechuan and Fuhkien . . . [necessitate] an impressive demonstration which can leave no doubt in the mind of the Chinese Government or the people in the interior that the United States Government is an effective factor in securing due rights for Americans resident in China. Regarding our proposition for an independent examination of the Cheng-tu business as a crucial test, it has been determined to push it to a successful conclusion on the assumption that if this be done, and the attitude of the United States for the protection of the lives and property of its citizens be conspicuously manifested, the necessity for such procedure on our part will, in all probability, not recur.[23]

By September 30, the Chinese had capitulated to all American demands, including the question of the best route to Szechuan.[24] As soon as this was announced, the British and French did indeed "offer trouble." The British minister, according to Denby, handed China an ultimatum insisting upon the punishment of Szechuan officials and a fleet was ordered to the area. Next the French minister made identical demands and threats. Proud that America had broken Chinese obstinacy on the Cheng-tu case, Denby informed Washington that a proclamation denouncing Liu Ping-chang and forever barring him from office had been published. It was a precedent Denby was pleased to have helped establish—never before had such a high official been so severely punished for an antimissionary riot in his jurisdiction.

In early August another antimissionary riot took place at Ku-t'ien, Fukien province. Ten British missionaries were killed, and one American, Mabel C. Hartford of New Hampshire, was wounded. American action in this case was swift. Denby was instructed, on August 12, to consult with the British but to "otherwise . . . act independently and carefully; abstain from joining in any course or policy which, however important to British interests, does not concern those of the United States."[25] The presence on the quickly formed joint commission of W. C. Hixson, American consul at Foochow, and Commander J. W. Newell of the *Detroit,* ensured a strong American voice in the proceedings. Such an investigation would combine the benefits of cooperation with those of independent action and thus avoid the delays and dissatisfaction experienced in the Szechuan situation.

For once, Denby felt confident that he was in tune with Department thinking. He sent off a rapid series of telegrams on the Ku-t'ien proceedings. On August 27 he noted that all was well, and many Chinese had been convicted. Several weeks later he cabled glad tidings of executions. In response to these reports Denby received first an angry telegram and then an even angrier letter. In both, Olney wanted to know precisely what Hixson and Newell were doing in Ku-t'ien. They were not there to take part in the Chinese judicial proceedings. These properly belonged to the Chinese officials involved. Olney reminded Denby that Hixson and Newell had been sent as observers for the Government, not as instruments of revenge. The government of the United States of America was not interested in vengeance, nor could it measure its sense of injury "by the number of decapitations" secured. Denby should try to keep the "higher purposes" of the United States constantly in mind. These were to secure evidence of guilt in high places and pursue *these* criminals mercilessly through negotiations with the Tsungli yamen.[26]

Olney's idealism aside, twenty-six Chinese were executed for their role in the Ku-t'ien uprising and the British members of the commission moved for a swift conclusion of the case. Olney agreed with Denby that, unless Hixson and Newell were dissatisfied with British findings, the United States would end the investigation when the British did.[27]

Meanwhile, the Cheng-tu investigating commission did not arrive on the spot until December 15, a full six months after the riots had occurred. By that time the leaders of the mob had already been executed and the governor-general degraded; the province was quiet once more. The commission nevertheless deliberated until December 28 and agreed to ask for property indemnification and personal reparation for the missionaries. On June 3, 1896, the case was closed. The Chinese, in their desire to settle quickly, agreed to indemnify the missionaries for lost property, house rent, cost of fleeing to safety (including passage to America for two missionaries who had returned home as a consequence of the riot), and the salaries of those who had been forced to suspend work during the period of disturbance.[28]

In Washington, William W. Rockhill, third assistant secretary of state, was considering the formulation of a general American policy toward antimissionary outbreaks. Before he had drafted instructions to Denby, however, another incident occurred. On May 12, 1896, in Kiang-yin, Kiangsu, a mob had destroyed the mission property of an American Presbyterian station.

A. C. Jones, American consul at near-by Chinkiang, quickly reported the missionaries' version of the riot.[29] A quack neighborhood doctor had been trying to extort money from the missionaries without success. In revenge and in the vague hope of receiving hush money from the missionaries, the man one day buried the body of a dead baby in the back yard of the mission. He and two confederates then called together a mob and dared the missionaries to dig for a child they claimed the missionaries had killed. Confidently the missionaries did so and found nothing. The doctor then took the spade, marched, the crowd following closely, to a spot in the back yard, and dug up the baby. The local magistrate was present and with this evidence before him he turned to the missionaries to ask for an explanation. But at this point the crowd of onlookers, consumed with rage, charged and ripped up the mission station while the magistrate vainly tried to quiet them.

Rockhill took charge of the case and instructed Jones to demand the severe punishment of the local magistrate who, Rockhill declared, was guilty for not informing his superiors of the possibility of trouble. Jones replied that the three men responsible for the plot had been arrested and sentenced to death; that no advance warning of the riot was possible as it had been completely spontaneous in nature; that the taotai of Chinkiang had prosecuted the case vigorously and ably. As for the local magistrate of Kiangyin, he had been dismissed on Jones's request but was being permitted to stay in office long enough to pay the indemnity fine of $9,007.12. Jones had agreed to this, for otherwise his friend the taotai would have been responsible for paying the indemnity himself. Rockhill was not quite satisfied. He urged Jones to keep an eye on the magistrate, to make sure he was dismissed as promised and that a proclamation giving the reason for his dismissal was published.[30]

The riot and massacre in Ku-t'ien, upon investigation, revealed the machinations of a secret society known as the Vegetarians, led by one Liu Hsiang-hsing. This secret society, organized in 1892, was connected with the larger and more powerful White Lotus Society. It came into conflict with both local Chinese authorities and missionaries, and its aims seem to have been both antidynastic and antiforeign. At least one element in the situation was the practical rivalry between missionaries and Vegetarians for the allegiance of Ku-t'ien's population. When, in response to a particularly outstanding defiance of local authority, some 210 soldiers were sent to Ku-t'ien, the Vegetarians blamed the missionaries and soon after attacked them at their summer cottages just outside of Ku-t'ien.

There is good evidence that at least one official was related by blood to the leader of the society, and two succeeding district magistrates were terribly ineffective against the rising threat of Vegetarian disorders. M. B. Rankin, in a study of this riot, notes that both officials and populace understood it as the result of rivalry between two equally heterodox secret sects. However, the ineffectiveness of local Chinese authorities against the sect was never shown to be deliberately antiforeign. As rebels, the Vegetarians were as much of a danger to the officials as they were to the missionaries. In Ku-t'ien, official feebleness was general, not simply in the area of protection of missionaries. In the riot in Kiangsu, as we have seen, a small-time extortionist was solely responsible. Though missionaries were hurt in all three incidents, the cause of each was quite separate and distinct.

Despite the widely differing origin of these events, the State Department supported Rockhill in his effort to arrive at a uniform policy.[31] In each of the above cases, local officials directly involved in the riot— either through weakness or sympathy with the mob—were severely punished. Rockhill wished to go far beyond this. Using the evidence gathered by the Szechuan commission (the only case where a high official was implicated), Rockhill generalized the guilt of Liu Ping-chang into a principle. In a long dispatch to Denby, Jr., dated July 28, 1896, Rockhill noted the Szechuan commission's conclusion that the simplest policy was to insist on the punishment of local officials without any investigation other than to establish that a riot had taken place. Rockhill agreed but expanded the point into two major demands that Denby should, at the first opportunity, present to the Tsungli yamen. China must formally recognize the residential rights of American citizens. More important, the Chinese government must agree to punish all persons directly or indirectly involved in any antimissionary outrage as well as the highest provincial official in whose province such an event occurred, "although his only fault may be ignorance."[32] In this way the highest provincial officials would be deterred from treating antiforeign feeling lightly.

It seems rather ironical that, to ensure the protection of missionaries, the United States should try to make use of the Chinese administrative code, with its theory of collective responsibility, when that very code, condemned as barbaric, had been one of the reasons for securing extraterritorial rights in the first place. Chinese law did indeed hold the governor-general of a province directly and personally responsible for all that occurred within his jurisdiction—yet at least one of the missionary aims was to replace this notion with modern Western concepts of individual legal responsibility. Such a contradiction is a common characteristic of nineteenth-century attempts to force the Chinese government to live up to its responsibilities as a central government while at the same time undermining its ability to behave as one. It is illustrated by the frequent demand that the Tsungli yamen act quickly in a particular case; at the same time the foreign power involved would send gunboats to the local area in question and *force* the authorities to comply with the stated demands. Time and again the one approach was sabotaged by the other—both in fact increased the weakness of the central government.[33]

In November 1896, Denby presented the Tsungli yamen with a list of demands on the missionary problem based on Rockhill's July dispatch. The Tsungli yamen replied that it could not commit itself in advance to punish officials whose only crime was ignorance or understandable carelessness.[34]

For months after his original request, Denby returned to this issue in written communications with the Tsungli yamen. He was urged to do so by the highest State Department officials. The Ku-t'ien case, for example, had been closed. Local officials were deprived of office, an indemnity was granted and paid. Denby reported that a great Christian revival had occurred in Ku-t'ien as a result of British forbearance in the settlement conditions.[35] The new secretary of state, John Sherman, replied that, in furtherance of the stated policy of the government, he must insist "in every case, on the punishment of all officials found guilty in any degree in connection with such occurrences." Denby returned to the struggle and sent a strong note to the Tsungli yamen with the following rhetorical question: "Why will you not hold your viceroys and governors responsible for outrages on foreigners as you hold them responsible for outrages on Chinese subjects? . . . A ringing earnest proclamation to every Yamen in China that not only degradation from office, but condign punishment will be awarded every official, high and low, in whose jurisdiction an anti-foreign riot shall occur would be hailed by the world with joy, and would insure peace."[36]

For some time the Chinese government continued to refuse Denby's demands. Then, in October 1898, the Chinese did publish two decrees that went far toward meeting American notions of justice to foreigners. On October 6 a decree was issued ordering local officials to protect Christian chapels, treat missionaries with courtesy, and settle fairly all disputes between Christians and the local population. Though not as strong as Rockhill had desired, the decree concluded almost in his words: "If, after this decree, riots still occur because of ineffective protection, the local authorities concerned will be severely punished and the viceroys and governors also will be held responsible."[37]

The treatment of antimissionary riots by the State Department in this period marks a change in China policy, slight but significant. With one eye on the extent of press reaction to the riots and with, perhaps, a sour memory of the outcry in the Japanese spy case, the government moved toward dispelling the impression that it was soft on China. Its ground of action was limited. Gunboats were not used. America's way was not yet that of Britain or France. Nevertheless, like those countries, an issue of national prestige and honor was constructed out of relatively minor incidents, and American demands were pressed, in one case over a period of several years, to success. Though losing money and subject to sniping lay attacks, the missionaries remained a major American investment in China and were not to be abandoned lightly. During the Spanish-American War the missionaries joined the expansionists with a will and were rewarded by increasing public interest and contributions.[38]

American Reaction to the Seizure of Kiaochow

Denby's efforts on the missionaries' behalf certainly conditioned his reaction to the Shantung crisis. His most immediate response was not to the political, but to the missionary aspect of the affair. He seemed to treat it as just another case of antimissionary feeling requiring prompt Western action. On November 23 he reported that the Germans had gone far toward establishing a harsh response to antiforeign riots as "permanent policy." He was confident that German actions would work toward greater foreign security in China.[39] Some of the flavor of treaty port reaction to the Kiaochow seizure can be felt in the hysterical praise for Germany in a *China Gazette* editorial: "Indications are abundant that the outraged Powers of the West have exhausted their patience and are at length determined to exact a heavy reckoning from the besotted and sanguinary Chinese mandarinate for the long and ever-growing list of crimes against humanity which the barbarous people of this country have for years been committing at the covert, if not the open, instigation, of their rulers."[40]

In general, the missionary reaction to German, Russian, and French encroachment on China was complacent, almost congratulatory. An article in the *Missionary Review of the World* noted that missionaries would benefit from the better government certain to be provided in areas run by Western powers. The *Review*'s missionary correspondents were not averse to the possibility of the partition of China; most felt the swift German retribution would have a salutary effect on Chinese behavior in the future. Henry Porter, an American missionary stationed in Shantung, wrote ecstatic letters to the board in praise of German policy. "The German Government," he declared, "deserves the admiration of all rightminded men, the world over." Foreigners in China had felt profoundly relieved when the kaiser's ships steamed into Kiaochow. Porter roundly criticized England for her failure to punish antimissionary actions adequately but excused America on the grounds of her "well known incapacity to deal with great subjects of diplomacy."[41]

Americans with specific business interests in China were disturbed and dismayed by the State Department's slow reaction to the threatening situation in the Far East. On January 4, 1898, *The Philadelphia Press* carried an interview with Secretary of State Sherman in which the secretary professed himself unconcerned with the partition of China. He thought partition unlikely, but even were it to occur American commercial interests would not be adversely affected.[42]

Clarence Cary, attorney for the American China Development Company, answered Sherman in an angry article for the March issue of the *Forum*. Cary explained that the Germans possessed the right, though they might delay exercising it, lawfully to exclude the goods of other nations through a discriminating tariff. This was also true of the area Russia had leased. Yet the United States showed no signs of acting so as to stop these clearly harmful developments. Our policy was one of drift; indeed the secretary of state refused to see the danger at all. However, the picture was not all black. "Happily," Cary wrote, "some of our merchants and traders, whose important affairs are thus seriously menaced, being men of energy and foresight, and used to fend for themselves, have now sought to instigate some action at Washington without longer waiting upon the somnolent policy of merely trusting to luck." Some sixty-eight New York and Philadelphia firms had combined to protest to several large Chambers of Commerce against America's lack of policy in the Far East. The New York Chamber in turn petitioned the State Department. In his article, Cary warned that Great Britain no longer appeared capable of safeguarding her own interests, much less those of the United States. Satisfied with the most minor German and Russian promises, Great Britain had ceased to protest. America must now look to its own.[43] For the time being, however, guarded observation remained United States policy in China, although an opportunity presented itself for a more positive policy.

Railroad Activity, 1898

Throughout January and February of 1898 Denby was busy reversing his earlier complacent reaction to Germany's seizure of Kiaochow. He warned that partition would hurt both missionary and trading interests, that exclusion from Russian and German spheres would be disastrous to American interests. Then in mid-February 1898, Denby informed the Department that Yung Wing, that relic of mid-century American-Chinese relations, had obtained Chinese consent to a charter to build the Tientsin-Chinkiang railroad as a joint foreign-Chinese enterprise. Yung Wing claimed American citizenship and had protested to Denby against Germany's opposition to his concession. The German complaint rested on their claim to priority on all enterprises in Shantung. Denby asked if he should intervene on the basis of the most-favored-nation clause in American treaties with China. He received an immediate telegraphic reply from Assistant Secretary of State William Day, the real power in the State Department during Sherman's incumbency, informing him that no Chinese could be an American citizen. Therefore the legation could not make any claims on Yung Wing's behalf.[44]

In a detailed report Denby explained that the Chinese government was very anxious to grant the charter to Yung Wing in order to circumvent German attempts at exclusive control of the province. When the German minister threatened to break diplomatic relations if the charter were granted, the Tsungli yamen backed down. Somewhat laconically Denby noted that Germany now claimed commercial and developmental supremacy in Shantung.[45]

Yung Wing did not give up easily. On February 28, 1898, he presented Denby with a sheaf of documents proving that he was in fact a naturalized citizen of the United States. These included an American passport and proof that he had voted in all federal, state, and municipal elections since his naturalization in 1852. The State Department referred the matter to the solicitor-general's office and, in early April, a decision was reached. The solicitor's report acknowledged that Yung Wing's possession of a certificate of naturalization and an American passport made refusal seem hard, but the courts were strict. Whatever his certification, a Chinese could not be a citizen.[46]

Rejected by the United States, Yung Wing sought the help of the British minister, Sir Claude MacDonald. Denby reported that British capital would be used. The Tsungli yamen also consulted MacDonald about German opposition to the Tientsin-Chinkiang trunk line. The Chinese felt that German demands amounted to a claim of alienation of

Shantung from China. On February 19, 1898, MacDonald reported to the Foreign Office that the German minister had confirmed Chinese suspicions. The minister had explained that for all practical economic purposes Shantung was a German province. Salisbury instructed MacDonald to deny any British admission of German preferential rights in Shantung and to pressure the Tsungli yamen to continue refusing the German claims. Eventually Anglo-German interests were compromised in the Tientsin-Chinkiang railroad project and that concession was then pressed on China by both the British and German ministers.[47]

American capital played no part in the construction of this important road; an opportunity for asserting American opposition to exclusive national spheres in China was lost. Clearly, if the McKinley administration had been interested, at this time, in making a strong stand against the growing danger of spheres of influence, Yung Wing's prospective charter was an ideal occasion. Even if the State Department were unwilling to compromise the harsh consistency of the Exclusion Acts, they could have protested on Yung Wing's behalf—as an individual who had once been an American, or was close to American interests. At no time, however, did the Department even weigh the issue. If Yung Wing's citizenship had been validated, some protest, out of obligation, might have been made; it would hardly have been out of strong conviction.

On April 14, 1898, the American China Development Company finally consummated its three years of effort in China with a contract for the Canton-Hankow railway. The contract included the right to operate coal mines adjacent to the right of way and an option to furnish funds for the Peking-Hankow railroad should the Belgians ever cancel their contract for that road. This was the only railroad project Americans secured in the battle for concessions. Within seven years it would be lost. In May, A. W. Bash appealed to the new secretary of state, William Day, on behalf of the company. Aware that the Franco-Belgian group was busy working against the American concession in hopes of gaining the right to build China's entire north-south railroad system, Bash asked for government protection against foreign interference. Day very properly, if somewhat unimaginatively, replied that instructions could not be issued covering contingent circumstances.[48] During the Spanish-American War the route of the Canton-Hankow line was surveyed, but no further action was taken because of the discovery that the original estimates were too low and a new contract would have to be negotiated.

Although events in the Far East continued to draw American press attention and were increasingly discussed in terms of how specific American interests would be affected, there was no move, either by the press or the government, toward a really active Far Eastern policy. The vigorous response to antimissionary riots in 1895 and 1896 was an indication to China and the world that America was, as it were, keeping its hand in. Nothing more positive occurred, or was urged, until after Commodore Dewey had proved American might against the Spanish fleet in Manila Bay. The group of businessmen who had become intensely interested in China from the time of her defeat in 1895 found the mere drama of events in the Far East was not enough to arouse public opinion or its leaders.

The vigorous government response to the missionary disturbances, however, did mark a change. Disregarding the niceties of the separation of church and state, which could be interpreted to preclude government intervention on behalf of sectarians, Secretary of State Olney was determined to demonstrate that the "United States government is an effective factor in securing due rights for Americans resident in China." When it seemed that cooperating with other foreign powers in missionary cases, as had been done in the past, resulted in a slighting of American demands, or a delay in the proceedings, Olney was prepared to establish independent inquiry commissions despite the protests of the Chinese. Moreover, for the first time a general approach to missionary riots was worked out, one that took full advantage of the *Chinese* legal system. Thus, the highest government official of the area in which such an outbreak took place would be held responsible, though his only crime was ignorance or, on the local level, helplessness in the face of concerted mob action. The formulation of this policy did much to predetermine American reaction to the Boxer uprising some three years later. The basic assumption was that China possessed a functioning central government that could control all areas of the empire if only it would. Perversity, duplicity, antiforeignism at the highest levels—these were adjudged to be the cause of provincial disturbances. Rather than modify foreign demands in order to help shore up the central government, American policy makers added to those demands. In the eyes of Chinese gentry and lower officials, there could be no greater sign of the dynasty's loss of power than the fact that a foreign country could interfere in the systematic operation of the bureaucracy. Dismissal of high officials on the instructions of foreigners weakened the dynasty both internally and externally. It was, conceivably, one reason for the unrestrained xenophobia of a portion of the court and the bureaucracy during the Boxer crisis.

five   Preparation for Action

In the spring of 1898, official American policy toward the encroachments of Germany and Russia on China was succinctly expressed in an informal exchange of notes with the British ambassador, Sir Julian Pauncefote. Pauncefote was instructed by his government to approach the McKinley administration with a suggestion for Anglo-American cooperation "in opposing action by foreign Powers which may tend to restrict freedom of commerce of all nations in China either by imposing preferential conditions or by obtaining actual cession of Chinese coast territory."[1] The note was part of a series of British efforts aimed at blocking Russia's acquisition of Port Arthur or Talienwan short of armed conflict. McKinley intimated his sympathy with British policy but declared that there was no "present reason for the departure of the United States from its traditional policy respecting foreign alliances and as far as practicable avoiding any interference or connection with European complications."[2]

Four months later, in July of 1898, the policy itself remained unchanged, but the self-abnegating tone that McKinley took toward China in the earlier reply was quite gone. Secretary of State William Day informed John Hay, then ambassador at the Court of St. James's, that the moment was not propitious for an Anglo-American effort in China. However, there was no assertion that China was a "European complication." Day explained McKinley's specific reasons for not interfering at that time.

> The President is engrossed with the prosecution of the war and the questions immediately arising out of it and he does not feel that this is an opportune time for action in that direction. In short, while we have so much on our hands, the President does not feel like adding to the load in any way where it is not absolutely necessary to do so. The outcome of our struggle with Spain may develop the need of extending and strengthening our interests in the Asiatic Continent.[3]

Though the administration's scale of priorities clearly placed the Caribbean before the Far East, it was already obvious that the outcome of the Spanish-American War would have a direct bearing on future American policy. Even at the height of the agitation over Cuba, developments in China worried McKinley. His negative judgment on the urgency of the Far Eastern situation was based, at least in part, on reasonably firm assurances received from both Germany and Russia that the ports they had recently acquired would not discriminate against the trade of other nations.[4] The value of these assurances has generally been underestimated and American acceptance of them pointed to as evidence of Secretary of State Sherman's senility and lack of concern with the Far East. Though it is true that Sherman himself was far less anxious about America's position in China than either Olney had been or Hay would be, his acceptance of German promises was well justified. England accepted them and, as regards commerce, though not railroad rates or investment projects, Germany did indeed open Kiaochow to the goods of all nations. Russian policy on Talienwan and Port Arthur was still unsettled, but the verbal commitment, made by Muraviev to the American ambassador to St. Petersburg as well as by the Russian ambassador in England to Salisbury, that the treaty tariff would apply to all foreign commerce, was an important one. As Salisbury wrote to the British ambassador to Russia, a treaty port (that is, one in which the treaty tariff of 5 percent ad val. would apply) "was not much inferior in value to a free port; and the course of policy it implied was more agreeable to our own contentions in that it preserved for the port in question the Conventional Tariff, which could hardly be set aside without violence to existing Treaties."[5]

In his annual message to Congress on December 5, 1898, McKinley referred to the assurances he had received from Germany, Russia, and England that the territories they had recently acquired would be open to international trade. McKinley noted that America would have no complaint provided American trade was not discriminated against.[6] Given the major concern with Spain then occupying the administration's attention, McKinley's satisfaction with the oral assurances he had received was reasonable. His message to Congress made clear the conditional nature of America's position. Should discriminatory threats appear, it would seem, some kind of action on the government's part could be expected.

The administration's further concern with the expansion of American commerce in China was demonstrated in June 1898, when Secretary of State Day, through the Secretary of the Treasury, proposed that Congress appropriate $20,000 for the organization of a commercial commission to China to investigate all aspects of American trade in that country. Day's letter incorporated two of the most basic assumptions made by Americans about China at that time: first, that America suffered from overproduction, which could only be relieved by a great expansion of exports abroad; second, that the Far East was the most likely market for American surplus goods. America, Day wrote, had important interests at stake in Asia. He asked that Congress, by establishing the commission, "enable the Department to give intelligent direction to future efforts to obtain a proper share for the United States in the development, which seems to be near at hand, of the vast resources of the Chinese Empire under modern conditions of industry and trade." Although favorably reported out of committee by both the House and Senate, Congress failed to appropriate the money; nor did a similar request meet with success in 1899 or 1900. The State Department, on its own initiative, however, began to publish commercial reports by consular officers in January 1898 in an attempt to give American businessmen a fuller understanding of the needs and opportunities of foreign markets.[7]

Rise of Popular Expansionism

In the March reply to Pauncefote's offer, McKinley had referred to America's traditional foreign policy with confidence. However, during the Spanish-American War, the supposed immutability of Washington's foreign policy was frequently challenged.[8]

By July 1898 the issue had crystallized sufficiently to be the subject of a *Literary Digest* survey. The *Digest* saw a party division even sharper than had existed on the silver question of 1896. The leading urban Republican press stood solidly in favor of expansion and territorial acquisition wherever possible. The leading Democratic papers were as solidly opposed. Increasingly, reference was made to the gains in China trade which territorial expansion in the Pacific would bring. The nondenominational New York *Independent* observed that although the Monroe Doctrine and the Farewell Address ordained a policy of mutual exclusion between America and Europe, "that has nothing to do with Asia or Africa. We are nearer China and the Philippines than European countries are. They have no more right of interference there than we have."[9] Somehow, from this mutual lack of right to interfere, the editors of the *Independent* drew support for a policy of active American intervention.

A few commentators drew the issue squarely. America, John R. Proctor argued, must choose between isolation or imperialism. It was time America abandoned the fetters of parochialism and took her "rightful place among the great World-Powers." Together with Great Britain and Japan, America must "proclaim a new Monroe Doctrine applicable to China"; the nation must protect Asian markets from being absorbed by European nations that would monopolize them. "The designs of the Powers in the Far East," Proctor warned, "will deprive this country of an already large market, which must increase to enormous proportions in the near future."[10]

Nor were some of the warnings against an imperial policy very appealing. William MacDonald, a professor of political science, answered Proctor's article in the October 1898 issue of the *Forum*. He defined imperialism "in the best sense in which the term is used" as a "theory of national policy in accordance with which the United States is to add to its territorial possessions, for the purpose of extending American trade and American political influence." It was the "cosmopolitan and international, as opposed to the provincial, idea." Yet MacDonald opposed it because of his belief that America was not up to fulfilling imperial responsibilities, whatever her national ambitions might be. He doubted if the civil service could be reformed sufficiently, if the public would readily consent to increased taxation to support the burdens of imperialism, or if the nation were fitted "for intimate and influential relations with world affairs."[11] MacDonald's arguments, in their extreme national modesty, even self-abnegation, seemed almost calculated to arouse an opposing mood of national pride.

But for most Americans, the clear assertion of a new departure was far less welcome than the attempt, however forced, to reconcile America's new course with the past. Part of Theodore Roosevelt's genius lay in his ability to understand this need and satisfy it. In his acceptance of the vice-presidential nomination Roosevelt did just that. "We are making no new departures. We are not taking a single step which in any way affects our institutions or our traditional policies . . . The simple truth is that there is nothing even remotely resembling 'imperialism' or 'militarism' involved in the present development of that policy of expansion which has been part of the history of America from the day when she became a nation."

Roosevelt equated Jefferson's acquisition of the Louisiana Territory with McKinley's decision to annex the Philippines. This was a common comparison and rather too loose to be stressed. Instead, Roosevelt boldly went on to claim that American behavior was not merely nonimperialistic but anti-imperialistic: "We made a great anti-imperialistic stride when we drove the Spaniards from Porto Rico and the Philippines and thereby made ready ground in these islands for that gradually increasing measure of self-government for which their populations are severally fitted."[12] Henry Cabot Lodge, for all his talk of a "large policy," also took refuge in semantic traditionalism. In a letter to the historian J. F. Rhodes, Lodge commented that he did not "think there is any such thing as 'imperialism,' but I am very clearly of the opinion that there is such a thing as 'expansion' and that the U.S. must control some distant dependencies."[13]

If, in the interests of national unity and the successful reelection of McKinley to office, the leaders of the Republican party chose to stand on such limited ground, other political figures were far more daring. Alva Adams, governor of Colorado, wrote a stirring article for the *Independent* in the summer of 1898. "I preach a new political gospel," he cried. "The war with Spain makes the United States a World Power. She is no longer a self-centered provincial country, but an imperial nation." Adams spoke glowingly of the "thrill of empire" and predicted great gains from the "new fields that the Pacific will open to our commerce."[14]

On specific issues there was much difference of opinion as to how far America should go. During the tense summer of 1898, when Anglo-Russian railroad rivalry in China seemed almost to threaten war, the *Literary Digest* calmly remarked that the issue had aroused interest in America but not because of any sense of direct national involvement. Contradicting its own analysis, however, the *Digest* quoted two large newspapers, the *Atlanta Constitution* and the *New York Times,* both of which urged that the United States act immediately to support Great Britain's "open door" policy against Russian exclusionism in the New-chwang railroad dispute.[15] The *Independent,* in a sharp editorial, declared that an Anglo-Russian war was to be preferred to the weakening of English power in Far East,[16] and the *Boston Herald,* though generally unsympathetic with the loud-voiced exponents of imperialism, felt very strongly about Russian gains in China—especially where they threatened British predominance. A long editorial in March 1898 argued that America would suffer "only slightly less" than England should Russo-German greed lead to China's dismemberment.[17]

The Possibility of a Base in China

The *Independent* was by no means unique in its vigorous support for Great Britain's continued power in China as against Russia's presumably exclusionist bid for control of north China and Manchuria. Yet, despite the way in which the acquisition of the Philippines focused attention on China and was in part justified in terms of increased prestige and trade in China, the government made no new move in that area. McKinley watched as support for a more active policy grew. He still refused to appoint the eminently qualified, but Democratic, Rockhill as minister to China. Instead, a solid party Midwesterner, Edwin Conger, was given the job Charles Denby had held so jealously for so long. The importance of the China post was recognized by McKinley despite his reluctance to employ Rockhill. In his journal, Charles Dawes, a close friend of the President's, noted that McKinley had rejected the appointment of Charles Page Bryan because of his sense that the Senate would demand a more mature and experienced man in the light of the certain complexities of Chinese diplomacy.[18] Rockhill was eventually recalled from his Grecian exile and, though nominally in charge of Pan-American affairs, acted forcefully as chief Asian adviser to the new secretary of state, John Hay.

Conger, following Denby's lines of interest closely, was quick to support American enterprise wherever he could find it. In July 1898 he wrote a long, regretful report on the final authorization of the Franco-Belgian syndicate's Peking-Hankow railroad contract. The loss of this concession by the American China Development Company was serious for more than commercial reasons. "We need the potency of such footholds as these *to offset in part the territorial acquisitions which are the policy of the other strong nations; but which, for the present at least, our traditions and policies forbid.* As yet, the Americans have secured only one line . . . and against the consummation of this, the Europeans are busily working."[19]

As in Day's letter to Hay, remarks about current United States policy were time-limited. Among the policy makers themselves there seemed to be an expectation of great change, although what form it would take was as yet unclear. In late August Conger sent the Department a general report on the importance of "ownership." "Next to controlling a desirable port and commodious harbor in China, the permanent ownership or possession of Manila and vicinity would be most invaluable to us in securing and holding our share of influence and trade in . . . this country."[20]

In November Conger wrote suggesting that Manila, the next best, was not after all good enough. Certain that the situation in China was changing rapidly, he urged that the United States, "either by negotiation or by actual possession," put itself in a position to "own and control at least one good port from which we can potently assert our rights and effectively wield our influence." Four months later Conger's ambitions for his country had grown by leaps and bounds. In an excited report on the Italian demand for a coaling station, Conger included a bold plan for America.[21]

Conger argued that this was the moment for America to choose and seize a base in China. Any delay might be fatal, for the area of available land was narrowing rapidly. With almost comic naiveté Conger noted that, by an oversight, Chihli, the metropolitan province, remained unclaimed. "This, however, with Tientsin as the entrepot for all northern China, is destined in the future to be commercially one of the most valuable permanent possessions in the Orient." He did not mention that, of all areas in China, Chihli was least open to foreign aggrandizement. Aside from the last ditch opposition its detachment would arouse among Chinese, no competing power in China could allow the political center of the empire to be exclusively dominated by any one country. Conger outlined the procedure other powers had used to obtain their spheres of influence and urged that America do the same. "The policy of the other powers seems to be to obtain possession of some unimportant harbor or bay, claiming as a perquisite temporary control of developments in the adjacent province, with a prior claim, thus established, to the entire province at the proper time." Conger admitted that using Taku for this purpose might arouse too much opposition from other powers; he suggested some less well-known port nearby. Conger's bold plan was acknowledged and filed by the State Department without further comment.[22]

Two American consuls also saw the occupation of the Philippines as an opportunity and a justification for the acquisition of territory in China itself. Anson Burlingame Johnson, a native of Iowa, was appointed consul to Amoy in the Spring of 1897. Charles Denby vividly described the position of a consular official in China in a dramatic article for the *Forum* written after he had safely retired from the East:

> In China there are 35 treaty ports; and at each one of them the Europeans and the Americans rule the natives who are resident in the concessions. They rule them absolutely, and generally peaceably and quietly. Sometimes, when a city of a million natives lies alongside a small European concession, there will be fear and terror in every home, and the pale-faced mother will not sleep at night: but the stalwart man is there and he has his rifle and his Gatling and perchance the flag of an American, or European, or Japanese gunboat flies on the river which flows by the town.[23]

When Johnson first arrived in Amoy he seemed glad of his Gatling and the protection of gunboat captains. Three months after his arrival Johnson wrote with appropriate awe of the work of missionaries in the Amoy area as "breaking through the wall of ignorance and superstition that everywhere enslaves the benighted millions." "While the English gunboats and the American men of war are given full credit for their part in removing the blockade . . . the pioneers in the work, once the landing was made, were not soldiers or merchants but . . . devoted missionaries."[24]

As he settled into his job, however, Johnson began to behave more like a gentry-official on the Chinese model than an embattled defender of white mothers and children. He raised money from Chinese and foreign merchants for the establishment of an Anglo-Chinese college at Amoy, the Tung Wen Institute, at which 189 students were taught Western subjects by an Oregon Bachelor of Arts. In 1900, under circumstances to be discussed later, Johnson raised $10,000 to pay rebellious Chinese troops when the taotai of Amoy found himself unable to pay their salaries. By late August 1900 even his attitude toward the missionaries had changed. He reported that antiforeign feeling in Fukien was entirely directed at the missionaries because of the missionaries' own involvement in secular matters. Johnson noted that he had been keeping a close watch on missionary activity in the Amoy area since 1898 and had a working agreement with the taotai whereby the latter promised to investigate promptly any charge of antimissionary propaganda, while Johnson undertook to make sure the missionaries confined themselves to religious activities.[25]

To this enlightened, sinified official, the acquisition of the Philippines was a singularly welcome event. He saw it as a chance to tie the United States and China still closer together. In July 1898 he wrote a long dispatch on the relationship between Amoy and the Philippine Islands. Of the large Chinese population living in the Islands, Johnson pointed out that 90 percent originally came from Amoy. Regular steamer lines serviced Amoy and Manila and there was considerable and profitable trade between the two ports. Johnson foresaw the logical and continued strengthening of this link between Manila and Amoy with America in charge at both ends. But he warned against possible conflicts with Japan over Amoy. "It would . . . be inimical to our interests for any other nation to secure any exclusive rights in this province especially in the vicinity of Amoy. It is reported in the press that Japan is now endeavoring to secure the exclusive right to develop the mines of this province."[26]

In early 1899 the first in a series of minor conflicts with Japan over Amoy occurred. Johnson's good friend, the taotai, warned him that the Japanese were requesting a concession on the small island of Kulangsu in Amoy harbor. The taotai felt the Japanese demand could be resisted if America lodged a strong protest; otherwise it was likely to be granted. On January 12 Johnson sent a strong dispatch to the State Department: "I wish to point out that it is more than likely that the United States will someday use Amoy and this magnificent harbor as a base of supplies in China in preference to Hong Kong. This has been suggested by naval officers out here and should this ever be deemed desirable, it would be impossible if Japan secures the hold she is now after . . . This is the one port in China we must preserve if we are to make of our new possessions in the Orient what is now anticipated." On March 2 Johnson sent an excited coded cablegram, informing the Department that Japanese demands for the concession had been made, but a firm protest by the United States could prevent its being granted. He was authorized to protest against any interference with American interests.[27] The Japanese, for the time being interested only in obtaining a small piece of property for consular purposes, shifted their demand from the island of Kulangsu to the shorefront of the city of Amoy and reduced the amount of land requested so as to remove all doubts as to their intentions.[28] Johnson had no objection to the new request, which was granted. The issue seemed to have been settled satisfactorily.[29]

Although Hay's instructions had authorized Johnson to do no more than remonstrate, when he discovered that Johnson had in fact insisted that the United States receive a concession should Japan be granted one, he did not object. As Hay wrote Henry Adams some years later, the "ideal policy is . . . to do nothing, and yet be around when the watermelon is cut. Not that we want any watermelon, but it is always pleasant to be seen in smart colored circles on occasions of festivity."[30]

If concessions were being distributed, America would expect equal consideration with the rest. If China were distributing slices of melon in the Amoy area, then we would expect our share. On the other hand, we were not so anxious as to *demand* a cut on our initiative. Hay's reply to Conger made it clear to both the consul in Amoy and the minister in Peking that the administration was not loath to acquire property in China. It was equally clear that no firm policy decision had been made on the matter one way or the other. It was still a policy of watchful waiting; if, as America looked on, any small pieces of territory should happen to be acquired, that was all to the good.

Meanwhile, Johnson took advantage of the entire incident to secure a lease on "certain desirable foreshore in the heart of the city for the New York tea firms." The Chinese, Johnson proudly reported, had previously refused to rent the property to foreign firms.[31]

By November 1899 Amoy was again quiet. Johnson summed up Japanese gains as being very limited in area and "far from conspicuous on account of its desirability." However, American-Japanese rivalry in the city continued. In March 1900 Johnson reported that the Japanese had, with great fanfare, opened a college in Amoy designed to rival his own Tung Wen Institute. The new college would teach both Japanese and English and had been well financed by contributions from Chinese and Japanese merchants in Formosa. Other rumors reached Johnson that Japanese surveyors were active in the Amoy area and that Japan intended to seize the entire province of Fukien at the first opportunity.[32]

In another area of the China coast, Consul John Fowler, an acerbic and rather quarrelsome man, was urging that America lease a naval base off the coast of Chekiang, the province in which he served. As early as January 1897 Fowler said that Chefoo, Shantung, would make a good naval base. In reply, the Department forwarded a letter from Commodore F. V. McNair of the Asiatic Squadron. McNair stated unequivocally that he deemed it "inadvisable that an attempt be made to establish a coaling station at any port, particularly so at the port of Chefoo"—and the matter was dropped. The Spanish-American War changed McNair's mind. Twice the Asiatic Squadron had been forced to depend on British goodwill to obtain essential coal supplies. McNair himself was now urging the government to establish a coaling station in North China. Fowler therefore renewed his suggestions in a long dispatch to the Department dated October 27, 1898.

> Owing to recent events in our history, and especially Admiral Dewey's experience in his efforts to obtain coal, and the fact that at no time since last November has it been possible for other than British men-of-war to secure proper steamer coal in North China . . . I venture to believe that my suggestions were sound, and had they been adopted, perhaps the political question in North China would not have assumed so acute a phase. . . . Knowing the keen interest taken in North China of late, at home and elsewhere, I have endeavored to convince by my reports that our commercial and other interests in North China are the most important we have in the Far East . . . and unless we are prepared to take a firm and decided stand, we may look for a rapid diminution of our interests, if not complete extinction.
>
> While it may be true that the United States does not care to interfere with Asiatic politics, we are now involved in them, and must decide whether we propose to be respected or annihilated commercially as well as politically, in the East.
>
> . . . I . . . most earnestly urge upon the Government that we secure a base on the China Coast . . . If we intend to protect our interests in North China, by our own guns, and by our own coal, and not be subjected to the position [we] are placed in today, we must have a base in North China.

Manila is well enough, but in order to be of use to us should be supplemented by a coaling station in North China.[33]

At Hay's direction this dispatch was immediately sent to the secretary of the navy for his consideration; Hay appended no comment of any kind. Acting Secretary of the Navy Allen acknowledged its receipt, but made no reply to Hay or to Fowler. Within the Navy Department, however, the subject was being carefully considered by the Bureau of Equipment, the section most directly concerned with coaling problems. On January 13, 1899, R. B. Bradford, chief of this bureau, sent a memo to the secretary of the navy actively endorsing Fowler's recommendation.

The Bureau cannot urge too strongly the necessity for establishing a coaling station near the mouth of the Yang-tsu-Kiang river, China.

The strategical position of Chusan is worthy of notice, lying as it does within 60 miles of the mouth of the Yang-tsu-Kiang but little more than 100 miles from the great commercial city of Shanghai.

Absolute sovereignty should be acquired over the island of Chusan, and the small islands near it for defensive purposes.

Allen's response was not too encouraging. After a delay of over eight months he finally replied to an anxious inquiry from Bradford that "the Department considered the recommendation of the Bureau on this subject . . . and gave instructions at that time to file the correspondence without further action."[34]

One month later Bradford placed the issue before the public in the hope of attracting wider support for the navy's position. In an article for the *Forum* Bradford systematically discussed every available coaling station across the globe. To protect American interest and property, to aid in the advancement of civilization, and to "protect innocent people from barbarous and inhuman treatment," Bradford wrote, America needed a strong navy and, in times of war, a strong navy was crippled without coaling stations; the more the better. He suggested that the Chusan Islands would be ideal, making no mention of Britain's prior claim on the archipelago. "With the recent concessions made by China in the way of granting territory to other first-class nations," he noted, "it would appear that the United States might, with becoming modesty, ask for one of these islands."[35]

In the summer of 1900, Bradford renewed his recommendations in the light of the new military situation in China. This time the secretary of the navy, Long, asked Bradford to put his suggestions in the form of a letter to the secretary of state for his signature. Bradford quickly complied and on July 31, 1900, Long sent the letter to Hay for his "favorable consideration."[36]

Bradford opened his argument with the comment that the "present outbreak in China [the Boxer Rebellion] developed so quickly and affects so many nations that it is only with difficulty and at great expense that we can supply our ships. These difficulties are likely to recur and perhaps in a greater degree." Bradford suggested that the current disturbed situation in China might be the ideal time to enter into negotiations for a coaling station and supply depot. He concluded his letter with an appeal to national pride as well as economy. "In addition it is to be noted that this country alone, of all those prominently interested in the maintenance of the affairs in Northern China, has no depot on or near that coast."[37] The fate of Bradford's recommendation is involved in the larger story of America's response to the Boxer crisis and will be dealt with in a later chapter.

Hay himself was cautious in all statements on America's territorial intentions in China. In a confidential letter to Paul Dana, editor of the *New York Sun,* written in March 1899, he confessed: "It is not very easy to formulate with any exactness the view of the Government in regard to the present condition of things in China. In brief we are, of course, opposed to the dismemberment of that Empire, and we do not think that the public opinion of the United States would justify the Government in taking part in the great game of spoliation now going on." Though not a very clear policy statement, this was at least definite in its notion of what we did *not* intend to do. Yet Hay went on:

> At the same time we are keenly alive to the importance of safeguarding our great commercial interests in that empire, and our representatives there have orders to watch closely everything that may seem calculated to injure us, and to prevent it by energetic and timely representations . . . We do not consider our hands tied for

future eventualities, but for the present we think our best policy is one of vigilant protection of our commercial interests without formal alliance with other powers interested.

In November 1899, Hay was equally careful not to bind America to any absolute renunciation of territorial ambitions when he responded to a worried question by Wu T'ing-fang, Chinese minister to the United States. Hay denied that the United States was considering the acquisition of territory in China. As in the letter to Dana, however, he went on to say: "If we should ever in the future, which I do not now anticipate, desire to treat with your Government for any conveniences of accommodations on the coast, we shall have pleasure in addressing ourselves directly to the Imperial Government of China."[38]

Changes in China

If victory in war had had a powerful effect on Americans, defeat remained China's teacher. The humiliating defeat by Japan had been a bitter experience for many Chinese. For a small group of intellectuals it was a galvanizing event that moved them, in three short years, to dramatic action. Between June and September 1898, a group of young reformers, led by K'ang Yu-wei, Liang Ch'i-ch'ao and T'an Ssu-t'ung, managed to attain a considerable degree of control over the government through a kind of palace revolution.[39] The reformers were able to influence the weak but painfully earnest Emperor Kuang-hsu to proclaim a stunning series of progressive decrees. Morally admirable, intellectually acute, the reformers yet lacked all political sense. In a country as regionally divided as China had become, their limited base of support was fatal. Nor did they capture the loyalty of a significant portion of their own class—the scholar-officials. When the opposition regrouped itself in the face of a decree that threatened to eliminate the sinecure jobs of many senior officials, the reformers turned to the military for aid.

In September 1898, Yuan Shih-k'ai, in charge of the "Newly Created Army," met with T'an Ssu-t'ung in Peking. T'an appealed to his loyalty to the emperor and to a reformed China. A military coup involving the final disposal of the empress dowager was suggested.[40] Such a coup would have saved the reform movement. However, Yuan Shih-k'ai, although he had expressed a serious interest in reform along the lines Kuang-hsu was then attempting, was far too cautious to commit himself completely to what would have then become a revolution. Instead he revealed T'an's plot to Jung-lu, governor-general of Chihli and a key supporter of the empress dowager. The empress dowager had prepared for all eventualities and she moved at once. On September 21, accompanied by Jung-lu's troops, she moved into Peking, arrested six reformers unfortunate enough to be caught, interned the emperor and, after a lapse of only four months, resumed control.[41]

Minister Conger's comments on these important events were laconic in the extreme. Although, like most Americans in China, Conger had excoriated the decadent Ch'ing government, he seemed totally unaware of the magnitude and importance of the reformers' attempt. His account of the summer's events was almost uninterested:

> Of course there is great excitement here; but the people themselves are so conservative, and they have so often heretofore witnessed the strength and conservatism of this remarkable woman that there is not the general alarm one might expect from such happenings . . . The belief is quite general that even the Empress Dowager and her ultra-conservative advisors have been somewhat aroused by passing events, and that material improvement, commercial development and educational progress will still be carried forward, though with somewhat slackened pace.[42]

Secular newspapers in the United States, even those, like the *Independent*, which were firm supporters of the missionary movement, were singularly harsh in their comments on both the attempt and failure of reform. On September 29, 1898, the *Independent* remarked that "China has during the past weeks puzzled and amused the world by its kaleidoscopic changes of policy." Two weeks later an editorial in the same paper demonstrated both a total lack of understanding of China and a nationalistic concern with what occurred there. "The sudden reversal of the political situation in China furnishes as conclusive proof as could be desired of the absolute incapacity of the Chinese Government to carry out any independent policy . . . The United States can scarcely look on with unconcern. Already American trade with China is large, and American interests in Chinese railways are increasing."[43]

The appointment of the American missionary, W. A. P. Martin, as president of the Imperial University upset many predictions as to the ultraconservative nature of the empress dowager's resumption of power. It is generally assumed that missionaries in China were bitterly disappointed by the failure of the reform movement and angered at British and American diplomatic indifference to it. Although this is undoubtedly true of missionaries *in* China, affiliated groups at home were less disturbed. *The Missionary Review of the World* took a very calm view of the emperor's deposition and was sympathetic with the empress dowager's position. Indeed by the summer of 1899 the Baptist Missionary Union's magazine felt reconciled enough to praise the empress for preventing her headstrong nephew from "precipitating turmoil and disorder, which would be a more effectual check to progress than her more conservative view."[44]

After the resumption of rule by the empress dowager, two parallel movements mark the development of American-Chinese relations. Along with cautious approaches to reform, the Chinese government began to take a hard line toward the demands of the European powers. Italy's request for the lease of San Mun Bay was firmly rejected. For all her talk of the Open Door, Britain supported the Italian demand, while the rest of the diplomatic corps in Peking maintained an attitude of benevolent neutrality. The Tsungli yamen, as it had so many times in the past, continued to resist; this time, however, it was the European power that gave way. Italy lowered her demands (on the new list was a rather pathetic request for a Chair of Italian Studies at the new Imperial University[45]) but continued to meet absolute rejection. Forced to back down at last, the Italian minister was recalled, and the Chinese tasted limited triumph for the first time in years. One month later, in March 1899, the Chinese responded instantly to the occupation of a Shantung village by German troops with a troop movement of its own. Signs of a growing popular antiforeign movement appeared just at the time the central government girded itself to maintain intact what remained of China's territorial integrity.

The reformers of 1898 had been greatly influenced by Western ideas, by the example of Peter the Great's dramatic reform of Russia, and by Japan's successful marriage of reform and revolution. Though their aim was to strengthen China so that, in addition to other gains, it might resist the depredations of the Western powers, the reformers were not anti-foreign. They were not twentieth-century revolutionaries able to combine a passion for modernization with hatred for the exemplars of that modernization. The reformers, bursting with plans but lacking the nationalist passion that might have ignited popular support, were able to make only limited gains under a weak emperor. To the European powers the reform movement was an interesting surface phenomenon. At no time did they allow the political changes in Peking to interfere with the progress of their demands on China. Indeed the height of the scramble for concessions coincided with the brief reform period.

Activation of American Public Opinion

At the same time that the Chinese government decided to resist, to the point of war, further foreign encroachments, the American public became increasingly and belligerently interested in the advancement of American economic gains in China. The American Asiatic Association, well financed by member companies, became an effective lobby for specific business groups as well as a vigorous supporter of any active American policy toward China. The August issue of the *Journal* printed with pride a speech made by Cushman K. Davis, then Chairman of the Senate Foreign Relations Committee. Davis spoke of American interests in the "ossified" Chinese empire as "vital." The *Journal* took implicit credit for bringing Davis to this view. In October it was able to reprint an editorial from the *Journal of Commerce* that praised the association for its "salutary influence in educating public sentiment into a recognition of the magnitude of the interests which this country has at stake in the Far East." The *Journal of Commerce* credited the association with being an important factor impelling the government to "adopt a more vigorous policy in China."[46]

The well-known missionary Gilbert Reid published several articles in the secular press urging the government to take an active role in China. In an analysis of American opportunities in China written for the *Forum* in April 1899, Reid noted that "our political power has failed to defend our commercial interests." Although spheres of influence were not legally recognized, Reid pointed out that the United States had to deal with Russia, as well as China, in Manchuria, with Germany in Shantung, with

England in the Yangtze Valley, and so on. Like so many men enchanted with the possibilities of the China market, Reid could not understand why American businessmen were not more active there. He concluded his article with an appeal to the government immediately to join Great Britain in support of the Open Door policy.[47] Reid's article exhibits several characteristics of the kind of publicity favorable to China that appeared regularly in the press and magazines of mid-1899. The Open Door policy, identified with Great Britain but never specifically defined, is strongly advocated. The vastness of the China market *and* the greatness of American interests existing in China are stressed. At the same time the somewhat contradictory wonder is expressed that America does not have *more* of an economic hold in China. In a vague way this lack is attributed to the unfavorable spheres of influence situation, and the Open Door policy is advocated once more.

Minor figures of the American intellectual elite, like C. K. Adams, president of the University of Wisconsin, wrote moving tributes to the prospects of American trade in China. Brooks Adams began the series of articles, later published as *America's Economic Supremacy,* that urged instant action in China against the great Russian menace. John Barrett, the Denbys *père et fils,* and other publicists associated with Asian topics found ready publishers.[48]

Continued Tribulations of the American China Development Company

The representatives of the American China Development Company, whose road was never smooth, were once more busy in China during the summer of 1899, not busy building road-beds, to be sure, but much involved in new negotiations. Not having the hands-off attitude of Secretaries Sherman and Day, Hay was ready to act in favor of the company against adverse contingencies known or unknown. As mentioned earlier, the company discovered that its original loan contract would meet only about 50 percent of the construction costs. Clarence Cary, the company's lawyer, was therefore sent to China to secure a supplementary agreement that would cover a larger loan. At the same time the company, whose ambitions consistently outran its ability to fulfill its contracts, hoped to

110

get extensive mining privileges in Hunan and expanded branch line rights.[49]

Cary found that Belgian and French emissaries of the Peking-Hankow syndicate were actively attempting to wrest the Canton-Hankow concession from the American group. Early in July 1899, he appealed to the consul-general in Shanghai, J. F. Goodnow, for aid. He asked that Goodnow inform Sheng Hsuan-huai that the United States government would back the demands of the Company. Aware of Day's earlier instructions on this matter, Goodnow hesitated to comply without further instructions from the Department. He told Cary to get his home office to put pressure on Washington so that appropriate instructions might be sent to China. On July 5 Goodnow duly received the permission needed in a telegram ordering him to use his good offices on behalf of the Development Company "to prevent injury or denial of vested rights."[50]

The negotiations remained deadlocked for another full year. In addition to combined Franco-Belgian pressure against the contract, the new American demands were exorbitant and the Chinese were determined not to grant them. On July 14 Conger received a telegram identical to that Goodnow had gotten earlier. He was to use his good offices "energetically" on the company's behalf. A covering letter referred specifically to the danger of unfair competition from foreign powers. Conger was not to favor one American company above another, "but in all cases where there are opportunities of competition between Americans and men of other nationalities, you will do what you can to see that your fellow citizens have a fair and equal chance with others." Cary was dissatisfied with the aid Conger gave him and complained to the Department. In defending himself, Conger sent back copies of letters proving that in the month of September alone he had made three strong representations to Sheng on Cary's behalf.[51]

In December 1899, Conger presented Cary to the Tsungli yamen in an effort to bring pressure on Sheng from within the Chinese government. The yamen refused any responsibility but it did offer an opinion on the company's demands for mining rights and branch lines. In supporting Sheng's refusal, the yamen pointed out that popular opposition to foreign mining enterprises in Hunan was too great to be bridged at this time. Cary was assured, however, that no other foreign company would get the concession. As for the branch lines, the yamen remarked that the company's demands were so extensive as to amount to a major concession; they could hardly be negotiated as a supplementary agreement to a more limited concession granted years before. In May of 1900 Hay was still doing his best for the company though it seemed certain their demands would not be met.[52]

On July 13, 1900, an agreement was finally reached. The company had the right to float bonds of up to $40 million for the construction of 710 miles of mainline, 130 miles of branch line, and 78 miles of siding. It is likely that the strained circumstances under which the agreement was signed—the Boxer upheaval was then at its height—had more to do with the conclusion of negotiations than Hay's efforts.

Yet, true to the tragicomic history of this enterprise, the new agreement contained the seeds of the final downfall of the American China Development Company. Article 17 of the Supplementary Agreement was, within two years, to cause the company and the State Department much difficulty. It provided that no transfer of rights to other nations or nationals would be permitted.[53] According to P. H. Kent, Cary informed Sheng that under American corporation law, there could be no legal prohibition on the sale of shares to any buyer. Cary's interpretation of the article was that the company *itself* could not be transferred to other nationals; no limit was placed on the disposal of shares. Kent speculates, probably correctly, that Sheng understood this reservation but neglected to inform anyone else of the article's true meaning.[54] Determined to maintain the semblance of balance of concessions that he had worked for, Sheng insisted on the article as the best guarantee available that America, and not Russia or France, would control this important line. The mischief this ambiguous article caused will be dealt with in a later chapter.

In a speech at the University of California in 1900 Whitelaw Reid provided the motto for a whole generation of American policy makers. "Duty first," he intoned, "but then Interest also." Reid was not being cynical. For the McKinley administration and its supporters, duty and interest were comfortably indistinguishable. In his first year in office McKinley told Robert La Follette that his greatest ambition was "to round out his career by gaining American supremacy in world markets." "It should be our settled purpose," he declared, "to open trade wherever we can, making our ships and our commerce messengers of peace and amity." Thus the decision to annex the Philippines was taken on the grounds of duty—to the Filipinos, to world peace, to the missionary movement—and of interest. Here China played a major role. The Philippines was to be one insular base in a series of naval stepping-stones to the China market.[55] Later, during the Boxer crisis, China justified the Philippines once more. Now it was clear to everyone that American possession of the islands alone permitted the United States to play its proper role in that upheaval. Cushman K. Davis expressed shock that anyone in California should oppose annexation of the archipelago in view of the possibilities for commerce in China. With the Philippines, he wrote Whitelaw Reid, "we can command what we please. Such a commerce as we ought to have would put 10 millions of people on the Pacific coast within not many years."[56]

With the territorial base the Philippines provided and the interest and enthusiasm for China their possession engendered, the United States was now ready for a major move in the Far East. Horace Porter, then American Minister to France, summarized the nation's position, as of November 1899, in a letter to McKinley. In three months, Porter observed, the United States had accomplished "what the great powers had sought in vain to do for over a hundred years, in having secured a chain of island ports in the Pacific, secured the Philippines, captured their trade, paved the way for a Pacific cable of our own, virtually taken possession of that ocean and occupied a position at Manila easily defended, only a couple of days time from the Chinese coast with no fear of Chinese or Russian armies at our back and yet near enough to protect our interests in the Orient."[57]

Yet a strange paradox remained. All that was needed to protect American interest in China had been secured. The interest alone was lacking. "Such a commerce as we ought to have," Cushman Davis had written, yet such a commerce did not exist. The reason for the disparity between reality and expectation was sought not in the nature of the American economy, but in the political situation in China. Now, in the formulation of the Open Door notes, there could be a merging of effort between those who sought a dominant power position for America and those concerned merely with increasing her trade. For in China, it was believed, trade and power were synonymous.

Between the spring of 1898 and the issuance of the Open Door note in September 1899, the McKinley administration had, through its inquiries into the intentions of Germany and Russia, manifested its concern with the trend of events in China. Although too occupied with the war with Spain to join England in a forceful statement of his administration's objectives in China, McKinley by no means ignored the Far Eastern situation. He watched as a rising wave of expansionist fervor caught the country; he watched as special interest groups organized themselves for the purpose of urging specific policies; he made sure that America made no commitment in regard to the eventual acquisition of territory on the mainland of China. Then, as had been the case with the Spanish-American War, McKinley moved when he felt the domestic mood was ready, even eager, to move. The only factor he did not, perhaps, watch closely enough was the internal condition of China.

In the early spring of 1899, American advocates of a new China policy were aided by the arrival of a master propagandist from Great Britain, Lord Charles Beresford. With his arrival the agitation for some form of American Open Door policy toward China increased.

six   The Open Door

The words "open door," first used to characterize British desires and then
to name actual American policy, are semantically interesting. They offer
rich metaphoric possibilities rare in diplomatic language. Doors may be
shut, broken down, forced open; they can be half-way, three quarters open.
Doors can even be multiplied—and some historians feel they make a distinction when they speak of an "open doors" instead of an "open door"
policy. Moreover, like all good political catch-phrases, "open door" has
immediately favorable connotations. An open door is, prima facie, more
fair, more desirable than a closed one—at least to those who would like
to get inside. Neither John Hay nor William Rockhill invented the phrase.
They were able to attach it to the policy they framed in part because
it had already become common coin. The difficulty that confronts the
historian is one of meaning, for the content of the phrase changed rapidly
in a short time period. By 1905 it had several layers of meaning; as a
result it was well on its way to meaninglessness.

Development of Open Door Concept
In part, the words "open door" refer back to an earlier period of Sino-
Western relations. The British were generally credited with having opened
China, that is, with having forced the Chinese government of the 1840's
to grant extensive trade privileges that violated the Chinese attempt to fit
its contacts with Western nations into its Asian trade pattern. Although
China was not completely open to trade by the late nineteenth century,
it was apparent that the greatest danger to free trade was no longer
Chinese obstructionism but European ambition.

One clear line of descent for the Open Door policy, as it was finally
enunciated by John Hay in 1899, lies in the history of the Imperial Maritime Customs Service under Sir Robert Hart. John K. Fairbank has
pointed out that the "constant purpose" of the Customs Service "was to
provide equal terms of competition both among individual traders and

among trading nations in China."[1] By keeping the treaty system intact and operating smoothly, the Customs Service ensured that equality—at least with respect to commercial opportunity. At the same time the integrity of China, within the framework of the unequal treaties, was also involved in the Customs' ideal. For the treaty system was seen as a contractual relationship protecting both sides. The greatest threat to the treaty system that occurred in over forty years of Customs administration in China was the scramble for concessions following the Sino-Japanese War. Spheres of influence threatened to make a mockery of the treaty system by confining its operation to ports long opened and excluding it from new areas of commercial opportunity. The threat of such spheres to the integrity of China was obvious.

One can argue, then, that the American Open Door policy was no more than the implementation of the ideas of Sir Robert Hart through the instrumentality of Alfred Hippisley and William Rockhill. However, the provenance of the ideas involved in the Open Door policy is beyond the scope of this study. The concern here is why, in 1899, that policy was adopted by the McKinley administration and how that event came about.

As has been noted, the British attempted to interest the United States in a cooperative effort to ensure equal trading rights in leases or concessions acquired by other powers in China. As stated by Joseph Chamberlain in February 1898, the British policy was that "any port occupied by a foreign nation shall be, *ipso facto,* a Treaty Port open to all on precisely similar conditions."[2] The United States professed itself satisfied with German and Russian assurances that Kiaochow and Talienwan, respectively, would be open ports.

By the spring of 1899, the meaning of the "open door" had been substantially narrowed. By acquiescing in Germany's position on concessions in Shantung, the British government had virtually admitted that within the spheres of influence capital investment was not "open" at all but was the prerogative of the preponderant power. Only if that power declined a particular concession or decided not to advance a projected development scheme, could other interested investors offer their bids. This became the rule within those provinces under the control of one power. As Great Britain fought the Franco-Belgian concession for the Peking-Hankow railroad on the grounds of infringement of Britain's preserve, so the

Russians fought, in the summer of 1898, British attempts to finance an extension road to Newchwang, which Russia considered deep in its sphere of influence. In November 1898, Chamberlain declared explicitly that it was not in England's interests "to give anything like a guarantee of integrity and independence of an empire which appeared to be decaying."[3]

Only in regard to trade were the British still hopeful of obtaining an Open Door agreement. Suggestions were made to Russia that, in exchange for a recognition of equal trading rights within each other's spheres, Britain would recognize Russia's special position in Manchuria. The Russian government, deeply divided on whether to make any arrangements with Britain at all, finally decided to agree to a limited accord on railroad rights. The British reluctantly accepted this reduced agreement and in April 1899, an exchange of notes between the two countries guaranteed that neither would seek railroad concessions in the other's sphere. The respective spheres were very loosely defined: the area north of the Great Wall for Russia, the Yangtze basin for England. As William Langer has pointed out, the exchange was most unequal and resulted in a feeling of intense dissatisfaction in England. The government admitted that the Yangtze valley could hardly be run as a province the way Manchuria could. It claimed, in the face of severe criticism, to be firmly in favor of the Open Door, determined to preserve British predominance in the Yangtze area and, at the same time, unprepared "to undertake the immense responsibility of governing what is practically a third of China."[4] In other words, the British government had settled for a truncated Open Door policy and a similarly partial sphere of influence policy.

In America the phrase "open door" was extensively used in relation to the tariff policy of the government in the Philippines. Recognizing the desirability of equal treatment to all in China, the administration was embarrassed by its domestic protectionist policy and worried as to what consistency would demand in the Philippines.[5] The high priest of protection, Senator Dingley, assured the press that the Open Door in the Philippines meant "equality of treatment and not free trade." Moreover this equality of treatment was intended to apply only during the period of military administration. If the Philippines should be admitted to the United States as a territory, extant trade rules would, of course, apply. The *Journal of Commerce* seized on the limited commitment to an Open Door in the Philippines and extended it to general United States policy in East Asia. What the Open Door would mean, it claimed, was: "a check to the policy of overriding treaty rights by a transfer of sovereignty over parts of China, and it is a notice to all concerned that the power newly in evidence in the Pacific proposes to retain all the privileges of trade which it possesses while freely granting . . . equality of opportunity to others." However, the *Literary Digest* noted that the *Journal of Commerce* was the only newspaper to draw such widespread conclusions.[6]

When Americans like Gilbert Reid referred to the British devotion to the Open Door, what they meant was the narrow commercial meaning that phrase had come to cover, that is, the nondiscriminatory entry of goods in trade. Neither territorial integrity nor equality of capital investment was included. In late February 1899, Americans interested in China welcomed Lord Charles Beresford, representative of the Associated Chambers of Commerce of England, as a spokesman for the Open Door policy. They found in Beresford a harsh critic of British policy. He asked that America declare a new policy for Asia that would go far beyond current British aims. The American Asiatic Association, familiar with Beresford's advanced ideas and in full agreement with them, welcomed him at a small dinner party in Abram S. Hewitt's home. He was greeted in the name of the "substantial identity between Great Britain and the United States in supporting the policy of the Open Door in China."[7]

Some days later the association gave a huge dinner party for Beresford at Delmonico's. Many men of importance were invited and several accepted, including ex-Governor Levi P. Morton, Whitelaw Reid, and General Woodford. After toasting the President and the Queen, Everett Frazar, president of the association, proposed a toast to "Commercial Opportunity in the Markets of the Far East." This somewhat unwieldy toast was followed by one to the "Open Door."[8]

Beresford's program rested on two general proposals: that the sphere of influence pattern was strangling trade and must be stopped and an Open Door policy substituted; that to make the Open Door meaningful, China's integrity must be preserved. To achieve the latter Beresford urged an alliance between Britain, Germany, Japan, and the United States. In addition the armed forces of China should be reorganized by foreign advisers so that it could become the effective protector of foreign trade.[9]

Beresford's speech to the assembled guests was in his best after-dinner style. He began with an assertion that "Commercial failure or success in the future" depended upon "the political line, upon the line of policy." Pointedly criticizing those in England and America who merely mouthed Open Door sentiments, Beresford declared that he saw no use "for us all hollering for the open door unless we put forward some way in which we are to keep it open." Over the mounting applause Beresford continued, "And that way should be . . . a clear, strong and definite proposition, which should be courteous to all nations." Beresford claimed that what he proposed was not new, for it primarily involved maintaining the existing treaties. He went on to say, however, that beyond that "The integrity of China should be assured, because without the integrity of China there is no use in talking about the open door." He was answered by applause. Beresford concluded his talk with an appeal to Anglo-American unity:

> We are of the same blood, with the same laws, the same literature, the same ideas, the same religion . . . We have a big, honest idea of what should be done with trade and commerce, and we have, even better than that, a grand, chivalrous, noble sentiment in regard to what should be done with weaker nations . . . I hope our friendliness will be cemented into an everlasting friendship, for I am absolutely certain that if that is so, not only will it push the interests of trade and commerce, but it will push the interests of humanity and of Christianity.[10]

Having thus appealed to race, religion, nobility, cupidity, and sheer sentiment, Beresford sat down to thunderous applause and three cheers.

Newspapers interested in China were quick to pick up Beresford's speech. The *Independent* noted that his concept of the Open Door was more extensive than that of most Americans: "It is a bold project, involving as it does an alliance with Great Britain, the United States, Germany and Japan; the reorganization and maintenance of the Chinese army; . . . the restraint of Russia and France . . . The question is highly interesting and one of great importance. It should be carefully and wisely considered by American Chambers of Commerce and at Washington." Placing these two on a plane of equality was not quite fair, yet the *Independent* had accurately pinpointed the two groups of people most concerned with Beresford's ideas. During the spring and summer of 1899, members of the American Asiatic Association made frequent trips to Washington to discuss China policy with Secretary of State Hay. In addition, the association charged its members about $100 each toward a fund to be used for the education of the general public. Between May and November $1,550 had been collected. During his visits to Washington John Foord, vice-president of the association, had been convinced that "To exercise its legitimate influence in shaping the course of this Government in dealing with questions affecting trade in China, it was absolutely essential that the public sentiment of the country should be better informed and should find more emphatic expression than heretofore."[11]

To the association's delight, newspapers and magazines during 1899 contained a growing number of articles on the danger to American interests of a partition of China, of being excluded from the vast China market, of failing to confront "the bear" with the force of "the eagle." Attention now focused on the "open door," as a catch-phrase and symbol of a policy that would avert the danger of exclusion from the China market. A strong editorial in the *Boston Herald* on March 14, 1899, urged an Anglo-Saxon union that would declare a "hands-off" policy to all the rest of the world and then jointly reform China. With Japan's cooperation, much could be done, the *Herald* assured its readers. In tones that suited the Asiatic Association and the more activist members of McKinley's administration, the *Herald* reprimanded the government for its total passivity. Though approving the general statements in favor of the Open Door made by the State Department, the *Herald* felt they were "without force or purpose."[12]

Nor was the association a silent observer. It did its best to feed the stream of publication urging a more vigorous policy. On June 10, 1899, the American Asiatic Association published a special number of its *Journal* and asked all members to distribute copies as widely as possible. The aim of the issue was to say in compact form "why the future of China is a question of supreme moment to the United States. Till the importance of that question is appreciated by the American people, it is useless to expect on the part of our government a policy as vigorous and resolute as the occasion demands." Among the longer items in the magazine was a reprint of an address by John Barrett, ex-ambassador to Siam and a strong advocate of a vigorous China policy, to the Chamber of Commerce of New York. Barrett opened by saying, "America is today the arbiter of China's future." China's future was relevant to every section of the American nation. Barrett predicted that in fifteen years China would consume all the wheat and flour supply of the Pacific states. Already the cotton manufacturers of the South "have millions of invested capital practically dependent upon the market of Manchuria being kept open." Iron and steel manufacturers, rolling stock companies, businessmen in every part of the country had a stake in Chinese trade.

Barrett urged that the American public speak out, for without clear public support, the government could not act. What they were to speak out for was less clear. Following Beresford closely in phraseology, Barrett was vague in his actual suggestions. It would be death to the Chinese empire for America to recognize spheres of influence as actual, binding entities. Yet Barrett saw no way for America to eliminate the spheres. He went on to propose that, should it be impossible to maintain China's integrity, "we should have a definite understanding with . . . the powers concerned, that they will guarantee the practical and permanent operation of the principles of the open door" within their respective spheres. Indeed, were China to be actually divided, it would be wise for America to seize a port herself.[13] Although Barrett declared that spheres of influence should not be accepted as *faits accomplis,* he then went on to discuss the arrangements America should make with powers that did control spheres. He noted the great damage partition would have on American trade, but instead of suggesting policies that would halt the trend he advocated joining in the division.

In October 1899, the American Asiatic Association managed to have two days set aside for China and Japan at the Philadelphia Commercial Convention. On October 18 Cornelius N. Bliss addressed the audience of the convention on China trade. A little confused as to what was really happening in China, Bliss declared that the United States asked for "no special 'sphere of influence' . . . which appears to be only another term for disintegration and ruin of China, but we hope to see her [China] ere long abandoning the policy of seclusion, coming forth in the light of her civilization and power and join the community of nations, to share in the prosperity that awaits the grand commercial development of the twentieth century." John Barrett also spoke, varying the phrases of his Chamber of Commerce talk. On this occasion he predicted that within the foreseeable future, based on a per capita projection, China might well consume $1,500,000,000 worth of American goods.[14]

121

On the question of spheres and the Open Door, Barrett's earlier ambiguity remained:

> We have everything to lose and nothing to gain by the dividing of China into such spheres . . . the U.S. undoubtedly stands today as the strongest influence for the integrity of the Chinese empire. Were we for one moment to indicate our acquiescence in such spoliation of this great kingdom, there would follow a scramble and rush for China's rich area that would astonish the world with its wantonness . . . We cannot think of rushing into an unwarranted expression of a bold, war-like policy, but we can exert a strong moral influence at Peking and elsewhere throughout the Far East that will protect and enlarge our interests.

The question of China's integrity was not only a commercial but a moral issue. It was the "question of the hour." Despite all these verbal reasons for committing the country to China's integrity, Barrett was ready to abandon it in a sentence. If spheres of influence could not be stopped they must be lived with.[15] The arbiter of China's destiny would settle for a guarantee of equal trading privileges within each sphere of influence.

Both Foord and Barrett had referred to the necessity of clear public support before the administration could be expected to act. To be sure, this is precisely how the interested but cautious Hay had described the situation to Foord. The administration had barely survived the torrent of agitation for war with Spain. Rather than leading that public movement it had just managed to keep up with it, maintaining the illusion of control through timely surrender. McKinley had repeatedly spoken of himself as "watching" the Far Eastern scene. More accurately, he and his political supporters were watching the American public. Should there be signs, clear, unmistakable, but yet early enough to be controlled, of a public demand for action in China, then the administration would act. It wanted neither to act before the moment nor to be caught unprepared when the time for action came.

The administration's difficulty is illuminated by Charles Beresford's report on his trip to America published on his return to England. Beresford had met with those most interested in a strong American Asian policy. He contrasted the attitude of the "commercial classes" in Japan and

America. "Both," he noted, "saw the necessity of keeping the Door open in China" but

> While on the Japanese side there was every indication of a desire to act in some practical manner in order to secure the Open Door, I could discover no desire on the part of the commercial communities in the United States to engage in any practical effort for preserving what to them might become in the future a trade, the extent of which no mortal can conjecture. On many occasions I suggested that some sort of understanding should exist between Great Britain and the United States for the mutual benefit of the two countries . . . but while receiving the most cordial support to this proposal, nothing of a definite character was suggested to me.[16]

Thus, though McKinley could be sure that *some* action in regard to China would be favored by the business community, it was not clear *how much* action they were willing to countenance. A policy must be devised that would satisfy the growing, but very vague, demand that something be done.

The business community, through groups like the American Asiatic Association, helped create a climate in which a new American China policy would be favorably received. But they did not offer clear prescriptions. The lineaments of policy would have to be worked out by the secretary of state himself in the full knowledge that to overstep the limits of public tolerance for new departures was to court disaster.

Writing of the Open Door Note

The story of the writing of the first Open Door note has been told many times. Nevertheless, it is essential to go over this ground once again, for the sequence of events is important and certain elements in the narrative have not been stressed sufficiently.

On August 3, 1899, William Rockhill dropped Hay a short, rather casual note expressing disappointment at having missed seeing him that week, as he wished to discuss the situation in China with him. Sometime in July Rockhill had introduced Hay to his old friend Alfred E. Hippisley of the Imperial Maritime Customs Service. He had recently received a letter from Hippisley that so impressed him he decided to send excerpts from it to Hay. In his letter Hippisley asked Rockhill to use his influence toward inducing the United States to make some move in support of the open door for ordinary commerce in China. Hippisley pointed out that although spheres of influence had achieved considerable solidity in the past few years, the special rights claimed *within* each sphere were thus far confined to preferential or exclusive rights to construct railroads and exploit mines. No claims had yet been made for the right to impose differential tariffs on merchandise coming into the sphere, although such a claim might be only a matter of time. Hippisley urged that the United States lose "no time in calling the attention of all the Powers to the changes now taking place in China . . . expressing her determination not to sacrifice for her annual increasing trade any of the rights or privileges she has received by treaty with China." Equality of opportunity for investment would not be affected, but Hippisley felt this had never really existed in any event.[17]

On the same day that he sent excerpts of Hippisley's letter to Hay, Rockhill wrote a long letter to Hippisley informing him that he had been discussing China with the secretary of state. Rockhill's notion of what Hay should do went beyond Hippisley's. He wanted Hay to make a declaration that "would be understood by China as a pledge on our part to assist in maintaining the integrity of the Empire." Rockhill reflected, however, that domestic politics made such a course difficult, "for it might be interpreted by a large part of the voting population . . . especially the Irish and Germans, as an adoption of the policy advocated by Great Britain." Rockhill, perhaps as a result of his own fluctuating career, was generally pessimistic about the likelihood of America's ever doing anything worthwhile. His interview with Hay, in which domestic politics naturally came up, resulted in a conviction that the administration would do nothing to commit itself; the preferred policy of drift would continue.[18]

On August 7 Hay thanked Rockhill for his letter and declared that he was ready to act along the lines suggested, "but the senseless prejudices in certain sections of the 'Senate and people' compel us to move with great caution."[19] Hippisley, whom long service in the Chinese government had made supranational as well as devious in the face of superior power, was ready to circumvent the "Senate and people." Replying to Rockhill's dispirited letter of August 3, Hippisley noted: "My object . . . in urging prompt action on the lines of my note of the 25th ult. was precisely to forestall any suggestion likely to prove injurious to the Administration that it was following the lead of or leaning towards England by inducing it to take the initiative by itself; then if England took similar action, she would follow America's lead."

Hippisley warned that the "russification" of north China was progressing at an alarming rate. Although the American minister to Peking disagreed, Hippisley insisted that the areas involved were precisely the districts trading most heavily with America. Playing skillfully on the administration's very caution, Hippisley argued: "I don't for a moment believe that American manufacturers will sit by with folded hands and see these districts closed without making an effort to retain them. Pressure will therefore be brought to bear upon the Administration and it may have no option but to take some such action as I have suggested."[20] Hippisley also remarked that the recently publicized interview given by Jacob Gould Schurman, president of Cornell, would probably have great influence. Schurman, head of the Philippine Commission sent by McKinley to investigate the islands in February 1899, had just returned to the United States. In San Francisco he was interviewed by newsmen on August 15: "It seems to me that the great question in the Orient is not Formosa nor the Philippines, but China . . . It is feared, now that Russia has taken Manchuria, it will try to encroach gradually on some or all of the other eighteen provinces of China, and when it gets them it will . . . put a duty on all foreign goods . . . China, it was agreed, should maintain its independent position, but its doors should be kept open. It means much to England and Japan and not less to America."[21]

Rockhill agreed that Schurman's views would have great influence on the decisions of the administration. He drily remarked, "Our Minister at Peking, as well as Dr. Schurman and most other Americans who have recently been out to China, have but the most superficial view of the country and practically no knowledge of its racial and administrative peculiarities . . . but not withstanding that, they are the ones who carry weight at home."[22] So long as that weight was applied in the right direction, Rockhill was not too upset at their ignorance.

Rockhill believed that simply insisting on the Open Door was not enough. Rather, the vague assurances of Great Britain, Russia, France, and Germany that they should like to insure the integrity of the Chinese Empire must be expressed in stronger and more formal terms.

The czar's ukase of August 14 declaring Dalny a free port seemed to

Hippisley to indicate Russian willingness to cooperate in some kind of Open Door agreement. Though he agreed with Rockhill that the safeguarding of China's independence and integrity was both important and valuable, he felt it too great an undertaking for so cautious an administration as McKinley's. Rather Rockhill should seek a modest declaration designed to secure certain minimal demands.[23]

Hippisley enclosed a copy of a memorandum on the Open Door, which he felt secured the greatest gains consonant with existing reality. Spheres of influence were a fact. The British government had accepted the notion of special mining and railroad rights within each sphere and it would be impossible to reverse this situation. However, some form of open door policy was not incompatible with a recognition of spheres of influence. The special mining and railroad rights could not be abrogated but they must be prevented from expanding so as to include total territorial jurisdiction and the power to impose discriminatory taxes on trade. Hippisley suggested that the powers be required to bind themselves in three ways with regard to policy within their spheres and leases:

> (1) . . . in no way interfere with any treaty port in such sphere or with the interests vested in it; (2) . . . unless the ports opened to trade in it are declared free ports, the Chinese treaty tariff . . . shall apply to all merchandise landed or shipped, no matter to what nationality such merchandise may belong and that the dues and duties so leviable shall be collected by the Chinese government; and (3) . . . levy no higher harbour dues on vessels of another nationality . . . and no higher railroad charges . . . than shall be levied on similar merchandise belonging to its own nationals transported over equal distances.[24]

Rockhill's concern with China's integrity interested Hippisley. Without waiting for Rockhill to answer the above letter, Hippisley wrote again on August 26. "Steps taken to secure the integrity of China," he reflected, "are taken not out of pure altruism but to maintain trade markets and to avoid international conflicts." Yet unless China took a determined stand on behalf of its own independence, Hippisley did not believe many foreign powers would be willing to bind themselves to the integrity idea. Hippisley was certain that China, left to go its own way, would maintain the obstructionist *status quo* at all costs, thus inviting internal rebellion, foreign intervention, or both—and destroying the integrity policy altogether. Therefore, sources of "trouble at home and of conflict abroad" must be removed in advance. Hippisley narrowed these down to antiforeign feeling and the internal Chinese trade tax, likin. To control the former, he proposed, as Rockhill had earlier attempted, to force the central government to publish new, more severe edicts ordering the provincial authorities to maintain order and protect the missionaries. On the taxation problem, which had exercised Imperial Maritime Customs officials for years, Hippisley suggested that the entire likin system be placed under foreign, perhaps American, control. In this way Hippisley felt that the two major objections foreign powers might make to guaranteeing China's independence could be overcome.[25]

Rockhill was delighted with Hippisley's memo and wrote his friend an enthusiastic letter. Never much of a politician, Rockhill's notions of exciting public opinion were rather limited. Still, he was determined to work out a plan of persuasion. First, he told Hippisley, he would write an article incorporating the August 21 memorandum into a review of Beresford's popular book, *The Break Up of China*. This would be published in the *Forum*. The review would be followed by a second article: "in which we could dwell upon the possibility of reform in China, showing what has been done and what can be done in that line. China is, and will remain, the one absorbing subject, so that I am awfully anxious to have all the data you can give me on the subject, that I may not make any mistake, and that my conclusions shall be practicable." Meanwhile Rockhill was pleased with the appearance of Barrett's New York Chamber of Commerce speech in the August *North American Review*. It was "sensationalistic" but the "ideas are all right in the main."[26]

Rockhill's rather limited campaign was stillborn. On August 24 he received a letter from Hay—then escaping the Washington heat in New Hampshire—that changed everything. Adee had sent on to Hay a memorandum containing Hippisley's suggestions and Hay decided to pursue the matter on a broad diplomatic front: "I have already received, from the representatives of the powers concerned, assurances that the recent extension of spheres of influence . . . will not result in restricting our commercial freedom of action in China. But I agree with you that some more formal engagement of that sort would be desirable. If you have time between now and next Wed. to set down your views on this question in the form of a draft instruction to Mr. Choate, Mr. White, Mr. Tower and Gen. Porter, I would be greatly obliged."[27]

Rockhill's response to this request, a memorandum dated August 28, is the key document in the whole Open Door exchange. For one thing, it demonstrates that, apart from his gratitude to Hippisley, Rockhill was more than a neutral transmitter of the Englishman's ideas. The various aspects of the Open Door had been discussed by many people, American and British, in and out of government, businessmen and missionaries, for some time. Hippisley's summer correspondence with Rockhill crystallized these ideas for the American and gave him the courage to act on them at the first opportunity. He was certainly indebted to Hippisley for the ideas contained in the August 28 memo. It would be unfair to say, however, that his were mere carbon copies of Hippisley's letters.[28]

A large part of Rockhill's memorandum consisted of a systematic critique of Beresford's recently published book, *The Break Up of China.* It was important to Rockhill to clear away some of the morass surrounding the Open Door concept and differentiate the policy he wished America to adopt from similar but less valid formulations. In addition to the general ideas Beresford had expressed during his speaking tour in the United States, the book included several specific reform suggestions based on Beresford's low assessment of the strength and efficiency of the Chinese government. He urged a reform of land tax collection, right of residence for trade purposes in the interior, abolition of likin, reorganization of the army by foreign observers, and a larger degree of general foreign supervision than had yet been suggested in reference to China. He consistently remarked on the identity of American and British interests.

In contrast to John Barrett, to Beresford, to Hay himself, Rockhill did not believe in the identity of interests between Great Britain and the United States. He made this clear in his memorandum to Hay. Nor was it merely a political attitude designed to placate Irish and German antipathies. In a letter to Henry Adams written months before the open door exchange, on March 6, 1899, Rockhill declared: "It seems to me we are letting ourselves be led by England like lambs to the slaughter. Why we suddenly believe in the disinterested friendship and identity of interests of that country I cannot conceive, when we are certainly its most dangerous competitor. This guff of Beresford is the veriest nonsense—so far as we

128

are concerned—I have ever heard, but we swallow it without a quiver or murmur."[29]

Rockhill's opinion of Beresford had not changed over the months. He was annoyed that, despite Beresford's faulty analysis, he should remain so influential in America. Beresford, he wrote Hay, had done more to influence American public opinion than almost anyone else. Yet, Rockhill complained, Beresford's criticisms of the Chinese government were unjust. The Chinese government had not defaulted on any of its financial obligations and was, however clumsily, trying to reform itself. The "unseemly haste" of some treaty powers in their "scramble for commercial advantages and acquisition of territory" was at least partially responsible for the growing antiforeign movement. Beresford's charges against China, as gleaned from British merchants in China, were all old complaints. Such grievances, likin among them, were proper subjects for diplomatic discussion. Indeed, concerted action by the powers might have settled them earlier. Beresford's proposal that foreign officers reform China's military was, to Rockhill, the weakest element in his scheme:

> That the existence of a strong and well-officered and disciplined army and navy in China might assist that country to ward off the attacks of a foreign foe, is likely; that, in the absence of such a force, and with the present aggressive policy of some of the Treaty powers, the creation of "spheres of influence" . . . should be held to be the only way of insuring China against complete partition, is comprehensible; but that the United States should lend a hand to the carrying out of either of these two policies seems absolutely suicidal to our vast and growing interests in that part of the world.

Most important, Beresford had spread the gospel of the Open Door in terms of opposition to spheres of influence. This led to the kind of confused thinking Barrett demonstrated. Spheres of influence existed. They were positive facts that would have to be taken into account before any sensible policy could be framed.

Then, what should America's "immediate policy" be? Rockhill urged that Hippisley's memorandum be accepted in its entirety. The points raised were all minimum demands. What America sought was *not* equality of opportunity, which could not be hoped for, however just. Rather, "absolute equality of treatment" should be insisted upon—this was realistic as well as essential to trade. Rockhill pointed out how important it was for the United States to initiate negotiations. Its advantage was not merely domestic, but would win the undying gratitude of the Chinese government, and increase American prestige and influence.[30] Thus, if America could not have the benefit of a sphere of influence, she would have the prestige of leading the struggle to neutralize them.

Deeply involved in the adoption of this scheme, Rockhill delayed answering Hippisley's last letter. On September 7 the Englishman wrote inquiring as to the fate of Rockhill's memorandum and adding some more thoughts on "independence and integrity." Unaware that Rockhill had left this out of his memo altogether, Hippisley expressed the fear that it might "cause difficulty," though only because the Chinese are so "foolish." "What are you to do with a government that . . . has to abandon the macadamizing of the entire length of Legation St. because the reactionary Hsu T'ung will not have the road touched in front of his house? But if the governments can agree among themselves to respect the integrity and independence of China, it should not be difficult for them to bring sufficient pressure to bear on China to induce her to embark on a real course of progress." Rockhill replied, on September 14, that as Hippisley himself had noted earlier, this aspect of the open door problem was too large and complex to be dealt with at present.[31]

For the time being, Rockhill dropped the question of China's territorial integrity. The public demand for action, limited to begin with, could be expected to remain satisfied with what the Open Door note would offer. On October 19, Rockhill informed Hay of a resolution adopted by businessmen interested in China trade at the Philadelphia Commercial Convention. The resolution called for "an emphatic declaration . . . by the government of the U.S. of its intention to protect to the fullest extent the rights which its citizens enjoy under existing treaties to pursue their trade in the Chinese Empire." Rockhill congratulated Hay on what the administration had done, confident that the framers of the resolution would be "fully satisfied."[32]

However, Rockhill had by no means changed his mind as to what the situation in China really required. He was beginning to develop the concept of an Asian balance of power in which no one power would predominate. America, he hoped, would be the fulcrum of that balance. At times he seemed to believe that the 1899 note itself would place America in that position. Months before the Boxer crisis Rockhill wrote Edwin Denby a highly optimistic account of what his labors had accomplished: "This country holds the balance of power in China. I hope sincerely that we may make good use of it, not only for our trade, but for strengthening the Peking Government so that it can find no means of escaping the performance of all its obligations to the Treaty Powers. What we have obtained will undoubtedly help to insure, for the time being, the integrity of the Chinese Empire, but, on its side, China can and must discharge its international obligations."[33]

The Open Door note was drafted by Rockhill on September 5 and on the 6th dispatched to the American representative in England, Germany, and Russia. Within a few days, it was circulated to Japan, Italy, and France. Actually, in the note sent to Great Britain on September 6, 1899, the integrity of China was, albeit in a subordinate clause, included:

> This Government is animated by a sincere desire that the interests of our citizens may not be prejudiced through exclusive treatment by any of the controlling powers within their so-called "spheres of interest" in China, and hopes also to retain there an open market for the commerce of the world, remove dangerous sources of international irritation, and hasten thereby united or concerted action of the powers at Peking *in favor of the administrative reforms so urgently needed for strengthening the Imperial Government and maintaining the integrity of China in which the whole western world is alike concerned.*[34]

This phrase was absent in the otherwise nearly identical notes sent to France, Russia, Italy, Japan, and Germany. It is important that, like Hippisley, Rockhill had a notion of how Chinese integrity might be obtained that always involved the reciprocity of the Chinese government itself. He did not owe this concept to Hippisley. It is inherent in his 1897 handling of the missionary issue. China must "discharge its international obligations." The powers, with America leading, might well make administrative reform one of those obligations; but without China's active participation all efforts would be rendered meaningless.[35]

The British response to the note was less enthusiastic than had been expected. Salisbury's major objection was to the words "leased territory" as used in the requests, that is, to the demand that the restrictions would apply to leased territory on the same basis as spheres of influence. Through Joseph Choate, American ambassador to England, Salisbury immediately protested that the phrase would perforce include Kowloon and Wei-hai-wei. Salisbury felt both should be exempt from the Open Door stipulations. An undated October memorandum from Rockhill to Hay explained that "leased territory" had been used in order to include Kiachow and the Russian holding at Dalny.[36] Rockhill did not feel it necessary to include purely military ports like Wei-hai-wei or Port Arthur but saw no way to distinguish between commercial and military leases.

On November 1, Choate reported a conversation he had had with Salisbury in an attempt to hurry British acceptance of Hay's note. The trouble was still the Hong Kong extension, which Salisbury felt had to be exempted from the "leased territory" category. Choate argued that if it were specifically excluded, other nations would make similar claims and the purpose of the note would be defeated. If all leases were excluded, important commercial ports like Kiaochow and Dalny would not be affected. Hay's solution, in a November 13 letter to Choate, was to ignore Kowloon; it would simply not be mentioned. If the British insisted on a specific exemption, Hay was ready to treat Kowloon as an integral part of Hong Kong.[37]

The note's terminology also bothered the Russians. Muraviev complained about the impossible confusion of treaty ports, spheres of interest and leased territory. Reading the note for its deepest meaning, Muraviev informed Cassini that, on first glance, he felt Russia could not object to the requests. Assuming the note referred, as far as Russia was concerned, "to the Chinese provinces from the Great Wall to the North," Muraviev remarked, "We have long considered that it would be advantageous for us by means of an exchange of opinions with the Washington Government . . . to induce the latter to recognize our privileged position . . . in this part of China."[38] This was not really a perverse interpretation. As we have seen, the premise of the note was an acceptance of spheres of interest as *faits accomplis*. Special railroad and mining privileges were recognized; the attempt was to limit the range of advantage enjoyed within the sphere.

Rockhill conducted the negotiations with Cassini in Washington. On November 24 he sent Hay a long memorandum of a conversation with Cassini. Cassini repeated Muraviev's complaint about the loose wording of the note: "the questions of 'free ports,' 'treaty ports,' and 'spheres of influence' were so mixed up . . . , they could not exactly determine what the United States desired." Cassini went on to discuss Russia's leased territory in China and the recent railroad agreement with Great Britain. All of these, he said, of course had to be protected. So far as the Liaotung peninsula and Dalny were concerned, Russia could enter no binding agreements. For the term of the lease these areas were a part of the Russian Empire and under Russian law. Perhaps without realizing how close he was coming to Hay's private arrangement with Salisbury, Cassini pointed out that Russia's position vis-à-vis its leased territory was the same as Britain's in Kowloon and Germany's in Kiaochow. Without committing his government, however, Cassini told Rockhill he thought his government would not object to equality of treatment within its sphere. Cassini was quite wrong. A few days after his talk with Rockhill he received a cable from Muraviev informing him that Witte strongly objected to the clause requesting nondiscriminatory railroad rates on goods passing into a sphere. Witte's objection applied to both the Russian sphere of interest and its leased territory. Cassini was also instructed to avoid making any agreement on leased territory whatsoever. Muraviev proposed a general, nonbinding answer to the American note.[39]

Rockhill had based his expectations of Russian cooperation on the czar's ukase regarding Dalny and an article by Prince Ukhtomskii, that appeared in the July *North American Review*. Rockhill felt these were reliable indicators of future Russian policy. However, the real lever in Russian acceptance of the Open Door note was the fear, in Muraviev's words, of "undermining the friendly relations existing between Russia and the United States and giving the occasion for the formation of a dangerous coalition of power against our interests in the Far East." In June 1898, Cassini wrote first to Muraviev and then to Lamsdorff about the danger to Russia of an Anglo-American alliance in the Far East.[40] Cassini saw no immediate signs of such an alliance but promised to watch developments with utmost care.

During Beresford's barnstorming United States tour, Prince Ukhtomskii, editor of the *St. Petersburg Vedomosti*, editorially espoused a Russo-American alliance in the Far East. In July 1899, the prince, a very influential man in Russian Far Eastern policy and head of the Russo-Chinese Bank, wrote a long preface for an article by Vladimir Holstrem that appeared in the *North American Review*.[41] The burden of both preface and article was that America should beware of any alliance with England. Russia alone truly desired China's independence and integrity. The continental similarity between Russia and America and the civilized manner in which both had expanded was stressed.[42]

Cassini was very frank with Rockhill as to Russia's fear of an Anglo-American alliance. In a conversation early in December 1899, Cassini assured Rockhill of the identity of Russian and American interests in China. He then discussed Chamberlain's recent speech, which, he felt, threatened France and looked to an alliance with Germany and America against France and Russia. "He [Cassini] then said that he could not conceive why Great Britain, if she was desirous as she said to adopt this policy in China, should not immediately have given the U.S. the assurances they wanted. I told him that no administration of the U.S., especially the present President, would adopt an English policy; that such a thing was an impossibility in the U.S.; that the Administration had solely in view the interests of the country."[43]

Given this desire to maintain America's friendship, or at least neutrality, in the Far East, Muraviev reluctantly accepted the Open Door declaration. His acceptance was as vague as possible. Ambassador Tower wrote Hay on February 12, 1900, that the Russian government hated to be bound by such written commitments. Indeed, powerful forces within the Cabinet were against responding at all. Tower felt the answer was made only "to maintain the relations subsisting between the two countries, which it would not on any account disturb. It went a great way, as Russian diplomacy goes, when it put into writing the answer which you now have."[44]

Hay's first taste of Russian diplomacy tried all his patience. Cassini had persistently delayed answering the note until Hay cleverly transferred the seat of negotiations to St. Petersburg—it was a technique he would use again with less success. To Henry White, Hay described Cassini's opposition to the note and his insistence that the Americans simply did not realize the implications of what they asked. Indeed *after* the answers were all published, Cassini had come to Hay and, "with a face as long as the moral law and with ghostly solemnity," had told Hay he only hoped his government would accept it. Hay reminded him that nothing was pending; a proposal had been made, Russia had replied favorably and the

United States had thanked her for the reply. Hay felt Cassini simply suffered from *"amour propre froissé."* Should Russia repudiate its own reply, it would isolate itself in the eyes of the world. But until that happened, Hay refused to worry about it. In June, Hay confided to Henry Adams, "We got all that could be screwed out of the Bear, and our cue is to insist we got everything." With the press, Hay's line was to imply that the government had a wealth of unpublished documents that gave it ample grounds for accepting the Russian answer as sufficient.[45]

Rockhill was fairly satisfied with what had been accomplished. He was convinced that the favorable response was due to America's strong and central position in the Far East.[46] Though this might be discouraging evidence of a lack of commitment to the Open Door principles, it was impressive testimony to America's influence.

Press reaction to the note and its European reception was varied. Not surprisingly, the *Journal of Commerce* called it "one of the most important diplomatic negotiations of our time." It predicted vast consequences; the permanent prevention of the dismemberment of China; the elimination of a casus belli among the powers, and of course, the assurance of expanding United States trade in the Far East. Leading Republican papers all over the country were full of praise. The *Philadelphia Press* hailed it as a greater achievement than the Spanish-American War; the *Boston Herald* praised Hay for his exceptional diplomacy; even the *New York Evening Post* had kind words for an administration it more often excoriated.[47]

The *Independent,* grown more fiercely expansionist during the debate over Philippine annexation, credited the administration with halting the partition of China, forcing recognition of the United States as a commanding force in international politics, winning a notable victory of American diplomacy and American character while at the same time underlining the change "in the development of both diplomacy and character" that had occurred. The United States, the *Independent* declared, had not only entered "the seas of European intervention in Asian matters," but had "quieted them, and received the thanks and congratulations of the very ones whose hostility it was believed that we must inevitably incur." The *Independent* was most pleased, however, by the "new departure" that the note marked. In a later editorial, the paper analyzed the healthy influence of Japan over China which, it felt, the United States should further encourage. If Japan was to be China's big brother, the tone of the *Inde-*

pendent's editorial indicated, the United States would be mother to both. The Open Door note had demonstrated, the editors crowed, that the United States "has something to say as to the future of Asia, and, if need comes, it will have something to do."[48]

The *Literary Digest* noted, however, that praise was not unanimous. The protectionist *New York Press* feared the consequences the note would have for the Philippines. How could the United States now close the door in the Philippines, which it should and must do, while demanding that it remain open in China? The *New Orleans Picayune* had similar worries with regard to Chinese immigration. How could the United States, with any consistency, shut the door against unwanted Oriental migrants? The *Springfield Republican,* whose isolationist position often sharpened its sense of international realities, pointed to the vagueness of the replies America had received: "The only assurance of an 'open door' still rests upon our ability to keep it open by force."[49]

Yet the generally favorable public response is not surprising—this was the kind of diplomacy that appealed to Americans—no complex treaties were involved, no concessions were made, no ambiguities existed. Moreover, it was all done by writing letters.[50]

During the spring of 1900 it became evident that China, perversely unaffected by Hay's brilliant diplomacy, was following an independent path toward convulsion and dismemberment. An American in January of 1900 might well have had a healthy sense of serving China as well as America's own interests; nine months later he would march from Taku to Tientsin and see the bodies of Chinese, slain by Americans, clogging the river: "And there were so many of them that they filled it from bank to bank and it was hard for steamboats to get along."[51]

seven   The Long, Hot Summer

The mythologizing of the Open Door note began almost at once and was led, appropriately enough, by its author, William Rockhill. We have seen how anxious Rockhill was to include a strong "integrity and independence" clause in the Open Door note and how a weak reference was, in fact, part of the September 6 letter to Great Britain. Now, in the course of explaining American policy to the public and instructing Minister Conger on its full implications, Rockhill referred increasingly to the maintenance of Chinese independence as if it had been achieved by the Open Door note.

One important portion of the note, the application of the equal treatment requirements to leased territories, was silently given up. In an article written for the *Forum* in May 1900, Rockhill reassured protectionists worried about the status of the Philippines and at the same time hinted that Muraviev had gained his point—leased territory would be ceded. Rockhill pointed out that American rights under previous treaties would lapse in such areas. Similarly any treaty rights which other countries had held with the Philippines were now null and void.[1]

Whether leased areas were indeed cessions was the subject of discussion in Peking in December 1899. Conger reported that a conference of the ministers and ambassadors in Peking as to the extraterritorial status of leased areas had resulted in general agreement that leased areas should be accepted as cessions. The Japanese alone protested, claiming that "sovereignty is too important a matter to pass thus with a lease, and . . . that China can, if she wishes, surrender jurisdiction over her own people, but they do not agree that these lessee governments shall or can exercise jurisdiction over other foreigners in the leased territory." Conger himself did not feel the problem to be too important: "Since these ports have practically passed from the control of uncivilized people, to a civilized, the paramount reason for exercising extraterritoriality . . . no longer exists."[2]

The State Department, although it made no comment on the degree of civilization flourishing in leased areas, did confirm that leases must be considered as cessions of territory belonging to the foreign power holding the lease. In February 1900 Conger was instructed to inform United States consuls in districts "adjacent to foreign leased territories" that they had "no authority to exercise extraterritorial consular jurisdiction or to perform ordinary non-judicial consular acts within the leased territory under their present Chinese exequaturs."[3] This admission of transferral of sovereignty, taken in conjunction with Rockhill's dictum on the Philippines, would seem to indicate that the Russian point was granted without a fight; indeed, without so much as a clear expression of the issue.

Conger, Rockhill, and "Integrity"

Conger's understanding of what Hay and Rockhill hoped to do in China was limited. Impressed by his colleagues, all of whom had had long diplomatic experience, much of it in China, Conger followed their lead whenever the State Department allowed. For example, disorderly troop behavior in the Peking-Tientsin area in November 1898 had led Conger to request a marine guard to protect the legation. Despite Hay's evident reluctance to have the guard remain in Peking after the trouble died down, Conger had insisted that the guard remain throughout the winter: "that . . . government which makes a show of power with a reasonably sustained threat to use it, is far more potent than the one which expects a like response to polite and courteous treatment . . . we cannot afford to lose the prestige and respect that fifty marines and two Gatling guns at Tientsin and Peking have given us."[4] It was an attitude he had learned over dinner with the diplomatic corps.

On January 27, 1900, Conger, without prior instructions, joined the other ministers in presenting identic notes of protest to the Tsungli yamen. The corps protested against a January 11 imperial decree which, by distinguishing between good and bad secret societies, in effect encouraged the Boxers, an antiforeign secret society then gaining frightening power. The diplomats asked that a new decree, ordering the total suppression of the Boxers, be issued immediately. There was nothing the State Department could do once the identic note was sent. However, in a long letter to Conger written March 22, 1900, Rockhill explained why the Department disapproved of his action.[5]

Rockhill did not object to the contents of the note but to its mode of presentation. A separate, if concurrent, note was preferable in view of the American attempt to maintain an independent posture in Asia. Rockhill went on to instruct Conger in the basic tenets of American policy since the Open Door note. It is here that the first sign of an increased valuation of the note is manifest. Rockhill, the supreme realist, who informed Hay in underlined sentences of the *fact* of spheres of influence, now began encouraging the view that America had acted *for* China in the circulation of the Open Door note.

Conger was instructed to avail himself "of every opportunity to impress upon the Yamen that this Government, by the recent assurances which it has obtained from the various great Powers holding leased territory or areas of influence in China, concerning freedom of trade in said regions and the maintenance therein of Chinese rights of sovereignty, has obtained thereby a renewed assurance of the policy of the Treaty Powers not to interfere with the integrity of the Chinese Empire." Having thus convinced the yamen of what had been secured for China, Conger was to remind the Chinese that corresponding obligations fell on their government, especially in regard to the treaty rights of foreign merchants and missionaries.

> Should the Chinese Government disregard these treaty duties, it is greatly to be feared that the policy now so happily inaugurated through the instrumentality of this Government will not bear fruit which, under other circumstances, it might, and that further guarantees in the nature of occupation of points within the limits of the Chinese Empire will speedily be demanded by the European Powers, the disintegration of China hastened, if not precipitated, the Empire disturbed and rebellion brought about.

Rockhill then returned to his pet project, that of forcing the Chinese government to accord the severest penalties to viceroys who failed, though only through ignorance, to protect foreigners. Rockhill never abandoned an idea.

> Your predecessor has on numerous occasions . . . called the serious attention of the Peking government to the concern with which the U.S. view the dilatoriness that Government has so frequently shown in suppressing anti-foreign movements in China and punishing all those directly or remotely involved in them, and more especially the high provincial authorities who are always directly

responsible to the Throne for their occurrences . . . You should not fail to impress these views on the Yamen, and to inform it that this Government is more determined than ever to see them carried out not only in the interest of our citizens and their rights, but for the unquestionable benefit of China itself.[6]

From Rockhill's verbose, opaquely written letter, it is clear that the administration was following a rather bold path with regard to the Open Door note. Just as Hay had made the most of Russia's limited acceptance of the Open Door principle, so it was hoped, that by referring, often enough, to the way in which America had secured China's integrity and independence, the powers would begin to feel that they had committed themselves to it; or at least China might believe it and be suitably grateful to America. More important, if the American people would believe it, the note would go far to fulfill Hippisley's promise of foiling the anti-imperialists and their followers. By representing itself to the American public as the savior of China's integrity, the charges of Republican imperialism might be deflected. From educating Conger, Rockhill now turned his attention to the American public.

In May 1900 Rockhill published a long article in the *Forum*. Entitled "The United States and the Future of China," the article contained a fairly lengthy discussion of recent history. With great sympathy for China, Rockhill related the sorry tale of the scramble for concessions and the progressive humiliation of the central government. "The true interests of China have never been considered," Rockhill wrote; "her ability to meet the obligations she was forced to incur have never been pondered; and the ultimate result on foreign trade has been ignored." It remained for the United States, strong in the glory brought by victory over Spain and admired as a new landlord in Asia, to make the saving move. The broad principles enunciated by the Open Door note were accepted by all, and the commercial world, safe in its enjoyment of all treaty rights, could proceed to develop and expand trade. But the results went beyond mere commercial gain. Temporarily, the threat of partition was lifted. Rockhill saw this pause as a breathing space for China. The declarations proved to Peking that no power menaced her integrity. Devoted to a peaceful development of China's trade and resources, the powers would stand aside while China worked out her own salvation.

But such generosity had to be paid for. Foreign aggression was very unlikely *if* China succeeded in maintaining order and protecting foreigners. Otherwise nothing could stand in the way of future Western encroachment. As in his instructions to Conger, Rockhill saw China's duty very clearly. If the government would but follow his proposal of punishing high officials, antiforeign riots would entirely cease. If China failed in her obligations, her fate was certain. "All of her well-wishers can but pray that she may not let the opportunity now afforded her by the United States pass away unused."[7]

Although he was well aware that a guarantee of Chinese integrity was politically impossible for America to give and not likely to come from any other power, in these two documents Rockhill seems to have been devising a verbal formula that would have the effect of a self-fulfilling prophecy—a public prophecy, which by its eloquence and cogency would compel the action of others in such a way as to fulfill its premise. If he could, through repetition, convince the Chinese that the powers had indeed agreed to hold off and allow China a chance to "put her house in order," perhaps rapid reform, iron-clad safety for foreigners, and more open trade arrangements could be accomplished. This being done, China, with the aid of America—the new balancing force in Asia—would have a strong lever against renewed European aggression. Such aggression, in Rockhill's imaginary political world, would have no excuse, no possible rationale, and might therefore be avoided.

Rockhill's analysis rested on his firm belief that the antiforeign riots, which had caused China so much trouble in the past, could be easily controlled by the central government. He either ignored, or was actually unaware of, the popular force of antiforeign sentiment; certainly he overrated the degree of control the central government had over provincial officials or the latter had over the people in their districts. Nor did Rockhill ever reflect that the United States itself was often quite unable to control antiforeign (anti-Chinese, anti-Italian, and closer to home, anti-Negro) mobs. Although pretending to hope for a reformed China, he yet wished to strengthen the autocratic hold of the government, to make an ineffective, absolutist system work with ruthless efficiency. Rockhill's ideal seems to have been a nicely ordered tyranny, advised by America and submitting to foreign pressure gracefully and efficiently.[8]

Rockhill's superficial understanding of the deeper forces at work in

China made it inevitable that he misjudge the Boxer movement and the response of the Chinese government to it. Thus on June 1, despite detailed reports from China on the strength and threatening attitude of the Boxers, Rockhill made his famous prediction: "I cannot believe that the 'Boxer' movement will be very long-lived or cause any serious complications. The day the Chinese authorities choose to put an end to it they can easily do so—I think they have now realized that they must act, and they will."[9]

The Mission Societies' Recovery

In the strange spring of 1900, while missionaries in the field reported the growing wave of antiforeign feeling, the missionary societies at home congratulated the administration on what it had done for China. In January 1900, both Baptists and Congregationalists reported greatly improved conditions. The Lutheran, Methodist, and Presbyterian missionary societies all reported that 1899 had been a fine year financially. All three, once deeply in debt, were now well in the black. The Methodist Missionary Society commented that 1899 had been prosperous in all things except "the most important item of all—increase of communicants." The editor of the *Independent* felt that an important element in the improved finances of mission societies was the increased interest of prominent business and professional people. Indeed the new president of the ABCFM was a "Christian businessman" who, it was confidently expected, would soon raise the level of contributions even higher. In a complex interrelationship difficult to untangle, the enthusiastic missionary response to foreign expansion had been handsomely repaid by the public; expansion itself, as Dr. Dunning pointed out, had turned the attention of the public to missionary work.[10]

A culmination of the 1899 recovery was the highly successful conference of foreign missions held in New York in April and May of 1900. In striking contrast to the failure of the 1897 conference, this one was very well attended. Ex-President Benjamin Harrison and President McKinley both addressed the crowds; prominent admirals, generals, and businessmen attended, and the president of the influential New York Chamber of Commerce served as chairman for the welcoming meeting.[11]

The link between the "expansionists of 1898" and missionary interests is emphasized by a contemporary newspaper poll. In July 1900, the *Boston Herald* conducted a fifteen-city poll of five occupational groups on the question of expansion. It found, in every city, that clergymen were the most ardent advocates of an expansionist policy. Rather piously shocked, the *Herald* reported that "without taking into consideration China's right as a nation to national existence, without apparently considering the moral phase of the question," ministers were found who expressed the earnest hope that the Boxer crisis would yield territorial benefits for the United States. In the face of secular criticism that missionary support for expansionism was based on the desire for new fields of labor, the editor of the *Independent* did not question the expansionist fervor of missionaries but protested that the motive was philanthropic rather than professional. When a reader asked if the *Independent* supported annexation of Cuba, the answer was a ringing "yes"—and Haiti, Santo Domingo, Canada, Mexico, Central America, South America, "and the rest of the world." The only proviso was that the United States wait till these countries wanted to be annexed. "We believe in enlarging the territory of American liberty," the *Independent* cried. Editorially, the *Independent* went quite far in its advocacy of righteous violence. "Peace," the editor conceded, "was a great good; and doubly harmful, therefore, is the attitude of those who advocate it in terms that would make it synonymous with selfish and cowardly shrinking from warring against the existence of evil." Only the "warlike power of a civilized people . . . can give peace to the world." Nations that expanded, like those that didn't "may both ultimately go down, . . . the one leaves heirs and a glorious memory and the other leaves neither."[12]

The Boxers

One of the most curious aspects of the Boxers is that it is possible to write about them with real sympathy. Fanatic, ignorant, ruthless, moved by absurd superstition and often greed, they were yet an authentic expression of revulsion against the West. The supercilious assumption that the Chinese would not and could not resist the powers was proved grossly false. More than merely antimissionary, the Boxers declared war against all foreigners, and their cry of "upholding the Ch'ing Dynasty and exterminating the foreigners" has, to modern ears, the rather familiar tone of vigorous nationalism. This is, of course, to romanticize as erroneously as did those nineteenth-century observers whose horror of the Boxers blinded them to the meaning of the movement. Yet, when one has lived most of one's adult life in an age of colonial independence movements, the Boxers become at once less exotic and their terroristic activities almost expected under the circumstances.[13]

The Boxer movement seemed to have no objective beyond throwing out the foreigners. It did not aim at social revolution and its relatively early adoption by ultraconservative government officials stultified any antidynastic ambitions its secret society origins might have encouraged. A recent examination of the antidynastic potential of the Boxers concludes that the movement was composed of diverse factions. That fragment of the Boxers that took as its slogan, "Overthrow the Ch'ing, Destroy the Foreigners," suffered a decisive setback when its leaders were arrested, and later executed, in the fall of 1899. At this same point in the history of the Boxers, an effort was made by some rigidly antiforeign Ch'ing officials to absorb the Boxers into local militia in order to take advantage of their antiforeign passion while at the same time deflecting their hostility from the dynasty to the foreigners. From October 1899 on, the banner of the main Boxer organization was "Support the Ch'ing, Destroy the Foreigners," and the court made every effort to keep it this way.[14]

Wavering between suppression of the movement and its pacification, the empress dowager listened to the arguments of all factions within the court. Officials like Chang Ju-mei and Yü-hsien, vigorously antiforeign, described the Boxers as a self-defense movement spontaneously created by the people to protect themselves from the injustices of Christian converts and their foreign supporters. Once the antidynastic leaders of the movement had been eliminated, the court was more ready to compromise and appease the Boxers, while the Boxers themselves were willing to adopt a pro-Manchu line. On the other hand, Tz'u-hsi could not ignore the arguments of such loyal officials as Chang Chih-tung and Yuan Shih-k'ai who insisted that, despite their new slogan, the Boxers were an uncontrollable element in the society and ultimately a grave danger to the dynasty. Should the movement get out of hand and succeed in challenging the authority of government officials, it would certainly turn against the court itself. Chang Chih-tung, in early June, telegraphed Peking that

144

the Boxers, in their sporadic resistance to government troops, their rioting, and their destruction of government property, were in fact "staging a rebellion on the pretext of anti-Christianity."[15]

However, the dynasty's moral and philosophic justification was that it rested on the popular support of the people. Their will could not be countered without disaster. Once accepting the Boxers, for a variety of reasons, as the genuine voice of the people, the court could claim that it had no choice but to support them. A gathering together of events in the spring and summer of 1900 determined the court's lenient attitude toward the Boxers. The growing strength of reactionary advisers like Yü-hsien was evidence of a decision to take a strong line against the demands of foreign powers. Indeed the advice of the antiforeign officials had, in the case of Italian demands, proved correct. The foreigners *were* contained by a show of readiness to use force. In mid-November 1899, a decree sent to all the provinces ordered resistance to foreign aggression and urged that all high officials stand firm against the ravening tigers that would tear China apart.[16] The Boxers, an expression of popular revulsion against foreign depredations, could hardly be condemned for so faithfully embodying the policy of the court itself. Furthermore, the court was aware of the basic social and economic conditions that had stimulated the rise of the Boxers. North China was, during the years 1897 through 1899 devastated by a series of natural disasters that set in motion a flow of some five million hungry refugees into Shantung and Chihli provinces. The open rebellion of bands of refugees, combining with roving groups of ex-soldiers frightened the court. Should the Boxers begin to organize the hungry migrants on the borders of the metropolitan province, the court might face a rebellion as huge in its dimensions as the Taiping uprising had been.[17]

For a time the empress dowager seems to have tried to keep a balance between those who would encourage and those who would suppress the Boxers. But she herself was deeply outraged at the most recent examples of foreign impudence and was not unattracted by Boxer claims to invulnerability. Moreover, the advice of Yü-hsien, in combination with the prodynastic position of the Boxers after October 1899, made her unwilling to order all-out suppression of the movement. It seems clear that, until June 9, the empress dowager was undecided as to what course to take. When the foreign ministers in Peking telegraphed to Tientsin for an increased legation guard (having already, in early June, called up guards to Peking far in excess of what the court had prescribed), the move was taken as an aggressive act.[18] Admiral Seymour, with 2,000 marines, including 100 Americans from the warship *Newark,* set off in dress uniform, flags flying, and boarded the train from Tientsin to Peking. On the other end of the line the ministers and their wives, at the anticipated time, went down to the train station to meet them.[19] While they waited, further down the line, at Lang-fang, the Seymour expedition met with the shock of Chinese resistance. Nervous, outraged, and terribly depressed the ministers returned to their legations when it became clear the saving train would not arrive. Seymour's defeat set off a chain of panic and riot in the whole area between Peking and Tientsin. The telegraph line was cut and the railroad wrecked. Within Peking, fierce mob outbreaks came closer to the legations. On June 11, the chargé of the Japanese legation was killed and on June 13 the Boxers entered Peking in force.[20]

With Boxers rioting within Peking and an international army fighting Chinese somewhere between the capital and Tientsin, the court was in a situation of such danger as to make sensible decision making impossible. In the past the government had had to balance between the two forces of internal rebellion and external aggression. Often the dominant foreign power would actively aid the government in its balancing act. Now, as a Chinese government would again experience in the 1930's, both forces seemed strangely united against the rather pitiful, confused men in nominal control of the government.[21] The most antiforeign of the men surrounding the empress dowager, like Prince Tuan, succeeded in defeating any suggestion that concentrated action against the Boxers be taken. When a member of the Tsungli yamen warned the empress dowager against the exaggerated claims of the Boxers, she answered with an ambiguity that belies any simple interpretation of her actions during these frantic weeks: "If we cannot rely upon the supernatural formulas, can we not rely upon the heart of the people? China is weak; the only thing we can depend upon is the heart of the people. If we lose it, how can we maintain our country?"[22]

This answer would seem to indicate that the empress dowager was more afraid of a sustained internal rebellion than she was of foreign aggression. She undoubtedly hoped that a thoroughly aroused populace might defeat the foreigners; Seymour's humiliation outside Tientsin would encourage such a conclusion. The empress dowager can perhaps be seen as taking a middle course between the moderate officials, anxious to reform China and fearful of foreign wars, and the extremists, whose one desire was to cleanse China of foreign poison. But it was a compromise that leaned to one side—that of the Boxers. Despite the fact that Boxers had attacked the railway station at Huang-ts'un, and had engaged in a pitched battle with imperial troops, a decree issued on June 6 appointed two officials to peacefully exhort the Boxers to disperse and return to their usual pursuits; otherwise they were to be suppressed. At the same time the pro-Boxer official Kang-i was sent on the same mission. Moreover imperial troops were ordered to withdraw and the general who had led the troops against the Boxers was reprimanded.[23]

In any event it was decided, on June 16, that a double course would be be pursued. Two officials were to proceed to the front and attempt to persuade the foreign forces to depart; simultaneously Boxers would be recruited into the army. At this point the confused episode of the forged demands occurred. On June 17 the empress dowager called an imperial council and revealed a list of four demands allegedly handed to the Chinese government by the foreign ministers. The demands amounted to a surrender of sovereignty: (1) a special place to be assigned to the emperor for residence; (2) all revenues to be collected by the foreign ministers; (3) all military affairs to be committed to their hands; and (4) rule to be restored to the emperor. After reading them out the empress dowager declared, "Now they [the powers] have started the aggression, and the extinction of our nation is imminent. If we just fold our arms and yield to them, I would have no face to see our ancestors after death. If we must perish, why not fight to the death?" According to Chester Tan, the demands were forged by Prince Tuan in hope of goading the empress dowager to declare war.[24] Though a forgery, they were exceedingly clever, for all the demands had been mentioned as high-priority desiderata by Western writers on China.

Action at the Taku forts on June 17 determined the court to declare war. In keeping with an imperial order to resist the advance of foreign troops, the officer in charge of the Taku forts refused, accordingly, to yield to a foreign ultimatum to surrender the forts and permit the warships to proceed up the Pei-ho. Hostilities broke out at 2:00 A.M. that

147

day and word reached the court on the nineteenth. On June 20 an imperial decree declared war against the powers.

The really curious state of affairs in Peking is underlined by the fact that just eight days after the imperial edict declaring war, a decree was issued to Chinese ministers abroad ordering them to inform the powers that China did not intend to fight all the powers and would order its troops to protect the legations and punish the rebels.[25] Thus the Chinese government itself was the first to use the "rebel theory"—China was not at war but involved in putting down a rebellion—and this in the very same week that imperial troops were besieging the legations and Boxers were being rewarded for their brave fighting. A not entirely satisfactory explanation of the many contradictory decrees issued between June and August 1900 is that the court saw the war as the powers' responsibility. With the ultimatum at Taku, the powers had forced the issue to a test of arms. Efforts would be made to restore peace; meanwhile China must fight as best she could.[26]

Perhaps the only explanation of shifting government policy lies in day-to-day events. The imperial government lacked any over-all plan. Once they accepted the allied ultimatum at Taku as a declaration of war, the die was cast until such time as military reverses, lack of support from the southern and central viceroys, and a growing realization of what it meant to fight so many countries at once, forced a reconsideration of policy. Seymour's early defeat, and his sixteen day struggle back to Tientsin, certainly encouraged the court to think that, unlikely as it seemed, China stood a fair chance of driving the foreign armies out. When Tientsin fell, on July 13–14, the effect was immediately felt in Peking. A cease-fire on the legations was declared on July 17 and lasted until the end of that month while peace feelers multiplied. Since the allies would not stop short of Peking, the court had no choice but to fight on. Moreover it must not be forgotten that the antiforeign passion of the Boxers was shared by a significant portion of high officials, including, at times, the empress dowager. An early acceptance of defeat; suppressing the Boxers, who, after October 1899, were prodynastic and antiforeign, at the order of the powers; allowing a large foreign army within the imperial city itself—all these impossible conditions were the *sine qua non* of peace. And for a second time in one decade, peace seemed too dishonorable an alternative.

148

United States Action and Reaction

On June 4 Conger sent a really alarming cable to Washington: "Situation worse. It is possible we may be besieged in Peking with Railways and Telegraphs cut." Four days later he cabled a request for permission to join his colleagues in presenting a series of demands to the Chinese. "The demand to be insisted upon and to state to the throne that unless Boxer war is immediately suppressed and order restored foreign powers will be compelled themselves to take measures to that end."[27] Hay was in an extremely delicate position. Conger's telegram implied united military action that could certainly lead to war. If he approved Conger's participation in such a joint effort he would, in effect, be committing the United States to an unknown degree of military action—possibly even to war, a decision reserved for Congress. Moreover, the United States was heavily engaged in the suppression of the Philippine insurrection. This involvement affected Hay's freedom of action in China in two ways. The moral ambiguities of the war then taking place throughout America's new domain were fully realized by Hay.[28] It was an ugly war, bound to grow uglier, in which the United States had constantly to resort to strange and tortuous justificatory arguments. The anti-imperialists, joined by the opposition Democratic party, were making great political capital out of it. Moving, with very little information, into a war in China, which could be described in terms as unpleasant as the Philippine action, would hand the Democrats a powerful political weapon. On a more technical level, the United States had limited military resources. Any forces sent to China would have to be withdrawn from the Philippines; an unlimited military commitment was beyond American means.

From every point of view, then, caution was the only sensible course. Though he approved Conger's June 9 request, Hay also cabled Conger to limit his cooperation. He was to act independently for the protection of American interests and join an international move only when absolutely necessary. Two days later he followed this with more specific instructions. "We have no policy in China except to protect with energy American interests and especially American citizens and the legation. There must be nothing done which would commit us to future action inconsistent with your standing instructions. There must be no alliances."[29] Conger's "standing instructions" were, most recently, Rockhill's long March dispatch, with its emphasis on American concern for China's

149

integrity. The great fear in the State Department was that the press of military expediency would force America into an anti-Chinese alliance inimical to McKinley's political interests at home and America's broader role as a balancer of powers. Thus, although a small force of Americans was part of the group that followed Admiral Seymour onto the train at Tientsin on June 10, Rear-Admiral Kempff did not take part in the bombardment of the Taku forts on June 17—an additional reason the administration could honestly regard itself as not at war with China.

The allied ultimatum to surrender the Taku forts seems to have been the really decisive factor in bringing the Chinese army into conflict with foreign forces. When Seymour's expedition left Tientsin it did so with the express permission of the Chinese authorities. On the march out they passed General Nieh's troops without hostility on either side. Meeting heavy Boxer opposition at Yang-ts'un, however, Seymour decided to turn back to Lang-fang and proceed by boat to Peking. By this time the action at Taku had taken place. Now he was faced with the combined force of Nieh's troops and Boxer irregulars and the order was given to retreat to Tientsin. As he makes clear in his memoirs, Seymour realized that the allied seizure of the Taku forts was responsible for the changed attitude of regular Chinese armed forces.[30] A contemporary American observer, Herbert Hoover, criticized the naval officers responsible for the Taku ultimatum. Given the lack of foreign troops on hand in China and the precarious position of Seymour midway between Peking and Tientsin, the officers "responsible for the taking of the Taku forts at such a time," Hoover said, "must have been insane." Hoover confirmed other reports that, until the taking of the forts, General Nieh's forces had been protecting the foreign settlement at Tientsin against the Boxers.[31]

The decision to seize the forts was made by the naval commanders on the scene without instruction from their home governments. The senior American officer, Rear-Admiral Kempff, was requested by the British admiral to sign an ultimatum on June 14. Kempff replied that he was "not authorized to initiate an act of war with a country with whom my country was at peace, that my limit was to protect American interests." Consultation with the German and Russian admirals led Kempff to believe that no ultimatum would be presented to the authorities in charge of the forts. However the fear that Taku would be cut off from Tientsin and several moves by the Chinese that seemed suspicious to the admirals, led to a decision, on June 16, to demand the surrender. Kempff refused to attend the meeting.[32]

Kempff's own ship was anchored too far out even to observe the exchange of fire closely. However, an ancient American gunboat, the *Monocacy*, commanded by Captain Frederick Wise, was right in the heart of the battle. Wise's orders were to protect American interests but not to fire against any Chinese force unless fired upon. Because of its position, the *Monocacy* was in danger from Chinese fire directed at a railroad station near its anchorage. Wild fire from the battery struck his ship and Wise, after picking up some women and children refugees, moved his ship some two miles upriver. For this he was bitterly reproached by Kempff, who decided that the *Monocacy* had been deliberately fired upon, despite Wise's most explicit report to the contrary. Wise was rebuked for not making "war in return." In response to the reputed attack on the *Monocacy*, Kempff ordered Wise, on June 18, to make "common cause and assist other foreign nationalities having military forces on shore for the protection of life and property of all foreigners."

A long dispatch to the secretary of the navy on June 20 complicates rather than explains Kempff's contradictory behavior. He had refused to join in the Taku ultimatum, because he thought it both contrary to government policy and unwise. However, the firing on the *Monocacy* was an act of war. "I regarded the situation," Kempff wrote, "as one for the protection of the National honor and the preservation of our people and have acted accordingly." Kempff virtually accused Wise of disobeying orders when, in fact, the captain had obeyed not only the letter but the spirit of Kempff's instructions to him.[33]

The explanation of Kempff's behavior lies in the ambiguity of his situation. Until June 18, his only order was to cooperate with Conger for the "protection of American interests." He was aware, moreover, that he had been severely criticized by his superior officer, Rear-Admiral George C. Remey, for lack of caution and for cooperation with foreign powers "to an extent incompatible" with American interests. Once the battle was joined Kempff faced a serious dilemma. Cooperation with the other powers might result in a reprimand from the secretary of the navy for going beyond his June 6 instructions. Remaining outside the battle, Kempff ran the risk of official, and perhaps public, criticism for failure to uphold the "national honor." Seizing on the wild shots that fell about the *Monocacy,* Kempff ordered his forces to cooperate with the attacking party. Indeed, it is difficult to see what else he could have done. Kempff realized that the attack on the forts meant a state of war between Chinese troops and those foreign forces committed to the protection of foreign life and property in China. On this latter point his instructions were clear. Whether the ultimatum was justified or not, it had been issued, and the result was a situation seriously endangering the very interests he was under firm orders to protect. The sacrifice of a junior officer's reputation did not seem too high a price to pay for easing America into the war without seeming to be the aggressor.[34]

Orders received from Acting Secretary of the Navy Hackett on June 18 assured Kempff that he had acted correctly. For the first time reference was made to the broader national interests America had in China: "[the] Department desires you to understand that it directs the *protection of American national interests as well as the interests of individual Americans.* Whatever you do let the Department know of the plan of the concerting powers in regard to punitive or other expeditions in order that this Government may properly discharge the obligations which its large interest put upon it."[35]

Thus, entering in a somewhat backward manner, America was now committed to concurrent military action in China. Contrary to Rear-Admiral Remey's insistence that the war in the Philippines was paramount, the Navy Department began to drain General MacArthur, commander of American forces in the Philippines, of both ships and men. On June 16 MacArthur complained that his force in the Philippines had been "disseminated to the limitation of safety." Nevertheless he was, on the same day, ordered to send a regiment to China. On June 22 MacArthur was asked to send still another regiment to China. He replied that the "detachment of regiments jeopardizes the entire enterprise" in the Philippines. However, he complied, commenting, as further demands for troops and transport came in, that he would "send troops to China when so ordered . . . with as much perfection and energy as though I believed in the wisdom of such policy." The only comfort held out to MacArthur was the value of demonstrating to the American public Manila's usefulness as a base of operations for action in China. This, in the face of public uneasiness over the brutal suppression campaign, was not to be scorned.[36]

Kempff's problems were not solved by joining in the military operations of the powers. Rather he found himself in ever greater difficulties as he struggled to stay clear of the bickering that divided the Russians from the British and the Germans from everyone. On June 25 he reported that his one object was to avoid "having our force made use of in assisting in carrying out any selfish designs and policies of other nations." Kempff thought that the small American unit then in China did not give him the flexibility that would allow him to both guard what was necessary and stay out of what was not. He wanted a large American force that could act independently of the other powers instead of being forced, for want of sufficient power, to cooperate in any project the others thought important. Certain that the other powers had ulterior motives, Kempff was determined not to sacrifice American lives for them. Secretary Long was sympathetic and reinforcements as well as personal encouragement were sent to the hard-pressed Kempff.[37]

The attack on Taku and the "four demands" determined the course of the empress dowager, and the consequent siege of the legations eased the delicate situation in which Hay and McKinley struggled to reassure the public they were neither too lax nor too forward in their actions. The difference the siege made is apparent in two editorials in the *New York Tribune*. An editorial on June 11 declared that Conger's concurrent representation to the Tsungli yamen and the presence of Admiral Kempff at Tientsin exhausted America's responsibilities. The *Tribune* felt it unlikely, as well as undesirable, that the United States would contribute more than the 300 marines already at Tientsin. On June 20, however, as it became clear the legations were cut off from all communication with the outside world and in mortal danger, the *Tribune* now remarked that the fight in China was the duty of "civilization toward barbarism, the duty of law and order toward riot and anarchy." It was the duty of the powers, the United States among them, to impose an orderly government on China "without the consent of the coolies and Boxers who are thus to be governed."[38]

However, McKinley found a lack of enthusiasm for major military action in China even among firm imperialists like Cushman K. Davis. In a long letter to Whitelaw Reid, Davis discussed the alternatives open to the administration in China. He was reluctant to have any part of the American force march in a combined European army against Peking.

Inevitably, he argued, America would then become involved in a struggle for "partition, concessions, definitions of spheres, and other advantages." The "commanding isolation" of the United States would become a thing of the past and freedom of action in Asia would be lost. Instead Davis wanted the administration to hold off in favor of future, greater glories. "If we can abstain," he wrote, "I am certain that within ten years we shall be the arbiter and this will be much better than to be one of many litigants. To be thus will be better in the long run for us, for civilization and humanity." Comforted, as McKinley and Hay could not be, by his vision, Davis was then able to keep calm when he contemplated the fate of the legations. Reid's reply, while in general agreement with Davis, underlined the administration's dilemma. The China situation, he wrote, was similar to that "in which the country found itself after the explosion of the Maine. None of us wanted war with Spain, and yet war was inevitable. None of us want now to go into the business of killing Chinamen, and yet the country will probably not permit American troops to be absent from the column which ultimately enters Peking." Like Davis, Reid thought the United States could exert major influence in China without the expense and danger of a large military effort. Yet the conclusion of his letter illustrated, once again, why McKinley had no choice but to send a substantial number of troops. If Conger were alive, Reid noted, "and if the Administration does not strain every nerve to save him, there will be a whirlwind."[39]

United States military participation increased radically after June 17. The *Oregon* and the *Brooklyn* joined the *Newark* and the ancient *Monocacy,* and Rear-Admiral Remey, who had previously objected to sending reinforcements to China, proceeded from Manila to Taku. General Adna Chaffee was appointed commander of United States forces on land and left for China in early July. By the end of August, 6,300 American soldiers were in China, with plans for at least another 4,000.[40]

Throughout June the administration was pulled in two directions. The magazine *Public Opinion* summarized press opinion for the month by reporting that, though most newspapers saw the necessity for sending reinforcements to China, all urged that the United States act independently to protect American nationals and treaty rights; any coalition for broader purposes was opposed. The administration took every opportunity to assure the public of America's limited aims. On the other hand, special interest groups urged more vigorous action and vehemently criticized McKinley's caution. Speaking for the missionary element, the *Independent,* on June 14, called for an American occupation of Peking, the deposition of the empress dowager and restoration of Kuang-hsu and the establishment of an international protectorate over China. "Do not tell us that we must avoid entangling alliances," the editors cried. "[That is] for babes, not men."[41] America must take part in the postwar settlement and ensure, by force if necessary, the integrity of China. Missionary groups in China similarly demanded full American participation and, according to John Lindbeck, called for a policy of "liberation" and the final crushing of the treacherous Chinese government. The American Asiatic Association petitioned McKinley on behalf of one hundred business firms demanding that America send adequate forces to China and cooperate closely with the European powers. At a public meeting of Americans in Shanghai, held on July 13, a strong petition was passed and forwarded to the President as well as to the press, and American consuls and naval officers in China. The resolutions called for naval support at all threatened points on the coasts and rivers of China. Convinced that Americans at home were unaware of the full dimensions of the crisis, the meeting issued a call to their fellow citizens to insist that McKinley send a larger military force. The small American contingent then in China was ludicrously disproportionate to America's interests and the necessity to entrust to other powers the job of protecting Americans was "humiliating." The Shanghai community mourned the loss of influence certain to follow current policy and emphatically urged strong, energetic cooperation with the other powers.[42]

Although the documentary evidence is slim, it appears that Hay was in favor of using the Boxer crisis as the occasion for a closer alliance with Great Britain. Like Brooks Adams and Henry Cabot Lodge, he was deeply apprehensive about Russian intentions.[43] In mid-June he asked Choate to report on the British attitude toward the Chinese situation and was somewhat disturbed by the reply. Choate assured Hay that the general desire was for England not to get involved in a partition of China. "But," he cautioned, "I cannot forget what Lord Salisbury once said to me in defining a 'sphere of influence,' that it was a sort of 'earmark' upon territory which in case of a break-up, England did not wish any other power to have." Nevertheless Hay was terribly frustrated by the obstacles in the way of forthright alliance with England. In a much-quoted letter to General John Foster, Hay lamented the "mad-dog hatred of England prevalent among newspapers and politicians." As a result, "Anything we should now do in China to take care of our imperilled interests would be set down to 'subservience to Great Britain.'" Furious, Hay concluded the letter with the angry words: "That we should be compelled to refuse the assistance of the greatest power in the world, in carrying out our own policy, because all Irishmen are Democrats and some Germans are fools —is enough to drive a man mad."[44] Since the British were at the time deeply and tragically committed in South Africa, the assistance Hay refers to could not have been very great. Indeed, it took no "mad-dog hatred" to realize that at this juncture the lines of assistance ran the other way across the Atlantic.

Later in the summer Hay received a letter from Henry Adams that, in somewhat extravagant language, expressed their common desire for an alliance with Great Britain as well as the recognition of its impossibility. Adams wrote that he foresaw Russia and Japan occupying North China. Who, then, would take care of the Yangtze? "There you are! Joint occupation of South China with England . . . you're a nice hand for such a job! Shades of G. W.! And Congress! And that giddy old Constitution! and the Senate! And the Supreme Court! Suppose you refuse! England must then go over to Germany and capitulate. She sinks anyway, but, that way, she disappears, and we too. Then it becomes a world of all Europe and Asia, with America as a fake-show in the Midway Plaisance." To which Hay replied, "Of course all you say is true. But what's the use of being so horribly clairvoyant." In a long letter to Brooks Adams, Henry confided his apocalyptic vision of the world scene:

> The Asiatic question has suddenly grown so serious that it has rather tended to force all Europe together . . . I imagine that today the whole financial world is united to hold up Russia, England and every other European interest in solidarity as against Asia . . . I have held, from the first Chinese outbreak, that Europe had got either to make a military partition of China, or a military occupation of it . . . Our government, of course, as it has always done, will pretend to do nothing, and will in fact run the whole machine.[45]

Adams' view of the alternatives—joint military occupation or joint military partition—obsessed him for the next few years. His overriding concern was that England, whose weakness and timidity "got on [his] nerves," be assured a large slice in any division. America must help her in this as she was our only ally in the coming struggle against Europe. If Russia were to organize China as a power, Western civilization was done for. "In that event," he wrote in 1903, "I allow till 1950 to run our race out."[46] Although their correspondence was intimate and extensive, Hay rarely joined Adams in his pessimistic prophecies on the fate of the world. On the importance of close alliance with England, however, he was in total agreement.

In 1900, however, no bilateral arrangement with Great Britain could be made and Hay would have to limit his efforts to independent American action taken in concert with all the other powers in China, including Russia. All through June the administration sought for a policy that would minimize criticism while satisfying the demands of all groups— merchants and missionaries in China, missionary and commercial groups at home, the demands of the public for national honor without the loss of too much national blood. Militarily, the American commitment was limited by the circumstance of the Philippine insurrection. Diplomatically, the State Department was restrained from entering into a forthright alliance with Great Britain that might have clarified America's position in China. Politically, McKinley had to avoid giving the anti-imperialist opposition a new campaign issue. At the same time, he realized that the aggresive bombast of the jingoes would probably not extend to the support of a long and costly war on the Asian mainland. It was impossible not to cooperate with the other powers in China. America could not relieve the legations alone; failure to relieve them would be disastrous. Yet full cooperation involved the danger, which Kempff, and later Chaffee, kept constantly before the President, of participation in some dark intrigue irrelevant or even inimical to American interests.

Under the general policy line of "independent action where possible, concurrent action where necessary," the administration met each development in the crisis as it came up. While the siege excited public opinion to the point where McKinley could, without fear of excessive criticism, send a substantial force to China, the arrangement with the southern and

central viceroys, described below, took the sting out of the anti-imperialists' arguments. Unless one of the powers acted so as to destroy the
tenuous concert, McKinley could hope to walk the thin line of limited war
with little danger to American interests or his own political ambitions.
Indeed, as many commentators pointed out, the practical demonstration
of Manila's value would probably do much to counter widespread dissatisfaction over the war against Aguinaldo.

Intervention

One of the most curious facts about the imperial declaration of war was
that it was purely internal. The decree of June 20 was not communicated
to Chinese legations abroad for delivery to the respective powers. Indeed,
as has already been pointed out, on June 29 Chinese representatives
abroad were specifically instructed to tell the respective governments
that China did *not* consider herself at war. More important, perhaps,
than the contradictory behavior of the court, was the decision of the
southern and central viceroys to use the "rebel" fiction in order to keep
their provinces out of the conflict. This notion, which was adopted on
the very day following the surrender of the Taku forts, was never precisely stated; rather, as one historian described it, it "evolved."[47] Of
course, had the powers so desired, they could have declared war on
China. Everything militated against this, however. No country was ready
to face the disorganization that a total disintegration of China would
cause. The partition of China, like that of the Ottoman empire, loomed
as a frightening possibility that no one in the Western foreign offices
desired; a threat to the very delicate balance of influence that did in fact
exist in the Far East at the time. Each country feared that its enemy
would gain more, or lose less, than itself. Because no country was very
sure who its enemies really were, a tenacious clinging to the status quo,
however difficult, was more desirable than forthright division of Chinese
territory. Total war and partition still might have occurred through acci-
dent or inertia. The vigorous diplomacy of the southern and central
Chinese viceroys, strongly supported by the United States, saved China
for other upheavals.

Liu K'un-yi, governor-general of Liang-Kiang, Li Hung-chang, governor-general of Kwangtung and Kwangsi, and Chang Chih-tung, governor-general of Hunan and Hupei, with the close cooperation of Sheng Hsuan-huai, director of railways and telegraphs, united to keep peace in the key central and southern provinces of China.

Prior to the actual declaration of war by the court, Sheng Hsuan-huai suggested to Li that, as hostilities had begun without direct orders from the court, they need not consider themselves at war. Li Hung-chang then wired all Chinese ministers abroad instructing them to seek a truce and negotiated settlement and to declare that the fighting at Taku was not ordered by the court. After the declaration of war, they seized on a phrase in an imperial edict of June 20 ordering the various provincial officials to unite to protect their territories; the insubordinate viceroys interpreted it to mean protection of foreigners against the Boxers.[48] As early as June 21 Liu K'un-yi had communicated with Wu T'ing-fang, Chinese minister in Washington, asking him to inform the President that, together with Chang Chih-tung, he was confident of being able to keep the peace and protect foreigners. Liu instructed Wu to urge that no American troops be sent to their provinces. They would be unnecessary and would also present obstacles to the viceroys' attempt to keep order.[49] Meanwhile, on June 20, the admirals and senior naval officers of the allied forces anchored off Taku had issued a public proclamation, signed by Kempff in the name of the United States, that clearly stated their limited aims. They would use force only against Boxers and those who joined them to prevent the Allies from rescuing their nationals in Peking.[50] Because the court had ordered that the advance of the allied forces be resisted, it was obvious the Allies would have to fight against imperial troops as well as Boxers. If the international expedition fought Chinese government troops, as they must, the viceroys could not be sure that they would uphold their limited declaration and refrain from an all-out war against China, which would inevitably involve their provinces. Obviously a more definite understanding was essential.

Sheng Hsuan-huai was the key tactician in the viceroys' maneuverings. On June 24 he suggested to Liu K'un-yi and Chang Chih-tung that the taotai at Shanghai be instructed to meet with the foreign consuls resident in the city and work out an agreement. The two viceroys agreed and, a few days later, the meeting was held. On June 26 the American consul-general at Shanghai cabled Hay that the viceroys of Nanking and Hankow had that day guaranteed peace in their provinces provided no foreign troops interfered.[51]

Wu T'ing-fang, in Washington, acted in close coordination with the viceroys. On June 27 he urged Hay to instruct American consuls to communicate directly with the viceroys. Hay checked with McKinley, commenting only that, though the proposal was a little irregular, given the paralysis of the government in Peking, it was advisable. The permission Hay thus gave local American officials to deal directly with their Chinese counterparts provided them with a freedom essential in the situation.[52]

On June 26 the Shanghai taotai, Yü Lien-yuan, and Sheng Hsuan-huai met the consuls and the neutralization of the Yangtze provinces was agreed upon. Goodnow reported that the admirals' proclamation of June 20 was the basic foreign text, although the Chinese had hoped to secure agreement to a more specific nine point agreement drafted by Sheng.[53]

The situation, though tenuous, was thus stabilized. Provincial authorities in Fukien, Kwangtung, and Kwangsi made similar arrangements with the resident consuls and, despite foreign efforts to station precautionary troops in delicate areas, the viceroys' efforts seemed successful.

The immense risk these viceroys ran should be pointed out. If, by whatever miracle, the foreigners should actually be driven out of China, their lives were forfeit. The sense of the risk they ran, as well as the fear that, at some future date, they might be called to account for their collaboration with the foreigners, may explain why men like Sheng Hsuan-huai and Wu T'ing-fang were as anxious as the kaiser himself to see the pro-Boxer ministers severely punished.

The Seige and the July 3 Note

Within the legations, the besieged ministers, missionaries, and refugee Christian converts made a fort of the legation quarter. Living on a diet of well-fed polo ponies, they held off the invader for fifty-five days behind breastworks made of finest Chinese silk. Mrs. Conger, a Christian Scientist, offered her female co-sufferers the limited comfort that "it was ourselves and not the times that were troublous and out of tune and insisted that while there was an appearance of war-like hostilities, it was really in our own brains."[54] This was precisely the attitude the liberal viceroys hoped more foreigners would cultivate.

Some of the ladies were more warlike. The wife of Mr. A. F. Chamot, a crack shot like her husband, killed seventeen Boxers in one day. Mr. Chamot's record was fifty-four. Together, over the whole period of the siege, they killed 700 Boxers.[55]

Then, on July 1 news of the murder of Baron von Ketteler, German minister to Peking, reached the angry, anxious world outside the riot-torn city. Goodnow cabled Hay the story, adding: "Viceroys Central and South China unitedly ask Consuls General, as representing governments, to agree not to attack their provinces regardless of what happens in Peking so long as they maintain order and protect foreigners. Fear holding back worst news Peking."[56] That evening Hay wrote his son, Adelbert, a letter full of the fear the news created everywhere. "News has just come in from Shanghai—which is a nursery of lies—that Baron Ketteler is murdered and the others in desperate danger. The President is in Canton, Ohio, and I have sent for the Cabinet. What an atmosphere of war and trouble I have breathed almost all my life!"[57] There was good reason to fear that all the ministers had been, or would soon be, murdered; this aroused, among the officials trying to keep most of China peaceful, a terror that the delicate structure built in the last weeks of June would collapse.

On July 3 the Chinese viceroys cabled an urgent message to all Chinese missions abroad to be circulated in all Western ministries urging that the arrangements for peace in south and central China be maintained. On the same day, the American government dispatched a circular note for similar distribution.

The connection between the murder of the bullying German minister (who attacked Boxers he came upon with his walking stick and joined in shooting them when possible) and the July 3 Chinese and American circular notes is central. The news of von Ketteler's death was itself the cause of renewed efforts to ensure peace and limited intervention in China. The viceroys understandably feared that the passion aroused by the news of the supposed massacre of the helpless ministers in Peking would lead to full-scale, vengeful war.

On July 3 Chang Chih-tung and Liu K'un-yi sent a joint telegram to the Chinese legations abroad promising to keep the peace in the areas they controlled.[58] Hay had, in fact, acted immediately in this direction as soon as he received Goodnow's July 1 cable. He ordered American troops to continue their restraint in the central and southern provinces so long as the local authorities maintained order. On July 3 Hay received a personal appeal from Liu K'un-yi through Goodnow. The viceroy urged that President McKinley take a leading part in controlling the other powers. America's leadership was China's only hope, Goodnow reported Liu as saying.[59]

On July 3 Hay called an emergency Cabinet meeting. The new, more dangerous situation created by Ketteler's murder and the uncertain fate of the rest of the ministers called for a more definitive declaration of policy than could be expressed through private negotiations between American consuls and Chinese officials. The circular of July 3 was the result.

Hay wired the President of his proposed circular note, stating that the critical situation demanded a policy declaration that would clarify America's position to the rest of the world. Each member of the Cabinet present at the July 3 meeting wired his support for Hay's suggestion. However, both the secretaries of war and navy wanted to send additional troops to China at once. Root told the President he believed the "sentiment" of the country demanded sending more troops and that the administration would be criticized if it did not do so. Hay urged waiting before dispatching any additional men. Although he did not say so, his probable motive was a desire to support the viceroys in every way he could. An additional American regiment might indicate his lack of confidence in them and could affect the situation in unpredictable ways. Root and Long agreed to follow Hay's lead and delay any new military move.[60]

It must be noted that it was essential for the administration to believe Wu T'ing-fang's repeated assurances that, except for von Ketteler, the legation quarters held their full quota of ministers and secretaries. Once the relief and rescue purpose of America's fairly sizable army in China was admitted to be hopeless, the soldiers must either be withdrawn or, as the viceroys feared, some formal declaration of war against China submitted. Congress was not in session in that steaming July 1900. To maintain the expedition in China under executive order, the only method available to him, McKinley had to insist upon the limited nature of the action.[61]

The last sentence of the note reads: "It is, of course, too early to forecast the means of attaining this last result [that is, to prevent a recurrence of such disasters]; but the policy of the Government of the United States is to seek a solution which may bring about permanent safety and peace to China, preserve Chinese territorial and administrative entity, protect all rights guaranteed to friendly powers by treaty and international law, and safeguard for the world the principle of equal and impartial trade with all parts of the Chinese Empire." This sentence alone broaches the subject of the future of China, but it affirms, in the clearest terms, American concern for China's integrity and independence. The note did not specifically renounce American territorial desires in China. The omission was directly related to the interest of the Navy Department in a coaling station in north China. McKinley, with this and other contingencies in mind, instructed Hay not to include any such self-denying pledge.[62]

The July 3 circular was a statement of American policy and required no response from the governments to which it was sent. Nor did any, except Great Britain, send a reply of any kind. However, as a public announcement of American purposes it was bound to carry weight in Europe. America now represented a power with some 75,000 troops stationed in the nearby Philippines. Its aims could not be ignored. The underlying purpose of the document was to assert America's steadfast opposition to using the opportunity presented by von Ketteler's murder as an excuse for an all-out war on China and subsequent partition of the country. To avoid this, the agreements with the southern and central viceroys were to be maintained. As has been pointed out, no power actually stood to gain from a decisive partition of China at this point. Hay, out of his own understanding of world affairs, and supported by information from Great Britain, was deeply afraid that Russia might be planning some coup in north China. If the circular was meant to warn any power in particular, it was Russia.

Analyzing his actions in a letter to his closest friend, Henry Adams, Hay explained: "The thing to do—the only thing, was to localize the storm if possible, and this we seem to have done. All the powers have fallen in with my modus vivendi in the Center and South."[63] The American press, too, felt that the stabilization of the crisis was due mainly to Hay's efforts. Nor is this view a chauvinistic overstatement of the facts. The United States was, in fact, the only country to state publicly and formally that such a modus vivendi existed and, because no country chose to protest, the powers can accurately be described as having "fallen in with [Hay's] modus vivendi." Some historians make light of Hay's diplomacy, attributing the powers' acquiescence to "political stalemate rather than conversion to principle." As Hay indicates in his letter to Adams, however, he did not seek to convert anyone to principle, but only to localize a situation of immense danger and complexity. However, the localization itself would go far to support what there was of principle in the circular note—the preservation of Chinese territorial integrity. The integrity section of the July 3 circular was not a sudden realization on the part of the United States of the importance of an undivided China. As has been pointed out earlier, a version of the integrity principle had been included in the September 1899 note to England, if not to the other powers. The statement of aim at the end of the July 3 note is not, in any sense, a contradiction of the underlying assumption of the earlier note. Spheres of influence were given facts and had to be dealt with. The *detachment* of territory from China, particularly Russian annexation of Manchuria under the cover of the Boxer crisis, had to be guarded against. In view of the fact of von Ketteler's murder and the possibility that all the ministers had been slaughtered, some dramatic move was necessary to prevent the abandonment of the careful fiction under which foreign forces fought Chinese soldiers but not the Chinese government.

It is hard to recapture the sense of disaster and catastrophe that engulfed the chancellories of the West throughout July. The British ambassador to France reported to Salisbury that M. Delcassé was positively distraught after the news of von Ketteler's death. The thought that all Europe could not rescue the besieged ministers was "overwhelmingly terrible" to him. Reports from Shanghai described the massacre of all foreigners in Peking in convincing detail. Consular dispatches constantly warned of the danger of an uprising in south and central China; in Tientsin, the foreign settlement fought desperately for its life and the prospect of a relief expedition to Peking seemed months away. On July 17, Ambassador Choate reported that, in England, "Nothing is thought of or talked of . . . but the final catastrophe at Pekin—and yet except that more troops are being sent—no one seems to have a clear idea of what action this catastrophe calls for."[64]

Each new story of disaster prompted panic and the possibility that the limited ends clearly stated in the July 3 note would be abandoned in favor of all-out war against China. On July 5, for example, Consul-General Goodnow cabled Hay: "Situation serious. Movement extending. Should allied forces north meet reverses must extend Central South China. Result, expulsion murder foreigners in interior. Ruin trade. Strong force necessary check Boxers North, support Viceroys South." McKinley's response was immediate. He at once suggested that American citizens be ordered to leave the Chinese interior for places of safety on the coast. Hay replied in a bold telegram the following day. The most important consideration, he told the President, was the effect such a withdrawal would have on the south and central viceroys. It would be a sign that the United States lacked faith in their pledges and might well increase tension in their still peaceful provinces. Another consideration was the immense responsibility such withdrawal would place on the government for the subsistence and repatriation of the missionaries later on. Finally, the missionaries themselves were in the best position to judge the situation; many had left the interior already, others seemed to feel that remaining was the wiser course. Before reaching this conclusion, Hay told the President, he had consulted with Secretary of War Elihu Root, who completely agreed with him. In this decision and others made in the enervating heat of that Washington summer, Hay showed himself determined to stand by the word of the viceroys as the only means of confining the disaster. With comic resignation he wrote Henry Adams on July 8 that if he "looked at things as you do in the light of reason, history and mathematics, I should go off after lunch and die, like Mouravieff. But I take refuge in a craven opportunism."[65]

Hay's letter convinced McKinley that evacuation of Americans from the interior would weaken the accord with the viceroys. Still worried by Goodnow's reports, however, McKinley contacted Secretary of War Root to see if more troops could be released, at once, for China. Root protested that MacArthur's description of the Philippine situation made this quite impossible. McKinley's reply was firm. If the danger was greater in China than in the Philippines, they must take the risk. To ease MacArthur's position, Root, with the President's approval, decided to withdraw three regiments from Cuba and most of an additional regiment from Puerto Rico. These would be sent to Manila, releasing more troops for China. On July 7 MacArthur was informed of this plan and ordered to send an additional force to Taku without waiting for the arrival of replacements from home.[66]

Every public statement made by the State Department was designed to support, diplomatically, the position taken in the July 3 note. On July 5, for example, Hay sent McKinley a draft of the consolatory message he planned to wire to the kaiser. Hay's version included a pessimistic reference to the fate of the other ministers that McKinley, intent on preserving the rescue aim of American forces in China, ordered deleted. In addition, McKinley suggested that Hay include a phrase restating the continuing effort of the United States to extend "stability and order" in China.[67]

American policy was further defined on the occasion of the appointment of General Adna Chaffee as commanding officer of American land forces in China. Chaffee's instructions were drafted by McKinley himself. According to the most recent reports, Conger and his entire staff had been destroyed. Nevertheless, the United States intended to retain its friendship with the Chinese people and those officials not involved in the outrages. Among the latter Chaffee was to count Li Hung-chang. He was ordered to aid any Chinese government or any "part thereof" in repressing the disorders, rescuing Americans, protecting their interests and property wherever the Chinese government failed to do so. Chaffee was to confer freely with other powers, seeking a "harmony of action along lines of similar purposes and interest." Later on the President remarked to a friend that he didn't care who led the allied armies. "What I want," he said, "is the friendship of China when the trouble is over."[68]

Two events that occurred on July 20 gave McKinley an additional lever to secure that friendship. All direct word from the legations had ceased in late June. Determined to find out whether Conger was alive, Hay capitalized on his excellent relations with Wu T'ing-fang, who in turn relied upon Sheng Hsuan-huai's contact with Jung-lu in Peking. Hay asked the harried minister to get a message through to Conger. Dispatched on July 11, it stated, simply, "Communicate tidings bearer." On July 20, the reply, dated four days earlier, finally arrived. "For one month," Conger wrote, "we have been besieged in British Legation under continued shot and shell from Chinese troops. Quick relief only can prevent general massacre." While the contents of the message were not comforting, Hay accepted it as proof that, as of July 16, Conger and the others were alive. Wu, and other Chinese officials through him, had been assuring Hay of just that for weeks. The administration's ready acceptance of the authenticity of the message confirmed the Chinese in their good opinion of American intentions. It should be noted that it took some courage to publish Conger's dispatch as genuine proof of his good health. Whitelaw Reid, despite the assurance of his own Washington news bureau that the note was authentic, doubted it. To C. K. Davis he confided: "I am trying to believe it; but the heathen Chinese is smart enough to have forwarded now, as of this date, a dispatch he may have suppressed weeks ago."[69]

The British Government was equally dubious, and Finley Peter Dunne's Mr. Dooley made wicked fun of the way in which the message was transmitted:

"A knock comes at the dure an' Woo enthers. 'Well,' says he, with a happy smile, ' 'tis all right.' 'What's all right?' says the sicrety iv state. 'Ivrything,' says Woo. 'I have just found a letter sewed in a shirt fr'm my frind Lie Much, th' viceroy iv Bumbang . . . I know 'tis gennoyine because it is an ol' dress patthern used be th' impress.' " The letter, Dooley goes on to relate, tells of the poisoning of the empress, the beheading of the emperor and the "warrum rayciption" given by the foreigners at Tientsin to the Boxers. " 'That,' says Woo, 'is wan way iv r-reading it. Read upside down it says that the impress has become a Swedenboorjan . . . I hope y're satisfied,' he says. 'I am,' says Jawn Hay. 'I'll tillygraft to Mark that ivrything is all r-right,' he says, 'an' that our relations with his majesty or her majesty or their Boxerships . . . are as they ought to be or worse or better, as th' case may be,' he says. 'Good,' says Woo, 'Ye're a man afther me own heart,' he says . . . 'I must write a secret message . . . to my corryspondint in Meriden, Connecticut, urgin' him to sind more impeeryal edicks iv a fav'rable nature,' he says. 'I've on'y had twinty so far, an' I'm gettin' scrivener's palsy,' he says."[70]

Understandably anxious to confirm the note, Hay added to his popularity by the homely American nature of the method he used. He asked Conger for the name of his sister and, some time later, received an answer unlikely to have been manufactured by the Chinese: "Alta."

The message accompanying Miss Conger's name was not encouraging and only portions of it were released to the press (the bracketed words were omitted in the press version): "All well; no fighting since sixteenth by agreement; enough provisions; [little ammunition;] hope speedy relief."[71]

On the same day Conger's dispatch arrived, Wu T'ing-fang brought McKinley a personal message from the emperor. Under the impact of the capture of Tientsin and the influence of the persuasive memorials of Chang Chih-tung and twelve other southern viceroys and governors, the court had agreed to send conciliatory letters to the United States, Germany, and France as earlier letters had been sent to England, Japan, and Russia. The letter to McKinley, dated July 19, declared that China had been "driven by the irresistible course of events" into a position where she had "unfortunately incurred well-nigh universal indignation." With impartial flattery the letter stated that China placed "special reliance" on the United States. The other letters contained similar personal appeals. The emperor then expressed the hope that McKinley would take the initiative in bringing about a concert of powers for the restoration of order and peace.[72]

Some powers doubted the authenticity of this note as well and none replied to it as carefully and thoughtfully as McKinley did. McKinley's reply set forth the limited aims of relief and rescue under which American soldiers fought in China. With Tientsin subdued, the manner in which the legations were relieved became of major importance. If, as the letter claimed, the imperial government was not behind the Boxer movement, then the United States would offer its good offices—in concert with the other powers—if the foreign ministers were definitely known to be alive and well and, most important, if they were put in full and free communication with their home governments. Moreover, as evidence of their good will, the Chinese government forces must contact the allied relief expedition and offer it all aid and assistance in the task of rescuing the legations. McKinley stuck by these conditions despite the urgent pleas of the Chinese to relax them. Whenever the State Department was assured that the ministers were indeed alive and therefore no expedition should be sent to Peking, Hay would insist that open communications and absolute safety for the ministers must first be established. Not till then would America make any move to mediate between China and the other powers.[73]

Some newspapers were critical of the mildness of the American reply. Responding to the rumor that all the ministers had been massacred, the *Atlanta Constitution* insisted that a special session of Congress be called and the entire strength of the country devoted to the "utter annihilation" of the Chinese government. The *Philadelphia Press* called for justice, "inexorable justice." And the *Independent* cried that there must be "punishment, at whatever cost of treasure or of life. China must learn that the nations of the West will visit terrible retribution for such an outrage." The anti-imperialist and Democratic press suffered an enforced silence on administration policy while the fate of Conger was still in doubt. Nevertheless, McKinley and his administration were constantly sniped at—increasingly as Root worked up to his intended quota of 15,000 American troops in China. (The actual number reached 6,300; a good portion of these arrived too late to participate in the relief of the legations.) The *Philadelphia Times* was relatively unrestrained, calling the dispatch of troops to China on executive order the worst kind of imperialism. The Democratic *Hartford Times* reacted to the rumor of Conger's death with great *sang-froid*. If Conger was dead there was no reason for American soldiers to be in China at all and they should be withdrawn at once.[74]

Important figures in his own party, however, were quick to congratulate McKinley on his handling of the crisis. Charles Emory Smith assured the President that his "answer to the Chinese application for mediation seems to me superb." George Perkins asked Colonel Montgomery, who cabled all messages to the President during his stay in Canton, to inform the President that McKinley's actions were being applauded in the best board rooms in New York, by Democrats and Republicans alike. A few days later Charles Dawes, McKinley's close friend, passed on further words of encouragement. The administration's Chinese policy was the general topic of discussion among businessmen, who were convinced America was now undisputed leader in the Far East.[75]

The most ambitious and certainly the most elegantly expressed interpretation of American policy in July 1900, was that of Henry Adams.

As stated in his *Education,* the central issue was the "inevitable struggle for the control of China," which his brother Brooks had predicted years ago. Observing the disasters in Peking, Adams was convinced that nothing could prevent Russia and Germany from dividing China and shutting America out. There was no recourse and Adams "laughed at Hay for his helplessness." Suddenly, Adams wrote, Hay moved alone to rescue the legations and save China. "Nothing so meteoric had ever been done in American diplomacy." The world sat back, shocked, and then "burst into a most tumultuous applause." Hay summarized his policy less theatrically in a private letter to Ambassador Choate. His constant aim had been to secure the safety and interests of Americans in China "without any thought of ultimate aggrandizement." Retribution would be exacted but without punishing the entire Chinese nation. Indeed Hay hoped to accomplish his ends with the aid of the highest officials in China.[76]

The relief expedition, after the setback of June 10, had been preparing itself for battle on an immense scale. Tientsin was captured in mid-July; on August 6 the expedition set out for Peking.

American participation in the Boxer expedition was the logical culmination of a China policy that had been shaping itself along interventionist lines since 1896. The new vigor with which antimissionary riots were met in 1896 and 1897, the strong diplomatic representations regarding American trade that had been made both to China and the powers in 1898 and 1899 made a policy of inactive cooperation with foreign forces during the Boxer crisis impossible. No longer would an American secretary of state leave the protection of nationals and their interests to the British. Now, danger to Americans required an American armed presence and, more than that, it was hoped that an American force would give the nation increased weight and influence in the diplomatic maneuvering that was sure to follow the suppression of the antiforeign movement.

The dispatch of large numbers of American troops to China was not an easy decision for McKinley. In addition to the logistical problem involved in diverting troops from the large-scale war against the Filipino insurgents, McKinley faced a serious political problem. The anti-imperialists could charge that America had so changed its ancient policy that it joined militaristic adventures whenever they occurred. The danger of partition of China was imminent; would not the presence of American troops in that nation inevitably lead to American participation in its dismemberment? Would not America find itself caught in a tangled web of European intrigue from which the country could not possibly emerge with honor? And what if the Boxer crisis led to a major war against China? How could America join the evil imperialistic ventures of Russia and France, of England and Germany? McKinley was, of course, aware both of the criticism and of the real dangers it described. He moved cautiously, but, perhaps fearing the even greater uproar that would ensue if he failed to rescue Conger, failed to demonstrate that America could protect its own interests, and failed to use what influence America had to prevent the very machinations the anti-imperialists condemned, he *did* move.

Once in, he did everything he could to limit the nature of the conflict, from a consistent clinging to the fiction that expeditionary troops were there to help put down a rebellion in which the Chinese government was not involved, to vigilant support for the south and central viceroys. When he wavered, Hay was there to strengthen his resolve, to help keep the lines of policy clear and distinct.

eight   The Problems of Peace

In early August the International Expedition began its triumphant march toward Peking. The route taken was the same the British had used some forty years before on their last military visit to the city. The expedition defeated successive Chinese armies as it went along and left behind it a trail of Chinese generals dead by their own hand.

On August 7, John Hay, exhausted by the trials of the summer, feeling sick and old, left Washington for his summer home in New Hampshire. In charge of the State Department he left the able, though half-deaf, Alvey A. Adee. Elihu Root, the new secretary of war, also remained in Washington and helped Adee in a variety of ways, including service as a speaking trumpet when Adee wanted to speak to the President over the long-distance telephone.[1] McKinley was in and out of Washington during August and September; both he and Hay were in frequent communication with Adee and each other by letter, telephone, and telegraph.

In mid-July Rockhill was sent to China, despite some missionary opposition, as special commissioner of the United States to China.[2] At the time it was not known if Conger lived, and if he lived, how competent he would be to resume his job after the rigors of the siege.

Adee, with both Hay and McKinley away, took little independent action. He wrote Hay that he had decided to stay close to his office "and hold on tight to the tiller."[3] On August 5 word reached Washington that the imperial government was ready to grant open communication with Conger. Justifiably frightened of what Conger might reveal, however, the capitulation was qualified. Messages must be uncoded, not in cipher. Uncertain whether or not to protest, Adee was in "telegraphic touch with the President a dozen times," and on McKinley's instructions submitted a strong protest. By August 9, the Chinese had granted McKinley's demand for free communication hoping, in return, to get his support for their plan to escort the envoys out of Peking and halt the advance of the allied expedition short of the capital. McKinley was firm in his insistence

172

on the *right* of communication; it was not a privilege which must be bargained for. Moreover, the Chinese had not cooperated militarily with the relief party. On these grounds, the President refused to consider negotiation prior to the rescue of the legations.[4] In Newport, Canton, and Washington, all over the United States in fact, people waited anxiously for news of the relief expedition.

Relief

After the temporary truce of mid-July, the bombardment of the legations was resumed. Mrs. Conger continued to supervise the reactions of the other ladies. Polly Condit Smith recalled a brush with the good American lady during one very heavy attack. Mrs. Conger had walked in on Mrs. Smith "lying on my mattress on the floor, not even beginning to dress for what I suppose half the women in the compound believed to be the beginning of the final fight. In a more than tragic manner she said: 'Do you wish to be found undressed when the end comes?' It flashed through my mind that it made very little difference whether I was massacred in a pink silk dressing gown . . . or . . . in a gold skirt and shirt waist. So I told her that in the light of experience I had come to the conclusion that, as it was absolutely of no benefit to anyone my being dressed during these attacks, I was going to stay in bed unless something terrible happened, when I should don my dressing gown and, with a pink bow of ribbon at my throat, await my massacre."[5]

Through what is now known to be Jung-lu's efforts, nothing terrible did happen. Word of the approaching relief expedition reached the besieged foreigners through complex and dangerous messenger routes; they had more concrete evidence of the approaching end when, on August 12, members of the Tsungli yamen attempted, on the empress dowager's orders, to negotiate a truce. Distrusting the Chinese too much to walk over to the yamen, the British minister replied, on behalf of his colleagues, that the Chinese negotiators would be received in the bullet-torn legation headquarters. Distrust, at least, was mutual. The yamen officials developed prior engagements and nothing came of the move. Indeed, the firing on the legations increased in intensity. The Chinese attack of August 13–14 was the most severe of the entire siege. One more last

173

minute attempt at negotiation came to nothing and then, on August 14, foreign troops entered Peking while, on a euphemistic "tour of inspection," the imperial family fled to the west.[6]

The news of the capture of Peking was ambivalently received in the United States. There was, of course, genuine relief that the beleaguered ministers were alive and well. There was also pride in the part America had played in the entire drama. On August 17, Brooks Adams wrote Hay: "The news today assured us that you have won for us the greatest diplomatic triumph of our time. No living minister in the world has done the like . . . we hold command in the East, with possible consequences which I cannot measure, but which are certainly greater than anything which has happened since 1870 . . . Your policy will prove to have carried us round one of the great corners in our history. The further we go forward, the larger your conception will look."

At the same time there was an almost immediate expression of anxiety for the future. Two *Literary Digest* surveys, one published August 25 and the other September 1, found that, almost without exception, the American press urged the government to secure reparations and guarantees for the future before withdrawing any troops. There was also unanimous opposition to the partition of China or, if the other powers insisted on such a course, American participation in the action. But the *Digest* found no paper that offered a plan for future American policy in China.[7]

The frank espousal of partition was rare and virtually confined to one man, Demetrius C. Boulger, who insisted that America share in a joint protectorate over China. "The American people," Boulger wrote, "have crossed the Rubicon of imperial responsibility." John Barrett, in the same issue of the *North American Review* that published Boulger's article, violently opposed partition and his attitude was far more representative. America, he wrote, must lead the fight against dismemberment, for only an intact Chinese empire could operate on the basis of the Open Door. Both Boulger and Barrett agreed on one key point: that America's role in the future of China could not end with the simple relief of the legations. Others, like the editor of the *Philadelphia Ledger,* were less ambitious. American troops, having accomplished what they were sent to do, should immediately withdraw. At all costs the United States must keep out of the ensuing struggle for power in the Far East.[8]

174

There was widespread anxiety in the United States that war with China might now begin in earnest. The province of Chihli was in a state of anarchy. The government had fled Peking; foreigners ruled Tientsin; pockets of armed resistance continued in the countryside north of the capital. It was known that the pro-Boxer officials, with a sizable army, continued to dominate the court. The powers rejected Li Hung-chang's repeated requests to call a halt to the hostilities and appoint plenipotentiaries. Indeed, fighting continued long after negotiations had begun in October. From December 1900 to April 1901, forty-six expeditions, composed mainly of German troops, were dispatched. There was nothing to prevent the empress dowager from declaring a war of resistance from her relatively secure position in Sian. Should she succeed in rousing the entire nation, the powers might become fatally bogged down in a massive war against all of China. The viceroys of south and central China were aware of the danger and moved quickly to avert it. In addition to using all their influence to persuade the court to adopt a conciliatory position, they asked the powers to assure the country that the persons of the emperor and empress dowager would be respected. The American response was an immediate reassurance on this point, which satisfied the viceroys. The United States also vigorously dissociated itself from the effort of the admirals at Taku to prevent Li Hung-chang from communicating with Chinese authorities in Tientsin. Rear-Admiral Remey was instructed to treat Li with the honors due an official plenipotentiary.[9]

The administration was faced with a series of immediate, limited problems. How it acted in each case would, of course, contribute to a broader definition of American policy. But the primary considerations were, so to speak, local and specific. The situation that developed in Amoy at the end of August is one example.

Amoy

The rumors of Japanese designs on Amoy that Consul Johnson had reported in the early spring of 1900 were more accurate than he knew. Gotō Shimpei, civil governor of Formosa in 1900, was in complete agreement with Kodama Gentarō, fourth governor-general of the island, on the desirability of developing Amoy as a "focal point for trade and gain in South China and the South Seas."[10] Yamamoto Gombei, Navy minister in the Yamagata cabinet, was similarly interested in an aggressive policy toward China and urged that advantage be taken of the Boxer rebellion and its contingent disturbances. A telegram of August 10, 1900, instructed Kodama to prepare for the takeover and occupation of Amoy on the grounds of protection of Japanese nationals. Russian independent military action in Manchuria and the recent landing of British troops in Shanghai were to be used as legitimizing precedents. On August 15 instructions from Katsura Tarō, the minister of war, developed the plan further. Upon orders from Tokyo, Kodama was instructed to be ready to bombard the Amoy shore batteries and move into the city in force. Gotō Shimpei himself proceeded to Amoy in preparation for occupying the city after its capture. The Japanese did not expect much effective resistance from the Chinese.

The pretext for action conveniently occurred the following week. Johnson cabled Hay on August 24 that a mob had burned a Japanese temple in Amoy that morning; Japanese marines had been landed; Chinese officials were busily attempting to restore order. Three days later he sent a more alarming wire. Despite the success of Chinese officials in keeping the peace, the Japanese were landing troops and guns. A full report, which Johnson wrote on the twenty-sixth, described the situation in detail. At nine o'clock on the morning of the temple burning, the Japanese consul had sent a circular letter to his foreign colleagues informing them that in order to protect the Japanese residents, marines had been landed in Amoy. As a rather presumptuous gesture of conciliation the consul had added that Japanese marines would protect the other foreign residents as well.[11]

Johnson, chosen by the consular body as chairman of the Defense Committee and Volunteer Defense Corps, which had been organized earlier in the Boxer crisis, immediately investigated the Japanese charges. He found that, contrary to the consul's report, it was not a temple which had been destroyed, but a house rented by Japanese priests and used as a chapel. Three days before the fire there had been a dispute between the priests and the owner of the house over the rent. On the night before the fire virtually everything that could be moved had been taken out of the house. At one o'clock on the morning of the twenty-fourth, the priest had reported to the consul that the building was on fire. When the taotai of Amoy heard about the fire, he immediately ordered his soldiers to aid in fighting it and, by morning, had posted soldiers all over the city.[12] Nevertheless, Japanese marines landed and the Japanese consul refused Chinese requests to have them withdrawn. On the following day another detachment of marines and several guns were landed. The Chinese, Johnson reported, were justifiably outraged. The leading merchants and propertied men of the city had subscribed to maintain an army of 200 men in addition to the regular army for the sole purpose of protecting foreign residents and preventing just such incidents as the Japanese had now manufactured. The Chinese believed that the Japanese priests had set the fire themselves—and Johnson was inclined to agree. The landing of marines was unnecessary in any event and their continued presence caused unrest and the first danger of antiforeign riots that Amoy had experienced all summer.

After writing his report, Johnson met with the German and British consuls to frame a joint protest to the Japanese consul. While they were discussing the wording, two hundred and fifty marines and four machine guns were landed right outside the American consulate. It was then felt that the situation called for more than written protests and the three consuls marched over to the Japanese consul to present their protests personally. Meanwhile panic had seized the city and Johnson reported the flight of some 30,000 residents followed by the looting of their homes and the further spread of fear among the Chinese. An active man, whose sympathy for the Chinese had been demonstrated on many occasions, Johnson did not wait for instructions to take action. Accompanied by some American businessmen and the British consul, Johnson walked around the city trying to quiet the people and assuring them that the marines would not open fire. These efforts were foiled by the Japanese, who placed a large gun on a hill overlooking the city and pointed it in the direction of the yamen. "Hence," Johnson remarked, "it was difficult to impress the people with mere words."[13]

The taotai seems to have placed himself fairly completely in the hands of his consular friends. On their advice he disarmed his choice troops in order to avoid clashes with the Japanese marines. On August 28 the taotai informed Johnson that he could not guarantee anyone's safety so long as the marines stayed. Meanwhile, a British man-of-war had joined the American gunboat *Castine* in Amoy harbor; a quick uncomplicated Japanese occupation of Amoy was no longer possible. Although Chinese continued to flee the city in thousands, there were no demonstrations against foreigners. The British landed a troop of marines, however, and Johnson was anxious to do the same.[14]

On the Japanese side, things had not gone according to plan. Kodama received orders from Tokyo on August 27 to proceed in accordance with the August 15 plan. Formosa was transformed into a floating fortress ready for war. According to the schedule, Amoy's forts were to have been stormed on the twenty-ninth, the foreign consuls informed of impending occupation on the same day and the occupation itself to be completed by August 31. However on August 28 Kodama received a telegram from Katsura calling the whole thing off. The cabinet, though it had not definitely decided against the invasion, was reconsidering the matter and all troop movements were postponed. By August 30, however, the British marines had landed and the Amoy plan was abandoned.[15]

Despite the decision in Tokyo, the Japanese marines remained in Amoy. The consul insisted he could not withdraw them on his own initiative and had had no instructions from his government on their disposition.[16] Johnson still feared a serious clash between Chinese and Japanese troops and, on September 3, cabled Goodnow for permission to land American marines from the ship *Castine*. Goodnow replied by midnight of the same day cautioning Johnson against a "mere counter-demonstration." Using this qualified permission and supported by the British consul, British naval officers and the captain of the *Castine,* Johnson presented a forceful protest to the Japanese consul. He was finally able to report a limited success: the Japanese marines would withdraw if the British left at the same time. In a joint meeting with the British consul and the taotai, a time was set and on September 8 Johnson cabled Washington that Amoy was, at last, free of Japanese troops.[17]

Johnson, whose efforts at cooperation with the Chinese officials antedated the Boxer crisis by several years, was heartsick at the behavior of the Japanese. Reflecting on the flight of some 100,000 Chinese during the week's uncertainty and fear, Johnson angrily pointed out how skillfully the Chinese officials had kept order throughout the uncertainty of the Boxer period.[18] Suddenly, contrary to all agreements, the Japanese had struck. The vulnerability of the Chinese, and their dependence on the more or less uncertain response of Britain and America, was evident.

The tense situation in Amoy was precisely the kind of complication the administration feared. The presence of American troops in China and the declared policy of the July 3 circular made it difficult for the limited aims of relief and rescue to be strictly adhered to. Quick British action in Amoy had obviated the need for a basic American policy decision. The dangers, however, were now clearer than ever. Though authorizing Johnson to land American marines, the Department had warned against giving the appearance of specifically opposing the Japanese—the purpose was to be protection of nationals solely. In an explosive situation, which a more aggressive Japanese policy would have created, such a distinction was more legal than actual.

The major question remained unanswered: how deeply was America committed to playing a role in Far Eastern matters? Should the United States assume responsibility for the postwar settlement or let those powers more frankly interested in the political balance of forces in Asia dictate the new establishment as they saw fit? Protecting China from the predatory interests of other nations required more than pious declarations. Gaining significant real estate in China similarly demanded decisive, often military, action. In either case the United States would come into conflict with her recent allies, a fact that circulars could not obscure.

The Russian Proposal

On August 14 the first telegram direct from Peking was sent to Washington. It was released to the press only in part: "Saved. Relief arrived today . . . Do not yet know where Imperial family is . . . Desperate effort made last night to exterminate us." Omitted was Conger's comment on the Chinese: "The base treachery and savage brutality of this Chinese Government is unparalleled. None of its members should in future be recognized by any civilized power. Its severe punishment alone can make China safe for foreigners." Recovering rapidly from his ordeal, Conger reacted from the two months of silence and isolation by flooding Washington with cablegrams. He began by sending strong policy recommendations to Washington—none of which were released to the press. On the sixth of September he urged that the Chinese ringleaders be punished and the government reorganized under foreign supervision. He categorically denied a New York press report that the Chinese government had

179

at any time tried to protect the legations. Conger was out for blood and the general feeling in Washington was that Rockhill's more detached attitude would be invaluable in the coming weeks.[19]

Russia's quiet but persistent pursuit of its own interests in north China raised the first major post-Boxer problem for the McKinley administration. Anxious to regain Chinese good will and neutralize any ill effect its participation in the international expedition might have had, Russia, through Count Witte, resumed its half-bullying, half-wooing relationship with the court-appointed negotiator, Li Hung-chang. Distrusted by the British for his past deals with Russia, ignored by Germany, whose kaiser was even then shipping Count Alfred von Waldersee to China, tolerated by America and Japan, both of whom were playing a waiting game, Li found support only from the Russians.[20] At the end of August the Russian government informed the Chinese that it would withdraw its troops from Peking to Tientsin and promised, as well, to evacuate Manchuria after a proper settlement. On August 25, in a circular note to all the powers, Russia proposed general military withdrawal from Peking on the grounds that the basic aim of the expedition had been achieved and that negotiations could not proceed until the Chinese government returned to Peking; the presence of foreign troops in the city only delayed this. Declaring its support for the current regime, Russia pledged its firm allegiance to an undivided China. The Russian occupation of Manchuria was explained as temporary; it had been essential to the protection of valuable railroad property.[21]

The Russian note caused intense concern in Washington. Although no reply was called for, McKinley apparently felt that, given the necessity in terms of domestic politics to define the conditions under which American troops remained in China, the opportunity for a policy statement should not be missed. McKinley was concerned about the undefined situation in Peking; he was also afraid that the arrival of Count von Waldersee would create a new crisis. Reluctantly accepted as commander-in-chief of the allied forces, von Waldersee sailed for China eight days after the capture of Peking. The Russian proposal was a brutal blow to Kaiser Wilhelm for it would add the final *opéra-bouffe* touch to the entire Waldersee expedition if Peking should now be evacuated. The fear in Washington was well-expressed by Root: "The approach of the much prepared Waldersee seemed a peril. There was a danger that after all the Emperor's windy eloquence he might feel the necessity of kicking up a row to justify the appointment of Waldersee. I was very glad therefore that the Russians gave us an opportunity to say that we would stay under a definite understanding and not otherwise."[22]

With Hay still away, the major task of drafting a reply to the Russian note fell to Root. Both he and McKinley wrote separate versions which were then combined during an all-day cabinet meeting. Some of the opacity of the result can be explained by the way in which it was drafted, but the major cause lay in the confusion of aims and ideas that it incorporated. The Russian circular had reaffirmed that country's adherence to the principle of Chinese integrity. Wishing to stress and even exaggerate Russia's commitment to this principle, the American reply on August 28 emphasized this section of the Russian note and expressed great satisfaction with it. In a further attempt verbally to solidify American policy, the reply went on to discuss the "purposes which all the powers have in common . . . which were specifically enumerated in our note to the powers of July 3."[23]

Using the words of the July 3 note itself, the reply to the Russians referred again to the "common" aims of the powers. Even if one granted the Russian contention that the original purposes of the expedition had been achieved, there yet remained the problems enumerated in the last paragraph of the July 3 circular, that of protecting "everywhere in China . . . foreign life and property," guarding legitimate foreign interests, aiding "in preventing the spread of the disorders to other provinces of the Empire" or their recurrence, preserving "Chinese territorial and administrative entity," and safeguarding "for the world the principle of equal and impartial trade with all parts of the Chinese Empire." With these "common" aims in mind, the question was then how to secure them. The United States suggested a joint occupation of Peking under an explicit agreement until such time as the Chinese government was in a position to negotiate new treaties.

Thus far it would seem that the Russian proposal had been, for good and clear reasons, firmly rejected. At the same time the United States was, by this oblique method, attempting to get a definite understanding from all the powers on the nature of continued occupation. The United States tried to make general and binding the policy aims of the July 3

181

circular. Convinced that only a joint occupation of Peking would give the powers any leverage with the Chinese government, and aware that the United States must be part of such an occupation if it wished to have any influence at all in the final settlement, the United States made an effort to elicit an agreement before negotiations with the Chinese began. But the basic indecision of the administration became apparent in the last part of the note: "Any power which determines to withdraw its troops from Peking will necessarily proceed thereafter to protect its interests in China by its own methods, and we think that this would make a general withdrawal expedient. As to the time and manner of withdrawal, we think that, in view of the imperfect knowledge of the military situation . . . the several military commanders at Peking should be instructed to confer and agree together upon the withdrawal . . . as they agreed upon the advance."

With a notable lapse of logic, the *Russian* plan to withdraw was taken as compelling *general* withdrawal under an agreement probably as difficult to reach as one determining the rules of occupation would have been. What America itself would do was not clear, nor did the final section of the note clarify McKinley's intentions: "Unless there is such a general expression by the powers in favor of continued occupation as to modify the views expressed by the Government of Russia and lead to a general agreement for continued occupation, we shall . . . withdraw our troops from Peking after due conference with the other commanders as to the time and manner of withdrawal."[24]

Obscure in all else, the August 28 note clearly reflected the pressures bearing on McKinley. He had to announce some decision as to the disposition of American forces in China. The national press, his own election-conscious party, his personal sense of responsibility, all made the anomalies of the Peking situation more and more difficult to tolerate. Unilateral withdrawal would appear, at home and abroad, as a denial of the very sense of world responsibilities and power that had been an important element in the decision to send troops to China in the first place. Influential missionary and business groups insisted that the United States retain its new position of power in the postwar agreements. America's substantial military force in China was a counter for influence; troop withdrawal might well render American negotiators totally powerless.

Since the note said so many apparently contradictory things, all readings were possible. Captain Alfred Thayer Mahan was so aroused that he wrote a stiff protest to the President. Mahan saw the note as an abandonment of American independence in favor of following Russia, a nation that sought its own ends "with the unscrupulous craft of the Asiatic." Russia sought American cooperation "in order to break up the concert, not by a general disagreement but by the principle that the withdrawal of one neutralises all." In the American press it was also widely interpreted as the first sign of a new alliance with Russia.[25] There were rumors of a rift between Hay and McKinley based on Hay's known anglophilic policy and his continued absence from Washington. Hay quickly denied the stories and did his best to explain the reasoning behind the note. In a long letter to Choate, Hay raged against the stupidity of "our yellows" and, to answer Choate's own doubts about the note, quoted at length from a letter Adee had written Hay earlier that week: "The point is that Russia has invited us and the other powers to no agreement. She does not propose to submit her action to the chances of a vote of the Powers. We on the contrary invite an international accord in the opposite sense, in the hope of persuading Russia to recede, but we are careful to avoid inviting them to join us in an anti-Russian league."

This was deep indeed. Not only did America hope to elicit a definite agreement on occupation or withdrawal but, on another level, there was an effort to force Russia to back down from her unilateral move. Indeed, general withdrawal would rob the Russian action of its unilateral aspect and a general accord on occupation might have forced the Russians to maintain their troops in Peking as well. What is so unusual about the note is that these anti-Russian, or at least mildly antagonistic, moves could be so widely received as a pro-Russian policy shift. Root, defending his draft perhaps, criticized the press harshly: "It appears that diplomacy as viewed from the opposition American view point has but two phases. If we agree with any Power on any subject there is a secret alliance; if we disagree there is a conspiracy to get up a war and foist a soldier on the back of every American laborer."[26]

As the note did not achieve any of its many purposes, the problem of troop withdrawal remained. Russia began a staged retirement to Tientsin and the American troops remained, under indefinite arrangements, quartered in the Temple of Agriculture. The August 28 reply, however, had committed America to some kind of troop reduction and McKinley was very anxious to begin. On September 5 he received a persuasive letter from Senator Morgan of Alabama, a leading member of the Senate Foreign Relations Committee, urging that the troops withdraw to the Philippines and await developments from there. Convinced that Germany, Russia, and Japan were determined to hold on to their concessions and expand them if possible, Morgan insisted that America must avoid being a party to any war brought about by the aggressive ambitions of these countries. Morgan felt the Chinese would be grateful to the United States if our troops were withdrawn—much as Witte reasoned in the Russian case. The Philippines was close enough to the scene of action for a quick return if that were called for. On September 9 McKinley heard from Adna Chaffee, commander of American land forces in China, who likewise urged a withdrawal of troops in order to encourage the Chinese government to return to Peking.

Secretary of War Root also argued for withdrawal—at least as far as Tientsin. Moreover, he felt that Minister Conger and the entire legation staff should accompany the troops to Tientsin. Root was certain no agreement on the terms of continued occupation would be reached. Both sound policy and the commitments made in the August 28 note required withdrawal. Drawing on General Chaffee's dispatches, Root argued that to remain would mean staying for a long period of diplomatic bargaining in which "we will be but a chip floating on the surface of the currents of intrigue and aggression of other Powers." Withdrawal did not mean an abandonment of American interests in China. On the contrary, Root urged a more radical policy than had yet been suggested. Essential American personnel should congregate at coastal points where they could be protected by the navy, and the expeditionary force should be withdrawn to Luzon. If China did not comply with the conditions stated in the July 3 note, Congress should authorize the dispatch of an adequate force to compel proper action by China. In this way, military power and diplomatic objectives would be fully consonant, and America's position much stronger than before.[27]

To this extent, then, the press was correct in its report of a rift within the administration, though the issue did not revolve around an alliance with Russia. Root, supported by the military in China and an important wing of congressional opinion, favored American withdrawal from the concert. Adee and Hay strongly urged the retention of troops in China and the continued exercise of American influence within the concert. Hay was convinced that America would indeed be just a chip in international seas if, at this crucial point, it left the powers to follow their own whims in China. McKinley tended to favor the safer course of withdrawal, but was open to persuasion.

With letters from Morgan, Chaffee and Root in mind McKinley anxiously asked Hay whether it was not best to get out of Peking at the earliest possible moment, in accord with our own declared intention if for no other reason.[28] Further action on withdrawal was halted by a direct request from Conger that the troops remain. In a dispatch dated September 12 Conger informed Hay that the Russians were in the process of withdrawing their troops from Peking and landing fresh forces in Manchuria. There was still no possibility of a restoration of Chinese authority. Conger felt continued allied military occupation of Peking was absolutely essential to future successful negotiations. As the August 28 note had anticipated in its final section, the determination of Russia to withdraw meant that it would "proceed thereafter to protect its interests in China by its own methods." But the conclusion of that premise, that this would make a general withdrawal necessary, was now ruled out by Conger.[29]

Hay cautioned the President against a too literal adherence to his own note. In a telegram from his New Hampshire retreat Hay reminded McKinley that the note did not bind the United States to any specific action. Freedom of alternatives was imperative in the amorphous state of Chinese affairs, Hay felt. He feared the President's legalistic interpretation of the American note. Only if Russia withdrew its *total* force should the United States, by the terms of its note, feel obliged to follow. Conger's wire settled the issue for the moment and Hay took the time to write Adee a long and thoughtful analysis of the confused position of the administration. The furor over the August note was an excellent example of the mindlessness of the American press, Hay wrote. Anti-administration papers had raged against a supposed Anglo-American alliance against Russia as well as against an equally mythical alliance with Russia. "If it turns out that we are *not* led by Russia, we shall be abused as wobbling and vacillating. So there is nothing for it, but to do as near right as we can, and leave the consequences to the newspapers."[30]

Far more distrustful of Russia than either Root or McKinley, Hay argued that by withdrawing completely, in concert with Russia, who had undoubtedly already made arrangements with China, America risked being entirely frozen out of the coming negotiations. Though it was important, for political reasons, to get American troops out at the earliest possible moment, it was even more important not to lose influence in the final negotiations. The basic weakness in America's position was obvious and Hay underlined it for Adee: "We do not want to rob China ourselves, and our public opinion will not permit us to interfere, with an army, to prevent others from robbing her. Besides, we have no army. The talk of the papers about 'our pre-eminent moral position giving us authority to dictate to the world' is mere flap-doodle."

Hay felt the ideal policy would be an alliance with England; but in the "present morbid state of the public mind towards England, that is not to be thought of—and we must look idly on" while England and Germany joined to run things in Peking.[31]

Hay's tone of detached analysis reflects both his physical separation from Washington and his readiness to follow McKinley's lead, offering only a restraining and guiding hand in the interest of greater flexibility. His attachment to an impossible ideal—a firm Anglo-American alliance —reinforced the piecemeal nature of policy making toward China. Hay possessed an over-all policy but knew he could not implement it; in default he satisfied himself with acid comments on the Senate and press.

By the second week in September it became clear that, whatever the true meaning of the August 28 note, the decision to withdraw had been postponed. Editorial reaction was divided and highly partisan. Those opposing withdrawal did so on the grounds that it would be seen by the world as a retreat, it would encourage Chinese intransigence and would create dissension among the powers. The administration could draw little guidance from the press. Newspapers which had supported intervention, favored a continuation of a strong policy. Others, like the *New York Evening Post,* which had reluctantly supported the government so long as the legation was still in danger, were anxious to pull out before anything catastrophic occurred. McKinley's compromise, gradual withdrawal without any broad proclamations on the subject, satisfied almost all requirements—at least until after November 4.[32]

The problem presented by the Russian circular note and the administration's own uneasiness in keeping troops in Peking without a definite program was not so much solved as delayed. The bold attempt to force the powers into an agreement through verbal fiat failed completely. Not only was the chosen instrument, the August 28 note, far too intricate and clause-ridden to make its purpose clear, but England and Germany, for different reasons, were far from ready to reach an agreement on either occupation or withdrawal. Intent on peculiarly Teutonic notions of glory, the kaiser was determined that von Waldersee would still see action in China. British distrust of Russia and the Chinese was so extreme as to make joint withdrawal quite impossible. Nor did the American note offer the British anything definite. Its references to a joint program of occupation were vague and hardly pointed to the kind of alliance that might have interested Salisbury. Indeed, as Hay had feared, during the last week of August, the British had come to a preliminary understanding with Germany on Chinese questions, and a formal alliance was being considered.

American troops were gradually moved from Peking to Tientsin on an independent basis. Enough troops remained to offer a show of power and a lien on influence in the coming peace talks. In the following months, the major problem was not with China but with the other Western powers. Framing the joint list of demands took far longer than it had to rescue the legations. America found itself in constant opposition to Germany and barely supported by either Britain or Japan. On point after point the talks broke down with Russia and America in united opposition to Britain and Germany. This unity, however, was merely a coincidence of views, not a matter of alliance or even identity of interests.[33]

Missionaries

In a confidential note to the head of the *Tribune*'s Washington bureau, Whitelaw Reid remarked that McKinley was following the wishes of the majority of his supporters in the strong steps he had taken to avoid foreign entanglements. But Reid worried that McKinley would have trouble with the "sober church-going element, who have been excited over the murders of missionaries." Any move which appeared to abandon the missionaries would be damaging, for they were as "troublesome and influential" as the Irish.[34]

The Germans had assumed the right to appoint a commander-in-chief because the German minister had been murdered by the Chinese; now the missionaries assumed that their greater suffering entitled them to a dominating position in the settlement of the Boxer crisis. A group of senior missionaries in Peking sent Minister Conger a memorandum demanding that the coming settlement include adequate punishment of the ringleaders, indemnification of native Christians, total educational reform, radical revision of the legal system, full indemnity for the missionaries including allowance for loss of time caused by the Boxers, traveling expenses and provision for a future rise in the price of building material and labor.[35]

Missionary opposition to a lenient policy toward China was expressed freely both publicly and privately. Rev. D. Z. Sheffield, on September 27, wrote a furious letter to the secretary of the American Board, in which he expressed the hope that after the November election McKinley would respond to popular indignation and join the other powers in the work of punishing China. Only Minister Conger escaped the censure of missionaries in China. The fact that he had lived through the siege, which made him unacceptable to the administration, made him a hero to the missionaries. "It is not," Sheffield explained, " 'blood-thirstiness' in missionaries to desire to see further shedding of blood, but an understanding of Chinese character and conditions."[36] On September 7, some four hundred American and British missionaries representing twenty societies met in Shanghai and adopted a strong policy statement. The missionaries urged severe punishment of all high officials involved in the uprising, from the empress dowager down. They insisted upon the restoration of the emperor to real power and foreign supervision of Chinese affairs.[37]

On October 5 American missionaries, merchants, and officials of the Tientsin Provisional Government met to protest the withdrawal of troops from China. Reporting to Judson Smith, the Reverend Henry Porter wrote that the missionaries considered the resolution so important they had sent it to the Associated Press and the *Chicago Record* to ensure widespread publication. Furious that the government had refused to join a punitive expedition against Paoting-fu, the Reverend Mr. Porter scornfully noted the sad contrast between the role America had played during the summer and its current timidity. Only the Germans understood the situation.[38]

When, on December 24, Li Hung-chang's credentials as negotiator were accepted, it was clear that the powers had decided to continue recognizing the empress dowager as the head of the Chinese government. Missionaries in China reacted violently against this decision. Their possible influence on government policy, however, was severely limited when their own home boards refused to second the protests.

The very vengefulness of the missionaries led to a radical change in public sentiment in America. Sympathy began to shift from the victims of the Boxers to the victims of the powers. The mission boards, anxious to capitalize on the crisis in order to increase contributions, were concerned by the alienation of public opinion. Partly as a result of this changed atmosphere at home and partly as a function of distance, missionary societies in America were more detached about the China issue than might have been expected. Anxious to clear missionaries of sole blame for bringing on the upsurge of hate and antiforeignism, the *Missionary Review of the World,* for example, published a studied critique of the Western record in China. J. T. Gracey, an associate editor of the *Review,* defended the missionaries by broadening the attack. The Boxers were the result of a clash between civilizations of two different orders, Gracey argued. Missionaries were a disturbing element, but they were no more destructive than the Western diplomat or merchant. "If the steam-engine is a democrat," Gracey wrote, "so is the missionary." The Presbyterian Board of Foreign Missions, in the *Presbyterian Banner,* placed major blame for the uprising on the brutality of German activities in Shantung and the presumptuous behavior of Roman Catholic missionaries all over China. The editor of the *Missionary Review* looked for meaning in the timing of the Boxer outbreak: it had occurred just at the close of the successful New York Ecumenical Conference; readers were encouraged to wait before judging events and perhaps the outline of divine purpose would become apparent. By October the *Review* thought it could discern the pattern of Providence. It speculated that the uprising was divine punishment for the opium Britain had forced on the Chinese, for the wars and spoliation all the powers had engaged in there. "The Western nations have been preparing their own chastiser," the editorial proclaimed.[39]

In September an interdenominational missionary conference met in New York to consider future mission policy in China. The Presbyterian Board brought to New York eight of its missionaries then on furlough from China and invited the secretaries of all other mission boards in the

189

United States and Canada to attend the conference. Some thirty-two delegates met on September 21 in two separate meetings: board secretaries at one, active missionaries at the other. Both groups were in general agreement. They concluded that the uprising should not discourage future conversion efforts. Mission stations should be reopened in a prudent fashion, the work gradually resumed and, it was hoped, expanded. In view of the increased public interest in China, it was unanimously agreed that a more aggressive policy at home should be adopted. As in the case of past missionary sufferings, they hoped that some good could be extracted from the events of the summer.[40]

A committee was appointed to prepare a joint letter to all American churches reaffirming the missionary obligation and urging a new fund-raising drive. The week of October 28 was to be designated a week of special prayer, a technique that had been used with some success earlier. Withdrawal from China was considered and rejected, for it would mean not only an admission of defeat and a postponement of missionary work but a consequent dimunition of new gifts.[41]

One of the most important decisions the conference reached was that the home societies would not attempt to interfere with government China policy. Some of the board secretaries had received urgent requests from missionaries in China to protest to Washington against the evacuation of troops from Peking and the reinstatement of the empress dowager. Though many delegates had strong opinions about what the government should do, none felt it proper for missionaries to give advice. They were particularly reluctant to admit that missionary work in China might require the help of armed troops. The conference concluded with a plea by the secretary of the Presbyterian Board to all missionaries then in America to take advantage of current public interest and contribute widely to the lay and secular press. All delegates felt that now was the time to make a new call upon the American churches.

One indication of the split that existed between the mission boards and their representatives in China is the effort some board secretaries made to justify the results of the conference to the missionaries. Judson Smith, of the ABCFM, for example, took pains to explain to the Board's noted missionary, Arthur Smith, the self-abnegating attitude of the conference toward the government. The missionary boards must not even *seem* to be trying to influence government policy one way or the other.

190

Individually members of the various boards would of course express themselves and exert such influence as they had. But for the boards to do so as an organized body would only open the way to lay charges of special pleading.[42] Smith felt a natural diffidence toward those who had very nearly died in the missionary cause. He could not muzzle them, yet he knew that the entire missionary enterprise in America was suffering from the exploits of the recently saved missionaries. He could do little more than demand explanations from the most prominent missionaries and pray for their quick return to America. His major worry was the behavior of the Reverend William Ament and his younger assistant, the Reverend E. G. Tewksbury.

Tewksbury and Ament came to the early attention of the *New York Sun*'s special correspondent, Wilbur Chamberlin. In a series of dispatches Chamberlin described the appropriation of palaces by the enterprising missionaries, their personal efforts at indemnifying native Christians, their attempts to force the American military to take a stronger stand against remnant "Boxers." Chamberlin described these events with relish. The piety of the missionaries, in uneasy harmony with their loud cries for vengeance, shocked Chamberlin. His reports created a tremendous stir in America and Judson Smith wrote gentle letter after letter asking Ament and Tewksbury to report. He also asked older missionaries whether the behavior of the two was proper.

Immediately after the relief, many missionaries had appropriated evacuated palaces. Tewksbury took one of Peking's best, an estate consisting of about fifty buildings, fully furnished. Although the palace had been looted several times, some $3,000 worth of silver was left, as well as a quantity of rich furnishings, domestic animals and fine fabrics. A little uncertain as to what Jesus would think of the sack of Peking, Tewksbury comforted himself by reflecting that "God is making up to us for some of the things we have lacked." Following the advice of Minister Conger to use whatever he found in the palace, Tewksbury, like Ament and other missionaries in Peking, auctioned off the contents of the house, as well as loot collected elsewhere in the city, to members of the legations, army officers, and other foreigners. The proceeds were used to care for the Chinese Christian refugees in Peking.[43]

Though the missionaries could make a good case for appropriating property abandoned by pro-Boxer princes in order to feed the starving refugees, they had a somewhat more difficult time when the property could not clearly be attached to the Boxers. Tewksbury's palace, for example, had belonged to a nine year old nobleman. And when the proceeds were used to build new churches and buy desirable tracts of city land not before owned by the church, the refugee aspect of their activities was somewhat diluted. Moreover, the Chinese Christians were, most disturbingly, yielding to terrible temptations. One missionary confessed that many converts had considerably bettered their condition and he was hard pressed to restrain their enthusiasm for advancement. There was some evidence that the refugee population would become permanent, taking advantage of the opportunities available to those Chinese connected with the foreign forces.[44]

The missionaries were most condemned, however, for their unashamed demands for vengeance and their individual indemnification trips into the countryside. Li Hung-chang and other Chinese officials were already acting to indemnify native Christians who had lost property in Boxer towns. In Shantung, Yuan Shih-k'ai had arranged for reparations to be paid locally to both native and foreign Christians. In addition, of course, the missionaries expected to receive reparations from the Chinese government through their respective countries.[45]

Nevertheless, Ament and Tewksbury, occasionally accompanied by soldiers, but more often alone (they found the army disappointingly lenient), made several profitable trips. Operating in the "Chinese manner" they sent a letter to the village elders before they arrived. The elders were advised to appoint two or three responsible men to come to some meeting place and negotiate with the missionaries. This done, the village would be assured security against foreign interference. If no negotiators arrived, the villagers could expect a visit from the troops. The indemnity conditions were as severe as those later arrived at by the powers. A cemetery for the martyred converts must be supplied as well as pensions for widows and orphans. A money compensation was levied for all destroyed property that was to equal one third *above* the value of the property. The indemnity would be distributed by the church and any balance retained by it for suitable missionary use. Furthermore, in any village where disturbances had occurred, a suitable location for a Christian chapel must be provided should the missionaries wish to establish one.[46]

Describing the fruits of his efforts, Tewksbury said he had used the money indemnity to buy rice at a low price to be sold high the following spring. In addition he had invested $1,500 in land near the Marco Polo bridge for use as a summer residence for missionaries.[47]

When Judson Smith questioned the propriety of the missionaries themselves collecting indemnity, Ament and Tewksbury both replied that the Chinese preferred this to being subjected to squeeze practices by the local officials. The missionaries in China thoroughly approved of Ament and Tewksbury, although they did not themselves engage in such indemnity proceedings. Only once did Ament step beyond the limits of what his colleagues thought just. Having to cover a large area, Ament would on occasion dispatch a "native helper" on a collecting mission. One of these men barely escaped arrest by the French for oppressing the villagers under pretence of punishing Boxers. Several missionaries wrote Smith that they did not approve of sending Chinese on indemnity errands without foreign supervision.[48]

The controversy over Ament's activities reached a climax between December, 1900, and March, 1901. On Christmas eve the *New York Sun* published a long attack that condemned Ament through quotations from the good doctor himself. Ament had declared the American policy in China soft and "not as good as the mailed fist of the Germans." The indemnity trips were described, with the unfortunate typographical error that thirteen times, instead of one third above the value of property was assessed. The article caught the attention of Mark Twain who, in the February *North American Review,* published a corruscating essay addressed "To the Person Sitting in Darkness." Twain praised Ament as the "right man in the right place"; a man representing the true "American spirit." "The oldest Americans," Twain added, "are the Pawnees," who never bothered to look for the specific author of a criminal act but punished an entire village instead. Twain wondered at Ament's ability to extract money from pauper peasants for other peoples' crimes for the purpose of propagating the gospel. "Sometimes," Twain said, "an ordained minister sets out to be blasphemous. When this happens, the layman is out of the running; he stands no chance." And Twain posed a question occurring to many Americans in the aftermath of the Boxer crisis. Shall we "go on conferring our Civilization upon the peoples that sit in darkness, or shall we give those poor things a rest?"

"Would it not be prudent to get our Civilizing tools together, and see how much stock is left on hand in the way of Glass Beads and Theology, and Maxim Guns and Hymn Books, and Trade-gin and Torches of Progress and Enlightenment (patent adjustable ones, good to fire villages with on occasion), and balance the books . . . so that we may intelligently decide whether to continue the business or sell out the property and start a new Civilization Scheme on the proceeds?"⁴⁹

Twain's article roused Judson Smith. He wrote a worried letter to Ament in which his desire to be fair to the missionary was almost drowned by his concern for the damage Ament was doing to the cause. He enclosed Twain's article and one that had appeared in the *New York Times* so that Ament would understand "the kind of comment that is made on our missionaries . . . and in particular upon what is supposed to have been your part in this work of extortion and braggadacio." Twain's article had received wide attention in the press and Smith warned that its effect was injurious to the missionary cause.⁵⁰

Until Ament could return to America and defend himself, Smith took on the job for him. On February 7 he wrote an open letter to Twain, which relied heavily on Ament's letters to the Board, and on March 24 he arranged for the *Sun* to print a long defense of his actions by Ament himself. In the latter Ament concluded his article with the philosophic reflection that "right is always right and wrong is always wrong, yet there are many actions that are relatively so."⁵¹

Twain could hardly let the issue lie, and in the April *North American Review* he returned to the battle with a piece on "My Missionary Critics." Answering Smith and Ament's articles point by point, Twain cited evidence to contradict their assertions. On the issue of missionary looting, he quoted a dispatch by a noted *New York Herald* reporter as well as an article by Sir Robert Hart in which a Chinese is overheard to remark: "For a century to come Chinese converts will consider looting and vengeance Christian virtues." While admitting his error on the issue of the amount of punitive indemnity collected, Twain charged that this evaded the major issue: did Ament operate on the basis of collective responsibility? Ament admitted, in his March 24 article, that collections were made indiscriminately, but boasted that many villagers contributed voluntarily. "Does the Board," Twain asked, "really believe that those hunted and harried paupers out there were not only willing to strip themselves to pay Boxer damages . . . but were sentimentally eager to do it?" As for the indemnity being only one third over the value and not thirteen times, Twain compared Ament to the girl who, having been rebuked for bearing an illegitimate child, "excused herself by saying 'But it is such a *little* one.'" The money, Twain insisted, was "tainted" money and could not be purified because it was used to defray "church expenses."

Ament had justified his behavior by citing Chinese custom. So that, Twain noted, as far as the Board was concerned, one of the ten commandments could be revised to read: "Thou shalt not steal—except when it is the custom of the country." Not that he was opposed to "the substitution of pagan customs for Christian, here and there and now and then, when the Christian ones are inconvenient." On the contrary, Twain declared, "I like it and admire it. I do it myself. And I admire the alertness of the Board in watching out for chances to trade Board morals for Chinese morals and get the best of the swap; for I cannot endure those people, they are yellow, and I have never considered yellow becoming." Thus, the punitive indemnity, though smaller than it had first been reported, was admitted, and Chinese morals approved, which, Twain concluded, "leaves me with a closed mouth, though with a pain in my heart."[52] In early May Ament returned and at once allowed himself to be interviewed by the press. Smith immediately asked him not to give any more interviews until he had conferred with the Board. "Such words as 'seize' and 'take' in your explanations . . . give peculiar offense to certain sensitive consciences in this country," Smith warned.[53]

The gap in attitude between the missionaries and both the government and public in America was recognized by the missionaries and expressed in the letters they sent their home boards. The Reverend Mr. Sheffield complained that the American press worried less about China's outrages against foreigners than about foreign abuse of China. Sheffield scorned all the "cheap talk about the United States being 'friendly' with China." A strong hand backed by military force was essential. The Germans were generally praised because, despite their admitted cruelty, they stood for law and order in China and their policies would facilitate missionary work. American policy was severely criticized. The American absence from the Paoting-fu expedition was mourned, for the purpose of that effort was not vengeance but, as the Reverend Henry Porter explained, "simple justice." Ament protested the American policy of treating Asian nations as though they were civilized, and Arthur Smith raged against both the government and the boards for their failure to demand indemnity for Chinese Christians. Mr. Porter informed Judson Smith that he and his colleagues were unanimous in their condemnation of America's soft and irresponsible policy.[54]

Despite the wholesale disapproval of Americans in China, the administration's policy was generally very well received at home. The secretary of the Presbyterian Board of Foreign Missions wrote Hay to express his sympathy with the administration and his admiration for McKinley's Christian statesmanship.[55] And whatever reservations Judson Smith may have had when he wrote to his missionaries, he was equally generous in his expressions of confidence in Hay and McKinley. Given the self-restraint of the mission societies in their decision not to urge specific policy measures on the administration, the missionaries, particularly after the withering attack of Twain and the *New York Sun*'s editorial writers, could not exert much influence on Hay or McKinley. Thus, one source of pressure for a hard line in China was neutralized. From the business interests the pressure was, on the whole, in the direction McKinley wished to go.

On November 1 the editor of a Baltimore newspaper sent Hay a marked copy of his journal, which reported the overwhelming support for McKinley coming from southern businessmen. A hand-written postscript from Hay to McKinley at the bottom of the article noted: "This is a remarkable showing, when we consider that all those electoral votes are to be given to Bryan." In regard to specific policy recommendations, the *New York Times* reported several petitions from businessmen to the State Department urging a rapid settlement of the Boxer dispute, at the expense, if need be, of those seeking punitive justice against the Chinese. One such petition was sent to Hay in mid-November by the leading cotton manufacturers of the South. The signatories, representing $15 million in capital, petitioned Hay to bring affairs in Peking to a speedy conclusion. Since the Boxer outbreak, southern mills had been working only half time. The petitioners asked that the Open Door policy be vigorously maintained and that any action threatening a partition of China be resisted with all possible power. An editorial in the *Journal of the American Asiatic Association* frankly admitted that, in view of the imminent elections, the association had no choice but to avoid pressing the administration on the Boxer issue. Pending McKinley's reelection, members of the association felt it best not to question any aspect of the administration's China policy.[56] Despite this remarkable freedom from organized pressure by the two most significant interest groups, the administration's policy makers were constantly aware of the coming national elections. Meanwhile, they were faced with the delicate negotiations in Peking, with daily diplomatic decisions of a new and unfamiliar complexity.

Despite early conflict with Germany on a series of minor and major points in the Protocol, for about one week in October it seemed to Hay that his Open Door policy was being massively supported by England and Germany. On October 16, an Anglo-German agreement was announced that contained an apparently firm commitment to the Open Door. Closer examination, however, revealed this part of the agreement to be extremely weak. The two powers undertook only to apply the principle to "ports on the rivers and littoral of China," a euphemistic way of excluding Manchuria from the guarantee. A gesture toward Chinese integrity was included: "[England and Germany] will direct their policy towards maintaining undiminished the territorial condition of the Chinese Empire." Germany gained much from the alliance, England little, and China nothing at all. William Langer points out that Germany, through the agreement, had forestalled any attempt by the British to establish themselves in the Yangtze and had secured British assurances on the continuance of the Open Door in that important area, without herself making any commitment to oppose Russian designs.[1]

The fourth clause of the agreement called for the other powers to accept the principles it embodied. Russia took the opportunity to assert the status quo nature of the agreement, underlining the absence of any Manchurian references. Hay tried to expand the meaning of the agreement, though he was quite aware of its true implications. Uncertain at first what the alliance portended, he made inquiries in Berlin and London. Henry Jackson, American ambassador to Germany, reported that the German government had tried to limit the agreement strictly to the Yangtze River valley; the vaguer wording was a compromise to satisfy Great Britain. Jackson warned Hay against thinking the agreement was anti-Russian and Hay concluded that Germany was simply interested in guarding herself against trade discrimination in the Yangtze. Nevertheless, Hay drafted a response to the agreement that deliberately ignored the known reality of the alliance in an attempt to milk its wording for the sake of the Open Door. In a memo to McKinley, Hay wrote that the American note should express gratification to both England and Germany for their firm stand on the Open Door and Chinese integrity.[2]

Some weeks later, however, Hay let out all his irritation in an angry letter to Henry Adams. He was appalled at Germany's vindictiveness in China and was pleased America had been spared the "infamy" of an alliance with her. The Anglo-German agreement, Hay literally reported, was no more than "a horrible practical joke on England." The British seemed unsure *why* they had signed it, though they assured Hay it was harmless enough.[3]

The Anglo-German agreement demonstrated what would be repeatedly evident during the Protocol negotiations: England could not be depended upon to support principles Hay thought the two countries held in common. Hay's attempt to lead the powers in a just settlement that would guarantee American interests and insure American prestige, all without resorting to threats of force, was doomed to failure. Painfully aware of the insufficiency of unarmed morality, Hay was constantly disappointed at his failure, but hardly surprised.

Chang Chih-tung and Liu K'un-yi, on the urging of the foreign powers, had been ordered to join Prince Ch'ing and Li Hung-chang as negotiators for the Chinese. Their main efforts were made in private interviews with selected foreigners during which they walked a very delicate line between loyalty and treason. Frightened by the foreign declaration, made early in the Boxer crisis, that all authorities at Peking, of whatever rank, would be responsible for acts of violence against the legations, they attempted to exonerate the empress dowager of any guilt in the affair. Should the powers depose her and reinstate the emperor, the viceroys faced an impossible dilemma. To support the emperor against his adoptive mother was impossible. They might well be forced to turn against the foreigners and destroy the very policy they had built up with such boldness during the summer. In a discussion with the British consul-general, Chang Chih-tung explained that the emperor could not possibly command the allegiance of the Chinese people if he allowed his mother to be disgraced by the powers. Liu K'un-yi made the same point in an interview with Rockhill. Moreover, like Chang, he attempted to put Tzu-hsi's actions in the most tolerable terms. She was guilty, Liu told Rockhill, only of having listened to bad advisers. At the same time it was essential to the viceroys' safety that the court punish, to the limit of the law, the pro-Boxer officials. Chang and Liu had gone to the very edge of rebellion in supporting the foreigners against the court. If their enemies remained in power, their lives were forfeit. The execution of these men, Liu told Rockhill, was more necessary to him personally than to any of the powers. Wu T'ing-fang likewise insisted upon punishment of the guilty, and Sheng Hsuan-huai advised Consul-General Goodnow that a threat to send a punitive expedition to Sian, coupled with a promise of safe-conduct for the empress dowager and the emperor, might scare the court into returning to Peking to negotiate.[4]

To forestall acceptance of the German proposal, Li Hung-chang had coincided. None of the powers was ready to risk a general uprising for the sake of deposing the empress dowager. All were intent on rooting out the pro-Boxer element in the court. When lower echelon appointments to the Yangtze area, made by the court from Sian in October, placed hostile Manchu officials under Chang and Liu, the foreigners successfully protested and they were removed. As Rockhill repeatedly wrote Hay, the Yangtze viceroys must be backed to the hilt. For at any moment the situation could degenerate disastrously. The Chinese knew, Rockhill informed Hay, that peace and trade were more important to the foreigners than they were to China. Nor had the Boxer disasters been on such a scale as to really shock the country. He saw the possibility of a renewed antiforeign campaign on an even larger scale than the Boxers. The court could afford to wait it out in Sian, indifferent to the slow progress of negotiation in Peking until such time as an antiforeign movement revived under more favorable circumstances. The only course, as Li Hung-chang and his associates urged, was the rapid conclusion of negotiations and the signing of a Protocol.[5]

However, conflict among the powers themselves was almost immediate. Germany demanded that the Chinese hand over to the powers for summary punishment a large number of pro-Boxer high officials. McKinley and Hay were both convinced that punishment of these officials must be left to the Chinese.[6] Only in this way could the authority of the central government be rebuilt. In a pattern that became consistent as disputed points multiplied, the United States firmly opposed German extremism; Russia, more concerned with Manchuria and hoping to gain Chinese friendship, supported the United States; England and Japan tipped the balance now one way, now the other.

To forestall acceptance of the German proposal, Li Hung-chang had persuaded the court to issue an edict variously punishing ten of the most rabid pro-Boxer officials and princes. The edict, issued on September 25, and America's firm opposition to the German position, succeeded in reducing the original demand for punishment by the powers. On October 2, Hay informed McKinley that the Germans considered the September 25 edict the first step in the direction of peace. In addition, the German minister suggested that the powers express their opinion on three points: whether the list proposed by China was satisfactory, if the penalties were sufficient, and how the powers might control their execution. McKinley, constantly concerned with the reestablishment of the central government's authority, urged that the third point be rephrased to read "in what manner are these punishments to be carried out."[7]

Having won this point, Hay allowed himself a moment of self-congratulation in a letter to Henry White:

> The success we had in stopping that first preposterous German movement when the whole world seemed likely to join it, when the entire press of the Continent and a great many on this side were in favor of it, will always be a source of satisfaction to me. The moment we acted the rest of the world paused, and finally came over to our ground; and the German Government, which is generally brutal but seldom silly, recovered its senses, climbed down off its perch and presented another proposition which was exactly in line with our position . . . The great viceroys, to secure whose assistance was our first effort and our first success, have been standing by us splendidly for the last four months. How much longer they can hold their turbulent populations quiet in the face of these constant incitements to disturbance which Germany and Russia are giving is hard to conjecture.[8]

A few days later Hay received a copy of a six point French proposal which, it was hoped, would serve as the basis for the joint note to be presented to China: (1) punishment of the principal culprits, to be designated by the representatives of the powers at Peking; (2) maintenance of the prohibition of imports of arms; (3) equitable indemnities for states, societies, and individuals; (4) establishment of a permanent legation guard at Peking; (5) dismantling of the forts at Taku; (6) military occupation of two or three points on the roads from Tientsin to Taku, which would thus always be open in the event of the legations' wishing to reach the sea, or for forces coming from the sea with the object of proceeding to the capital.[9]

On the whole, Hay found the proposals reasonable. In consultation with McKinley he listed several minor reservations. The arms embargo, he felt, was both unrealistic and undesirable. China could manufacture her own arms; moreover, the United States was anxious to trade in all commodities, including weapons. Congressional approval would be necessary before America could establish a legation guard or join in occupying points on the Taku-Tientsin road. As for the indemnity, Hay seconded an earlier Russian suggestion that the matter be taken to the Hague should the powers prove unable to agree on an "equitable" figure. In accepting the French proposal, Hay suggested that the powers preface it with a pledge to "preserve the territorial integrity and the administrative entity of China." No one responded to this attempt to have the July 3 "integrity" clause and the Open Door note formalized in an international treaty. Rockhill saw the advantage of incorporating an integrity proviso in the final settlement and was hopeful that it could be done.[10] As the weeks of bickering wore on, however, it was increasingly obvious that the powers were uninterested in giving general guarantees to China; their total concern was with getting specific ones from her.

On McKinley's instructions, Hay ordered Conger to work against including unqualified demands for the death penalty in the joint note. On October 27, McKinley wrote Hay that he thought the ministers should first advise the Chinese government that they had evidence of the guilt of the pro-Boxer officials they wished to have executed; only after the Chinese government indicated a definite refusal to punish these men adequately should more severe action on the part of the powers be considered. After months of debate this was accepted.[11]

Through all of Hay's instructions to Conger, one note is constantly sounded: ask only the possible. Thus America successfully convinced the other powers that they should drop their demand for Tung Fu-hsiang's head, as he was then in command of troops surrounding the exiled court in Sian. Yet Rockhill despaired of the negotiations. "The Chinese Commissioners are ready to sign any instrument the Representatives here may see fit to place before them," he angrily wrote Hay in early January, "but these brilliant geniuses have only just made up what they are pleased to call their minds to the form of protocol they want signed." Earlier, Rockhill had suggested that the negotiations with China be held in Europe where the overbearing attitude of the military commanders would not be felt and men of superior quality to those currently negotiating in Peking might take charge. McKinley welcomed the suggestion and proposed such a transfer on January 3 only to have it rejected due to Japanese and German opposition.[12]

A final draft of the joint note, consisting of twelve articles, was ready for signing in early December. Determined to make the note as little like an ultimatum as possible, Hay instructed Conger to substitute for "irrevocable" demands the phrase "absolutely indispensable" conditions. On December 4, Conger wired that the majority preferred the word "irrevocable," though they might be persuaded to change if Hay was adamant. On the seventh Conger received a telegram from Hay ordering him to "sign as majorities." Unwilling to buck the opposition of his colleagues and totally insensitive to Hay's impeccable diction, Conger did not question the strange wording of the telegram and signed the note with the word "irrevocable" included. The telegram, which referred to the draft using the phrase "absolutely indispensable" and not "irrevocable," should have read "sign as transmitted." On December 19, Conger received a blistering wire of inquiry from Hay that insisted on the omission of the word despite the fact that Conger had already signed the note. Advised by Rockhill that further delay was dangerous, Hay acquiesced in the error.[13]

Finally, on December 24, the joint note was handed to the Chinese for consideration. It was clear to Li Hung-chang that there could be no alternative and, on January 16, it was accepted by the Chinese, though the negotiators were instructed to argue it "article by article" in the succeeding conferences.[14]

A Base for the Navy

On July 31, 1900, Rear-Admiral Bradford, chief of the Navy's Bureau of Equipment, had prepared a long memorandum urging the acquisition of a base on the China coast. The military exigencies of the Boxer situation and the political weakness of China combined to convince Secretary of the Navy Long that the time was opportune for such an action. Bradford's memo was sent, over Long's signature, to the State Department. On October 23, Long repeated the request, this time specifying Samsah Bay in Fukien as the desired location. Hay delayed almost a month and then, on November 16, included a "most confidential" paragraph in his general cable of instructions. Conger was instructed to do what he could to secure a naval station at Samsah inlet.[15]

Conger's reply was not encouraging. Given the stress America had placed on China's integrity, it was a most inopportune moment to ask for a piece of territory. Furthermore, the Sino-Japanese nonalienation agreement on Fukien made it necessary to "consult" Japan, who was unlikely to agree. In fact, Conger's siege experience had soured his earlier enthusiasm for an American sphere of interest or large area of territory in China. Nothing could compensate for the burden of ruling in China. "The Chinese can be governed easily in Chinese ways but, I apprehend, would be most difficult to control by Western men or methods. It will be better to continue our declared policy, and try to keep the doors open for our influence and trade in some other way."[16] Referring to Conger's wire, Hay, on December 10, rejected the Navy's demand. He also sent a copy of Conger's wire to the American minister in Japan, asking him to find out "informally and discreetly" if Japan had any objection to United States possession of Samsah Bay. They emphatically did and for the time being the matter was closed.[17]

Hay's transmission of the Navy's request to Conger was hardly an abandonment of the Open Door principles. Indeed, he had never opposed American possession of a coaling station on the China coast. Hay was careful in all his dealings with China not to deny positively that the United States might, in the future, make some territorial demand. At the same time he was fully aware of the bad timing of the Navy's plan. In the midst of what he knew to be difficult and protracted negotiations, the Navy's request, had it become generally known, might well have served as an unwelcome precedent to Germany, Russia and other land-hungry powers. Hay could not well refuse to make inquiries on behalf of the Navy. Conger's negative reply, which Hay could have predicted, served to convince the Navy of what Hay had known all along. There is no evidence that Hay considered entering the "concessions-scramble" at this juncture.

Secretary Long was apparently satisfied with the State Department's refusal, but Bradford was a much harder man to convince.[18] Turning his attention to the possibility of obtaining the Chusan Islands from the British, he asked Long, on January 14, 1901, what steps had been taken to acquire this site for the United States. Long passed the question on to Hay and learned that no progress had been made whatsoever. Under the vigorous direction of Admiral Dewey, now president of the General Board, the Navy continued to press Hay.[19]

Throughout 1901 and 1902 the General Board, in conjunction with Bradford's Bureau of Equipment, kept up a steady pressure on the Department of the Navy to secure a suitable base in China. Periodically, the secretary of the navy would send copies of Bradford's or Dewey's memoranda to Hay. The State Department's consistent response was that the time remained unsuitable for such negotiations. Involved in a nonmilitary effort to restrain Russia in the north and expand Chinese trade through a revised treaty of commerce, Hay could hardly press the Navy's suit. He delayed as best he could without, however, interfering in any private efforts the Navy made.

In the spring of 1902, Vice-Consul Carl Johnson in Amoy, after consulting Captain Sperry of the *New Orleans,* who was then stationed in that port, obtained title to a piece of foreshore property that he thought might interest the Navy. By subleasing his private property to the government it would be possible to avoid protests from other foreign consuls. Johnson cited the example of the French consul at Foochow as a precedent. That gentleman had sublet a small island in Amoy harbor to his government. He urged that the same use be made of his property: "On account of the large traffic between here and the Philippines all Americans in Amoy are anxious that we should acquire something that would give us standing here."[20]

Dewey was not particularly interested in the prestige of the small group of American merchants in Amoy. The survey that accompanied Johnson's letter was more convincing than his argument. At the Navy's request Hay instructed Conger to inquire whether the Chinese would object to the use of the area as a coaling station. They did not. A Navy survey was ordered and Bradford remarked that the foothold his Bureau desired on the China coast might at last be realized in Amoy.[21]

The result of the survey was ambiguous. Rear-Admiral R. D. Evans reported the site suitable for storing coal. However it could not be fortified and Evans was, in principle, opposed to establishing undefendable stations. Uncertain of the General Board's attitude toward "footholds," however, Evans suggested that the property might be useful as a bar to Japanese schemes in Fukien.[22]

Dewey was unenthusiastic. On June 18, 1903, he advised that the Amoy plan be discarded:

> The General Board is opposed to establishing coal depots on the Asiatic station in places that would not be useful as advanced bases in time of war. In time of peace, the ordinary commercial facilities, and the resources of the fleet itself, based upon the Philippines, are sufficient. Even if the right were granted to fortify and defend Amoy, which of course is out of the question, that port would under no probable conditions of the future serve as an advanced base. It is too near our primary base in the Philippines, and too far from the probable theatre of operations.

After three years of surveying the possibilities, the Navy found that the Chusan Islands remained the only desirable location. Dewey urged that efforts now concentrate on this possibility. The British, however, made no move to relinquish their lien on this territory and, unless the present American position on Taiwan be counted, the United States never obtained a coaling station on Chinese soil.[23]

Hay had taken a neutral stand on the issue of the coaling station. Given the political situation in China it would have been difficult, if not impossible, for him to press the Navy's suit. Any peremptory territorial demands would have ruined the image of the United States as an impartial arbiter among greedy contending forces, an image Hay had done much to construct.

The administration attitude toward Russia was extremely pragmatic. Legitimate fear of Russian domination rather than anglophilism moved both Rockhill and Hay. Rockhill distrusted all powers in the Far East.

206

He was never convinced that British and American interests were identical; he was aware that Japan might be the major threat to a balance of powers as early as the Sino-Japanese War and, of course, he recognized that Russia's ambitions would destroy his vision of an Asia in which no one power predominated. Rockhill wanted America to make its position in the Far East so secure it would not have to ally itself with any other power. When this did not materialize, Rockhill worked on the basis of meeting each threat individually as it arose. Hay, to be sure, distrusted and feared Russia. Yet, he too operated on a pragmatic, problem-solving basis. The mere fact that Russia proposed withdrawal from Peking in August 1900, did not make Hay reject the notion. Rather, he fully supported McKinley's efforts to turn the Russian move into something suitable to American purposes—though he might have done it more skillfully himself.[24]

The Boxer upheaval allowed Russian troops to move into Manchuria in force, and by October 1900 Russia was in almost full control of south Manchuria. In November the Tatar general, Tseng Ch'i, opened negotiations for a truce in Manchuria with Admiral Alexeieff, governor-general of the Liaotung Peninsula. Prevented from communicating with either Li Hung-chang or the court, Tseng was forced into signing a highly unfavorable, if temporary, agreement.[25] The document was published by the London *Times* on January 3, 1901, and caused a flurry of excitement in Europe, Japan, and America. Strong protests by Japan and the firm determination of the Chinese not to ratify the Tseng-Alexeieff agreement finally resulted in a Russian retreat. Witte was convinced that little could be gained from insisting on what was, after all, only a modus vivendi between two military commanders. The center of negotiations then shifted to St. Petersburg and the intensity of Russian pressure was increased. Yang Ju, Chinese minister to Russia, was presented with a new list of demands modeled closely on the Tseng-Alexeieff agreement.

Skillful fencing by the Chinese had won them one advantage—time. By the end of January 1901, the Protocol in Peking had been signed. Detailed negotiations remained and foreign troops still occupied key areas of the country. Still, with the other European powers united, at least temporarily, in joint negotiations with China, the Chinese could hope to appeal for help against Russian demands in Manchuria.

On February 16, the Russians placed twelve demands before Yang

Ju. Manchuria was to be returned to China as an act of the czar's "friendly feeling" for China and the "hostile acts" committed against Russians in that area would be forgiven. However, Russia would retain extensive rights of protection over its railroad property in Manchuria; China could not, without prior Russian approval, grant mining or railroad privileges to any other power in Manchuria or Mongolia nor could China build railroads in these areas herself; permission to build the South Manchurian line was demanded and a catch-all clause stated that the claims of the China Eastern Railway Company for reparations could be "commuted for other privileges."[26]

Without precise knowledge of the new demands but certain of their nature, Japan immediately attempted to gain British support for a strong joint protest. At Japan's suggestion, Britain, Germany, America, Austria, and Italy all informed China of their firm disapproval. The Japanese minister to Peking pointedly remarked that the Manchurian arrangement would be taken as a precedent by other powers leading, inevitably, to the total partition of China.

The key Chinese viceroys were divided on what course to follow. Both Liu K'un-yi and Chang Chih-tung distrusted Russia and Li Hung-Chang more than they did Japan and England. They felt an appeal to the powers for help against Russia was the only way to ensure the return of Manchuria, more or less intact, to China. Li, on the other hand, felt that Manchuria could be restored only through an agreement with Russia; that the other powers would not support China forcefully enough, leaving her, in a crisis, to deal with an angry and more demanding Russia. Indeed, it was easier for the powers to pressure China than Russia, though they well knew that China, unaided, was quite incapable of resisting Russian demands if they were backed by force.[27]

The court used both approaches. Yang Ju was instructed to continue negotiations with Russia, working for modifications in the latest Russian proposal. At the same time Liu K'un-yi and Chang Chih-tung were ordered to ask the other powers to intervene on China's behalf. Although the response of the powers was not encouraging, the court continued to reject Li Hung-chang's advice to sign the treaty in its original form. Yang Ju was instructed to continue urging a reduction in the terms. The court's stand was successful to a limited extent. The treaty was significantly modified, though it still retained extensive rights for Russia in

Manchuria. However, it now took the form of an ultimatum. Lamsdorff indicated that this was the most China could hope to gain. If the treaty were not signed in fifteen days, negotiations would be broken and Russian troops would continue to occupy Manchuria indefinitely.

Chang Chih-tung cabled Yang Ju advising him to ignore the Russian ultimatum. The treaty, he argued, would serve as a precedent for the total dismemberment of China. Offending the Russians might mean the loss of Manchuria but signing would alienate the other powers and endanger all the provinces. Yang Ju was not entirely convinced. In a telegram to Li Hung-chang he reflected: "I wonder whether the other Powers would intervene against Russia or would follow Russia's example and seize our territory. Upon this hinges our preservation or extinction."[28]

Chang Chih-tung's reasoning was supported by other high Chinese officials including Yuan Shih-k'ai and Sheng Hsuan-huai. Moreover foreign consuls in the Yangtze ports were in unanimous agreement that signing the treaty would result in the immediate partition of the country. Their logic does not stand examination. However, China was accustomed to arguments which involved country *A* kicking her twice if she did not firmly resist the one kick country *B* was intent on administering. As the Japanese consul-general in Shanghai put it, the agreement violated China's treaties with the other powers who, in order to protect their rights and to maintain the principle of equal opportunity, would seize Chinese territory.[29] It was a strange, but not impossible, reading of the Open Door.

Hay sent a strong note of protest against the Russian treaty to Wu T'ing-fang. He stressed the injustice of separate negotiations in particular:

> The preservation of the territorial integrity of China having been recognized by all the Powers now engaged in joint negotiations . . . it is evidently advantageous to China to continue the present international understanding upon this subject. It would be therefore unwise and dangerous in the extreme for China to make any arrangement or to consider any proposition of a private nature involving the surrender of territory or financial obligations by convention with any particular power, and the Government of the United States, aiming solely at the preservation of China from the

danger indicated and the conservation of the largest and most beneficial relations between the Empire and other countries . . . and in a pure and friendly spirit . . . desires to express its sense of the impropriety, inexpediency and even extreme danger to the interest of China of considering any private territorial or financial arrangements, at least without the full knowledge and approval of all the Powers now engaged in negotiations.[30]

Not satisfied with this, Hay instructed the consuls in Nanking and Hankow to confer at once with Liu K'un-yi and Chang Chih-tung and stress the depth of America's conviction that a private Sino-Russian deal would seriously injure China.[31]

The court weighed the dangers and, fearing everything equally, delayed coming to any decision.[32] There was an element of self-serving in the advice of the viceroys who urged the court to risk losing Manchuria to Russia by defying her rather than acquiesce to a treaty that set such dangerous precedents for their own provinces. Li Hung-chang's interest in Manchuria was deep and consistent throughout his long career. Certain that Russia would detach Manchuria entirely if China continued to resist an arrangement which would leave her with at least nominal sovereignty, Li warned against trusting the other powers to intervene against Russia. On the other hand, Chang Chih-tung, with great imagination, urged the court to use the Open Door for Chinese purposes. Combining, with great art, the traditional Chinese notions of treating all barbarians equally and using one barbarian to fight the other, Chang's policy suggestions modernized both. The Chinese Open Door could become a weapon of considerable defensive power. Chang outlined a three-part policy in early March. China should ask England, Japan, the United States, and Germany to persuade Russia to postpone negotiations for a time. Second, the entire question should be submitted to the joint arbitration of the powers. Finally, China should promise to open Manchuria to international trade under conditions of equal opportunity for all in concessions and commerce in return for positive aid in resisting Russian demands for exclusive privileges in that area. In this way, all the powers would have a specific economic interest in Manchuria that would, judging from their past behavior, ensure their forceful action in defense of their privileges. The court chose a middle course. Ministers abroad were instructed to ask the governments to which they were accredited to urge Russia to delay the negotiations. In addition they were, in strict confidence, to promise that Manchuria would be open to foreign trade.

On March 23 Yang Ju was ordered not to sign the treaty and, two days later, the court instructed Li Hung-chang to urge the Russians to submit the Manchurian problem "to arbitration by the United States or the Netherlands." Li was also to ask the Russians to delay negotiating a separate treaty until "after the conclusion of the collective agreement with the Powers." Liu K'un-yi, responding to Hay's protest against concluding an agreement "without the full knowledge and approval" of the other powers, discreetly distributed copies of the treaty to the various foreign consuls on April 1. Japan's reaction was immediate and violent. It was at once made clear to both Germany and England that Japan was ready to go to war on the Manchurian question if it could be certain of European support, or at least benevolent neutrality.[33]

As China continued to refuse to sign and Russia could not be sure Japan would peacefully accept the agreement even if China did sign, the Russian government finally backed down.

Through a rare exercise of will the Chinese government had succeeded in forcing the Russians to withdraw from an advanced position. However, Russian troops remained in Manchuria, and the Chinese victory amounted only to a bare maintenance of the status quo ante. Lamsdorff now agreed to evacuate the three provinces on two conditions: that order be restored (a state which Russia would define) and that the actions of the other powers "not serve as obstacles to this withdrawal."[34]

However, the basic policy decision remained. Unless China submitted the entire question to the joint arbitration of the powers, the latter had no basis for intervention. The court's present policy merely stalled the Russians, it was hardly a solution. The only alternative to joint arbitration (which would certainly enrage Russia and might be rejected by the powers, leaving China to face Russia alone) was the unilateral opening of Manchuria. In late March and again in July, Liu K'un-yi and Ching Chih-tung memorialized the court to take this decisive step. Liu argued that the best policy was to use the trade of other countries to counterbalance Russia. With some reason the court pointed out that China had no control over Manchuria so long as Russian troops occupied it. To open an area China did not really possess was meaningless and could only lead to a complete breakdown in negotiations with Russia. Whatever the other powers *said,* they were unlikely to forcibly restrain Russia for China's sake. To hold Russia off until the negotiations in Peking were concluded, was too great a gain to be risked.

For the time being, the situation in Manchuria was stabilized. The effects of Russian occupation in Manchuria, however, had already made themselves felt on American trade. Hay was increasingly disturbed by the reports of the vigorous consul in Newchwang, Henry Miller. In October 1901 Miller asked Conger to arrange for a gunboat to spend the winter anchored at Newchwang. "Chinese merchants and businessmen have more consideration and respect for countries represented by their Navy . . . This feature of Chinese sentiment is to my mind undervalued generally by our country . . . The Chinese merchants cannot understand why there has not been a U.S. gunboat in this river for more than a year past when our imports here are greater than that of any other country, and their conclusion is that the United States will not protect its trade interests."

Rear-Admiral Remey disapproved of any American military demonstration unless the government intended to contest Russian occupation. The few American citizens in Newchwang had never been more secure, though Remey admitted their trade might suffer for want of an American military presence. Hay ignored the admiral's advice and orally requested Secretary of the Navy Long to take immediate steps to winter a ship at Newchwang. The following spring Miller expressed his satisfaction with the effect the gunboat *Vicksburg* had had. The Chinese had shown a new interest in the possibility of trade with Americans. The gunboat was symbol of the determination of the United States to maintain its rights in Manchuria.[35]

Hay was ready to take limited action, such as sending a gunboat to Newchwang, to encourage and protect American trade interests in Manchuria. In the long run, however, it was not in the government's power to maintain America's trade position in Manchuria; Hay could work to keep the door open, but he was dependent on the interest and ambition of the business community to make the effort worth while.[36]

212

The Protocol

In a letter to Whitelaw Reid written before the protracted protocol negotiations had really gotten underway, Hay described the aims of the United States in China: "I take it you agree with us that we are to limit as far as possible our military operations in China, to withdraw our troops at the earliest possible day consistent with our obligations, and in the final adjustment to do everything we can for the integrity and reform of China, and to hold on like grim death to the open door."[37] The tone of acknowledged limitation that runs through Hay's letters of this period is echoed in Rockhill's letters from Peking on the progress of negotiations. From January 1901, when the Chinese accepted the joint note, till the following September, when the protocol was finally signed, Rockhill fought a losing battle against the excessive, destructive demands of the other powers. In May 1901, he summed up American progress in a letter to Hay. The harshness of initial demands had been modified. The terms remained onerous, Rockhill granted, but without American interference they would have been worse.

Rockhill noted that on two occasions American efforts had restrained uncalled-for German military expeditions; that the construction of an international fortress adjacent to the gate of the imperial palace had been abandoned due to American efforts; and that some innocent men had been kept off the death list prepared with such diligence by the ministers. He added that: "The U.S. has been able to exercise a moderating influence on the councils of the Powers, while maintaining the concert which, clumsy as it undoubtedly is, is still, so long as it exists, a tolerable guarantee of the maintenance of Chinese integrity and of equal trade privileges for all the world."[38]

Certainly moderation had been one of Hay's objectives. In repeated instructions to Rockhill and Conger, however, he mentioned several specific items he hoped would be included in a final settlement. These included the establishment of a ministry of foreign affairs to replace the Tsungli yamen, posthumous honors to those Chinese officials who had been executed for their proforeign views during the Boxer era, the protection of American merchants and missionaries, the naming of Peking as a treaty "port," revision of the commercial treaty with China, and an equitable indemnity.[39]

No reform of the missionary position was incorporated in the final

Protocol. In mid-September 1901, Chang Chih-tung presented a proposal for missionary control that attempted to limit the scope and influence of missionary work. Conger, returned from home leave and again minister to Peking, felt that the status quo ante was preferable to reform. Rockhill noted on the bottom of Conger's dispatch that the missionary question was in a hopeless tangle. Chang Chih-tung asserted that missionaries had no official rank, while the Roman Catholic priests claimed, on the basis of an 1899 edict that established equivalencies between the Catholic hierarchy and Chinese officialdom, that they did. "The Catholics," Rockhill noted, "insist upon this right; the Protestants exercise it but insist on being considered less meddlesome than the Catholics. On every point they are at loggerheads . . . That our Protestant missionaries require restraining in their ardor there can be no doubt. How is it going to be done? The Lord only knows."[40]

The missionary interest, with the fillip of martyrdom and sacrifice, remained powerful enough to resist Chinese moves to control it. While falling far short of missionary expectations, the Protocol did provide for severe punishments in case of antiforeign riots. For their sufferings during the crisis American missionary societies and individuals received a total of $1,500,000.[41]

Several other points in Hay's instructions were fully met by the Protocol. The Tsungli yamen was replaced by a Ministry of Foreign Affairs with precedence over the other departments in the government; although not part of the Protocol, posthumous honors were eventually accorded to the anti-Boxer ministers; and provision was made for the negotiation of new commercial treaties.[42]

It was hoped, by Rockhill and Hay, that such revision could be carried on jointly with Great Britain with the further aim of effecting a general fiscal reform. The Open Door would be applied to all of China (by implication Manchuria was thus specifically included). Great Britain had no desire, however, to tie its revision to American interests, and by the end of October 1901, had appointed its own commissioners to negotiate separately with China.[43]

The negotiation of the American treaty, signed in October 1903, became intricately involved in the continued problem of Russia's presence in Manchuria. In the years following the signing of the Protocol, Hay maneuvered between two impossibilities: a frank confrontation with

Russia, using the threat of force, or an abandonment of the Open Door with respect to Manchuria. His aim was to secure the maximum trade advantages for the United States with the minimum risk of a showdown with Russia and its attendant humiliations if forced to back down. Thus Hay wrote Roosevelt that America must recognize Russia's exceptional position in north China. In this regard Hay granted Russia no more than he had already granted to Germany in Shantung, Japan in Fukien, and France in southwest China. Reluctantly but realistically Hay recapitulated America's limited aims in north China: "What we have been working for two years to accomplish, and what we have at last accomplished, if assurances are to count for anything, is that, no matter what happens eventually in northern China and Manchuria, the U.S. will not be placed in any worse position than while the country was under the unquestioned domination of China."[44]

The star-crossed history of the American China Development Company continued to plague American policy makers. In early 1901 a dispute between F. W. Whitridge, attorney for the company, and Wu T'ing-fang, Chinese minister to Washington, grew to major proportions. In January, Whitridge requested that the company's contract be amended so as to include a "most-favored-nation clause." "The Government of China undertakes and agrees to grant to the American China Development Company all the advantages whatsoever which it may hereafter grant to similar enterprises . . . in respect to rates of interest, price of the issue of bonds, and other obligations, the division of profits, the length of the concession . . . and any other advantages whatever."

The request was presumptuous enough, but in view of the fact that, in violation of the contract as it was understood by the Chinese, the company was no longer controlled by Americans, Whitridge was virtually begging for trouble. Wu noted that he had had no communication from the company for some time and before answering Whitridge's request he demanded to be informed on the state of the company's stock, which, he had heard, was no longer in American hands. Instead of placating Wu, Whitridge's answer was bound to inflame him: "I have not sent you any information as to the affairs of the company, because I do not think that anything has occurred in its affairs which concerns you, your Government, or any other person except its stockholders . . . I am happy to be able to tell you that the American China Development Company has not sold out to a Belgian or any other foreign or domestic syndicate."

Although this was patently false and Hay, through Rockhill, must have been aware of the fact, the government decided to back the company against the Chinese government in this and subsequent contract struggles.[45]

The issue of the return to American control of the old concession in Tientsin is another example of the attempt made by the administration to maintain its enhanced position in China even at the expense of the new store of goodwill it felt it had gained from the Chinese government during the Protocol struggle.

In 1861, along with Great Britain and France, America had been granted a concession in the city of Tientsin. Because of the lack of a sufficient number of American residents to make use of it, the concession had been virtually abandoned although no formal return to China was made. Shortly after the fall of Tientsin, the Russians took over about two miles of territory as a "concession." The Russians informed the other powers that this area was Russian "by right of conquest." As a direct consequence of this every other nation expanded its concession at Tientsin or, if they had never had one before, claimed one.[46]

Minister Conger strongly urged that the United States resume control over the 1861 concession. Although it took both money and citizens to operate a concession and, Conger admitted, America lacked both, in the interests of United States prestige, Conger felt the government should insist on a concession. However, as two prominent Chinese companies now occupied the land involved, the Chinese were understandably reluctant to comply. On October 11, 1901, Conger reported that his negotiations with Li Hung-chang had come to a standstill. Li declared that he was anxious to please the United States and would consent to ousting the Chinese involved if Hay was adamant, but he was obviously most reluctant to do so.[47]

In a memorandum on Conger's dispatch, Rockhill pointed out that no American was living in the area. "Of course," Rockhill continued, "the abandonment of our claim may lead to some adverse comment on the part of some Americans and we may 'lose face' a little, but I think that even this is better than a great big white elephant." It was decided that a provisional extension of the British concession to include the old American concession (and specifically reserving American commercial and residential rights) would be acceptable. However it was considered important to keep open the possibility of eventual recovery of American interests. Thus, while deciding not to press the matter, the administration nevertheless made clear its desire not to lose face—even a little.[48]

The end of the Boxer affair marked a new relationship between the United States and China. In its first encounter with difficult multipower negotiations, the United States had made its weight felt on the side of moderation, winning some, but not all of its points. The gain in power and influence, however, would have to be maintained at this new level to be effective. In its struggle with Russia, the United States would compromise the principles of the Open Door, attempting to gain without force of arms what, perhaps, only force could have secured. As China changed, fighting for the semblance of nationhood, America would come into conflict with her as well. For the Open Door, like the Monroe Doctrine, was merely an expression of American economic and political self-interest. Insofar as China interfered with America's attempt to neutralize the forces in the Far East and the increase of American influence there (as in the anti-American boycott of 1905), the United States would stand against her as well.

Curiously enough, the Open Door policy, often considered so uniquely American, was becoming an element in Chinese diplomacy as well. If its vague tenets suited the American fondness for "fair play and no favor," it was also amenable to Chinese notions of treating all barbarians with equal hospitality. Used as a counterbalance against powers attempting to monopolize privileges in China, it was consonant with the venerable Chinese policy of setting barbarians against each other to China's advantage—or at least safety. In a provocative study, Kosaka Masataka has pointed out that, for China, the Open Door was a means of maintaining the integrity of China, while for America, the integrity of China was a means of maintaining the Open Door.

Chang Chih-tung urged the court to open ports to trade on a quid pro quo basis. In Manchuria, a general opening would be useful insofar as it gave other powers a material reason for opposing Russian encroachment. So long as the powers felt they must pressure China for every trade concession, they could hardly unite to oppose a third party. But if China were to *join* those powers more interested in trade than territory, there was a chance for success. China might then become a participant in an Anglo-Japanese alliance, for example, instead of the object of such an alliance. Indeed, Chang Chih-tung explained his policy in words that could have been used by Rockhill with reference to American goals in China. The principle of Chinese diplomacy was to treat all nations equally without discrimination. Foreign operation of Chinese mines was not necessarily harmful. However, no province should exclusively belong to one country.[49]

Unfortunately it was too late. Several provinces were already controlled by one power. So long as China could not fight to prevent one power from attaining predominance, and so long as America would not back a similar aim by force of arms, the Open Door would mean only the right of all to exploit China with equal ferocity.

ten   Conclusion

Much of American history, diplomatic and internal, can be analyzed in terms of a search for unity, for defined, comprehensible nationhood. In quite another context, David Riesman has written of a situation in which, as local allegiances break down, "*national* unity is bought at the price of chauvinism."[1] The tensions of late nineteenth-century America gave rise to the need to achieve national unity, and few were loathe to pay the price of chauvinism. A sense of one's own nation is most easily grasped in terms of its current enemy. A world divided into blocs clearly labelled friend and foe is, perhaps, the simplest path to patriotism. Those Americans who tried to understand the position of their country as it emerged victorious from the Spanish-American War leaned increasingly to a bipolar analysis. There was America, sometimes seen standing alone against the world, sometimes paired with Great Britain, and there was Russia and her stalwarts. In between lay vast areas of unexploited territory over which warfare, diplomatic or military, must be waged. The post-1898 theorizing of men like A. T. Mahan, Brooks Adams, Charles Conant and W. W. Rockhill reveals the changed perspective brought about by the Spanish-American War and America's new role in Asia. Their writings at the turn of the century offer a fascinating picture of how these influential men saw the world in which they lived.

After the Spanish-American War, A. T. Mahan wrote more and more specifically about the coming struggle in Asia. In a series of articles dealing with the lessons that the war had taught America, Mahan described an inevitable confrontation between the United States and Russia: "The quiet, superficially peaceful progress with which Russia was successfully advancing her boundaries in Asia . . . was suddenly confronted with the appearance of the United States in the Philippines."[2] Like the cavalry swooping down to save a threatened frontier outpost, America's entrance into Asia, in Mahan's view, was a move to save civilization from the northern menace.

Although the importance of Asia and its control was always clear to Mahan, it was not until 1900 that he devoted serious, concentrated attention to it. Mahan recognized the changed nature of expansionist thinking since 1898. Prior to the Spanish-American War, most expansionists saw Hawaii as a defensive position, not as a stepping-stone. After the war, Hawaii became a stop on the way to Asia, and not an end itself. At the same time conditions in Asia had changed, compelling a "readjustment of ideas, as well as national policies and affiliations." With Asia as the focus of national rivalries, Mahan saw the world split between the sea powers and the land powers—a dichotomy natural to his oceanic way of thinking. The divisions were not altogether exclusive, however. Russia and France, as the land powers, stood on one side; on the other Great Britain, Japan, and the United States. But Mahan had trouble with Germany. Clearly on her way to "sea power" status, Mahan was not sure which way Germany would lean.[3] (One of the characteristics of this period was the uncertainty as to who America's enemies really were—one solution was to create imaginary enemies who would do for the time being.)

Mahan always spoke of China as an *object* to be acted *upon,* not as an autonomous nation whose actions and aspirations had to be taken into account in policy calculations. Since dispossession of China's large population and subsequent colonization by the sea powers was out of the question, it was necessary to "develop China through the Chinese." To do so, certain basic changes were necessary. First, the capital of China must be moved from Peking, where it fell under the shadow of Russia, to the Yangtze River Valley. This area would then become "the core around which to develop a new China." If this were not feasible, then Mahan suggested a more radical policy. "It may perhaps be for the welfare of humanity that the Chinese people and territory should undergo a period of political division, like that of Germany anterior to the French Revolution." Though the Chinese resembled "sheep without a shepherd" they could not be treated as "sheep to be owned." The implied, but unstated, corollary was that they must be treated as sheep to be led. Mahan, a moral man with a host of absolute values to guide his political thinking, recognized the theory of natural rights. But in the case of "inefficient" countries, these natural rights suffered a sea change. No people were entitled automatically to control the country in which they and their ancestors had lived. For countries like China the relevant natural right was that of humanity in general. Political fitness, and the ability to administer a country "in such a manner as to insure the natural right of the world at large that resources should not be left idle" alone gave a people the right to rule itself.[4]

Because it was right, as well as politically feasible, for China to be run by external powers, the major question was which powers and how they should operate. Mahan's ideal was a balance of contending forces in which no one country would predominate. One way to achieve such an equilibrium would be for China to be divided according to the area each external power controlled. Prey to his own version of the yellow peril, Mahan was frightened by the vision of a powerful united China. Partition *before* China developed into a modern nation-state would therefore be essential. Just as the development of China should not outrun the requirements of "healthy growth," so "kindliness" and "conditions of equity" toward the Chinese people must be maintained by the presence of armed force and by "just self-assertion, taking the shape of insistence upon equality of opportunity."[5]

The policy toward China which Mahan proposed was two-pronged: (1) the prevention of any one country from attaining preponderant influence over China; and (2) the insistence upon "an open door for commodities and ideas." The latter, however, must be supported by force whenever necessary and not left to the workings of "moral influence."[6]

An American and a Christian, Mahan was also concerned with the state of China's soul. He warned that one day China might well acquire power commensurate with her mass and would then demand her share of the world's goods. While there was still time, therefore, it was essential to instill Christian values so that "time shall have been secured for them [the Chinese] to absorb the ideals which in ourselves are the result of centuries of Christian increment."[7] Otherwise the world might one day be faced with a dangerous, materialistic, and hugely powerful country unrestrained by either God or the Constitution.

The Spanish-American War influenced Brooks Adams as well. It clarified, for him, what America must do to prevent that stagnation which, as his law of civilization and decay had demonstrated, was the certain fate of the inactive power. In *America's Economic Supremacy*, published in 1900, Adams spelled out the meaning of his law for America's future. He saw the world polarized into two opposing blocs—Russia, and with her France and Germany, against America and England. The battlefield for the inevitable, titanic struggle would be China. In a period of increasing economic competition, to stand still was to decline while expansion meant life. "China is the only region which now promises almost boundless possibilities of absorption." If America would only ally herself with Britain, the center of trade would remain safely in the West, and human society "would be absolutely dominated by a vast combination of peoples whose right wing would rest upon the British Isles, whose left would overhang the middle provinces of China, whose center would approach the Pacific, and who would encompass the Indian Ocean as though it were a lake." But the situation was critical. America's domestic market could no longer absorb her industrial surplus. If she did not sell abroad in an open market, America would suffer gluts and depressions as never before.[8]

In the *Law of Civilization and Decay* Adams had described all civilizations as following the same line of development—from dispersion through concentration to stagnation and ultimate dispersion once more. But now he differentiated between two paths that concentration had historically followed.[9] One was through individual activity, the other through collectivism. In general, he felt, Eastern races had tended toward collectivity, the West toward individual effort. The Anglo-Saxon was the most "individual of races and it reached high fortune under conditions which fostered individuality to a supreme degree." Yet it had operated most effectively in a world still open to extensive expansion, and when steam had just begun to make communication more rapid. The world had changed; no longer were the pioneer qualities those that commanded success. Now it was evident that, "other things being equal, the administration of the largest mass is the cheapest." And in a period of intense economic competition, that unit which operated most cheaply and efficiently would undersell its rivals. American trusts illustrated Adams' point nicely, and he was convinced that as it was in domestic competition so it would be internationally. "But the concentration whose result is an elimination of waste," Adams wrote, "is nothing but a movement towards collectivism, and the relative rise of the people who excel in collective methods, has been accordingly contemporaneous with the advent of the great trusts in the West."[10]

The collectivizing countries were Russia and Prussia, not England and America. The United States was a wasteful country with an anachronistic administration. Its foreign service was helpless—underpaid, lacking in all intelligence services. Its army had no general staff; its Treasury Department was without adequate banking facilities. Until the end of the nineteenth century America had been able to operate in its wasteful fashion because a liberal margin of profit enabled intense individual efforts to counterbalance waste and inefficiency. But those days were gone. Either America must expand, or it must resign itself to a stationary period during which competition would eventually force it to abandon its individualistic system for a collective one. "But if we are not prepared to reduce our scale of life to the German or perhaps the Russian standard, if we are not prepared to accept the collective methods of administration . . . we must be prepared to fight our adversary, and we must arm in earnest." The enemy was known and formidable. Germany and Russia in combination would shut America out of every market they could. Indeed, were it not for Great Britain's firm stand they might well have allied with Spain and crippled the United States permanently during the war. Should France, Germany, and Russia—the three land powers —combine to occupy the Chinese interior and then exclude our goods, America would be forced to collectivize or die. Either the great trusts would amalgamate and take control of the government, or the central corporation, the government, would absorb the trusts. In either event "the Eastern and Western continents would be competing for the most perfect system of State socialism."[11]

Thus, only by expanding into Asia could America hope to preserve her cherished system of free enterprise. And by expanding she would not merely preserve the status quo but win an empire besides. With Manila as a base and China kept open to American commerce, by force if necessary, there was nothing to prevent the establishment of an empire rivaling Rome, London, or Constantinople in wealth and power.[12] The organization, civil and military, of such an empire would be the task of the next half-century.

Adams never really faced the domestic consequences of his proposals. As a social scientist he claimed only to state the alternatives. America must expand or she would be forced to contract her economy, collectivize it, and with a living standard similar to Russia's, face world competition on an entirely new basis. If she expanded into Asia and thus obtained markets for her industrial surplus, perhaps collectivization would not be necessary. Yet his own logic forced him to admit that the organizational pattern of the business trust was the cheapest and most economical. And in a period of extreme international economic competition only the cheapest, most efficient nation could hope to survive. Like so many progressives, he feared the economic power of the trusts, recognized their value, and did not know how to utilize them without allowing the government to fall into the hands of a powerful minority ruling for personal profit. All his conclusions imply this problem, but he neither states the issue clearly nor attempts to solve it.[13] Rather, he retreats to a plane of scientific objectivity wherein he sees what America must do if it is to continue as a powerful state and urgently pleads that it do so at once. Nor does the vision of an imperial America displease him. If the United States blocked Russian domination of North China: "Our geographical position, our wealth, and our energy preeminently fit us to enter upon the development of Eastern Asia, and to reduce it to a part of our economic system . . . The Chinese question must, therefore, be accepted as the great problem of the future, as a problem from which there can be no escape; and as these great struggles for supremacy sometimes involve an appeal to force, safety lies in being armed and organized against all emergencies."[14]

The Boxer uprising and its aftermath convinced Adams that his analysis of the world scene was correct. Moreover, the role America had played in China seemed a fulfillment of his prophecy. America was the New Empire. In a book of that title published in 1902, Adams completely abandoned his 1896 objections to the trusts and welcomed them as the instruments of American power. "Institutions are good which lead to success in competition, and are bad when they hinder . . . Nature eliminates those who do not satisfy her requirements, and from Nature's decree there is no appeal." Intellectual flexibility and a single standard of judgment, that of utility, must guide America in the future.[15]

Examining the events of the last half-century, Adams was convinced that "the seat of Empire" had passed from Europe to the United States. The rapid, confusing, and catastrophic events in the Far East were explicable in terms of the universal struggle for economic survival. The new wave of social energy, as Adams saw it, was passing from the East, which

Russia represented, to the West. In the Far East, Japan, which had rapidly assimilated Western civilization, represented Western influence —"therefore the kernel of the catastrophe impending in the Orient is the struggle for survival between Russia and Japan." Adams saw the coal and iron beds of Shansi and Honan as possessing the key to the future. Moved by a common urgency, the European nations threw themselves upon China in the years following the Sino-Japanese War, furiously contesting for control of Shansi. But they were too late, for, with the Spanish-American War, America had taken a territorial stand in Asia.[16]

In Adams' view 1894 had been the decisive year. China's sorry fight had shown the world just how weak she was. Japan's major bid for a share in the spoils had strengthened the determination of Germany and Russia to exclude Japan and divide China before it was too late. American passivity had fooled the land powers into thinking she was weak and indifferent. But the result of Europe's aggressive policy toward China was only to provoke the Chinese to rebel and the Boxers had shocked a world unaware that Chinese could fight back. Only Japan and America were prepared for what happened, and they were united in their determination to preserve China's integrity at all costs. According to Adams, American and Japanese troops alone acted effectively during the Boxer crisis. Hay's circular note of July 3, 1900, was, in Adams' eyes, an ingenious diplomatic stroke whereby the United States took a definitive lead in Asian politics. Still the Far Eastern situation remained unstable. Two rival economic systems—marine and land—continued to confront each other, competing for the prize of domination in Asia and the world.[17]

In the last pages of *The New Empire*, Adams examines the economic, political, and military strengths of the powers and concludes that they are all weak compared to the United States. America seemed indeed to have achieved economic supremacy over the world. Central America, with the completion of the Panama Canal, would become a part of the American system. Already we had expanded into Asia, checking the expansion of Russia and Germany. Great Britain was rapidly becoming an American dependency and if things continued in this way, if we were willing to fight for our empire, "the United States will outweigh any single empire, if not all empires combined. The whole world will pay her tribute."[18]

A thoroughgoing Darwinist, Adams was convinced that nature abhorred the weak and that only those nations that triumphed both in peaceful competition and in war could survive. In this industrial survival of the fittest America was emerging triumphant. In the *Law of Civilization and Decay,* he had pointed to the moral that other empires had taught us. In *America's Economic Supremacy* he had outlined a plan by which America might yet survive, despite the intensification of economic competition. In *The New Empire,* he read the recent history of America as a vindication of his prophecies. We had expanded into Asia. We were supreme among nations. Perhaps America would show the world a second law: how to achieve a Roman empire and neither decline nor fall.

The most sophisticated approach to America's problems and their imperial solution was taken by Charles Conant, an editor of the influential *Banker's Magazine* and a highly original economic theorist. Arguing for a policy that the English economist J. A. Hobson was to deplore, Conant urged that the United States adopt finance imperialism. In a series of closely reasoned articles (which appeared in the *Atlantic Monthly,* the *North American Review,* and the *Forum* between September 1898 and August 1900), Conant analyzed the familiar lament that America suffered from overproduction. Conant argued that the root of the problem lay in surplus *capital.* An increasing proportion of income was being saved but, because of a lack of good investment opportunities, was not being spent. The current overproduction was due, not to a lack of domestic purchasing power, but to a lack of demand. Excess saving leading to an accumulation of unconsumed goods was at the heart of America's economic instability. To keep the economy from stagnating it was essential that investment fields be found abroad. And the only significant field of investment left in the world was China. Conant did not deny that other solutions existed. Socialism was one. His argument against this alternative for America is still a common one. Socialism destroyed incentive and was thus both morally abhorrent and economically unsound. The creation of new demands was another possible solution. Conant's major argument against this was that it would take too long before it could have a major impact on the economy. So aside from war, whose destructiveness he detested, the only answer Conant saw was a consistent policy of finance imperialism. By this he meant the assured control of a share in the equipping of undeveloped countries, especially China, with the "means of production and exchange."[19]

The exclusive policy of France, Germany, and Russia, as illustrated by their spheres of influence policy, must be either stopped by force or imitated. Conant warned that this was no mere question of political and naval prestige, but of the very facts of economic survival. Colonial possessions alone offered developed nations a proper and profitable field for fixed investments and the continuing employment of excess capital. In a country like China, investment opportunity depended on the home government's vigor in pressing the claims of private investors. This the United States must now do. Conant predicted that Russia would in another generation be the chief competitor of England and America for the commercial and military supremacy of the world. He felt that Russia's highly centralized, absolutist form of government offered that nation distinct advantages in the struggle for control of undeveloped countries over a democracy. To act effectively, America would have to streamline its administrative institutions. The control of foreign policy by the Senate was particularly burdensome in a situation where quick decisions were essential. Like Brooks Adams, Conant felt that America's anachronistic system of foreign policy formulation could not successfully compete with that of a country like Russia. Conant urged that the United States learn the techniques of centralization from Russia, as Russia should learn a greater internal liberalization from America. Indeed, he saw the possibility of the two countries moving closer together as each assimilated the best of the other's system.[20]

John Hay died before he could write, free from the restraints of office, an account of what he had hoped to accomplish in China. His closest adviser on China policy, however, William W. Rockhill, did compose two long articles that looked back on his years of greatest activity in the State Department and attempted to explain the successes and failures of the policies he had helped formulate.

According to a recent biographer, Rockhill was a great admirer of the Chinese and all their works. This love for China is seen as the basic motivation for much of his later activities and the rationale for his China policy.[21] Yet his private correspondence more often expresses scorn and contempt for Chinese individually and collectively, however much he genuinely admired their culture and studied their past history. To a personal friend he wrote quite frankly about his reaction to Li Hung-chang's 1896 visit to America: "We are expecting Li Hung Chang here in Washington . . . and I am sorry to say that I will have to take part in receiving him in New York and probably here. I don't like dancing attendance on any kind of a dirty Chinaman, on Li any more than on any other. I have never met in my life more than one or two Chinamen who were gentlemen at heart and who could appreciate and accept in a proper spirit courtesies shown them, but I have got to grin and bear it." In a speech to the Naval War College in 1904 Rockhill listed as a "fundamental fact" about China the weakness and corruptness of the government and sole devotion of the people "to their individual interests."[22] The roots of Rockhill's China policy lay elsewhere than in his supposed love for China.

Like Adams, Mahan, and Conant, Rockhill too saw the world as polarized between land and sea powers. Control of China by the land powers necessitated a weak, inefficient Chinese government kept in colonial subjugation. Control by the sea powers on the other hand, because they required only free access to the seaboard ports and to the Yangtze River, would favor the development of a strong, responsible, and highly centralized government.[23] Thus, what was good for the sea powers would be good for China as well.

Rockhill saw a major change in American Asian policy after 1898. Prior to that date, policy was directed solely at protecting American interests and insuring our treaty rights. After that date, America became *politically* interested in China. The main goal now was a balance of powers designed to deny preponderant political control to any one state. To the maintenance of this balance of power, China's integrity was essential and the logical policy of the United States would be to guarantee that it was maintained. To Rockhill, the Open Door policy or, as he preferred to call it, the "Hay Doctrine," was as essential to America's welfare as the Monroe Doctrine. He saw the two as "the great and unchangeable principles of American foreign policy."[24]

Ten years later in 1914, in a speech to the Asiatic Institute, Rockhill regretted that America had allowed Japan to take the lead in balancing the powers in Asia. During the Russo-Japanese War, Japan had moved to stop Russia's advance in Manchuria, a job that properly belonged to America. Thus the United States "let pass out of its hands the duty and responsibility of maintaining it [the open door] and the honor of retaining the commanding role in the affairs of the Far East which would have been ours."[25]

Between 1895 and 1905, China had moved from the periphery to the heart of American concern. For a brief time, following the Boxer crisis, it had seemed that America indeed had a leading position in the affairs of the Far East. During the struggle with Russia over the opening of new ports in Manchuria in connection with the commercial treaty of 1903, Roosevelt felt confident enough of public concern to write, privately it is true, that he believed he could take the nation to war over the issue. American aims in 1903 were limited and were achieved without the use of force. When war did come over Manchuria, it was, to Rockhill's regret, Japan that assumed command.

Mahan, Conant, Adams, and the businessmen and politicians who dominated American thinking at the end of the nineteenth century were firmly convinced that the United States suffered from an overproduction of goods and a surplus of capital. In their view a radical expansion of foreign trade was the only feasible alternative to economic stagnation. On the basis of this analysis, which McKinley and his advisers shared, theorists of imperialism urged a variety of policies that would aid American commercial domination of the Far East. Yet neither commerce nor investments expanded at the expected rate. Despite the pleas of American consuls in China and the earnest advice of China experts, American merchants continued to send goods that were inappropriate for the China market and to send those goods badly packaged. Few firms kept permanent agents in the Far East, fewer tried to discover the particular needs of the trade. Although, in 1899, 50 percent of American cotton exports was shipped to Manchuria and north China, the trade was lost in the first decade of the century only in part because of unfavorable political conditions. A major cause was that American merchants made no effort to fight for the trade.

Moreover, a strange imbalance characterized American China policy in these formative years. In terms of economic interests, north China and Manchuria were vital to the United States. Yet our policy was most directly tied to that of Great Britain, which had already, in effect, recognized Russian special interests in that area. Even when Britain was prepared to take an advanced stand on Manchuria (as in 1901, when England hoped to secure American support for a joint protest over Sino-Russian negotiations) the United States held back. A strong independent protest was made but joint action was rejected. It is possible that the interests involved, which were mainly southern, could not exercise sufficient pressure on McKinley, whose strong business ties were in the Midwest, not the South, or even the East. In a politically sensitive year (1899–1900) the administration did respond positively to southern pressure to take a strong stand against a restrictive Russian trade policy in Manchuria, for the Republican party was still wooing the southern vote. But in a non-election year, the South found it was unable to exercise enough influence to overcome McKinley's reluctance to involve the nation in what might become a fighting issue.

The general criticism of American China policy, that it was never ready to back up its pronouncements by force of arms is, however, only partially true. America did use force during the Boxer crisis; Theodore Roosevelt did respond in a militant fashion to Japanese bellicosity in 1907–1908. America did not go to war to safeguard Chinese integrity (against Russian encroachments for example) but neither did Britain, whose concern with the maintenance of trade privileges was equal to America's. Prior to the Second World War, Britain never fought any power but China in the Far East. Except in relation to missionaries, the United States, in contrast to Britain, France, Germany, Japan, and Russia, was slow to use the threat of force against the Chinese government in order to gain its ends.

Looked at in this light, American pacifism is hardly so startling. The only war fought in the Far East prior to the Second World War, which was not against China itself, was the Russo-Japanese War. And clearly, a war on the mainland of Asia was not one entered into lightly.

What America did not do that it could have been expected to do, was to join the Anglo-Japanese alliance. But why should the United States commit itself when the alliance, in its normal operation, would aid, not obstruct, American interests. Why *not* ride Great Britain's coattail?

To be sure, Hay and Rockhill fully recognized that, in Asia, commerce, politics, and finance were inseparable. Rockhill's concern for American *political* weight in China was almost obsessive. The difficulty, again, was the lack of commercial and financial interest that might give substance to political maneuvers in the Far East. The impulse to attempt to play a role in Asia from a limited power base was difficult to resist. In these early years America somehow came to feel that having influence in Asia was a categorical imperative for a world power. America was a world power, therefore it must take a key part in Far Eastern affairs despite an insufficiency of concrete interests that might impel and support such a role.

The fact that America did not assume a role comparable to Japan's in its militancy was a great disadvantage to China. In the situation of the dynasty at the end of the century, the balancing of barbarians was the only viable foreign policy. But they had to be barbarians with real stakes. It was a dangerous game, which, in given instances, proved successful. China felt that America was a disinterested power (in the territorial sense). China wanted America on her side and, therefore, to an extent, wooed her. But America was never the key barbarian China thought it would be, and a potentially powerful element in the balancing game was thus eliminated. China continued to occupy American attention, though the failure of the Taft administration's complex schemes in Manchuria illustrated that, in the main, American businessmen had all but abandoned their old vision of the great China market.

In Asia, American policy had clearly gone beyond the simple pressure of economic facts, though economic facts, real or imagined, were part of the rationale for action. Unwilled events, such as the Boxer rebellion, were handled primarily with an eye to the domestic situation and with a deep-seated fear that the administration might fall behind the impulses of the public or stand too far in the vanguard.

The Open Door passed into the small body of sacred American doctrine and an assumption of America's "vital stake" in China was made and never relinquished. Tragically, definitions of the precise nature of America's vital interests in Asia have been rare, yet the idea that this country has a major role to play there remains fixed in the foreign policy of the United States.

Notes, Bibliography, Index

Abbreviations Used in the Notes

FRUS   Papers Relating to the Foreign Relations of the United States, 1894–1904, U.S. Department of State, Washington, D.C.

BPP   British Parliamentary Papers

ABCFM   American Board of Commissioners for Foreign Missions

Notes

Introduction

1. Oscar Handlin, *The American People in the Twentieth Century* (Cambridge, Mass., 1954), p. 6. By 1900 almost 40 percent of the population lived in cities. My discussion of this period is much indebted to Professor Handlin's books and articles.

2. Richard Hofstadter, *The Age of Reform: From Bryan to F. D. R.* (New York, 1956) provides a good account of this period in chaps. 1 and 2. More dramatically, Henry Adams, in *The Education of Henry Adams,* Modern Library edition (New York, 1931), p. 338, describes how, in the year of the depression, men "died like flies under the strain, and Boston grew suddenly old, haggard, and thin."

3. Hofstadter, *Social Darwinism in American Thought* (Boston, 1944), chaps. 1, 2, and 9. The bloody Pullman strike, which occurred in the summer of 1894, contained all the elements that so terrified middle-class America: destruction of property, violence, socialist overtones (it was led by Eugene Debs), and even the hand of the insidious foreigner (German-born Governor Altgeld did his best to prevent federal intervention).

4. Henry Adams, *Education*, pp. 344–345.

5. John Higham, *Strangers in the Land* (New Brunswick, N.J., 1955), pp. 69–73.

6. *Ibid.*, p. 77.

7. I have in mind here the shipbuilders and iron and steel interests involved in the Navalist movement.

8. After the Spanish-American War, a fourth concept emerged more fully —that the most important area of future commercial activity lay in East Asia, particularly China.

9. Alfred T. Mahan, "Possibilities of an Anglo-American Reunion," *North American Review,* 159:558 (November 1894).

10. *Ibid.* The most concise account of Mahan's thinking is in Harold and Margaret Sprout, *Rise of American Naval Power, 1776–1918* (Princeton, 1946), chap. 13.

11. Adams was perhaps the most influential of the systematic imperialist ideologues of his day, though William A. Williams' portrait of him as a kind of *éminence grise* of American imperialism is, I think, overdrawn. See

William A. Williams, "Brooks Adams and American Expansion," *New England Quarterly,* 25:217–232 (June 1952) and "The Frontier Thesis and American Foreign Policy," *Pacific Historical Review,* 24:379–395 (November 1955). There are two biographies of Brooks Adams: Thornton Anderson, *Brooks Adams, Constructive Conservative* (Ithaca, 1951) and Arthur F. Beringause, *Brooks Adams: A Biography* (New York, 1955). Timothy P. Donovan deals with both brothers in *Henry Adams and Brooks Adams: The Education of Two American Historians* (Norman, Okla., 1961). Brooks has written perhaps the best portrait of himself in an essay on his brother, "The Heritage of Henry Adams," which appears in a reprint of Henry Adams, *The Degradation of the Democratic Dogma* (New York, 1958), pp. 14–123. A recent article by Charles Hirschfeld argues that Adams was a "progressive of the nationalist school." I feel Hirschfeld minimizes the irrational element in Adams' thought and makes a too simple equation between *Realpolitik* of the Adams-imperialist variety and a "viable and realistic response to events in the Western world in the twentieth century." "Brooks Adams and American Nationalism," *The American Historical Review,* 69:371–392 (January 1964).

12. Brooks Adams, "Heritage of Henry Adams," p. 89.

13. Brooks Adams, *The Law of Civilization and Decay* (New York, 1903), pp. ix, x.

14. Theodore Roosevelt to Cecil Spring Rice, May 29, 1897, in *Letters of Theodore Roosevelt,* ed. Elting E. Morison (8 vols., Cambridge, Mass., 1951–1954), I, 618–621.

15. Williams, "Adams and American Expansion," p. 227.

16. Roosevelt to John Hay, June 17, 1899, *Letters of Theodore Roosevelt,* II, 1021. Brooks Adams was himself afraid of his possible insanity. He recalls that he told his wife, before marrying her, that he was "eccentric almost to madness" and that if she married him it must be on "her own responsibility and at her own risk." Brooks Adams, "Heritage of Henry Adams," p. 89.

17. Roosevelt to Spring Rice, August 5, 1895, *Letters of Theodore Roosevelt,* I, 553–556. In my opinion the best general study of Roosevelt's life and work remains Henry F. Pringle's immensely readable *Theodore Roosevelt: A Biography* (New York, 1956). A shorter, more interpretive study is John M. Blum's *The Republican Roosevelt* (Cambridge, Mass., 1954).

18. Theodore Roosevelt, review of Charles H. Pearson's *National Life and Character, Sewanee Review,* 2:354 (May 1894). It is interesting to compare Roosevelt's attitude toward the century with that of Henry Adams: "We have done well on massacres this last year," he wrote his brother in 1896, "and counting the deaths from exposure this winter in Armenia, I doubt whether civilization has ever had such reason to be proud." Henry Adams to Brooks Adams, Feb. 18, 1896, *Letters of Henry Adams, 1892–1918,* ed. Worthington C. Ford (Boston, 1930), pp. 99–101.

19. Roosevelt to Henry Cabot Lodge, Dec. 27, 1895, *Selections from the Correspondence of Theodore Roosevelt and Henry Cabot Lodge, 1884–1918*, ed. Henry Cabot Lodge, 2 vols. (New York, 1925), I, 204–205. See also Roosevelt to Lodge, Apr. 29, 1896, in *Letters of Theodore Roosevelt*, I, 535–536.

20. Roosevelt to Spring Rice, Aug. 13, 1897, *ibid.*, I, 644–649; Roosevelt to Spring Rice, Dec. 2, 1899, *ibid.*, II, 1103–1104.

21. Joseph R. Levenson, *Confucian China and Its Modern Fate: The Problem of Intellectual Continuity* (London, 1958), pp. 53, 88–91, 79ff.

22. See Benjamin Schwartz, *In Search of Wealth and Power: Yen Fu and the West* (Cambridge, Mass., 1964).

23. See Levenson, *Liang Ch'i-ch'ao and the Mind of Modern China* (Cambridge, Mass., 1953).

24. Max Muller to Sir Edward Grey, Oct. 28, 1910, FO 129/373, No. 388. I am grateful to Professor Schiffrin for the use of his copy of this document from the Archives of the Foreign Office, Public Record Office, London.

25. *Ibid.*

Chapter 1
Official Neutrality, Private Intervention

1. See John K. Fairbank and Ssu-yü Teng, "On the Ch'ing Tributary System," *Ch'ing Administration: Three Studies* (Cambridge, Mass., 1960), pp. 107–246.

2. Hilary F. Conroy's *The Japanese Seizure of Korea, 1869–1910: A Study of Realism and Idealism in International Relations* (Philadelphia, 1960), is the best recent account of the background of conflict in Korea and its consequences.

3. As, for example, the 1636 expedition of 100,000 Manchu soldiers across the Yalu into Korea to suppress pro-Ming loyalists. See John K. Fairbank and Edwin O. Reischauer, *East Asia: The Great Tradition* (Boston, 1960), p. 444.

4. Mary C. Wright, "The Adaptability of Ch'ing Diplomacy: The Case of Korea," *Journal of Asian Studies*, 17:363–381 (May 1958).

5. Article I, Treaty of Kianghwa, in H. B. Morse, *The International Relations of the Chinese Empire*, 3 vols. (Shanghai, 1918), III, 9.

6. The American treaty contained no reference to Korea's status and a covering letter (insisted upon by Li Hung-chang) from the Korean king to the President, which referred to Korea's dependent status, was ignored by American authorities. In a letter to Minister J. R. Young, Secretary of State Frelinghuysen noted the contradiction between the treaty and the letter and instructed Young to "make it clear that we have not regarded the aid lent us by Chinese officials in bringing about this treaty . . . as in any way an

assertion of China's administrative rights over Korea . . . but that we regarded Korea as *de facto* independent, and that our acceptance of the friendly aid found in China was in no sense a recognition of China's suzerain power." Frelinghuysen to Young, Aug. 4, 1882, quoted in Paul H. Clyde, *United States Policy Towards China: Diplomatic and Public Documents, 1839–1939* (Durham, N.C., 1940), p. 170.

7. *Ibid.*, p. 173.

8. William L. Langer, *The Diplomacy of Imperialism, 1890–1902*, rev. ed. (New York, 1956), p. 172.

9. Morse, III, 14.

10. Fred H. Harrington, *God, Mammon and the Japanese: Dr. Horace Allen and Korean-American Relations, 1884–1905* (Madison, Wisc., 1944), pp. 226, 234.

11. *Ibid.*, pp. 236–237.

12. Morse, III, 17.

13. Harrington, *Horace Allen*, pp. 309–311.

14. *Ibid.*

15. There are several very interesting accounts of the war written soon after the peace treaty was signed. See for example, Venone Volpicelli (Vladimir, *pseud.*), *The China-Japan War* (London, 1896), and J. Inouye, *The Japan-China War* (Shanghai, 1895 or 1896). Both are detailed and well illustrated, but their viewpoint is strongly pro-Japanese and perhaps they make the Chinese seem more incompetent than they actually were.

16. Langer, pp. 174–175.

17. Yang Ju to Tsungli yamen (Oct. 30, 1894, KH 20, 10th month, 2nd day), *Ch'ing-chi wai-chiao shih-liao* (Historical materials on foreign relations in the latter part of the Ch'ing dynasty; Taipei reprint, 1962), 99:3. 1 should like to thank Professor Chang Hao of Ohio State University for his generous help in translating this and other relevant documents from the Chinese.

18. Charles Denby to Walter Q. Gresham, March 22, 1895, *FRUS, 1895*, pt. 1, p. 197.

19. Denby to Richard Olney, June 20, 1895, *China Dispatches*, vol. 98. U. S. Department of State Archives, Foreign Affairs Division, National Archives, Washington, D.C.

20. William Pethick to James H. Wilson (Dec. 1, 1888), Wilson Papers, Library of Congress, Washington, D.C. The colonel, as Denby preferred to be addressed, had fought in the Civil War on the Union side, though he came from Virginia. Active in Democratic politics, he was rewarded in 1885 with an appointment as minister to China. He served there until July 11, 1898, when McKinley replaced him with a deserving Republican. In his retirement he wrote a book on China and became an early and most prolific China expert.

21. *Public Opinion*, 17:620 (Sept. 27, 1894).

22. S. Kurino, "The Oriental War," *North American Review,* 159:536 (November 1894).

23. *Public Opinion,* 17:444 (Aug. 19, 1894); *The Review of Reviews,* 11:220 (Mar. 15, 1895). British opinion changed in more complex ways. British merchants in China remained neutral, seeing the war as an opportunity to force long-standing commercial demands on China. *The Review of Reviews* reported British sympathy at the beginning of the war as being "unmistakably with the Chinese" (10:220, Sept. 15, 1894), but noted, one month later, that through military victories Japan had won new respect and power (10:318, Oct. 15, 1894). As Japanese victories became overwhelming, articles warning Britain of the danger to her position in Asia multiplied. Japan was seen as a new and unprecedented threat. See in particular, 10:533 (Dec. 15, 1894), 11:377 (Apr. 11, 1895), pp. 528–529 (June 15, 1895).

24. Augustine Heard, D. W. Stevens, and Howard Martin, "China and Japan in Korea," *North American Review,* 159:300–320 (September 1894).

25. *Ibid.,* pp. 300, 316.

26. *Missionary Review of the World,* 8:319 (April 1895). All volume numbers for this periodical refer to the New Series.

27. *Ibid.*

28. William W. Rockhill to Alfred Hippisley, Oct. 30, 1894, William W. Rockhill Papers, 1882–1914, Houghton Library, Harvard University, Cambridge, Mass.

29. Gresham to Edwin Dun, Nov. 6, 1894, Gresham to Denby, Nov. 8, 1894, *FRUS, 1894,* appendix I, pp. 76, 77.

30. *American Review of Reviews,* 10:250 (September 1894). While recognizing China's claim to some kind of suzerainty over Korea, the *Review* argued that Japan had gone to war to prove to the West her advanced state of civilization and thus convince England that the unequal treaties should be abrogated. Maintaining a righteous, impartial position, the *Review* held that America's real interest lay in bringing peace to the Far East, thus gaining the love and respect of both China and Japan.

31. *Literary Digest,* 10:125–126 (Dec. 1, 1894).

32. See for example, *ibid.,* p. 146.

33. See Denby, Jr., to Gresham, July 24, 1894 and Gresham to Denby, July 26, 1894, *FRUS, 1894,* p. 95. Although published too late to be of direct help to me, a detailed account of this aspect of Gresham's diplomacy during the Sino-Japanese war can be found in George E. Paulsen's "Secretary Gresham, Senator Lodge and American Good Offices in China, 1894," *Pacific Historical Review,* 36:123–142 (May 1967).

34. Gresham to Denby, Jr., Aug. 18, 1894, *FRUS 1894,* p. 103.

35. Denby, Jr., to Gresham, Aug. 21, 1894, *ibid.,* p. 104; T. R. Jernigan to Denby, Jr., Aug. 25, 1894, enclosed in Denby, Jr., to Gresham, Sept. 8, 1894, *ibid.,* p. 115.

36. Gresham to Denby, Jr., Aug. 26, 1894, *ibid.,* p. 105.

37. Gresham to Denby, Jr., Aug. 29, 1894, *ibid.,* p. 106.

38. Denby, Jr., to Gresham, Aug. 31, 1894; Denby, Jr., to Gresham, Sept. 1, 1894, *ibid.,* pp. 108–110.

39. The consul-general, however, had asked Denby for permission to deport them or, alternatively, to keep them under his protection until the war was over. See Jernigan to Denby, Jr., Aug. 21, 1894, enclosed in Denby, Jr., to Gresham, Sept. 8, 1894, *ibid.,* p. 114. On the same day on which Denby wrote his extenuating report, Jernigan notified him that he had quickly deported seven Japanese students whom the Chinese suspected of spying. Jernigan also informed Denby that he had surrendered the two accused Japanese spies but felt the action to be "unspeakably brutal." Jernigan to Denby, Jr., Sept. 1, 1894, enclosed in Denby, Jr., to Gresham, Sept. 8, 1894, *ibid.,* p. 116.

40. Denby, Jr., to Gresham, Sept. 1, 1894, *ibid.,* p. 110.

41. Denby to Gresham, Dec. 31, 1894, *China Dispatches,* Vol. 97.

42. *Literary Digest,* 10:151 (Dec. 8, 1894).

43. *Ibid.,* p. 152.

44. *Ibid.*

45. George Gray, "Two Years of American Diplomacy," *North American Review,* 160:423–424 (April 1895).

46. *Outlook,* 50:974 (Dec. 8, 1894); *Public Opinion,* 17:671 (Oct. 11, 1894).

47. The following account is based on the Wilson Papers.

48. See letters from Wilson to John J. McCook for 1897 and 1898. Wilson was deeply involved in the agitation preceding the Spanish-American War. With John J. McCook, banker to the Cuban junta, he was an active lobbyist in the rebels' cause.

49. Wilson to Rockhill, Dec. 20, 1895, Rockhill Papers.

50. During this visit Wilson put Pethick in contact with Charles Cramp, head of a large shipbuilding firm. See Pethick to Wilson, Aug. 31, 1894, Wilson Papers.

51. There is, as yet, no adequate biography of this remarkable man. For a detailed account of some aspects of his career see Stanley Spector, *Li Hung-chang and the Huai Army* (Seattle, 1964).

52. Pethick to Wilson, Sept. 24, 1894, Wilson Papers.

53. Wilson to D. W. Stevens, Sept. 23, 1894; Pethick to Wilson, Sept. 29, 1894, *ibid.*

54. Stevens to Wilson, Sept. 30, 1894, *ibid.*

55. Pethick to Wilson, Sept. 29, 1894, *ibid.*

56. John W. Foster to Denby, Sept. 28, 1894, *ibid.* Foster's letter was not solely concerned with the hope of making Li Hung-chang emperor. He also discussed the possibility of an American loan to China. Foster had learned, through the Chinese minister to Washington, that the Chinese gov-

ernment was making inquiries about an American loan. Foster had met with a group of New York bankers and had then spoken to the Chinese minister once more. He had urged on him the benefits to China of dealing with American bankers, who, in contrast to their European counterparts, were independent of the government and presented no threat to Chinese autonomy. He hoped Denby would speak to the Tsungli yamen along similar lines.

57. Wilson to Denby, Sept. 28, 1894, *ibid.*

58. Stevens to Wilson, May 3, 1894; Wilson to Foster, Aug. 10, 1895, *ibid.*

59. Very early in the war, for example, Denby reproached the Tsungli yamen for having appealed to the United States for its good offices and for requesting help at the same time from England, Russia, France, Germany, and Italy. Denby called the action "contradictory and embarrassing." With disarming frankness, the Chinese replied that their "condition was such that they were compelled to look for aid wherever they might hope to find it." Denby to Gresham, Nov. 10, 1894, *China Dispatches,* vol. 97. See also Denby to Gresham, Mar. 20, 1895, *ibid.,* vol. 98.

60. A noted Chinese historian of the war suggests that the Chinese did rely heavily on Denby for aid in non-substantive matters regarding the negotiation of peace with Japan. Before making any final move, either in the dispatch of an envoy or the preparation of an edict to accompany him, the Tsungli yamen would send the document to Denby for a final check. *Liu-shih-nien lai Chung-kuo yü Jih-pen* (China and Japan during the last sixty years), Wang Yün-sheng, comp., 6 vols. (Tientsin, 1932–1933), II, 226, 255.

61. Denby to Gresham, Dec. 8, 1894, *China Dispatches,* vol. 97.

62. Denby to Gresham, Dec. 26, 1894; Denby to Gresham, Jan. 17, 1895, *ibid.*

63. Denby to Gresham, Feb. 17, 1895; Gresham to Denby, Feb. 18, 1895, *ibid.*

64. Gresham to Denby, Apr. 13, 1895, *ibid.,* vol. 98.

65. Denby to Gresham for late January through February 1895, *ibid.,* vol. 97. Enraged by the Japanese rejection, the empress dowager wished to recall the plenipotentiaries immediately and resume the war. Among the arguments used to dissuade her was a plea from Denby, transmitted by a high official, that such an action would result in a loss of "face" for the American minister, as he had been intimately involved in the dispatch of the two envoys. The Chinese historian who records this fact, however, makes no comment on how important Denby's "face" was to the empress dowager. *Liu-shih-nien-lai Chung-kuo yü Jih-pen,* II, 226. See also John W. Foster, *Diplomatic Memoirs,* 2 vols. (Boston, 1909), II, 113–156. Foster's account of the negotiations is detailed and most interesting.

66. Denby to Gresham, Mar. 5, 1895, *China Dispatches,* vol. 97.

67. Pethick to Wilson, Sept. 17, 1895, Wilson Papers.

68. *History of the Peace Negotiations, Documentary and Verbal, between China and Japan, March–April 1895,* reprinted from the *Peking and Tientsin Times* (Tientsin, 1895).

69. The negotiations are well summarized in Langer, pp. 178ff.

70. See Nathan A. Pelcovits, *Old China Hands and the Foreign Office* (New York, 1948), pp. 167–171.

71. Denby to Gresham, Jan. 17, 1895, *China Dispatches,* vol. 97. Denby remarks that Japan had a great opportunity to improve the commercial position of all nations in China.

72. Denby to Gresham, Apr. 29, 1895, *ibid.,* vol. 98. Although Denby's role in the peacemaking was less than he had wished, the cumulative effect of his service, and that of Minister Dun in Tokyo, was to enhance the prestige of the United States in both Japan and China. Yang Ju, the Chinese minister to the United States, was impressed with the repeated expressions of friendship offered him by Gresham. Yet he noted that the State Department seemed not to have a very clear concept of the situation in the Far East nor any definite ideas on how to implement the help it so frequently proferred. See Yang Ju to Tsungli yamen, Aug. 29, 1894 (KH 20, 7th month, 29th day), Oct. 30, 1894 (KH 20, 10th month, 2nd day), Nov. 24, 1894 (KH 20, 10th month, 27th day), Apr. 30, 1895 (KH 21, 4th month, 6th day), *Ch'ing-chi wai-chiao shih-liao,* 94:25, 99:3, 100:14, 110:19.

Chapter 2
Early Investment Schemes

1. Wilson to Foster, Dec. 14, 1884, Wilson Papers. The Wilson Papers are invaluable for a study of these embryonic business deals in China.

2. Wilson describes this trip in *China: Travels in the Middle Kingdom* (New York, 1887). A second edition appeared in 1894, and a third in 1901.

3. Ellsworth C. Carlson, *The Kaiping Mines, 1887–1912* (Cambridge, Mass., 1957), is an excellent study of the varying fortunes of this important enterprise.

4. *Ibid.,* pp. 18–19, 21.

5. Wilson sent a model of American-designed track "and a small train operated by clock-work," which was installed in the Imperial Palace grounds. The French, however, sent a full scale model of their own design, which was first established in Tientsin and then given as a gift to the empress dowager. See Tyler Dennett, *Americans in Eastern Asia: A Critical Study of United States' Policy in the Far East in the Nineteenth Century* (New York, 1922), p. 598 and P. H. Kent, *Railway Enterprise in China* (London, 1908), p. 30.

6. Albert Feuerwerker, *China's Early Industrialization: Sheng Hsuan-huai (1844–1916) and Mandarin Enterprise* (Cambridge, Mass., 1958), p. 12.

7. *Ibid.*, pp. 13–14; Kent, p. 33.

8. Pethick to Wilson, February 11, 1887, Wilson Papers.

9. Carlson, p. 24.

10. Kent, pp. 33ff.

11. Feuerwerker, p. 14.

12. Li Kuo-ch'i, *Chung-kuo tsao-ch'i te t'ieh-lu ching-ying* (The initial development of railroads in China; Nan-kang, Taiwan, 1961), chap. 3, *passim.* I am grateful to John Schrecker of Princeton University for directing my attention to this important recent study.

13. Kent, p. 34.

14. *Ibid.*, pp. 36–38. That Li's plans went considerably beyond the talking stage is demonstrated both by the completed branch to Shanhaikwan and the huge quantity of railroad materials the Japanese captured at Port Arthur —materials stored there for the purpose of further work on the Manchurian line. See *ibid.*, pp. 42–43.

15. Feuerwerker, p. 14.

16. Pethick to Wilson, Aug. 11, 1887, Wilson Papers.

17. The Wharton Barker Papers in the Library of Congress, Washington, D.C., are very complete. All correspondence relating to Barker's business deals in China can be found there.

18. One of China's early self-taught experts in foreign affairs, Chang Yin-huan was part of the reformist clique that tried to transform the empire in 1898. For his part in the reform movement he was exiled to Sinkiang by the empress dowager. During the Boxer crisis, a sudden court decision to have him executed was carried out. Fang Chao-ying, "Chang Yin-huan," in *Eminent Chinese of the Ch'ing Period* (Washington, D.C., 1943), ed. Arthur W. Hummel, I:60–63.

19. Contract signed by William L. Paine addressed to Chang Yen Hoon, Nov. 28, 1886; copy of same contract, slightly altered, signed by Barker and Mitkiewicz on same date.

20. Allen Johnson, ed., *Dictionary of American Biography* (New York, 1928), I, 606–607.

21. Barker to Liang Sheng, Feb. 8, 1887, Barker Papers.

22. Barker to M. M. Moore, May 10, 1887, *ibid.*

23. Mitkiewicz to Barker, Mar. 10, 1887, Mar. 18, 1887, *ibid.* The Chinese were anxious to receive shares in a joint-stock company to be organized before the party left for China to secure the actual concession. Under American incorporation laws, this was apparently impossible. Instead, Barker had certificates that would be convertible once a company was formed. See Barker to Mitkiewicz, Mar. 19, 1887, Mitkiewicz to Barker, Mar. 20, 1887, *ibid.*

24. Paine to Barker, Apr. 12, 1887, *ibid.*

25. Stern to Barker, Apr. 25, 1887, May 23, 1887, May 27, 1887, and May 30, 1887, *ibid.*

26. Feuerwerker, pp. 117–118. See also reference to S. P. Ma (Ma Chien-chang), *ibid.*, p. 142.

27. Stern to Barker, June 10, 1887, June 12, 1887, June 14, 1887, Barker Papers.

28. Li Hung-chang to Barker, July 2, 1887; Barker to Stern, July 2, 1887, *ibid.*

29. Stern to Barker, July 14, 1887, July 18, 1887 (cable and letter of same date), *ibid.* By the end of May, Barker had already spent $49,000 in salaries and charges and had issued credits for $25,000 more. See Barker to Frances Murphy, May 30, 1887, *ibid.*

30. Li Hung-chang to Barker, n.d., 1887; "rescript of Li Hung-chang," n.d., 1887; see also Liang Sheng to Barker, Aug. 5, 1887, *ibid.*

31. Edward LeFevour, "Western Enterprise and the Ch'ing Bureaucracy in the Late 19th Century," conference paper, London School of Oriental and African Studies, pp. 13–14. Mr. LeFevour's study refers to railroad loan negotiations carried out by Russell and Company during the summer of 1887. In his study, which focuses on the activities of Jardine, Matheson and Company, he quotes from several Jardine letters that discuss the "comprehensive, gigantic scheme" won by an American syndicate directed by Russell and Company. I have found no other information on the Russell and Company project and can only surmise that, relying as they did on the vaguest Shanghai and Peking rumors, the Jardine people had confused Barker's syndicate with a separate undertaking by Russell and Company. It is clear from the Barker papers that Russell and Company did everything they could to sabotage his efforts. This may have been general business rivalry or it may have been the fact that Mitkiewicz had scooped Russell and Company on some specific enterprise. I believe the Jardine reference must be to the railroad venture described to Barker by Stern in mid-June of 1887. The lines involved were, indeed, "comprehensive" and "gigantic." One would run from Shanghai to Tientsin, with the possibility of a 1,000 mile route from a northern terminus to Nanking and from Hankow to Canton. As a condition, the syndicate would have to lend China money at an interest rate of less than 4.5 percent per annum (a figure previously offered by the French. The usual rate was 6 percent and above.) See Stern to Barker, June 14, 1887. The scheme, as Stern explained it, would give the syndicate the right to build the road, furnish materials and equipment and receive from 25 to 50 percent of the profits. As the project developed, the railroads were subsumed under the more inclusive bank proposal, one clause of which specifically referred to bank loans for a line from Peking to Tientsin and from Shanghai to Canton. Russell and Company did bid for a contract for the Tientsin-Taku line, but this could hardly have been the "comprehensive" scheme the Jardine agents fought so vociferously. See Dennett, *Americans in Eastern Asia,* p. 599.

32. *North China Herald,* 39:141–142 (Aug. 5, 1887).

33. *Ibid.,* pp. 154–155.

34. Consul E. G. Smithers to Barker, July 18, 1887, Barker Papers.

35. *North China Herald,* 39:155 (Aug. 5, 1887); see also Denby to Bayard, Aug. 13, 1887, *China Dispatches,* vol. 81.

36. Smithers to Mitkiewicz, Aug. 15, 1887, Barker Papers.

37. Denby to Bayard, Aug. 13, 1887, *China Dispatches,* vol. 81.

38. Denby to Bayard, Sept. 9, 1887, *ibid.*

39. Li Kuo-ch'i, chap. 4, *passim.*

40. Chang Yin-huan to Makietchang (Ma Chien-chang), Aug. 3, 1887; Chang Yin-huan to Barker, Oct. 22, 1887, Barker Papers; Chang Yin-huan, *San-chou jih-chi* (Diaries of Three Continents; Peking, 1896), 4:99b.

41. Barker to S. P. Makiechung (Ma Chien-chang), Oct. 5, 1887. Ma's name is variously romanized in Barker's papers as S. P. Ma, S. P. Makietchang, S. P. Makiechung and Makutchang. His elder brother, Ma Chienchung, is referred to as Makutchong, Makietchang, and, at one point, Barker speaks of them collectively as "the brothers Ma Kiet Chang." In the text I consistently use the Wade-Giles romanization of their names as it is in this form that they can be found in Western reference books.

42. There are many copies of the 12 Articles in Barker's papers. One complete version is enclosed in a letter from Ma Chien-chang to Barker, dated Oct. 5, 1887.

43. T. G. Morrow to Barker, Sept. 5, 1887, Barker Papers; E. Frazar to Barker, Oct. 6, 1887, *ibid.,* enclosing several newspaper clippings; LeFevour, "Western Enterprise and the Ch'ing Bureaucracy," p. 296; references to Russell and Company's machinations can be found in J. R. Young to Barker, Oct. 4, 1887; Balch to Barker, Dec. 11, 1887, Barker Papers. Balch, a European contact of Barker's, informed him that the attack on Mitkiewicz had been instigated by Russell and Company. Company officials had succeeded in having the New York police request information on Mitkiewicz's record of Scotland Yard. It was discovered that he had served five years in an English jail. On the element of European intrigue see Young to Barker, Oct. 19, 1887, *ibid.* William Rockhill, in a letter to John H. Wilson, Oct. 22, 1887, Wilson Papers, ascribed the failure of the Barker scheme to the "opposition of the Shansi bankers at Tientsin." The efforts of the German government to obstruct the scheme are described in Helmuth Stoecker, *Deutschland und China im 19. Jahrhundert* (Berlin, 1958), p. 204. Stoecker states that Barker failed to obtain sufficient funds to carry out the project. It is true that Barker had difficulty raising money but this was only *after* Li Hung-chang had already cancelled the project. Lack of funds was not the cause of the scheme's failure.

44. *North China Herald,* 39:423 (Oct. 19, 1887).

45. Young to Barker, Sept. 26, 1887, Oct. 4, 1887, Barker Papers.

46. Denby to Bayard, Sept. 9, 1887, *China Dispatches,* vol. 81; Bayard to Denby, Sept. 21, 1887, Instruction Book, vol. 4.

47. Denby to Bayard, Sept. 27, 1887, Oct. 3, 1887, *China Dispatches,* vol. 81.

48. Li Hung-chang to Tsungli yamen, Aug. 16, 1887, *Li Wen-chung kung ch'üan-chi* (The complete works of Li Hung-chang; Shanghai, 1921), 5:485.

49. Edict to the Grand Councillors, Sept. 28, 1887, *Ta-Ch'ing li-ch'ao shih-lu* (Veritable records of successive reigns of the Ch'ing dynasty; Taipei, reprint, 1963–1964), 5a9–5b6 Oct. 6, 1887, 9b5–9b10 (pp. 2265 and 2267). Under the direction of Robert Irick, Director of the Chinese Materials and Research Aids Service Center, a thorough search of the *Ta Ch'ing li-ch'ao shih-lu,* the archives of the Tsungli yamen and several other relevant documentary collections was made. Apart from the two edicts cited above, no information on Li Hung-chang's bank project could be found.

50. Li Hung-chang to Tsungli yamen, Oct. 7, 1887, *Li Wen-chung kung ch'üan-chi,* 6:234.

51. Ma Chien-chang to Barker, Oct. 5, 1887, Barker Papers.

52. The *New York Sun,* for example, reported with relish that Li Hung-chang had "abruptly terminated all dealings with the Russian imposter and smashed his whole scheme."

53. Denby to Bayard, Oct. 18, 1887, *China Dispatches,* vol. 81; Bayard to Denby, Nov. 29, 1887, Dec. 15, 1887, Instruction Book, vol. 4.

54. J. R. Young to Barker, Oct. 14, 1887, Oct. 19, 1887, and Oct. 24, 1887, Barker Papers.

55. Barker to Smithers, Jan. 31, 1888; Barker to Li Hung-chang, Jan. 31, 1888; Barker to Ma Chien-chang, Mar. 26, 1888, May 12, 1888, Barker Papers. From January through July, Barker had an interesting correspondence with Yung Wing and Yung Wing's patron, an American named McDowell. Yung was anxious to become Barker's agent in China, working through Li Hung-chang and Chang Yin-huan. He claimed that Ma Chienchang was corrupt and unreliable—a Chinese Mitkiewicz. He urged Barker to surrender to Chang all papers relating to the original concession. The Chinese, Yung Wing noted, like to tie things up. According to him the original concession was worthless and Barker should simply forget about it. However, as Chang Yin-huan had told Yung Wing, "what cannot be given openly may be given confidentially." Barker angrily refused to surrender the papers, insisting that the concession might be revived. Familiar with the Chinese scene, on good terms with Chang Yin-huan, Yung Wing might have been an excellent associate had Barker's ambitions been less extreme. In a long letter to McDowell, Yung explained that the ideal way to proceed was that suggested by Li Hung-chang (Barker should establish a bank in Tientsin). "The establishment of a Bank purely on a Treaty right basis with the secret cooperation of the Viceroy is a far more satisfactory and safe plan than to have it a joint co-partnership of Chinese and Americans." Chinese would be solicited to subscribe up to 50 percent of the capital stock but would have no voting power. Yung Wing to McDowell, May 13, 1888, *ibid.*

In this way, the bank would be free from all complications that destroyed the first scheme and entirely under American protection. Barker rejected Yung Wing's approach and their association ended. See correspondence between Barker and McDowell for May 1888, *ibid.*

56. Barker to Ma Chien-chang, Mar. 7, 1888, *ibid.*

57. Li Hung-chang to Barker, May 3, 1888; Ma Chien-chang to Barker, May 15, 1888, *ibid.*

58. Barker to Li Hung-chang, July 6, 1888; Ma Chien-chang to Barker, July 18, 1888; Barker to Li Hung-chang, Aug. 17, 1888, *ibid.* On the loan negotiations see telegraphic correspondence between Barker and Ma during October 1888. See also Ma Chien-chang to Barker, Jan. 18, 1889, and Barker to Ma Chien-chang, Jan. 5, 1889, *ibid.*

59. Ma Chien-chang to Barker, Nov. 21, 1889, *ibid.*

60. LeFevour, "Western Enterprise and the Ch'ing Bureaucracy," p. 1; Le Fevour, *Western Enterprise in Late Ch'ing China: A Selective Survey of Jardine, Matheson and Company's Operations, 1842–1895* (Cambridge, Mass., 1968), p. 112.

61. Pethick to Wilson, Jan. 19, 1891, Wilson Papers. See also Wilson to Pethick, Mar. 8, 1891, *ibid.* It should be remembered that no other foreign investors were seizing these opportunities either—mainly because the Chinese government firmly resisted the idea of foreign-controlled concessions. The first railroad concessions granted by China to a foreign country were to France in June 1895. In other words, the concessions followed the resounding defeat of China in the Sino-Japanese War, wherein by virtue of its role in securing the recession of the Liaotung Peninsula, France felt it had a reasonable claim on China's gratitude. Moreover, France backed its demands with threats of force at a time when China was utterly unable to defend herself.

62. Even at the height of the Venezuelan crisis, for example, rumors that Russia was negotiating a secret treaty with China received prime news space and, according to the *New York Herald,* journals which had been extremely anti-British did a complete about-face, seeing England's cause as that of civilization itself. *Literary Digest,* 12:33 (Nov. 9, 1895).

63. *Ibid.,* 12:32.

64. *Ibid.,* 12:3 (Nov. 2, 1895).

65. *Ibid.*

66. *Ibid.,* 13:580 (Sept. 5, 1896).

67. *Ibid.,* 13:567 (Aug. 29, 1896).

68. *Ibid.,* 13:580 (Sept. 5, 1896).

69. Charles S. Campbell, Jr., *Special Business Interests and the Open Door Policy* (New Haven, 1951), pp. 19, 20, 10.

70. *Our Commercial Relations in the Orient,* tables prepared under the direction of Oscar P. Austin, Chief, Bureau of Statistics, Department of Commerce and Labor (Economic Club of New York, Mar. 29, 1909).

71. Kerosene, exported primarily to Manchuria, increased in export value after 1898. When the demand for oil in America and Europe began to decline, Standard Oil for the first time gave serious attention to the Far Eastern market, devoting money and care to the proper marketing of American kerosene in Manchuria and exerting much effort to combat the unfair competitive advantages of Russia, and later, Japan. See Ralph W. and Muriel E. Hidy, *History of the Standard Oil Company (New Jersey): Pioneering in Big Business, 1882–1911* (New York, 1955), pp. 547–552. Dana C. Munro, in a valuable study of American commercial interests in Manchuria, shows that Standard Oil did not give up without a struggle, unlike the cotton interests which made no effort to retain the American import lead in Manchuria through proper marketing techniques. See Dana C. Munro, *American Commercial Interests in Manchuria,* publication no. 654, American Academy of Political and Social Science, reprinted from the *Annals* (January 1912).

72. Wilbur J. Chamberlin to wife, Nov. 18, 1900, *Ordered to China* (New York, 1903), p. 150.

73. Langer, chap. 12.

Chapter 3
Investment and Speculation

1. The most complete account is by William Braisted, "The United States and the American China Development Company," *Far Eastern Quarterly,* 11:147–165 (February 1952). See also Kent, pp. 110–121.

2. Foster to Wilson, Apr. 23, 1895; Wilson to Foster, Apr. 25, 1895, Wilson Papers. In a letter to Mrs. Foster, dated July 4, 1895, Wilson anxiously inquired who Bash and Dolph were. He got the answer from John W. Foster in a letter dated July 8, 1895, *ibid.*

3. Denby to Gresham, May 10, 1895, *China Dispatches,* vol. 98.

4. *Ibid.*

5. Denby to Gresham, May 12, 1895; Edwin F. Uhl to Denby, May 14, 1895, *ibid.*

6. Denby to Gresham, May 17, 1895, *ibid.*

7. Denby to Gresham, May 30, 1895; Olney to Denby, June 22, 1895, *ibid.*

8. Charles Denby, Jr., was for a time an agent for Louis Spitzel and Company, a firm with a very poor reputation for honesty. More legitimately he became Burnham, Williams and Company's agent at a salary of $300 per month with a 2.5 percent commission on any railroad business he might obtain for them. This arrangement was to take effect after he left the legation, although it had been arranged beforehand. See undated memorandum, Pethick to Wilson (probably written early in 1898), Wilson Papers; Burn-

ham, Williams and Company to Denby, Jr., Mar. 6, 1896, and Apr. 26, 1895, *ibid.*

9. Charles Denby, Jr., to Burnham, Williams and Company, Sept. 11, 1895; Wilson to Burnham, Williams and Company, Oct. 23, 1895, Wilson Papers.

10. A. W. Bash to Wilson, Aug. 1, 1895; Bash to Wilson, Oct. 4, 1895; Wilson to Bash, Oct. 15, 1895, Wilson Papers.

11. In May 1895, John Hay wrote Whitelaw Reid that he would be sorry to lose Brice from the Senate. "He is such an agnostic in politics," Hay remarked, "that he votes generally right when his party is wrong and his house has been the greatest social center ever known in Washington . . . Their entertaining has been so constant and so splendid that their guests lose all sense of individual obligation." Hay to Whitelaw Reid, May 2, 1895, Whitelaw Reid Papers, Library of Congress, Washington, D.C.

Brice had been active in Democratic politics for over a decade and was a friend of such prominent businessmen as William C. Whitney and H. B. Payne. A sound money Democrat, Brice had entered the Senate when, as William Allen White noted, a senator "represented principalities and powers in business." Matthew Josephson, *The Politicos, 1865–1896* (New York, 1938), pp. 427, 444.

12. Pethick to Wilson, Aug. 14, 24, 29, 1896, Wilson Papers. John W. Foster, who remained in China for a while after the peace treaty negotiations, was also aiding the Brice syndicate. In two letters to Wilson written in 1896, he told his friend that he felt the Brice group would open the way for many more American concessions in China. Foster had warned them that they must be serious in their efforts or make way for some other group. They had agreed but pointed out the difficulty of raising money until after the election. Foster to Wilson, Aug. 9 and Sept. 21, 1896, Wilson Papers.

13. Clarence Cary to Wilson, Oct. 24, 1896; Wilson to Cary, Oct. 25, 1896; Wilson to Pethick, Oct. 26, 1896; Wilson to Jacob Schiff, Sept. 1, 1896, Wilson Papers.

14. Wilson to McCook, Oct. 27, 28, 1896.

15. Clifton R. Breckenbridge to Gresham, Feb. 5, 12, 1895, U.S. Department of State Archives, Foreign Affairs Division, *Russia Dispatches,* National Archives, Washington, D.C., vol. 46; Breckenbridge to Olney, Apr. 4, 1896, *ibid.,* vol. 48; Wilson to Pangborn, Feb. 15, 1897, Wilson Papers.

16. McCook to Olney, July 10, 1896; James M. Peirce to Olney, July 11, 1896, Richard Olney Papers, Library of Congress, Washington, D.C.

17. McCook to Wilson, Nov. 11, 17, 18 and 30, 1896, Dec. 19, 1896; Wilson to McCook, Oct. 13, 1896, Wilson Papers.

18. McCook to Wilson, Dec. 19, 1896, Wilson Papers. Wilson's dislike for Washburn was in part due to the latter's role in the Bash-Brice syndicate. Possibly more important, however, was Wilson's belief that Washburn, while

a senator, had been in the pay of the Canadian Pacific Railroad, whose incursions into United States carrying-trade Wilson fought for years. See Wilson to Senator Cullum, Feb. 16, 25, 1890, Mar. 26, 1897; Wilson to Pethick, Nov. 25, 1896, Wilson Papers.

19. Wilson to Pethick, Nov. 25, 1896; Wilson to Denby, Nov. 26, 29, 1896, Dec. 29, 1896; Wilson to Pethick, Dec. 23, 1896, Wilson Papers.

20. Barker to Ma Chien-chang, Jan. 17, 1895; Ma Chien-chang to Barker, Mar. 11, 19, 1895, Barker Papers.

21. Barker to "Dear Sir," Aug. 30, 1895; Charles P. Cheney to Barker, Aug. 29, 1895, ibid. Cheney worked as a fund raiser for the scheme. Barker to Garland, Aug. 31, 1895, gives an accounting of funds received, ibid.

22. Barker to Chang Chih-tung, Oct. 14, 1895; Barker to Li Hung-chang, Oct. 26, 1895, ibid.

23. Pethick to Wilson, Oct. 22, 1895, Wilson Papers. Actually Barker did run for president some five years later, with Ignatius Donnelly as vice-presidential candidate. Barker ran on the Peoples' (Anti-Fusion) party ticket and received the lowest popular vote—50,232 (as compared to Debs' 94,768 and McKinley's 7,219,530). Encyclopedia of American History, ed. R. B. Morris (New York, 1953), p. 266.

24. Barker to Ma Chien-chang, Oct. 28, 1896, Barker Papers.

25. Garland to Barker, Feb. 17, 21, 1896, ibid.

26. F. Holden to Barker, Feb. 18, 1896; Barker to Holden, Feb. 21, 1896; Holden to Barker, Mar. 9, 1896, ibid.

27. Burr and DeLacy law firm to Gresham, Jan. 12, 1895, U.S. Department of State, Foreign Affairs Division, Miscellaneous Letters, National Archives, Washington, D.C. (April 1895, pt. 1). Barker never gave up his dream of making money in China. As the years passed he began to sound more and more like Count Eugène Stanislaw Kostka de Mitkiewicz himself. In 1898, Barker contacted the count and, for a short time, it seemed that Barker might be able to raise a large capital fund once more. A friend advised him, however, that "large capitalists are generally men of such important affairs that it is not easy to get them to even discuss new businesses." Moreover, the number of men ready "to join a blind pool for business at such a distance" were very few indeed.

For a while Barker tried to interest Count Cassini, Russian ambassador to the United States, in using him to promote anti-British feeling in America in exchange for privileges in a joint Russian-American railroad venture in China. Lacking cash, he tried to obtain the new Chinese minister's favor by nominating him to the American Philosophic Society and for an honorary Doctor of Law degree at the University of Pennsylvania. In 1905 and 1918 he organized phantom Oriental-American Associations. The brochures for these companies contained fantastically imaginative accounts of Barker's activities in China in 1887. In one he claimed that, had his original bank concession been granted, "there would have been no war between China and Japan, no war between Japan and Russia, and . . . the Chinese revolution . . . would have been much further on." The final descent to the pathetic occurred in 1917, when Barker described himself, in an article, as "Advisor to Li Hung Chang, as Prime Minister, on China's Financial, Transportation and Industrial Problems." He firmly believed himself the "only man in America" able to play a leading role in China's development.

See Barker to Count Cassini, Nov. 21, 1898, Dec. 4, 1898; Charles C. Dodge to Barker, Dec. 10, 1898, Jan. 6, 1899; Wu T'ing-fang to Barker, Dec. 7, 1899; Statement of Possibilities, n.d., 1898, 1905; article printed by National Editorial Service, Inc., 1917, Barker Papers.

28. Olney to Denby, Dec. 19, 1896, *FRUS, 1897*, p. 56.

29. Pethick to Wilson, Feb. 1, 1897, Wilson Papers. According to Pethick, Sheng Hsuan-huai wanted to have all of China's railroads under Chinese control with subordinate foreign management responsible to Chinese directors and with as much Chinese material used in construction as possible. Trying to obtain the lowest terms on railway loans, Sheng had been encouraging offers from many different countries, and trying to play one off against the other. Li Hung-chang, Pethick felt, was ready to settle with the Bash-Brice group at once, but Prince Kung and other members of the Tsungli yamen ruled that there should be no interference with Sheng Hsuan-huai's handling of the affair. He had been "appointed with full power" and he must "be left with a free hand and take the consequences, good or bad."

In the same letter Pethick remarked that the 1896 Russo-Chinese treaty had, in effect, made China a protectorate of Russia in return for concessions in Manchuria. He feared that China would lose all of Manchuria in this way and had been urging that China protect herself, by giving liberal concessions in railways, mines, and forests to Americans. Pethick's neutralization scheme anticipates that of Taft and Knox.

30. Langer, pp. 400–409. See also Andrew Malozemoff, *Russian Far Eastern Policy, 1881–1904* (Berkeley, 1958), chap. 4, for a detailed account. Li Hung-chang pared Russian demands to the bone. The concession was not granted to the government directly but to the Russo-Chinese Bank; a branch line to the Yellow Sea was categorically refused; Chinese repurchase rights after 36 years guaranteed; in return, China received a fifteen-year defensive alliance. See also Kent, pp. 97ff.

31. Denby to Olney, Jan. 10, 1897, *FRUS, 1897*, pp. 56–57.

32. Charles Campbell, in his study of special business interests in China in the late nineties, claims that Sherman's damper may well have seriously harmed the Development Company's chances for securing the Peking-Hankow concession. This is very unlikely. As a commercial outfit, the Development Company had presented Sheng Hsuan-huai with a reasonable proposition, though it involved a high degree of American control of the road during the term of the loan. The Belgian group, on the other hand, offered Sheng extremely liberal terms, so liberal that Sheng could not use

them as a bargaining point with the Americans, for the latter could not possibly offer a better contract. Wilson to Denby, Nov. 25, 29, 1896; Wilson to Pethick, Dec. 23, 1896; Wilson to Rockhill, Nov. 25, 1896, Mar. 6, 1897, Wilson Papers; John Sherman to Denby, Mar. 8, 1897, *FRUS, 1897,* pp. 59–60; see also Campbell, Jr., *Special Business Interests,* p. 29.

33. Edward H. Zabriskie, *American Russian Rivalry in the Far East, 1895–1914* (Philadelphia, 1946), pp. 34ff. The American China Development Company also failed to reach any agreement with the Russians. Count Cassini told Bash the Russians could and would develop Manchuria without American help. By 1896, Bash's efforts in this direction ceased. C. B. Gorelik, *Politka SShA B Manchzhurii B 1898–1903 GG. I Doktrina "Otkrytykh Overei"* (Policy of the U.S.A. in Manchuria, 1898–1903, and the Doctrine of "Open Doors"; Moscow, 1960), pp. 25ff, discusses American attempts to build into Manchuria. Gorelik quotes from a letter that Pethick wrote Cassini, on behalf of the Development Company, arguing that a concession giving the company the right to build a line crossing Manchuria from south to north (to a point on the Trans-Siberian railroad) and one from Mukden to the Korean border, would be of great benefit to Russia. The project also involved exclusive mining and timber rights in Manchuria as well as prohibition of concessions to any other company in this area for a period of thirteen years. Pethick wrote that the plan would strengthen the Trans-Siberian railroad, that it would exploit the resources of Manchuria, and give income to the Chinese government without "in any way introducing a disturbing element in the political life of the area." *Ibid.,* p. 26.

A joint American-Russian effort, Pethick said, would mean more rapid completion of a line connecting Russia directly with China. Pethick told Cassini that he realized Manchuria and north China were within the Russian sphere of influence. According to Gorelik, the Russian government was not interested in the project and had no desire to complicate its relationship with China on behalf of an American company. *Ibid.,* p. 27. Gorelik interprets Pethick's action as an early move in America's attempt to establish political and economic supremacy in Manchuria. In describing Russia's success, Gorelik recounts Russia's long and intimate relationship with China and their mutual interest in opposing Japanese aggression. *Ibid.,* p. 28. (I am grateful to Professor Henry Rosovsky of Harvard University for translating the relevant portions of Gorelik's book.)

34. Denby to Sherman, May 24, 1897, *China Dispatches,* vol. 102.

35. E-tu Zen Sun, *Chinese Railways and British Interests, 1898–1911* (New York, 1954), p. 41; Kent, chap. 11. Kent has an excellent summary of the fight over the Peking-Hankow concession including British protests and their result.

36. McCook to Wilson, undated letter (probably spring of 1897), Wilson Papers. Rockhill to Fleming Cheshire, Dec. 12, 1896, Rockhill Papers. On

several occasions in 1896, Rockhill sent Wilson copies of reports on railroads written by Denby and by the American consul-general in St. Petersburg. At one point Wilson even asked Rockhill to cable Denby, at the State Department's expense, to find out whether the Bash-Brice group had signed a contract for the Peking-Hankow line. Olney, to whom the matter was referred, gave permission for the Department's cable facilities to be used—at Wilson's expense, since the matter was not an urgent one to him. Rockhill to Wilson, Jan. 13, 20, 1896; Oct. 24, 28, 1896, Rockhill Papers.

This casual attitude on Olney's part goes far, I think, to modify Gorelik's picture of the American government standing close behind the Development company in their concession efforts. A few days later, Rockhill apologized for not having sent the cable. He said he would have done it if Olney had been away. Rockhill to Wilson, Nov. 1, 1896, Wilson Papers.

37. McCook to Wilson, Jan. 26, 1897; Alba B. Johnson to Wilson, Apr. 3, 1897; McCook to Wilson, Aug. 12, 1897, Wilson Papers.

38. Johnson to Wilson, Apr. 3, 1897; Rockhill to Wilson, Apr. 1, 3, 1897; Foster to Wilson, Apr. 3, 1897, Wilson Papers.

39. Rockhill to Wilson, May 26, 1897; McCook to Wilson, May 28, 1897; Wilson to Rockhill, May 13, 29, 1897; McCook to Wilson, July 28, 1897, Wilson Papers. See also Wilson to Rockhill, May 12, 1897, Rockhill Papers, M. G. Seckendorf to Reid, May 7, 1897, Reid Papers.

40. Wilson to Pethick, Sept. 7, 1897, Wilson Papers.

41. Breckenbridge to Olney, Apr. 4, 1896, *Russia Dispatches,* vol. 48.

42. Breckenbridge to Olney, Aug. 15, 1895, *ibid.,* vol. 47.

43. Ethan Allen Hitchcock to Cridler, Aug. 26, 1897, *ibid.,* vol. 51. Attached to the letter is a clipping from a newspaper describing Hitchcock's background.

44. Hitchcock to Sherman, Jan. 4, 1898, *ibid.,* vol. 51. See also letter and cable to McKinley, Dec. 28, 1897, *ibid.*

45. Hitchcock to Sherman, Mar. 7, 1898, *ibid.,* vol. 51; Apr. 9, 25, 1898, May 12, 21, 1898 (this last addressed to Day), *ibid.,* vol. 52.

46. A. S. Moss Blundell to Peirce, Dec. 6, 1898; Hay to Peirce, Dec. 8, 1898; Peirce to Hay, Dec. 9, 1898; Peirce to Blundell, Dec. 8, 1898; Peirce to Hay, Dec. 16, 1898; Hitchcock to Hay, Dec. 23, 28, 1898, *ibid.,* vol. 53.

47. Hitchcock to Sherman, Mar. 31, 1898, Feb. 8, 1898, *ibid.,* vol. 51; Reid Diary, entry for Nov. 19, 1898, Reid Papers.

48. Peirce to Hay, Nov. 19, 30, 1898, *Russia Dispatches,* vol. 53.

49. A. A. Adee memorandum attached to Peirce to Hay, Feb. 25, 1899, *ibid.,* vol. 54.

50. For a somewhat different account of the development of Russo-American hostility in China, see Thomas J. McCormick, *China Market: America's Quest for Informal Empire, 1893–1901* (Chicago, 1967), pp. 80–84. For an interesting view of Russian diplomacy in this period that argues that

Witte's aims were no different from Kuropotkin's, see H. P. Ford, "Russian Far Eastern Diplomacy: Count Witte and the Penetration of China," Ph.D. thesis (University of Chicago, 1950).

Chapter 4
Threat of a Closing Door

1. Langer, p. 478, is inclined to put major blame on France and Russia, not Germany, though he calls the German action a "frontal attack" on China. While it is true that France obtained the first railroad concession ever granted to a foreign power, it is hard to see how this and subsequent Franco-Russian gains forced Germany to a policy of territorial aggression. It seems to me there is a qualitative difference between the two policies and that Germany began the more damaging trend.

2. Quoted in *ibid.,* p. 454; Kaiser Wilhelm to Bülow, as quoted in *ibid.,* p. 452. The kaiser also said that thousands of "German Christians will breathe easier, when they know that the German Emperor's ships are near; hundreds of German traders will revel in the knowledge that the German Empire has at last secured a firm footing in Asia; . . . and the whole German nation will be delighted that the government has done a manly act."

3. *Ibid.,* pp. 470–471, 475–476, 479. Some notion of the arrogance of these foreign demands can be gained from a dispatch written to Salisbury by the British minister. Between February 4 and February 20, MacDonald wrote, he had been to see the Tsungli yamen four times for the purpose of "extracting some concessions in return for the rejection of the offer of a guaranteed loan from Great Britain after it had in principle been accepted." MacDonald to Salisbury, Feb. 20, 1898, BPP, *China, No. 1* (1899).

4. Langer, pp. 464, 467; Morse, III, 121; Langer, pp. 395, 702, 682.

5. John M. H. Lindbeck, "China Missionaries and American Foreign Policy: The Boxer Period," chap. 1. See also Paul A. Cohen, *China and Christianity: The Missionary Movement and the Growth of Chinese Anti-foreignism, 1860–1870* (Cambridge, Mass., 1963), esp. chap. 10.

6. A brief account of the career of a not atypical American missionary can be found in Marilyn Blatt, "Problems of a China Missionary: Justus Doolittle," *Papers on China,* 12:28–50 (Harvard University, East Asian Research Center, 1958). For an account of what missionaries could do at their best, see Peter Duus, "Science and Salvation in China: The Life and Work of W. A. P. Martin," *ibid.,* 10:97–127 (1956).

7. In 1895, the American Board of Foreign Missions was $116,000 in debt; the American Baptist Missionary Union was $203,600 in debt and the Presbyterian Board carried a deficit of $250,000. For figures on the American Baptist Missionary Union see *Missionary Review of the World,* 8:299

(April 1895); for the American Board of Commissioners of Foreign Missions see *ibid.* (January 1895), p. 43; for the Presbyterian Board of Foreign Missions, see *ibid.* (June 1895), p. 459.

8. *Ibid.,* p. 2 (January 1897).

9. Editorial by Arthur L. Pierson, *ibid.,* p. 219 (March 1897); report of Dr. Storr's address, *ibid.,* p. 320.

10. Anna W. Pierson, "A Woman's Missionary Rally," *ibid.,* 8:517 (July 1895).

11. *Literary Digest,* 11:451 (Aug. 17, 1895); 11:483 (Aug. 24, 1895). The *New York Tribune* insisted that "the Chinese Government . . . be held to the strictest accountability . . . if need be at the cannon's mouth." But the same article questioned the propriety of the missionary presence in China.

12. *Literary Digest,* 11:483 (Aug. 24, 1895).

13. *Ibid.,* p. 484.

14. *Ibid.,* 12:139 (November 1895); 11:454, 452 (Aug. 17, 1895).

15. See Denby to Olney, July 26, 1895, *FRUS, 1895,* pt. 1, p. 96; Jernigan to Denby, Oct. 25, 1895, U.S. Department of State Archives, Foreign Affairs Division *Consular Dispatches: Shanghai,* vol. 43, National Archives, Washington, D.C.

16. Denby to Uhl, June 13, 1895, *FRUS, 1895,* pt. 1, pp. 87–89.

17. Denby to Olney, July 9, 1895, *ibid.,* p. 91. This dispatch encloses a report by the Protestant missionaries at Cheng-tu to British Consul J. W. Tratman, *ibid.,* pp. 91–94; Denby to Olney, July 12, 1895, *ibid.,* p. 95.

18. Jernigan forwarded this petition directly to the Department adding his endorsement and hinting that he would not mind being the "consul of high rank," called for by the petitioners. Jernigan to Olney, Oct. 25, 1895, *Consular Dispatches: Shanghai,* vol. 43. Jernigan, later dismissed on grounds of petty peculation, was reprimanded by the Department for having taken an active role in drafting the Shanghai committee's resolutions. He denied that he had done so but added, vitiating his claims to neutrality, that China was at the threshold of great change and, "to enhance our interest on all lines of trade and commerce, no proper occasion should be omitted to impress upon China that the government of the United States is not only the most just, but the most powerful, in the world." Jernigan to Olney, Nov. 12, 1895, *ibid.*

19. Denby to Olney, July 26, 1895, *FRUS, 1895,* pt. 1, p. 96.

20. Denby to Olney, Aug. 13, 1895; Adee to Denby, Aug. 13, 1895; Denby to Olney, Aug. 14, 15 and 19, 1895, *ibid.,* pp. 104, 105, 108–109, 110–111.

21. Adee to Denby, Aug. 20, 1895; Denby to Olney, Aug. 15 and 31, 1895; Adee to Denby, Sept. 4, 1895, *ibid.,* pp. 112, 109, 122, 125.

22. Translation of a cablegram from the Tsungli yamen to Yang Ju dated Sept. 7, 1895 and handed to Adee Sept. 9, 1895, Adee to Denby, Sept. 4,

1895, *ibid.,* pp. 128, 130; Denby to Olney, Sept. 5, 1895, *China Dispatches,* vol. 99.

23. Yang Ju to Olney, Sept. 7, 1895; Olney to Denby, Sept. 19, 1895, *ibid.,* pp. 128, 138.

24. The Chinese wanted the commission to take the faster water route, which would come into relatively little contact with hostile elements of the population, cost less in guards and accommodations, and place less burden on the officials through whose provinces the commission passed. The Americans insisted on the land route, feeling its value lay precisely in the effort provincial officials would have to make, the demonstration effect on the people of seeing an elaborate American caravan proceeding to investigate antimissionary activities with a full panoply of Chinese guards and bearers. See Denby to Olney, Sept. 19, 1895; Olney to Denby, Sept. 20, 1895; Denby to Olney, Sept. 24, 1895, and Olney to Denby, Sept. 24, 1895, *ibid.,* pp. 140–141, 145.

25. Denby to Olney, Aug. 19, 1895; Adee to Denby, Aug. 12, 1895, *ibid.,* pp. 111, 102–103.

26. Denby to Olney, Aug. 27, 1895, Sept. 18, 1895; Olney to Denby, Sept. 19 and 21, 1895, *ibid.,* pp. 118, 139–143.

27. Olney to Denby, Nov. 30, 1895, *ibid.,* p. 172.

28. Denby to Olney, Mar. 24, 1896, *FRUS, 1896,* pp. 48–49. This dispatch encloses a communication from the Tsungli yamen to Denby dated March 19, 1896, which reviews the entire case and its settlement, *ibid.,* pp. 49–50. On June 3, 1896, Denby reported to Olney on the financial terms of the settlement, which had not been closely scrutinized by the Chinese in their anxiety to close the case. Denby to Olney, June 3, 1896, *ibid.,* pp. 52–53.

29. Denby to Olney, May 30, 1896, *ibid.,* p. 72. This dispatch encloses the report of Consul A. C. Jones to Denby dated May 20, 1896, *ibid.,* pp. 72–74.

30. Rockhill to Jones, July 22, 1896; Jones to Rockhill, July 24, Aug. 29, 1896, Oct. 24, 1896; Rockhill to Jones, Oct. 12, 1896, *ibid.,* pp. 74–83.

31. On the Ku-t'ien riot see Mary B. Rankin, "The Ku-t'ien Incident (1895): Christians Versus the Ts'ai-hui," *Papers on China,* 15:30–62 (Harvard University, East Asian Research Center, 1961). See also the report of Commander Newell, Nov. 1895, enclosed in Denby to Olney, Dec. 18, 1895, *FRUS, 1895,* pt. I, pp. 174–189.

32. Rockhill to Denby, July 28, 1896, *FRUS, 1896,* pp. 58, 59.

33. One small example of what the Tsungli yamen was up against can be found in the case of the Kiangyin riot. The local missionaries were suddenly conscience-stricken and convinced of the innocence of one of the three men about to be executed. Protest meetings were held in Shanghai and a petition sent to Denby who went to the Tsungli yamen to ask for a retrial, but the Tsungli yamen was firm. In accordance with foreign demands they had instructed the taotai of Chinkiang to act severely, and he had. No further inter-

ference with local justice would be tolerated. To drive the point home, the yamen reminded Denby that they were forced to act severely in order to protect the government from the consequences of missionary riots. Denby to Olney, Aug. 13, 1896, *ibid.*, pp. 78–79.

34. In this note to the yamen, Denby included a demand for the clear right of missionaries to reside and buy land anywhere in China—a proclamation to this effect to be published and distributed. The Tsungli yamen replied that such rights were provided for in the treaties. Denby to Olney, Feb. 25, 1897. This dispatch encloses a communication from the Tsungli yamen to Denby dated Feb. 19, 1897, *FRUS, 1897,* pp. 60–63.

35. Denby to Sherman, Mar. 24, 1897, *ibid.*, p. 64. In her study of the riot, M. B. Rankin concludes that the revival was, on the contrary, due to the harshness of the penalties imposed. This convinced the people of Ku-t'ien that, after all, the Christians were more powerful than the Vegetarians, and they joined the Church for the same reason they had earlier joined the Vegetarians—protection. See Rankin, pp. 52ff.

36. Sherman to Denby, May 15, 1897; Denby to Sherman, July 10, 1897, *FRUS, 1897,* pp. 66–69.

37. Chester C. Tan, *The Boxer Catastrophe* (New York, 1955), p. 58.

38. See *Literary Digest,* 21:78ff (July 21, 1900), for a good summary of articles illustrating missionary attitudes toward imperialism. In contrast to the dismal 1897 rally, an ecumenical conference of foreign missions held in New York in 1900 was addressed by ex-President Benjamin Harrison and President McKinley. It drew gratifying crowds, was given extensive press coverage, and was able to report increasing contributions. See below, Chap. 7.

39. Denby to Sherman, Nov. 23, 1897, *China Dispatches,* vol. 103.

40. Enclosed in John Fowler to Day, Dec. 1, 1897, *Consular Dispatches: Chefoo,* vol. 3.

41. Delavan L. Peirson, "The Crisis in China," *Missionary Review of the World,* 11:137 (January 1898); Rev. W. B. Hamilton, abstract of article which appeared in the *Independent, ibid.,* 11:316–317 (April 1898); undated article by Henry Porter, "The German Mission in Shantung" (North China Mission), American Board of Commissioners for Foreign Missions Archives, Houghton Library, Harvard University, file 16.3.12.

If one looks at American reactions to the German seizure of Kiaochow on a more general level, the picture is varied. According to the *Literary Digest,* the signing of the lease convinced the American press that, despite the kaiser's prose style, William was not, after all, a "clown." The *Journal of Commerce,* which numbered several men deeply interested in China on its staff, began publishing alarming reports on Far Eastern affairs early in January 1891. Convinced that Russia and Germany were determined to exclude American goods, the *Journal* urged a policy of cooperation with Japan and

Great Britain so as to ensure a continued market for American goods in China. *Literary Digest,* 16:2 (Jan. 1, 1898); *ibid.,* 16:31–32 (Jan. 8, 1898).

42. Campbell, p. 30.

43. Clarence Cary, "China's Complications and American Trade," *Forum,* 25:35–36, 49 (Mar. 1898); Campbell, pp. 35–36; Cary, "Complications," p. 45.

With Cary and John Foord in the lead, a Committee on American Interests in China was formed. James McGee of Standard Oil, Everett Frazar, head of the China Trading Company, S. D. Brewster, partner in a prominent cotton exporting firm and E. L. Zalinski of the Bethlehem Iron Company were other early members. The petition Cary mentioned in his *Forum* article was sent to the State Department by the Chambers of Commerce of Boston, San Francisco, and Philadelphia, as well as New York. Sherman, an increasingly feeble secretary of state, hastened to assure the New York Chamber that he was carefully watching Chinese affairs, and the American attachés in Berlin and St. Petersburg were instructed to inform their respective governments that the United States was not indifferent to their actions in China. Campbell, pp. 30ff, describes this group in some detail.

44. Denby to Sherman, Jan. 31, 1898, Feb. 19, 1898; Day to Denby, Feb. 21, 1898; Denby to Sherman, Feb. 21, 1898, *China Dispatches,* vol. 103. See also Pethick to Wilson, Feb. 13, 1898, Wilson Papers.

45. Denby to Sherman, Feb. 21, 1898, *China Dispatches,* vol. 103.

46. Denby to Sherman, Feb. 28, 1898, *ibid.* Solicitor General's Office to Adee, Apr. 12, 1898, *ibid.,* vol. 104. This opinion was based on several cases in which Chinese naturalized before the Exclusion Act of 1882 were denied citizenship. In 1892 the Supreme Court had ruled: "Chinese not born in this country have never been recognized as citizens of the United States, nor authorized to become such under the naturalization laws."

47. Sir Claude MacDonald to Marquis of Salisbury, Feb. 19, 1898, FO 377/Ref. 17/1340, no. 48. See also MacDonald to Salisbury, Feb. 25, 1898, *ibid.,* no. 47. (I am indebted to Professor May for the use of his microfilm copy of these documents from the Archives of the Foreign Office, Public Record Office, London.) The German and British banking groups involved reached an agreement on the division of interests in the line and then the concession was secured by joint Anglo-German effort. See Sun, p. 179, n 45. Mrs. Sun notes that the Foreign Office pressed for the Tientsin-Chinkiang line before British businessmen had expressed any interest in the venture. She concludes that in this, as in several other cases, concessions were valued in some measure for the political weight they might add to Britain in her competition with other powers in China. *Ibid.,* p. 41. See also British correspondence on this subject in BPP, *China, No. 1,* 1899.

48. Bash to Day, May 3, 1898; Day to Bash, May 13, 1898, quoted in Braisted, "American China Development Company," pp. 149, 150.

Chapter 5
Preparation for Action

1. Adee to Hay, undated memorandum of 1898, Hay Papers. This note contains both the Pauncefote statement and McKinley's reply with the recommendation that they do not appear in *FRUS, 1898.*

2. Pauncefote to Salisbury, Mar. 17, 1898, FO 4/2361. McKinley told the ambassador he was very much concerned over the actions of Russia and Germany in China and that the problem had "occupied his attention for some time past."

3. Day to Hay, July 14, 1898, Hay Papers.

4. The confusion of terms ("free port," "open port," "treaty port") used in asking for and receiving assurances was truly frightful. The Russian ambassador to London clarified his government's use of terms in the course of correcting a speech Salisbury had made to the House of Lords on February 8, 1898, in which he informed the lords that Russia had agreed to make Talienwan a "free port." De Staal objected that the English term " 'free port' appears to correspond to the French term 'port franc,' i.e., a port where goods imported are exempt from all import dues, whereas a treaty port, while being equally open to international commerce, subjects it nevertheless to the observance of the Customs Regulations and Tariffs in force in the country where the port is situated." (In other words, the Russian government used the terms "treaty port" and "open port" interchangeably; "free port," however, meant something quite different, being a port where goods could enter free of any duty whatsoever.) De Staal informed Salisbury he could not anticipate which policy his government would choose. Salisbury to Nicholas O'Conor, Feb. 8, 1898, BPP, *China No. 1,* 1898, and de Staal to Salisbury, Feb. 10, 1898, *ibid.* Salisbury did not help matters much by conceding: "The word used by your Excellency was, I understand, 'ouvert,' and it would have been better if I had said 'an open port' instead of using the word 'free,' which seemed to me to be the equivalent, but which is, of course, in some degree ambiguous." Indeed, they were two different things entirely. Salisbury to de Staal, Feb. 15, 1898, *ibid.* Langer, p. 469, mentions this exchange but in such a way as to confuse matters further. He notes that Britain gave up its earlier demand that "Talienwan be made a treaty port" when assured by de Staal that the port would be open—only to have de Staal protest that the Russians meant a "treaty port" and "not a free port." The implication is that Salisbury felt cheated, and that the Russians had further violated the principle of open trade in China; both are incorrect. The czar's ukase of August 1899 did make Talienwan a free port. The only reservation was that the Russians retained the right to establish a customs barrier between the port itself and the rest of the Liaotung Peninsula. In this event, however, the Russians promised that any tariff levied would apply equally

to all foreign goods regardless of nationality. Muraviev to Charlemagne Tower, Dec. 18–30, 1899, *FRUS, 1899,* p. 142.

5. Salisbury to O'Conor, Feb. 8, 1898, *China No. 1,* 1898. The standard study of this period makes light of German assurances on Kiaochow. Prior to the czar's ukase of August 1899, Griswold states, Talienwan had "merely been declared an open port—i.e., that foreign commerce would be admitted, subject to the Russian tariff." There was nothing "mere" in such an assurance, and the tariff to which goods were to be subject was not Russian but Chinese. A. Whitney Griswold, *The Far Eastern Policy of the United States* (New York, 1938), p. 57 and p. 72, n. 1.

6. McKinley speech in *FRUS, 1898,* p. xxii. Just one week after Paunce-fote's inquiry of March 8, Sherman cabled Hitchcock in St. Petersburg asking him to determine what policy Russia intended to pursue in the leased territories. Hitchcock replied that Muraviev had assured him that China retained sovereign rights in both territories. Port Arthur was strictly a military base but Talienwan would be "open [to] existing treaty rights of all nations." Hitchcock expanded on this in a letter written the same day. Muraviev had told him that Russian policy was "to develop home industries for supplying her home markets, under a protection policy, aided by increased transportation facilities." She would be glad to have foreign commerce "contribute" to the "maintenance and profit" of the leased territories. Sherman to Hitchcock, Mar. 17, 1898; Hitchcock to Sherman, cable and letter of Mar. 19, 1898, *Russia Dispatches,* vol. 51. On German trade policy in Kiaochow, see Morse, III, 109–110.

7. Letter from secretary of treasury transmitting letter of secretary of state, June 14, 1898, House Document 536, U.S. Documents, 55th Congress, 2nd session, 1897–1898, *House Documents,* vol. 64. It is understandable that, in the midst of the war, Congress would be too preoccupied to concern itself with such a project. Later on, more inclusive proposals of consular reform detracted from the wisdom of a commercial commission that, at some cost, would only make a single visit and a single report.

8. Henry Watterson, editor of the *Louisville Courier-Journal,* and an early spokesman for the New South, became an early advocate of a new America as well. On less theoretical grounds, the *Tradesman,* of Chattanooga, Tennessee, heartily supported a policy of assertion of American power, particularly in the Far East, where the paper foresaw a glorious opportunity for southern cotton interests. *Literary Digest,* 17:3, 4 (July 2, 1898), *ibid.,* p. 361 (Sept. 17, 1898). A *Journal of Commerce* survey made in June 1899, showed a considerable expansion of mills and spindlage in the South. Most of the increase was due as much to the expectation of growing exports to China as to the general economic recovery of the nation. Quoted in *Independent,* 51: 1715–1716 (June 22, 1899).

9. *Literary Digest,* 17:32ff (July 9, 1898); *Independent,* 50:714 (Sept. 8, 1898).

10. John R. Proctor, president U.S. Civil Service Commission, "Isolation or Imperialism," *Forum*, 26:14–26 (Sept. 1898).

11. William MacDonald, "The Dangers of Imperialism," *ibid.*, pp. 177–187 (Oct. 1898).

12. Letter of Theodore Roosevelt accepting the nomination of the Republican National Convention of 1900 for vice-president of the United States, September 15, 1900 (pamphlet published by the Republican National Committee, New York). Given the agonized debate over whether the United States should annex the Philippines, there is a touching irony in the Russian ambassador's puzzled comment to Muraviev, the foreign minister: "What do the American's intend to do about the Philippines? If you can believe them, they simply want to annex them." Cassini to Muraviev, June 22, 1898, quoted in Zabriskie, app. I, p. 203.

13. Lodge to J. F. Rhodes, Aug. 6, 1900, quoted in John Garraty, *Henry Cabot Lodge* (New York, 1953), p. 204.

14. Alva Adams, "A New Political Gospel," *Independent*, 50:169, 170 (July 21, 1898).

15. *Literary Digest*, 17:272, 273 (Sept. 3, 1898).

16. The following week, on August 18, the *Independent* continued to sound a muted war cry. Its editor urged Great Britain to resist Russian presumption at all costs. *Independent*, 50:427–428 (Aug. 11, 1898); *ibid.*, p. 503 (Aug. 18, 1898).

17. The editorial stated: "We have ten times as much reason for defending our great interests in the east as we have of fighting a sentimental war with Spain over which class of people shall misrule Cuba." After the British took Wei-hai-wei, the *Herald* was gently disapproving. Its major complaint was that now America could no longer depend on England "to fight our battles for us" in China. As opposed to the *Independent*, however, the *Herald* did not advocate that America fight her own battles either. *Boston Herald* (Mar. 27, 1898), p. 12; *ibid.* (Mar. 29, 1898), p. 6.

18. Charles G. Dawes, *A Journal of the McKinley Years*, ed. B. N. Timmons (Chicago, 1950), p. 139.

19. Conger to Day, July 31, 1898, *China Dispatches*, vol. 104.

20. Conger to Day, Aug. 26, 1898, *ibid.*

21. Conger to Hay, Nov. 3, 1898, Mar. 1, 1899, *ibid.*, vols. 105 and 106. Conger's interest in a coaling station may not have been entirely unprompted. In September 1898, a representative of the American China Development Company, in whose success Conger was very interested, suggested to him that the company's bargaining power would be considerably increased if the United States had a naval base along the south China coast. Lyman to Conger, Sept. 20, 1898, quoted in Braisted, "American China Development Company," p. 150.

22. Conger to Hay, Mar. 1, 1899, *China Dispatches*, vol. 106.

23. Denby, "Why the Treaty Should Be Ratified," *Forum*, 26:646–649

(Feb. 1899). Denby preferred holding the Philippines to seizing territory in China. See "Shall We Keep the Philippines?", *Forum*, 26:80 (Nov. 1898).

24. A. B. Johnson to Denby, Sept. 1, 1897, *Consular Dispatches: Amoy*, vol. 14.

25. Johnson to Hay, May 5, Aug. 30 and 23, 1900, *ibid*.

26. Johnson to Hay, Jan. 12, 1899, *ibid*. Johnson hoped to prevent the application of the Chinese Exclusion Acts to the Philippines. He felt this would be both unfair to the Chinese and disastrous to the development of the Islands. Johnson pointed to the British development of Singapore as the proper model for American efforts in the Philippines. The sensible use of cheap Chinese labor, he believed, was vital.

27. Johnson to Hay, Jan. 12, 1899, and Mar. 14, 1899, *ibid.*, Johnson to Hay, Mar. 2, 1899; Cridler to Johnson, Mar. 9, 1899, *ibid*.

28. When Amoy was made a treaty port in 1842, British merchants and the first consul gravitated naturally to the cool and convenient island of Kulangsu in Amoy harbor. However, it was believed essential to establish residence rights within the Amoy city wall and the consulate was set up there in 1845. In 1903, Kulangsu became a formal International Settlement. John K. Fairbank, *Trade and Diplomacy on the China Coast: The Opening of the Treaty Ports, 1842–1854* (Cambridge, Mass., 1953), I, 201–203.

29. Johnson to Hay, Nov. 21, 1899, *Consular Dispatches: Amoy*, vol. 14.

30. Conger to Hay, Mar. 23, 1899; Hay to Conger, Mar. 24, 1899, *China Dispatches*, vol. 106; Hay to Henry Adams, July 8, 1900, Hay Papers.

31. Johnson to Hay, Oct. 5, 1899, *ibid*.

32. Johnson to Hay, Nov. 21, 1899, and Mar. 5, 1900, *ibid*.

33. John Fowler to J. B. Moore, Oct. 27, 1898, *Consular Dispatches: Chefoo*, vol. 3. Fowler's dispatch can also be found in files relating to the acquisition of a naval base in China (1897–1903). U.S. Department of the Navy Archives, Secretary's Office, National Archives, Washington, D.C. RG 80/5664/3.

34. Cridler to Acting Secretary of the Navy Allen, Dec. 23, 1898, and Allen to Hay, Dec. 24, 1898, U.S. Department of the Navy Archives, RG 80/5664/3. Fowler had suggested Chefoo or Chusan Island as most suitable to American purposes. The disposition of Chusan lay with Great Britain under a non-alienation agreement with China made in 1846. Fowler suggested that the British might exchange their rights over Chusan for one of the islands in the Philippine group. R. B. Bradford to Secretary of the Navy Long, Jan. 13, 1899; Allen to Bradford, Sept. 21, 1899, *ibid*.

35. R. B. Bradford, "Coaling Stations for the Navy," *Forum*, 26:732–747 (Feb. 1899).

36. Long to Hay, July 31, 1900, U.S. Department of the Navy Archives, RG/80/11324/3.

37. Bradford's report is enclosed in *ibid*.

38. Hay to Paul Dana, Mar. 16, 1899; Hay to Wu T'ing-fang, Nov. 11, 1899, Hay Papers.

39. The best secondary works on this period are John K. Fairbank and Teng Ssu-yü, *China's Response to the West: A Documentary Survey, 1839–1923* (Cambridge, Mass., 1954), pt. 5; Levenson, *Liang Ch'i-ch'ao*, chaps. 1 and 2; and the primarily documentary collection, *Sources of the Chinese Tradition*, Wm. Theodore de Bary, Wang-tsit Chan and Burton Watson, comps. (New York, 1960), chap. 26.

40. Li Chien-nung, *The Political History of China, 1840–1928*, tr. and ed. Teng Ssu-yü and Jeremy Ingalls (Princeton, 1956), p. 159.

41. The reform movement and its failure is a complex and fascinating subject, whose intricacies I have treated somewhat cavalierly. Neither the reformers nor their conservative opponents were simple men. The rivalries involved extended beyond the ideological to the purely, perhaps imponderably, personal. Fairbank and Teng have noted that if the empress dowager herself, through some sleight-of-hand, could have been placed in the forefront of the movement, the opposition would have been considerably nullified—nor was the empress dowager unimaginable in such a role. To attain real power, the emperor had to get rid of the empress dowager's influential, sycophantic followers. In so doing, however, he directly threatened the empress dowager and, indeed, forced her into the opposition. The court factions, north and south, themselves largely personal in origin, were divided on reform. The Chinese-Manchu division may also have been significant in aligning forces and in determining the empress dowager's final move. Fairbank and Teng, *China's Response to the West*, p. 175.

42. Conger to Hay, Sept. 24, 1898, *China Dispatches*, vol. 105.

43. See Lindbeck, "China Missionaries," chap. 2; *Independent*, 50:873–874 (Sept. 29, 1898); 50:1067 (Oct. 13, 1898).

44. See for example *Missionary Review of the World*, 11:939 (Dec. 1898). The editorial points out that the reforms were very radical, that the empress dowager was probably more in favor of reform than she was usually given credit for, and it speculated that perhaps she feared she could not have enforced such extreme reforms at that time. See also *Missionary Review of the World*, 12:448–449 (June 1899), which expresses a view very similar to that of the only comprehensive Western study of the reform movement yet written, Meribeth E. Cameron's *The Reform Movement in China, 1898–1912* (Stanford, 1931).

45. Conger to Hay, Aug. 28, 1899, *China Dispatches*, vol. 107.

46. *Journal of the American Asiatic Association*, 1:8 (Aug. 1898), 19 (Oct. 31, 1898). This praise was hardly surprising given the overlapping membership of the *Journal of Commerce's* staff and the association's executive board.

47. Gilbert Reid, "American Opportunities in China," *Forum*, 27:238, 239–240 (Apr. 1899).

48. C. K. Adams, "Colonies and Other Dependencies," *ibid.*, p. 46 (March 1899). Charles Conant's important articles on America and the Orient began to appear at this time as well; the first was published in the September 1898 issue of *North American Review*.

49. Braisted, "American China Development Company," p. 151.

50. J. F. Goodnow to J. Hill, July 5, 1899, *Consular Dispatches: Shanghai,* vol. 46.

51. Hay to Conger, July 14, 1899, and July 15, 1899; Conger to Hay, Nov. 25, 1899, and Dec. 6, 1899, *China Dispatches,* vols. 106 and 107.

52. Hay to Conger, May 7, 1900, *ibid.,* vol. 108.

53. Braisted, "American China Development Company," p. 152.

54. Kent, p. 115.

55. Whitelaw Reid, "Our New Interests," address at University of California, Mar. 23, 1900, printed for the university in 1900; Margaret Leech, *In the Days of McKinley* (New York, 1959), p. 142; Thomas J. McCormick, "Insular Imperialism and the Open Door: The China Market and the Spanish-American War," *Pacific Historical Review,* 32:155–169 (1963).

56. Cushman K. Davis to Reid, Apr. 20, 1899, Reid Papers.

57. Horace Porter to McKinley, quoted in Wayne Morgan, *William McKinley and His America* (Syracuse, 1963), pp. 476–477.

Chapter 6
The Open Door

1. Fairbank, *Trade and Diplomacy,* p. 463.

2. Joseph Chamberlain to Arthur Balfour, Feb. 3, 1898, quoted in Griswold, p. 45.

3. Langer, p. 681.

4. *Ibid.,* p. 684. A brief, lucid account of these maneuvers can be found in *ibid.,* p. 679.

5. See Hay to Henry White, Nov. 23, 1898, Hay Papers. Hay explained that the President was in favor of an "open door" in the Philippines, which would admit goods of other nations to the islands "on an equal footing with ourselves." It did not mean absolute free trade.

6. *Literary Digest,* 17:680, 682 (Dec. 10, 1898).

7. See Gilbert Reid, "American Opportunities in China," pp. 239ff; *Journal of the American Asiatic Association,* 1:30 (Mar. 11, 1899).

8. *Ibid.* Letters of regret were received from the President, the secretary of war, the secretary of the navy, the secretary of state, Governor Theodore Roosevelt and Cushman K. Davis. Hay gave a dinner for Beresford in Washington later in the month.

9. *Ibid.,* p. 35.

10. *Ibid.,* pp. 36–42.

11. *Independent,* 51:573 (Feb. 1899); *Journal of the American Asiatic Association,* 1:58 (Nov. 13, 1899).

12. *Boston Herald* (Mar. 14, 1899), p. 6. The Sunday *Herald* of March 12, 1899, pp. 35ff, ran a three page supplement on nineteenth-century China trade stressing its role in making New England great. The explicit point was that the "open door" existed in the 1840's, making profitable trade possible. As the situation of free competition changed to one of exclusive spheres of influence, New England suffered from a severe decline in this important trading area.

13. John Barrett, reprint of address to New York Chamber of Commerce, pp. 46–50; *Journal of the American Asiatic Association* (special issue), 1:1 (June 10, 1899).

14. *Ibid.,* 1:61 (Nov. 13, 1899); *ibid.,* p. 66.

15. *Ibid.,* p. 65.

16. Charles Beresford, *The Break-Up of China* (London and New York, 1899), pp. 443–444. I do not think it evades the issue of causation to stress the interrelationship of such factors as the demands of special interest groups, the ideology of men like Rockhill and Hay, and the fearful, strained attentiveness of the politicians of the 1890's to public opinion. Campbell's too limited approach focuses on the role of businessmen out of all proportion to their real influence. I would agree with Harvey Pressman that Campbell's "special business interests were more a permissive than a major causal factor." Harvey Pressman, "Hay, Rockhill, and China's Integrity: A Reappraisal," *Papers on China,* 13:61–79 (Harvard University, East Asian Research Center, 1959).

17. Rockhill to Hay, Aug. 3, 1899; Hippisley to Rockhill, July 25, 1899, Rockhill Papers.

18. Rockhill to Hippisley, Aug. 3, 1899, *ibid.*

19. Hay to Rockhill, Aug. 7, 1899, *ibid.* Hay had other reasons for moving with caution. Although he took full advantage of Rockhill's knowledge and experience in things Chinese, Hay was independently interested and had other sources of information. In January 1899, he had received advance warning of Beresford's arrival from Consul-General Wildman in Hong Kong, Wildman felt that the present state of American trade with China did not warrant "any great expense on our part towards aiding England to maintain the open door policy." Wildman to Hay, Jan. 6, 1899, quoted in Tyler Dennett, *John Hay: From Poetry to Politics* (New York, 1933), p. 287, n. 1.

20. Hippisley to Rockhill, Aug. 16, 1899, Rockhill Papers.

21. *New York Times* (Aug. 16, 1899), p. 9.

22. Rockhill to Hippisley, Aug. 16, 1899, Rockhill Papers.

23. *Ibid.;* Hippisley to Rockhill, Aug. 21, 1899, Rockhill Papers. Hip-

pisley was fully aware of the fact that even in 1899 the administration was looking to the next election, when its Philippine policy would be, in America's clumsy referendum, "tested," at the polls. He reminded Rockhill that an administration claim to have served the cause of civilization in China would be "a trump card" for McKinley and a serious defeat for such anti-imperialist agitators as Bryan.

24. Hippisley to Rockhill, Aug. 21, 1899, Rockhill Papers.

25. Hippisley to Rockhill, Aug. 26, 1899, *ibid.*

26. Rockhill to Hippisley, Aug. 26, 1899, *ibid.*

27. Hay to Rockhill, Aug. 24, 1899, Hay Papers.

28. Rockhill to Hay, Aug. 28, 1899, Rockhill Papers.

29. Rockhill to Henry Adams, Mar. 6, 1899, Rockhill Papers.

30. Rockhill to Hay, Aug. 28, 1899, *ibid.*

31. Hippisley to Rockhill, Sept. 7, 1899; Rockhill to Hippisley, Sept. 14, 1899, Rockhill Papers. Rockhill's correspondence with Hippisley slowed down after the exciting summer exchange. On October 13, Rockhill took a parting shot at Lord Beresford: "Lord Beresford made a speech in N. Y. . . . He did not, however, say anything new or important in any way. It seems to me he is more a bag of wind than anything else. I think it would be quite unnecessary to enlist his assistance over here to carry out what must be recognized by all as *our* policy in China." (Italics in original.) Rockhill to Hippisley, Oct. 13, 1899, Rockhill Papers.

32. Rockhill to Hay, Oct. 19, 1899, *ibid.*

33. Rockhill to Edwin Denby, Jan. 13, 1900, *ibid.*

34. Italics inserted. The note was sent to Japan on November 13, 1900, to Italy on November 17, 1900, and to France on November 21, 1900. The notes and replies are printed in *FRUS, 1899,* pp. 128–142.

35. Clyde, pp. 201–215, includes a very convenient parallel column reprint of Hippisley's August 21 memorandum, Rockhill's August 28 memorandum to Hay, the Rockhill first draft, and the final draft of the September 6 note to England.

36. Joseph Choate to Hay, Nov. 1, 1899; Rockhill to Hay, n.d., October 1899 memorandum, Hay Papers.

37. Choate to Hay, Nov. 1, 1899; Hay to Choate, Nov. 13, 1899, Hay Papers. This was in fact done. England's acceptance of the September note states that the government was prepared to make a declaration in the sense desired (only) "in regard to the leased territory of Wei-hai Wei and all territory in China which may hereafter be acquired by Great Britain by lease or otherwise." A letter from Choate to Hay, dated March 3, 1900, Hay Papers, indicates that Hay had agreed to some delicate falsification of the British Blue Book on China for 1899. It was felt undesirable to "show the world that the Hong Kong extension was specially excluded." Instead a new exchange of notes "antedating them for the purpose," was to be drawn up and substituted.

38. Muraviev to Cassini, Nov. 19, 1899, quoted in Zabriskie, p. 55.

39. Rockhill to Hay, Nov. 24, 1899, Rockhill Papers. See also Zabriskie, pp. 55ff. for an excellent account of Russo-American negotiations. Zabriskie quotes extensively from the reports of Tower to Hay which can also be found in *Russia Dispatches,* vol. 55. See especially Tower to Hay, Dec. 28, 1899.

40. Rockhill to Hay, Aug. 28, 1899, Rockhill Papers; Muraviev to Witte, Dec. 31, 1899, quoted in Zabriskie, pp. 58–59; Cassini to Muraviev, June 22, 1898, Cassini to Lamsdorff, June 23, 1899, quoted in *ibid.,* app. I, pp. 203–205. Although the Russian acceptance was limited, it *was* an answer. There had been strong opposition within the Russian government to answering the note at all. The definition of Russia's sphere as being the "Chinese provinces north of the Great Wall" demonstrates that it was understood by both Russia and America that Manchuria was to be included within the scope of the note's application—indeed the note made little sense with regard to Russia if this were not the case.

41. Prince Esper Ukhtomskii, a close friend of the czar's and an advocate of Pan-Asianism under Russian guidance, was president of the Russo-Chinese Bank and an important figure in Russian expansionist circles. Langer, p. 402; Ernest R. May, *Imperial Democracy: The Emergence of America as a Great Power* (New York, 1961), p. 265, attributes the article to an attempt to put pressure on Great Britain in a pending railroad negotiation. Ukhtomskii hoped "that the threat of a Russian deal with America would make them more businesslike." I think it more likely that the article was a continuation of Muraviev's 1898 instructions to Cassini to create as many conflicts as possible between the United States and Great Britain. The tone of both article and introduction is defensive—combatting the felt russophobia of men like Hay and Brooks Adams.

There existed in America considerable pro-Russian sentiment, based both on the "historic" friendship between the two countries, and upon more current economic considerations. The depth of this sentiment and the lines of interest that divided the russophobes from the russophiles remains to be explored. Ukhtomskii's article was actually an introduction to a piece by Vladimir Holstrem: "Ex Oriente Lux: A Plea for Russo-American Understanding," *North American Review,* 159:6-32 (July 1899).

42. It should be noted that some Americans, when they counted Russia as white European and not yellow Oriental territory, were very prone to see Russian expansion in just this light. As Theodore Roosevelt wrote Cecil Spring Rice in August 1899: "Russia's march over barbarous Asia does represent a real and great advance for civilization." What stopped Roosevelt short of complete admiration was his concern for English predominance: "But I feel that to have England's power curtailed even by this Russian advance would be a great calamity." Roosevelt to Spring Rice, Aug. 11, 1899, in Morison, II, 1048–1053.

43. Cf. Gorelik, pp. 41ff. Gorelik stresses the efforts of czarist diplomacy to prevent the formation of a three power pact between the United States, England, and Japan.

44. Tower to Hay, Feb. 12, 1900, Hay Papers. It should be noted that Germany too was very concerned about a possible American-British-Japanese entente.

45. Hay to White, Apr. 2, 1900; Hay to Henry Adams, June 15, 1900, Hay Papers. Rockhill's defense of the acceptance of Russia's vague answer is interesting. In a letter to Hippisley he reflected: "All the Powers have practically accepted the proposals of the U.S. although I am fain to omit that the acceptance of Russia is not as complete as I would like it; in fact, it has what we call in America a string attached to it. Nevertheless, I think it prudent to accept it, for none of the European Powers are prepared to have this question made the subject of heated debate and controversy, and those who have given their unconditional acceptance . . . would withdraw . . . if they perceived that the Powers might get arrayed in hostile camps against each other on this subject." Rockhill to Hippisley, Jan. 16, 1900, Rockhill Papers.

46. Rockhill to Edwin Denby, Jan. 13, 1900, *ibid.*

47. *Literary Digest*, 20:35 (Jan. 13, 1900); 20:365 (Apr. 7, 1900).

48. *Independent*, 52:137, 138 (Jan. 11, 1900), 52:841–842 (Apr. 5, 1900).

49. *Literary Digest*, 20:36 (Jan. 13, 1900).

50. Leech, pp. 516, 515. Miss Leech also notes, with the decision to retain the Philippines, "The President . . . made the extension of American markets in the Far East a leading policy of his administration."

51. Chamberlin, p. 80, a letter to his wife, Oct. 1, 1900.

Chapter 7
The Long Hot Summer

1. William W. Rockhill, "The United States and the Future of China," *Forum*, 29:330 (May 1900).

2. Conger to Hay, Dec. 11, 1899, *FRUS, 1900*, p. 385.

3. Hay to Conger, Feb. 3, 1900, *ibid.*, pp. 386–387.

4. Conger to Hay, Nov. 30, 1898, *China Dispatches*, vol. 105.

5. Conger to Hay, Jan. 29, 1900, *FRUS, 1900*, pp. 93–96. Conger joined in presenting a second identic note in early March. Conger to Hay, Mar. 10, 1900, includes the note and the Chinese reply, *ibid.*, pp. 102–108. Hay to Conger, Mar. 22, 1900, *ibid.*, pp. 111–112. The letter was signed by Hay but everything from its phraseology to its tortuous syntax indicates that Rockhill wrote it for the secretary's signature. The version printed in *FRUS* is incomplete. For the full text see Instruction Book, vol. 6.

6. Hay to Conger, Mar. 22, 1900, Instruction Book, vol. 6. It should be noted that Hippisley too felt China owed much to America. Commenting on the American China Development Company's negotiations, he told Rockhill he felt China could hardly deny the company's requests in view of what American diplomacy was doing for her.

7. Rockhill, "United States and the Future of China," pp. 324–331.

8. Writing as an "old friend" of Yuan Shih-k'ai, Rockhill congratulated Yuan on his appointment as viceroy of Chihli on December 6, 1901. Correspondence between Rockhill and Admiral Tsai Ting-kan indicates that Rockhill had become Yuan's paid adviser in 1914. The relationship ended with Rockhill's death that same year. Financial arrangements are discussed in Tsai Ting-kan to Rockhill, Mar. 13, 1914, and Tsai to Mrs. Rockhill, Dec. 31, 1914, Rockhill Papers.

9. Rockhill to Hay, June 1, 1900, *ibid.*

10. *Independent*, 52:20, 25, 36, 37, 44, 37, 78, 25 (Jan. 4, 1900).

11. *Ibid.*, 52:1021ff (Apr. 26, 1900), p. 1079 (May 3, 1900); *Missionary Review of the World*, 13:411ff (June 1900) and pp. 546ff (July 1900), contains extracts from the New York newspapers.

12. Julius W. Pratt, *The Expansionists of 1898: The Acquisition of Hawaii and the Spanish Islands* (Baltimore, 1936), chap 8, *Boston Herald*, July 31, 1900, p. 2; *Independent*, 52:1146 (May 10, 1900); 51:2576 (Sept. 21, 1899), 51:2637 (Sept. 28, 1899), 51:3201 (Dec. 21, 1899).

13. The best study of the Boxer movement, its origins and aftermath is Tan, *The Boxer Catastrophe*. Vincent Purcell's recent *The Boxer Uprising: A Background Study* (Cambridge, Mass., 1963), contains additional detail on the origin and beliefs of the Boxers (see especially chaps. 8–11). Almost every missionary present in China at the time of the siege later wrote a book about it. These, and the diaries kept by the besieged diplomats and their dependents, have been put to good anecdotal use in Peter Fleming's *The Siege at Peking* (London, 1959).

14. Purcell, pp. 199–217. One segment of Boxers remained anti-Manchu throughout, see *ibid.*, pp. 209–210.

15. *Ibid.*, p. 209; Tan, p. 65.

16. Purcell, p. 202.

17. *Ibid.*, pp. 174–179. Purcell argues that demands by the legations to suppress the Boxers may have precipitated the entire crisis, pp. 245ff.

18. Tan, pp. 70ff.

19. Fleming, p. 73, gives the most vivid account of this incident.

20. Tan, pp. 72ff.

21. Joseph Levenson, *Confucian China and its Modern Fate,* pp. 146ff.

22. Quoted in Tan, p. 72.

23. Purcell, pp. 248–249.

24. Tan, pp. 73ff.

25. *Ibid.*, p. 75, 97.

26. *Ibid.,* p. 98; Purcell, pp. 245ff. The court quite understandably saw the presence of a force of foreign troops like Seymour's—some 2,000 men— as an unbearable threat to the safety of the government itself. The ministers' refusal to halt Seymour's advance determined the court's attitude and confirmed its fears.

27. Conger to Hay, June 4 and June 8, 1900, *China Dispatches,* vol. 108.

28. As Hay's closest friend, Henry Adams, put it: "I turn green in bed at midnight if I think of the horror of a year's warfare in the Philippines; . . . we must slaughter a million or two foolish Malays in order to give them the comforts of flannel petticoats and electric railways . . . I am certain that every member of the administration thinks as I do. We all dread and abominate the war, but cannot escape it. We must protect Manila and the foreign interests, which, in trying to protect the natives from Spain, we were obliged to assume responsibility for." Henry Adams to Elizabeth Cameron, Jan. 22, 1899, *Letters of Henry Adams, 1892–1918,* ed. W. C. Ford, p. 208. Henry's brother, Brooks Adams, was consistently closer in spirit and outlook to Theodore Roosevelt than he was to either Hay or, after the early 1890's, his own brother. In October 1899, he wrote Henry in a tone of optimism his brother found impossible in the gloom of the turn of the century. "For my part," Brooks declared, "I go with the tide. I am all for the new world—the new America, the new empire . . . Every day I live here my conviction deepens that we are the people of destiny." Brooks Adams to Henry Adams, Oct. 14, 1899, quoted in Beringause, p. 186. Henry might have agreed that America was the country of destiny, but what the destiny was he disliked to contemplate.

29. Hay to Conger, June 8, 1900, and June 10, 1900, Instruction Book, vol. 6.

30. Admiral of the Fleet, the Right Honorable Sir Edward H. Seymour, *My Naval Career and Travels* (London, 1911), pp. 344ff. William Braisted, *The United States Navy in the Pacific, 1897–1909* (Austin, 1958), pp. 81ff.

31. Interview with Herbert Hoover, *New York Sun* (Nov. 19,1900).

32. Correspondence between the Foreign Office and the British consul in Tientsin indicates that the Foreign Office had no advance knowledge of the ultimatum. See BPP, *China, No. 3,* 1900, for month of June. McKinley was following the situation very closely and Kempff's dispatches are all included in the McKinley Papers. See Kempff to Secretary Long, June 9, 12, 16, and 17, 1900.

33. Kempff to Long, June 17, 1900; Wise to Kempff, June 17, 1900; Kempff to Wise, June 19, 1900; Kempff to Long, June 20, June 22, 1900; Wise to Kempff, June 23, 1900; Kempff to Long, June 25, 1900, McKinley Papers.

34. Long to Kempff, June 5, 1900; Remey to Long, June 6, 1900, McKinley Papers.

35. Acting Secretary of the Navy Hackett to Kempff, June 18, 1900, McKinley Papers.

36. MacArthur to Adjutant-General Corbin, June 16, 1900; Corbin to MacArthur, June 22, 1900; MacArthur to Corbin, July 18, 1900; Corbin to MacArthur, July 16, 1900, McKinley Papers.

37. Kempff to Long, June 25, July 1, 1900; Benjamin F. Montgomery to George Cortelyou, July 1, 1900, McKinley Papers. (Montgomery was the telegrapher at the White House who transmitted all messages for the President while the latter was at Canton through the President's secretary, George Cortelyou.)

38. *New York Tribune* (June 11, 1900), p. 1; *ibid.* (June 20, 1900), p. 8. The *Tribune* argued, however, that of all the powers, Japan was best equipped for the job of restraining China. The Chinese would "yield to the Japanese where they would furiously resist any other nation." Apparently the *Tribune* had forgotten the war of 1895.

39. Davis to Reid, July 4, 1900; Reid to Davis, July 20, 1900, Reid Papers.

40. Leech, p. 520.

41. *Public Opinion,* 28:772 (June 21, 1900); *Independent,* 52:1454 (June 14, 1900); Leech, p. 519.

42. Lindbeck, "China Missionaries," chap. 4; Campbell, p. 71; Enclosed in Adee to Cortelyou, Aug. 28, 1900, McKinley Papers.

43. In late June, before the publication of the July 3 circular, Lodge wrote to White that only by acting together with England and Japan could the United States "prevent the absorption of China by Russia, and keep the Empire open for our trade and commerce, which is all we want." Lodge to White, June 29, 1900, quoted in Allan Nevins, *Henry White and Thirty Years of American Diplomacy* (New York, 1930), p. 137. By mid-July Lodge's fears were quieted. He wrote Rockhill that "Russia has utterly failed to meet the situation, and I think it is plain that whatever happens she will never get control of China, which I once feared she would." Lodge to Rockhill, July 16, 1900, Rockhill Papers.

44. Choate to Hay, June 20, 1900; Hay to Foster, June 23, 1900, Hay Papers.

45. Henry Adams to Hay, June 26, 1900, *Letters of Henry Adams,* pp. 290–291; Hay to Henry Adams, July 8, 1900, Hay Papers; Henry Adams to Brooks Adams, July 29, 1900, in Harold D. Cater, ed., *Henry Adams and His Friends* (Boston, 1947), p. 496.

46. See also Henry Adams to W. W. Rockhill, July 12, 1900, *ibid.,* p. 492; Henry Adams to John Hay, Nov. 7, 1900, *Letters of Henry Adams,* pp. 299, 300; Henry Adams to Elizabeth Cameron, Mar. 22, 1903, *ibid.,* p. 402.

47. Langer, p. 694. Tan, p. 75, gives the date of the edict declaring war as June 21. Li Chien-nung, p. 177, n. 2, puts it a day earlier, June 20. Although not sent abroad, the edict was communicated to the legations. The

ministers were told "that if they wished to open hostilities, they must lower their flags and return to their nations instantly." Li Chien-nung, p. 176. The diplomatic corps in Peking had no power to open hostilities on the government to which it was accredited unless so instructed by their governments. Nor did the ministers plan to risk their lives by leaving the legation quarter at that time. Instead, they requested a conference with the Tsungli yamen, which was refused. See also Purcell, pp. 255, 256, n. 1.

48. The following account is based on Tan, chap. 4.

49. Memo of interview between Wu T'ing-fang and John Hay, June 22, 1900, *FRUS, 1900,* pp. 273–274. Hay replied that McKinley had authorized him to say no expeditions into peaceful areas were planned. The British were threatening to occupy the Woosung and Kiangyin forts as well as the Shanghai arsenal. The British consul claimed that Liu K'un-yi had offered the British joint occupation of these places. J. C. Ferguson, an American close to both Sheng Hsuan-huai and Liu K'un-yi, told the American consul-general, J .F. Goodnow, that in fact the British consul had warned the Shanghai taotai that the fleets of all the other nations had aranged to seize the Woosung forts and he had asked the taotai if he didn't want England to take "joint control so as to keep the others out." Goodnow said it was impossible to get a clear story but that it was evident the English were anxious to occupy the forts and constantly plotted toward that end. (Goodnow to Cridler, June 29, 1900, *Consular Dispatches: Shanghai,* vol. 46.) In August Goodnow reported that the consular body at Shanghai was under tremendous pressure from resident merchants of all nationalities to land troops in Shanghai. The consuls agreed this would increase distrust and unrest and was therefore unadvisable. Admiral Seymour, however, without consulting anyone, had put in a request to his government for troops to garrison Shanghai. (Goodnow to Hay, Aug. 8, 1900, *ibid.,* vol. 47.) On August 10, a confidential telegram from Goodnow to Hay informed the secretary that the British had ordered two regiments of Sepoys to proceed to Shanghai. The British consuls claimed that a special arrangement had been made with the viceroy allowing only British soldiers to land. Goodnow felt this was a bluff, but that it was used at all demonstrated the anxiety of the British not to arouse American or Chinese hostility. (Goodnow to Hay, Aug. 10, 1900, *ibid.*) According to an August 7 telegram from Goodnow, Liu K'un-yi unwillingly acquiesced in the landing of British troops. American troops were not landed, despite Goodnow's recommendations to that effect, although America's right to do so if the need arose, was affirmed. See Goodnow to Hay, Aug. 7, 1900, and Sept. 1, 1900, and Braisted, *United States Navy in the Pacific,* p. 98.

50. Proclamation by Senior Naval Officers of Allied Forces in China, June 20, 1900, signed by Kempff as second-in-command, U.S. Department of Navy Archives, United States Naval Force, Asiatic Station RG/45.

51. Tan, pp. 92, 80. Tan credits Sheng, this "bold and brilliant official,"

with initiating most of the important measures taken during this period. Goodnow to Hay, June 26, 1900, *Consular Dispatches: Shanghai,* vol. 46.

52. Hay to McKinley, June 27, 1900; Hay to Goodnow, June 27, 1900; Goodnow to Hay, June 27, 1900, McKinley Papers.

53. Tan, p. 81; Goodnow to Cridler, June 29, 1900, *Consular Dispatches: Shanghai,* vol. 46. Tan, p. 81, has a complete list of the articles. Salisbury objected to being bound by a contractual agreement that would prevent the British from judging each case "on its merits." See Tan, p. 244, n. 1, for British moves in the Shanghai area.

54. Fleming, p. 148.

55. Interview, *New York Sun* (Jan. 2, 1901).

56. All through July and August, Goodnow was sending reports received from couriers within the legations to Washington. The fears of Hay and the others were well-justified. On July 18, for example, Goodnow sent this alarming cable: "Bombarding legations June 30 with Krupp cannon. Reliable. Sixty foreigners, 100 Chinese massacred Tai-yuan, Shansi." On August 1 Goodnow reported: "MacDonald courier 21st reports continuous artillery attack the 16th; holding American, German, Russian legations, and part wall: food ammunition short. Sixty killed; 120 wounded." Goodnow to Hay, July 1, 18, Aug. 1, 1900, *Consular Dispatches: Shanghai,* vols. 46 and 47.

57. Hay to "My Dear Boy," July 1, 1900, Hay Papers.

58. Feuerwerker, p. 72, refers to this as a formalization of the June 27 Shanghai meeting. Clearly this is mistaken. Goodnow's July 1 telegram to Hay conveys the urgency with which the two viceroys viewed the new situation. They asked that peace be maintained "regardless of what happens in Peking." This could only be a reference to the news of von Ketteler's death. Goodnow to Hay, July 1, 1900, *Consular Dispatches: Shanghai,* vol. 46. The naval commander at Chefoo, for example, noted the "new condition of affairs since the murder of the German Minister . . . and the rumored probable declaration of war against China by Germany." Rodgers to Kempff, July 4, 1900, McKinley Papers.

59. Hay to Goodnow, July 1, 1900; Goodnow to Hay, July 3, 1900, *Consular Dispatches: Shanghai,* vol. 46; McKinley to Hay, July 3, 1900, Hay Papers.

60. Exact information on the formulation of the July 3 circular is surprisingly difficult to find. Events were proceeding at such a pace that decisions seem to have been taken verbally and very rapidly. From the telegrams quoted in Charles S. Olcott, *The Life of William McKinley* (Boston and New York, 1916), II, 231–234 it is clear that the note was discussed at the Cabinet meeting Hay had called for July 3.

61. As Miss Leech says, McKinley's optimism "was a matter of policy, as well as personal inclination. To abandon hope for the legations was to

divest the intervention of the motive of rescue and relief." Leech, p. 521.

62. Circular note of July 3, 1900, to the powers cooperating in China; sent to the U.S. embassies in Berlin, Paris, London, Rome, and St. Petersburg and to the missions in Vienna, Brussels, Madrid, Tokyo, the Hague, and Lisbon. *FRUS, 1901,* app. I, p. 12; Leech, p. 522.

63. Hay to Henry Adams, July 8, 1900, Hay Papers.

64. Monson to Salisbury, July 5, 1900, *British Foreign and State Papers* (London, 1905), 95:116–117; Choate to Hay, July 17, 1900, Hay Papers.

65. Goodnow to Hay, July 5, 1900; McKinley to Hay, July 5, 1900; Hay to McKinley, July 6, 1900, Hay to Adams, July 8, Hay Papers.

66. Stenographic report of telephone conversation between McKinley and Root quoted in Olcott, II, 236–237; Corbin to MacArthur, July 7, 1900, *Correspondence Relating to the War with Spain* (Washington, D.C., 1902), I, 423.

67. Exchange of telegrams between Hay and McKinley reprinted in Olcott, II, 234–235.

68. Corbin to Chaffee, July 19, 1900, McKinley Papers; Olcott, II, 252.

69. Hay to Conger, July 11, 1900, Conger to Hay, July 20, 1900, *FRUS, 1900,* pp. 155, 156; M. G. Seckendorff to Nicholson, July 20, 1900, Reid to Davis, July 20, 1900, Reid Papers; Choate to Hay, July 25, 1900, *FRUS, 1900,* pp. 345–346.

70. Finley Peter Dunne, "Minister Wu," in *Mr. Dooley's Philosophy* (New York, 1900), pp. 83–89.

71. Hay to Conger, July 21, 1900, *FRUS, 1900,* p. 156, Conger to Hay, n.d., *ibid.,* p. 159. *FRUS* marks this cable, received August 16, as the reply to Hay's July 21 cable. Hay had, however, already received it via Goodnow, in a dispatch dated August 5, 1900. See Goodnow to Hay, *Consular Dispatches: Shanghai,* vol. 47.

72. Emperor of China to the President of the United States, July 19, 1900, *FRUS, 1901,* app. I, pp. 13–14.

73. President of the United States to the emperor of China, July 23, 1900, *ibid.* For examples of Chinese efforts to get the terms reduced and Hay's firmness in response to these efforts, see Hay to McKinley, July 29, 1900, McKinley Papers. From mid-July through August 15, the McKinley Papers contain many examples of this situation.

74. *Public Opinion,* 29:102 (July 26, 1900); *Literary Digest,* 21:35 (July 7, 1900); *Independent,* 52:1747 (July 19, 1900); *Public Opinion,* 29:9 (July 5, 1900), *ibid.,* p. 103 (July 26, 1900).

75. Charles Emory Smith to McKinley, July 25, 1900; George Montgomery to Cortelyou, July 24, 1900; Charles W. Dawes to McKinley, July, 29, 1900, McKinley Papers.

76. Henry Adams, *Education,* pp. 291, 392; Hay to Choate, July 17, 1900, Papers of Joseph H. Choate, Library of Congress, Washington, D.C.

Chapter 8
The Problems of Peace

1. Leech, p. 524.

2. Hay to McKinley, July 23, 1900, Hay Papers. Hay wrote McKinley that he had received assurances from John Barrett that many influential men on the missionary boards strongly favored Rockhill's appointment. Hay told the President that the underground feeling against Rockhill was probably due to the fact that Rockhill approached oriental theologies as a student rather than as a sectarian. Hay to Rockhill, July 19, 1900; Hay to Rockhill, July 27, 1900, *FRUS, 1900,* pp. 156, 157.

3. Adee to Hay, Aug. 5, 1900. See also, Hay to Adee, Aug. 11, 1900, Hay Papers.

4. Adee to Hay, Aug. 5, 1900, Hay Papers; Montgomery to Cortelyou, transmitting dispatch from Fowler, Aug. 9, 1900; Adee to Conger, Aug. 13, 1900, McKinley Papers.

5. Quoted in Fleming, pp. 148–149.

6. Tan, pp. 110ff; for Jung-lu's role see especially pp. 113–115.

7. Brooks Adams to John Hay, Aug. 17, 1900, Hay Papers; *Literary Digest,* 21:211ff (Aug. 29, 1900); *ibid.* 241ff (Sept. 1, 1900).

8. *Literary Digest,* 21:241 (Sept. 1, 1900); *ibid.,* p. 212 (Aug. 25, 1900).

9. Adee to McKinley, Aug. 20, 1900; Adee memorandum, Aug. 20, 1900; Long to Remey, Aug. 24, 1900; Adee to McKinley, Aug. 21, 1900; unsigned memorandum dated Aug. 21, 1900, probably written by Adee for the President, McKinley Papers.

10. Marius B. Jansen, *The Japanese and Sun Yat-sen* (Cambridge, Mass., 1954), p. 99. Kodama and Gotō were strongly supported by Katsura Tarō, minister of war in 1900. As governor-general of Formosa in 1896, Katsura had written a plan for Japanese expansion southward with Amoy as the starting point. The account of Japanese plans is drawn from Jansen, pp. 99–103.

11. Johnson to Hay, Aug. 24, 1900, Aug. 26, 1900, *Consular Dispatches: Amoy,* vol. 14. This was in keeping with instructions from Katsura to avoid conflict with the other foreigners if at all possible.

12. Johnson to Hay, Aug. 26, 1900, *ibid.*

13. Johnson to Hay, Aug. 29, 1900, Aug. 30, 1900, *ibid.* Johnson cabled that 20,000 more Chinese had fled the city. He also reported that the taotai had no funds to pay his soldiers, who threatened to mutiny as a consequence. The taotai told Johnson that he had no money, the native banks were closed and he had no means of raising any funds. He begged Johnson for $10,000, which Johnson managed to raise and with which the troops were then paid.

14. Johnson to Hay, Aug. 29, 1900, *ibid.*

15. See Jansen, p. 101ff.

16. Johnson to Hay, Sept. 5, 1900, *Consular Dispatches: Amoy,* vol. 14. Gotō Shimpei learned from Saigo Tsugumichi that Itō Hirobumi's opposition had broken the unanimity of the cabinet on the Amoy plan. As head of the Privy Council, Itō, fearful of European complications, had convinced Foreign Minister Aoki that the move was too risky. Yamagata used the Russian example as sufficient justification for any action Japan might take in south China. However, on August 26, the cabinet had received a report that Russia was considering withdrawal from Manchuria. "By using this, Itō had been able to delay the invasion in order to check the report. By the time it proved unfounded the arrival of foreign warships in Amoy harbor had made the invasion impossible." Jansen, p. 102.

17. Goodnow to Hay, Sept. 3, 1900; Goodnow to Johnson, Sept. 3, 1900, *Consular Dispatches: Shanghai,* vol. 47; Johnson to Hay, Sept. 8, 1900, *Consular Dispatches: Amoy,* vol. 14.

18. Johnson to Hay, Aug. 30, 1900, *Consular Dispatches: Amoy,* vol. 14.

19. Conger to Hay, Aug. 14, 1900, Sept. 6, 1900, Sept. 3, 1900, *China Dispatches,* vol. 108; Leech, p. 527.

20. Langer, p. 696. Both Witte and Lamsdorff had been opposed to Russian participation in the expedition to begin with. General Kuropatkin, however, insisted that the Boxer crisis was an opportunity to expand Russian influence in Chihli and should not be missed. Some 4,000 Russian soldiers joined the allied forces. See also Malozemoff, chap. 6. Russian endeavors to show their friendship for the Chinese began as early as August 12, when the Russian consul in Shanghai offered Li the use of a Russian ship to take him to Peking. See Tan, p. 128.

21. The Russian note was orally communicated to Adee on August 28. *FRUS, 1901,* app. I, p. 19. Langer, p. 698, analyzes the circular as a temporary victory for Witte's policy over Kuropatkin's more aggressive desires. According to Malozemoff, pp. 133ff, all Russian statesmen and military men, including even Kuropatkin, were glad when the action in Chihli was over.

22. Quoted in Hay to Choate, Sept. 8, 1900, Hay Papers.

23. Leech, p. 525; memorandum in response to the Russian chargé's oral communication made on Aug. 28, 1900, Adee to United States representatives in Berlin, Vienna, Paris, London, Rome, Tokyo, and St. Petersburg, *FRUS, 1901,* app. I, p. 20.

24. *Ibid.*

25. A. T. Mahan to McKinley, Sept. 2, 1900, McKinley Papers; see *Literary Digest,* 21:301 (Sept. 15, 1900).

26. Hay to Choate, Sept. 8, 1900, Hay to Adee, Aug. 31, 1900, Hay Papers; Root to Hay, Sept. 2, 1900, quoted in Philip C. Jessup, *Elihu Root* (New York, 1938), I, 383.

27. Senator J. T. Morgan to McKinley, Sept. 5, 1900; Chaffee to McKinley, Sept. 9, 1900; Root to McKinley, Sept. 11, 1900, McKinley Papers.

28. McKinley to Hay, Sept. 14, 1900, Hay Papers.

29. Conger to Hay, Sept. 12, 1900, *China Dispatches,* vol. 108. Adee later informed Hay that the President had been on the verge of cabling Chaffee to withdraw at once when Conger's telegram was received and settled the problem for him. Adee to Hay, Sept. 14, 1900, Hay Papers.

30. Hay to McKinley, Sept. 17, 1900; Hay to Adee, Sept. 14, 1900, Hay Papers.

31. Hay to Adee, Sept. 14, 1900, Hay Papers.

32. *Literary Digest,* 21:322, 301 (Sept. 15, 1900). The *Post* urged that Russia be trusted; most newspapers protested on specifically anti-Russian grounds, *Public Opinion,* 29:291 (Sept. 6, 1900). The *New York Press,* generally a pro-administration paper, asked the unpleasant rhetorical question whether the retreat policy was not a "surrender of the country's commercial future in Asia to the exigencies of its political present in America?" *Literary Digest,* 21:367 (Sept. 29, 1900). The Democratic *New Haven Register,* on the other hand, protested on the basis of the administration's alleged underhanded economic motives: "We have accomplished our errand unless there is a hidden commercial motive, which we prefer not even to suspect." *Public Opinion,* 29:259 (Aug. 30, 1900). Southern newspapers were frank in supporting just such commercial intentions. The *Memphis Commercial Appeal,* the *Atlanta Constitution,* and the *New Orleans Picayune* urged continued occupation for the sake of insuring American commercial interests in China. The Atlanta paper was most specific: "Cotton is King, and we must remain in Peking to see him duly crowned." *Ibid.,* p. 292 (Sept. 6, 1900).

33. Zabriskie, p. 63.

34. Reid to M. G. Seckendorff, Sept. 30, 1900, Reid Papers.

35. Enclosed in Conger to Hay, Aug. 22, 1900, McKinley Papers.

36. D. Z. Sheffield to Judson Smith, Sept. 27, 1900, Feb. 26, 1901, Mar. 26, 1901, ABCFM, North China Mission.

37. Lindbeck, chap. 6.

38. Henry D. Porter to Judson Smith, Oct. 10, 1900, ABCFM, North China Mission. Lindbeck, chap. 5. Lindbeck quotes a Presbyterian missionary as saying that the German punitive raids in Shantung would soon clear that area for the missionaries' return. Other missionaries made invidious comparisons between America's velvet glove approach to China and Germany's mailed fist.

39. J. T. Gracey, "The Clash of Civilizations in China," *Missionary Review of the World,* 13:623–626 (August 1900); extract from *Presbyterian Banner, ibid.,* pp. 631–635; *ibid.,* p. 639; Arthur T. Pierson, "Mysteries of God's Providence in China," *ibid.,* pp. 737–742 (October 1900).

40. This account is drawn from the article by the Reverend Arthur J. Brown, secretary of the Presbyterian Board of Foreign Missions, "A Notable Conference of Mission Secretaries," *ibid.,* pp. 852–858 (November 1900).

41. *Ibid.,* p. 855.

42. Judson Smith to Arthur Smith, Nov. 14, 1900, ABCFM, file 2.1, Foreign Letterbooks. Smith also commended Sheffield on an article the latter had written for the *North China Daily News,* but explained that he would not reprint it in America because of its harsh criticism of government policy. Smith to Sheffield, Nov. 9, 1900, *ibid.*

43. Rev. E. G. Tewksbury to "My Dear Ones," Aug. 26, 1900; Tewksbury to "My Dear Father," Sept. 9, 1900; Tewksbury to Judson Smith, Feb. 18, 1901, ABCFM, North China Mission; Chamberlin to his wife, Nov. 25, 1900, Dec. 28, 1900, to his sister, Nov. 4, 1900, pp. 163, 212, 128–129; see also Chamberlin's reports and editorials on the subject in the *New York Sun,* Nov. 18, Sept. 23, 1900, Jan. 20, 28, Feb. 7, 8, 9, 1901 as well as articles in late March of 1901. See also letters of Reverend William Ament to Judson Smith, Aug. 28, 1900, Nov. 13, 1900, Dec. 27, 1900, Feb. 18, 1900, ABCFM, North China Mission.

44. Sheffield to Smith, Nov. 15, 1900; Tewksbury to Smith, Feb. 18, 1901, ABCFM, North China Mission.

45. John J. Heeren, *On the Shantung Front: A History of the Shantung Mission of the Presbyterian Church in the U.S.A., 1861–1940, In Its Historical, Economic and Political Setting* (New York, 1940), pp. 130–131; Sheffield to Smith, July 9, 1901, ABCFM, North China Mission.

46. Tewksbury to Smith, Feb. 19, 1901, ABCFM, North China Mission. In a letter to Smith written Nov. 13, 1900, Ament complained that American soldiers, on a punitive expedition undertaken in late September, had shown "so much leniency to the Boxers that no real good was accomplished."

47. Ament to Smith, Nov. 13, 1900, ABCFM, North China Mission.

48. Judson Smith to Ament, Jan. 2, 7, 1901, ABCFM, Foreign Letterbooks; Sheffield to Smith, Dec. 14, 1900, ABCFM, North China Mission.

49. Mark Twain, "To the Person Sitting in Darkness," *North American Review,* 172:161–176 (February 1901). Albert B. Paine writes that Twain "never wrote anything more scorching, more penetrating in its sarcasm, more fearful in its revelation of injustice and hyprocrisy" than this essay. "Every paper in England and America commented on it editorially, with bitter denunciations or with eager praise, according to their lights and convictions . . . It was really as if he had thrown a great missile into the human hive, one half of which regarded it as a ball of honey and the remainder as a cobblestone. Whatever other effect it may have had, it left no thinking person unawakened." Albert Bigelow Paine, *Mark Twain, A Biography: The Personal and Literary Life of Samuel Langhorne Clemens* (New York, 1912), III, 1129.

50. Judson Smith to Ament, Feb. 13, 1901, ABCFM, Foreign Letterbooks.

51. *New York Sun* (Mar. 24, 1901).

52. Twain, "My Missionary Critics," *North American Review,* 172:520–534 (April 1901). See also Smith's reply, "The Missionaries and their Critics," *ibid.,* pp. 724–733 (May 1901).

53. Judson Smith to Ament, May 2, 1901, ABCFM, Foreign Letterbooks.
54. Sheffield to Smith, Feb. 26, 1901, Apr. 7, 1901; Porter to Smith, Oct. 10, 1900; Ament to Smith, Nov. 13, 1900; Arthur Smith to Judson Smith, Jan. 31, 1901; Henry Porter to Judson Smith, Oct. 28, 1900, ABCFM, North China Mission.
55. Presbyterian Board to Hay, Oct. 22, 1900, McKinley Papers.
56. R. H. Edmonds to Hay, Nov. 1, 1900, McKinley Papers; *New York Times,* Nov. 16, 1900; *Journal of the American Asiatic Association,* 1:109 (Nov. 26, 1900).

Chapter 9
Temporary Solutions

1. See Langer, pp. 699–703.
2. Hay to McKinley, Oct. 26, 1900, Hay Papers.
3. Hay to Henry Adams, Nov. 21, 1900, Hay Papers. See also Choate to Hay, Oct. 31, 1900, Choate Papers. A remark by Salisbury confirmed all of Hay's disgust with the agreement: " 'Well,' said he, 'one of my colleagues, the Duke of Devonshire, who likes to speak his mind freely . . . said "I don't see that this amounts to anything." ' "
4. For this declaration see Salisbury to Viscount Gough, July 2, 1900, *British Foreign and State Papers,* 95:1103; Rockhill to Hay, Oct. 25, 1900; memorandum of conversation between Wu T'ing-fang and Secretary Hill, Sept. 25, 1900; Goodnow to Hay, Oct. 18, 1900, McKinley Papers.
5. Rockhill to Hay, Oct. 25, 1900, McKinley Papers.
6. Adee to Hay, Sept. 18, 1900, Hay Papers.
7. For Li Hung-chang's efforts in this regard see Tan, p. 138; Hay to McKinley, Oct. 2, 1900, Hay Papers; German chargé to Hay, Sept. 18, 1900, *FRUS, 1901,* app. I, pp. 23–24; Hill to German chargé, Sept. 21, 1900, *FRUS, 1901,* app. I, pp. 24–25; German chargé to Hay, Oct. 2, 1900, Hay to German chargé, Oct. 2, 1900, *FRUS, 1901,* app. I, pp. 25–26; McKinley to Hay, Oct. 2, 1900, Hay to McKinley, Oct. 3, 1900, Hay Papers.
8. Hay to White, Oct. 16, 1900, Hay Papers.
9. French chargé to Hay, Oct. 4, 1900, *FRUS, 1901,* app. I, pp. 26–27. The most complete account of the negotiations can be found in John S. Kelly's recent, *A Forgotten Conference: The Negotiations at Peking, 1900–1901* (Paris and Geneva, 1963).
10. Hay to McKinley, Oct. 4, 1900, memorandum of Oct. 10, 1900, Hay Papers. For the text of the American reply to the French proposals, see Hay to French chargé, *FRUS, 1901,* app. I, pp. 27–28; Hay to Rockhill, Oct. 22, 1900, Instruction Book, vol. 6; Rockhill to Hay, Dec. 10, 1900, *China Dispatches,* vol. 109.
11. Hay to Conger, Oct. 29, 1900, *FRUS, 1900,* p. 224; McKinley to Hay,

Oct. 27, 1900, Hay Papers. As late as December 8, the British were insisting that the death penalty be specifically mentioned in the joint note. Choate to Hay, Dec. 8, 1900, Hay Papers. The punishment question continued to plague the negotiators. In February 1901, Wilbur Chamberlin drily noted that, if the Chinese agreed, there would be one decapitation per minister: "I should hate to see any of the Ministers disappointed. A head is such a rare souvenir too." Chamberlin to wife, Feb. 8, 1901, p. 252.

12. Rockhill to Hay, Jan. 5, 1901, Hay Papers; Rockhill to Hay, Dec. 15, 1900, *China Dispatches,* vol. 109; Hay to Conger, Jan. 3, 1901, *FRUS, 1901,* app. I, p. 357; Rockhill to Hay, Jan. 19, 1901, *China Dispatches,* vol. 110. McKinley withdrew his suggestion on January 11, 1901. For British correspondence on the subject see *British Foreign and State Papers,* 95:866, 873–877.

13. Hay to Conger, Nov. 27, 1900, *FRUS, 1900;* Rockhill to Hay, Dec. 1, 1900, *China Dispatches,* vol. 109; Conger to Hay, Dec. 4, 1900, *FRUS, 1900,* pp. 235–237; Hay to Conger, Dec. 5, 1900, Hay to Conger, Dec. 17, 1900 and Dec. 19, 1900, Conger to Hay, Dec. 20, 1900, *FRUS, 1900,* pp. 238–242; Rockhill to Hay, Dec. 20, 1900, *China Dispatches,* vol. 109; Hay to Conger, Dec. 21, 1900, *FRUS, 1900,* p. 242.

14. Tan, pp. 153–156, describes the advice sent to the court by the leading viceroys. Chang Chih-tung raised serious objections to the note. Li Hung-chang's insistence that the only alternative was to break negotiations altogether finally convinced the empress dowager to sign. For the text of the joint note see Conger to Hay, Dec. 23, 1900, *FRUS, 1901,* app. I, pp. 59–60.

15. Long to Hay, Oct. 1900, U.S. Department of Navy Archives, RG 80/11324/3; Hay to Conger, Nov. 16, 1900, Nov. 19, 1900, Instruction Book, vol. 6.

16. Conger to Hay, Nov. 23, 1900, Dec. 7, 1900, *China Dispatches,* vol. 109.

17. Dewey to Long, Nov. 25, 1903, U.S. Department of Navy Archives, RG 80/11324/3.

18. Adee to Rockhill, Dec. 6, 1901, Rockhill Papers, describes Bradford as "daft on the subject of acquiring naval stations or coaling depots everywhere."

19. Bradford to Long, Jan. 14, 1901, Jan. 26, 1901; Dewey to Long, Nov. 25, 1903, U.S. Department of Navy Archives, RG 80/11324/3.

20. Carl Johnson to Bradford, Mar. 5, 1902, *ibid.,* RG 80/14173.

21. Conger to Hay, Sept. 22, 1902, *ibid.;* abstract of documents by Bradford, Dec. 11, 1902, *ibid.*

22. R. D. Evans to Department of State, Apr. 21, 1903, *ibid.*

23. Dewey expected future conflicts in China to occur in the north; Amoy would be of little use in this case. He specifically dissented from Bradford's idea that Amoy would serve as a useful foothold and from Evans' remark that the lease would give America a needed voice in the disposition of terri-

tory around Amoy. Dewey to Long, June 18, 1903, *ibid.* William Braisted points out that England had "lost that primacy in the Yangtze which would have permitted her to consent unilaterally" to an American base in the Chusan Islands. A detailed account of naval efforts to obtain a China base can be found in Braisted, *United States Navy in the Pacific,* pp. 124ff.

24. It has been argued that the pernicious influence of the russophobic Brooks Adams blinded American policy makers to the dangers of Japanese expansion while turning them against Russia. An American alliance with Russia, this approach suggests, might well have influenced the czar in favor of Witte's moderate economic imperialist program and dissuaded him from supporting the aggressive territorial imperialism of powerful military leaders. There is little evidence to support this contention; nor, on the face of it, would American interests have benefited from the successful implementation of Witte's plans. Indeed, American economic interests in Manchuria might well have suffered more than under the erratic efforts of Kuropatkin and his cohorts. See William Appleman Williams, *American Russian Relations, 1781–1947* (New York, 1952), chap. 2. Williams describes Russia (before 1903) as having helped "serve American interests by checking Japanese expansion." *Ibid.,* p. 47.

25. It is important that Japan, in her abortive effort to seize Amoy, used the Russian example in Manchuria and the British troop landing in Shanghai as legitimizing precedents. In all three cases, protection of nationals and their property was the justification. The best account of Sino-Russian negotiations in this period is Tan, chaps. 8–10. Zabriskie, chap. 4, contains more Russian material and Malozemoff, chaps. 6 and 7, gives a very sympathetic account of Russian policy.

26. Tan, pp. 178ff gives the text of the February 16 agreement.

27. *Ibid.,* pp. 182ff describes, in some detail, the arguments put forward by each side.

28. Quoted in *ibid.,* pp. 190, 191.

29. *Ibid.,* p. 201.

30. Hay to Wu T'ing-fang, Feb. 19, 1901, Hay Papers. A specific exception to the general policy on releasing diplomatic correspondence to the press was made in this instance. The *Sun,* on March 27, 1901, published an accurate account of the correspondence that had passed between Russia and America on the Manchurian question. Without reluctance the State Department admitted to the *Sun's* reporter that it was most anxious to thwart Russian actions in that area.

31. Rockhill to Nanking and Hankow consuls, Mar. 2, 1901, *China Dispatches,* vol. 112.

32. The following paragraph draws heavily on a paper by Kosaka Masataka entitled "Chinese Policy in Manchuria, 1900–1903," seminar on Ch'ing Documents (Harvard University, 1961).

33. Quoted in Tan, pp. 203, 202, 206ff. In a private conversation with

Hay, Cassini learned that the United States did not object to any efforts Russia made to prevent future riots. However, Hay insisted that American trade should not be made to suffer. Cassini was ready to offer such assurances, but already the Russian government had decided to abandon the agreement. Mutual distrust between Germany and England as well as Japan's unwillingness to risk a war while uncertain of the other powers' attitude, postponed the Russo-Japanese war some three years. Zabriskie, p. 71.

34. Malozemoff, p. 150.

35. Correspondence on this incident appears both in the U.S. State Department Archives and in the U.S. Navy Department Archives, RG 45: Miller to Conger, Oct. 12, 1901; Rear Admiral Remy to Long, Oct. 12, 1901; Conger to Hay, Nov. 12, 1901; Miller to Conger, Mar. 29, 1902.

36. See Munro, pp. 158ff. Munro shows that from 1900 on, Russia tried to divert trade from Newchwang, where American merchants were very well established, to Dalny through the use of discriminatory rates on the China Eastern Railway. At first this stimulated all foreign trade into Manchuria, not merely Russian. American cotton goods were imported in as great quantities as before. However, Russian oil entered Dalny duty free and was granted extremely low carriage rates. The effect on United States kerosene export figures was immediate. From 1901 to 1902 American kerosene exports to Manchuria fell from 3,172,000 gallons to 603,180. The Russian advantage, however, soon proved illusory. Shipment via the China Eastern Railway was actually more expensive, even with rate reductions, than sea transport via Newchwang. Munro shows that Russia could not monopolize Manchurian commerce without a far greater disregard for the open door than she was ready to display in 1903. After the Russo-Japanese War, the situation changed radically. The subsidized Russian lines were gone and American kerosene dominated the market, *ibid.*, p. 159. The depression of 1907–1908 seriously affected American trade with Manchuria and, after a brief recovery, the American position of leadership was permanently lost to Japan. Munro makes the final point that neither Japanese nor developing Chinese industries "could . . . have overcome the established reputation of American goods in so short a period if the exporters of the United States had made any intelligent effort to retain their hold." *Ibid.*, p. 164.

37. Hay to Reid, Sept. 20, 1900, Hay Papers.

38. Rockhill to Hay, May 25, 1901, *China Dispatches,* vol. 115. The text of the Protocol can be found in *FRUS, 1901,* app. I, pp. 312–318.

39. Hay to Conger, Nov. 16, 1900, Dec. 29, 1900, Instruction Book, vol. 6.

40. Conger to Hay, Sept. 23, 1901; Rockhill memorandum on this dispatch, Nov. 9, 1901, *China Dispatches,* vol. 114.

41. The commercial treaty of 1903 included an article on missionaries that specifically asserted missionary rights to residence in all parts of China, purchase and sale of land, and the prompt attention of Chinese officials to

complaints by missionaries and native Christians. It also exempted Christians from those taxes that were levied for religious purposes. Clyde, p. 223.

42. Article XI, Protocol, *FRUS, 1901,* app. I, p. 317.

43. Conger urged the joint negotiation of commercial treaty revision, and commented that "Great Britain would like to do most of the work herself and gain corresponding credit, since she claims that, up to this date, she is largely responsible for whatever commercial rights anyone has in China." Conger to Hay, Sept. 4, 1901, *China Dispatches,* vol. 114. A Rockhill memorandum on this dispatch notes that satisfactory treaty revision must include the total abolition of likin. This, however, required a compensating increase in the tariff on imports; otherwise China would lose too much. Cooperation was indispensable for successful tariff revision. "Great Britain has, however," Rockhill wrote, "regardless of these considerations, already appointed a Commission to negotiate separately with China . . . I fear the result will not prove very satisfactory." Rockhill, Oct. 31, 1901, *ibid.* For a lucid summary of the commercial treaty negotiations, see Stanley F. Wright, *Hart and the Chinese Customs* (Belfast, 1950), pp. 753–765. American businessmen in China were far less concerned with the abolition of likin than were British businessmen or the State Department. According to the American Asiatic Association, only 7 percent of likin collections were made in north China where 75 percent of American trade was conducted. Rockhill and Hay, however, were both convinced of the urgency of total abolition and the commercial treaty of 1903 included this provision in Article 4. General Sharretts, American adviser to the tariff commission, however, had bluntly stated his opposition to the abolition of likin if it were to be replaced by surtaxes harmful to American trade. The British were much exercised over his statements and demanded to know whether he spoke for the government. They were reassured that Sharretts was not an official negotiator. See Adee to Hay, Aug. 7, 1902, Hay Papers; Goodnow to Hay, Feb. 22, 1902, Mar. 1, 1902, and Mar. 25, 1902, *Consular Dispatches: Shanghai,* vol. 48; Choate to Hay, Aug. 11, 1902, Choate Papers.

44. Hay to Roosevelt, May 1, 1902, Hay Papers. The complex history of the negotiation of the 1903 treaty is beyond the scope of this study. I refer to it only to give some sense of the continuity of problems that faced the United States after the Boxer settlement.

45. Acting chargé Squiers to Hay, Mar. 12, 1901, transmitting copies of correspondence between Wu T'ing-fang and F. W. Whitridge, *China Dispatches,* vol. 112. Whitridge to Wu, Jan. 10, 1901, Jan. 14, 1901; Wu to Whitridge, Jan. 12, 1901, *ibid.* The struggles of the American China Development Company against the efforts of the Chinese government to cancel their much violated contract continued until 1905 and is well told in Braisted, "American China Development Company." In essence American and Chinese interests coincided. Neither wished to see the concession in the hands of the Franco-Belgian syndicate. Uncomfortably, Hay, Rockhill, Conger, and

other officials found themselves trying to shore up the company in the interests of American prestige. A melancholy note in Hay's diary for Friday, December 30, 1904, concisely indicates his attitude: "At Cabinet meeting I said a few words about asphalt in Venezuela and railroads in China and the difficulties of fighting for shady American enterprises in foreign countries." Hay Papers. The role of Theodore Roosevelt in the death struggle of the company can be found in Howard K. Beale, *Theodore Roosevelt and the Rise of America to World Power* (Baltimore, 1956), pp. 203–211. Goodnow's dispatches for 1904 and 1905 (*Consular Dispatches: Shanghai*) transmit copies of telegrams from key Chinese officials and local gentry to Sheng Hsuan-huai that indicate the extreme pressure Sheng was under to cancel the contract.

46. Conger to Hay, Nov. 14, 1900, *FRUS, 1901*, p. 39, reported the Russian occupation and urged that the United States make a strong protest. The Russian circular itself can be found in Conger to Hay, Dec. 31, 1900, with sub-inclosure, James Ragsdale to Conger, Nov. 8, 1900, *ibid.*, p. 41. See Morse, III, 325–326, for a concise account of the Tientsin controversy.

47. Conger to Hay, Dec. 31, 1900, *FRUS, 1901*, 40; Conger to Hay, Oct. 11, 1901, *China Dispatches*, vol. 115. This dispatch reports the negotiations Conger conducted from September through early October 1901.

48. Hay stated the Government's position: "The Government of the United States will . . . expect to have equal favors and facilities with other Powers for military purposes at Tientsin should it at any future time become necessary to carry out the purposes of the protocol with respect to keeping open communication between Peking and the sea; and if effective assurance in this regard be given we may leave the question of a commercial concession in abeyance until the development of commerce in that quarter shall make it necessary to claim privileges and facilities on the same footing as other Powers . . . It is to be remembered that circumstances have materially changed since the United States relinquished its holding at Tientsin . . . we have entered into conventional arrangements . . . which may make it not only expedient but necessary to secure a position of equality at Tientsin in matters of commerce and international policy." Rockhill memorandum on Conger's Oct. 11, 1901 dispatch, dated Nov. 20, 1901, *ibid.;* Hay to Conger, Sept. 12, 1901, Nov. 27, 1901, *FRUS, 1901*, pp. 54, 59.

49. See Kosaka.

Chapter 10
Conclusion

1. David Riesman, "Containment and Initiatives," Council for Correspondence *News Letter,* no. 23:25 (Feb. 1963).

2. Alfred T. Mahan, *Lessons of the War with Spain and Other Articles* (Boston, 1899), pp. vii–viii.

3. Alfred T. Mahan, *The Problem of Asia and its Effect upon International Policies* (Boston, 1900), pp. 11, 37–44, 63.

4. *Ibid.*, pp. 66–67, 87, 98.

5. *Ibid.*, pp. 111–112.

6. *Ibid.*, pp. 167–170. Mahan went so far as to suggest that America should think of abandoning the Monroe Doctrine as it applied to South America. It was essential to concentrate the nation's strength, and the Far East was more important to the United States than was South America. *Ibid.*, p. 201.

7. *Ibid.*, p. 93.

8. Brooks Adams, *America's Economic Supremacy,* Marquis Childs, ed. (New York, 1947), pp. 79, 83.

9. "Concentration" is never specifically defined. Adams uses it interchangeably with "consolidation" and "civilization." In context it seems to be another word for "progress" in terms of material, scientific, and economic advances. In the *Law of Civilization and Decay,* it had pejorative connotations because, in its final form, it presaged decay. But often he uses the term descriptively to distinguish between primitive and complex societies.

10. Brooks Adams, *Economic Supremacy,* pp. 44, 99, 45.

11. *Ibid.*, pp. 100–104, 106.

12. *Ibid.*, p. 105.

13. William E. Leuchtenberg dealt with this intriguing problem in a later period. See his fascinating article, "Progressivism and Imperialism," *Mississippi Valley Historical Review,* 39:483–504 (December 1952). Among the more interesting ramifications of imperialism as an ideology is its role in social reform. A provocative treatment of this subject for British imperialists is Bernard Semmel's *Imperialism and Social Reform: English Social-Imperial Thought, 1895–1914* (Cambridge, Mass., 1960). The proto-fascist element in Brooks Adams' theories is a neglected aspect of his thought.

14. Brooks Adams, *Economic Supremacy,* p. 194.

15. Brooks Adams, *The New Empire* (New York, 1902), pp. xxiv–xxv.

16. *Ibid.*, pp. 186, 190, 191.

17. *Ibid.*, pp. 191–193, 194, 195.

18. *Ibid.*, pp. 208, 209.

19. The articles were later printed in book form; the following references are to the book. Charles A. Conant, *The United States in the Orient* (Boston, 1900), pp. 5ff, pp. 24ff.

20. *Ibid.*, pp. 32, 33, 74, 111, 175, 60, 197ff.

21. See Paul A. Varg, *Open Door Diplomat: The Life of W. W. Rockhill* (Urbana, Ill., 1952), p. 29.

22. Rockhill to Cheshire, Aug. 19, 1896; Rockhill, "The United States

and the Chinese Question," speech at Naval War College, Newport, Aug. 5, 1904, Rockhill Papers.

23. *Ibid.*

24. *Ibid.*

25. Rockhill, speech given at the Asiatic Institute, New York, Nov. 12, 1914, Rockhill Papers.

Bibliography

I. Manuscript Sources: Official and Private Papers

OFFICIAL

Archives of the American Board of Commissioners for Foreign Missions, Houghton Library, Harvard University, Cambridge, Massachusetts.

Archives of the Department of Navy, Secretary's Office: Files relating to the acquisition of a naval base in China, 1897–1903.

Archives of the Department of State, Foreign Affairs Division, National Archives, Washington, D.C.

PRIVATE

Barker, Wharton, Collection in the Division of Manuscripts, Library of Congress, 1870–1920, 12 volumes, 27 boxes.

Choate, Joseph Hodges, Collection in the Division of Manuscripts, Library of Congress, 1861–1917, 39 volumes, 42 boxes.

Hay, John, Collection in the Division of Manuscripts, Library of Congress, 1859–1914, 15 volumes, 110 boxes.

McKinley, William, Collection in the Division of Manuscripts, Library of Congress, 1847–1902, 261 volumes, 156 boxes.

Olney, Richard, Collection in the Division of Manuscripts, Library of Congress, 1830–1917, 153 volumes, 15 boxes, 3 bundles.

Reid, Whitelaw, Collection in the Division of Manuscripts, Library of Congress, 1861–1912, 101 volumes, 179 boxes.

Rockhill, William W., Collection in Houghton Library, Harvard University, Cambridge, Massachusetts, 1882–1914, 20 volumes.

Root, Elihu, Collection in the Division of Manuscripts, Library of Congress, 1898–1937, 73 volumes, 312 boxes.

Wilson, James H., Collection in the Division of Manuscripts, Library of Congress, 1861–1920, 13 volumes, 76 boxes.

II. Printed Sources: Official Documents and Documentary Collections

British Foreign and State Papers, XCIV (1900–1901), XCV (1901–1902), London, 1904, 1905.

British Parliamentary Papers, *China,* 1898–1901.

Correspondence relating to the War with Spain and conditions growing out of same including the insurrection in the Philippine Islands and the China Relief Expedition, between the Adjutant-General of the Army

287

and Military Commanders in the United States, Cuba, Porto Rico, China, and the Philippine Islands, from April 15, 1898 to July 30, 1902, in two volumes, Washington, D.C., 1902.

Clyde, Paul H., *United States Policy Towards China: Diplomatic and Public Documents, 1839–1939,* Durham, N.C., 1940.

Department of State, *Papers Relating to the Foreign Relations of the United States,* 1894–1904.

Wang Liang, editor, *Ch'ing-chi wai-chiao shih-liao* (Historical materials on foreign relations in the latter part of the Ch'ing dynasty), Peiping, 1932; Taipei, Taiwan reprint, 1962, 112 *ts'e.*

Wang Yün-sheng, compiler, *Liu-shih-nien-lai Chung-kuo yü Jih-pen* (China and Japan during the last sixty years), 6 volumes, Tientsin, 1932–1933.

Ta-Ch'ing li-ch'ao shih-lu (Veritable records of successive reigns of the Ch'ing dynasty), 4,485 *chüan,* Taipei, Taiwan reprint, 1963–1964.

III. Periodicals and Newspapers

American Review of Reviews, 1894–1901.
Forum, 1894–1901.
Boston Herald, 1895–1900.
Independent, 1894–1901.
Journal of the American Asiatic Association, 1899–1901.
Literary Digest, 1894–1903.
Missionary Review of the World, 1894–1901.
North American Review, 1894–1902.
Outlook, 1894–1900.
Public Opinion, 1894–1901.
Review of Reviews, 1894–1896.
New York Sun, 1900–1902.

IV. Letters

Cater, Harold D. (editor), *Henry Adams and His Friends,* Boston, 1947.

Chamberlin, Wilbur J., *Ordered to China,* New York, 1903.

Ford, Worthington C. (editor), *Letters of Henry Adams, 1892–1918,* Boston, 1930.

Gwynn, Stephen, *The Letters and Friendships of Sir Cecil Spring Rice,* 2 volumes, Boston, 1929.

Lodge, Henry C. (editor), *Selections from the Correspondence of Theodore Roosevelt and Henry Cabot Lodge, 1884–1918,* 2 volumes, New York, 1925.

Morison, Elting E. (editor), *Letters of Theodore Roosevelt,* 8 volumes, Cambridge, Mass., 1951–1954.

Thayer, William R., *Life and Letters of John Hay,* 2 volumes, Boston, 1915.

V. Books, Articles, Pamphlets

Adams, Brooks, "The Plutocratic Revolution," Address before the New England Tariff Reform League, June 15, 1892, Boston, 1892.

———— *The Law of Civilization and Decay,* 2nd edition, New York, 1903.

———— *America's Economic Supremacy,* Marquis Childs edition, New York, 1947.

———— *The New Empire,* New York, 1902.

———— "The Heritage of Henry Adams," in Henry Adams, *The Degradation of the Democratic Dogma,* Capricorn reprint, New York, 1958, 13–122.

Adams, Henry, *Education of Henry Adams,* Modern Library edition, New York, 1931.

Beresford, Charles, *The Break-Up of China,* New York and London, 1899.

Cary, Clarence, *China's Present and Prospective Railways,* New York, 1899.

Conant, Charles A., *The United States in the Orient,* Boston, 1900.

Conger, Sarah P., *Letters from China,* Chicago, 1909.

Dawes, Charles, *A Journal of the McKinley Years,* Chicago, 1950.

Foster, John W., *Diplomatic Memoirs,* 2 volumes, Boston, 1909.

History of the Peace Negotiations, Documentary and Verbal, between China and Japan, March–April, 1895. Reprinted from the *Peking and Tientsin Times,* Tientsin, 1895.

Li Hung-chang, *Li Wen-chung kung ch'üan-chi* (The complete works of Li Hung-chang), 9 volumes (165 *chüan*), Shanghai, 1921.

Mahan, Alfred T., "Current Fallacies upon Naval Subjects," *Harpers' Monthly Magazine,* XCVII (1898), 42–53.

———— *Lessons of the War with Spain and Other Articles,* Boston, 1899.

———— *The Problem of Asia and its Effect upon International Policies,* Boston, 1900.

Pearson, Charles, *National Life and Character,* London, 1893.

Roosevelt, Theodore, Review of Charles Pearson's *National Life and Character, Sewanee Review,* II (1894), 354–368.

———— *Letter of Theodore Roosevelt accepting the nomination of the Republican National Convention of 1900 for Vice President of the United States,* Republican National Committee, September, 1900.

Seymour, Edward H., *My Naval Career and Travels,* London, 1911.

Wilson, James H., *China: Travels in the Middle Kingdom,* 3rd edition, New York, 1901.

VI. Secondary Works

Anderson, Thornton, *Brooks Adams, Constructive Conservative,* Ithaca, N.Y., 1951.

Bailey, Thomas A., "America's Emergence as a World Power: The Myth and the Verity," *Pacific Historical Review,* XXX (1961), 1–16.

Beale, Howard K., *Theodore Roosevelt and the Rise of America to World Power,* Baltimore, Md., 1956.

Beard, Charles, *The Idea of National Interest,* New York, 1934.

Beringause, Arthur F., *Brooks Adams: A Biography,* New York, 1955.

Blatt, Marilyn, "Problems of a China Missionary—Justus Doolittle," *Papers on China,* XII (1958), 28–50.

Bowers, Claude, G., *Beveridge and the Progressive Era,* Boston, 1932.

Braisted, William, "The United States and the American China Development Company," *Far Eastern Quarterly,* XI (1952), 147–165.

——— *The United States Navy in the Pacific, 1897–1909,* Austin, Texas, 1958.

Cameron, Meribeth E., *The Reform Movement in China, 1898–1912,* Stanford, 1931.

Campbell, Charles S., Jr., *Special Business Interests and the Open Door Policy,* New Haven, Conn., 1951.

Carlson, Ellsworth C., *The Kaiping Mines, 1887–1912,* Cambridge, Mass., 1957.

Cohen Paul A., *China and Christianity, the Missionary Movement and the Growth of Chinese Antiforeignism 1860–1870,* Cambridge, Mass. 1963.

Conroy, Hilary F., *The Japanese Seizure of Korea, 1869–1910. A Study of Realism and Idealism in International Relations,* Philadelphia, 1960.

Croly, Herbert, *Willard Straight,* New York, 1924.

Dennett, Tyler, *John Hay: From Poetry to Politics,* New York, 1933.

——— *Americans in Eastern Asia: A Critical Study of United States' Policy in the Far East in the Nineteenth Century,* New York, 1922.

Dennis, A. L. P., *Adventures in American Diplomacy, 1896–1906,* New York, 1928.

Donovan, Timothy P., *Henry Adams and Brooks Adams: The Education of Two American Historians,* Norman, Okla., 1961.

Dunne, Finley Peter, *Mr. Dooley's Philosophy,* New York, 1900.

Duus, Peter, "Science and Salvation in China: The Life and Work of W. A. P. Martin," *Papers on China,* X (1956), 97–127.

Fairbank, John K., *Trade and Diplomacy on the China Coast: The Opening of the Treaty Ports, 1842–1854,* 2 volumes, Cambridge, Mass., 1953.

———— and Reischauer, Edwin O., *East Asia, The Great Tradition*, Boston, 1960.

———— and Craig, Albert M., *History of East Asian Civilization*, vol. 2, *East Asia: The Modern Transformation*, Boston, 1960.

Fairbank, John K. and Teng, Ssu-yü, *China's Response to the West: A Documentary Survey, 1839–1923*, Cambridge, Mass., 1954.

———— "On the Ch'ing Tributary System," *Ch'ing Administration*, 107–246, Cambridge, Mass., 1960.

Feuerwerker, Albert, *China's Early Industrialization, Sheng Hsuan-huai (1844–1916) and Mandarin Enterprise*, Cambridge, Mass., 1958.

Fleming, Peter, *The Seige at Peking*, London, 1959.

Garraty, J., *Henry Cabot Lodge*, New York, 1953.

Gelber, L. M., *The Rise of Anglo-American Friendship: A Study in World Politics, 1898–1906*, New York, 1938.

Gorelik, C. B., *Politka SShA Manchzurii B 1898–1903 GG. I Doktrina "Otkrytkyh Dverei,"* (Policy of the U.S.A. in Manchuria, 1898–1903, and the Doctrine of "Open Doors"), Moscow, 1960.

Griswold, A. W., *The Far Eastern Policy of the United States*, New York, 1938.

Handlin, Oscar, *The American People in the Twentieth Century*, Cambridge, Mass., 1954.

Harrington, Fred H., "The Anti-Imperialist Movement in the United States, 1898–1900," *Mississippi Valley Historical Review*, XXII (1936), 211–230.

———— *God, Mammom and the Japanese: Dr. Horace Allen and Korean-American Relations, 1884–1905*, Madison, Wisc., 1944.

Hidy, Ralph W. and Muriel E., *History of the Standard Oil Company (New Jersey): Pioneering in Big Business, 1882–1911*, New York, 1955.

Higham, J., *Strangers in the Land*, New Brunswick, N.J., 1955.

Hirschfeld, Charles S., "Brooks Adams and American Nationalism," *American Historical Review*, LXIX (1963–1964), 371–392.

Hobson, J. A., *Imperialism: A Study*, 3rd edition, London, 1938.

Hofstadter, Richard, *The Age of Reform: From Bryan to F. D. R.*, New York, 1956.

———— *Social Darwinism in American Thought*, Boston, 1944.

Inouye, J., *The Japan-China War*, Shanghai, 1895 or 1896.

Jansen, Marius B., *The Japanese and Sun Yat-sen*, Cambridge, Mass., 1954.

Jessup, Philip C., *Elihu Root*, 2 volumes, New York, 1938.

Josephson, Matthew, *The President Makers*, New York, 1940.

———— *The Politicos, 1865–1896*, New York, 1938.

Kelly, John S., *A Forgotten Conference: The Negotiations at Peking, 1900–1901*, Paris and Geneva, 1963.

Kennan, George, *American Diplomacy, 1900–1950*, New York, 1952.

Kent, P. H., *Railway Enterprise in China*, London, 1908.

Kosaka, Masataka, "Chinese Policy in Manchuria, 1900–1903," Ch'ing Documents Seminar Paper, Harvard University, Cambridge, Mass., 1961.

LaFeber, Walter, *The New Empire, An Interpretation of American Expansion, 1860–1898*, Ithaca, N. Y., 1963.

Langer, William L., *The Diplomacy of Imperialism, 1890–1902*, 2nd edition, New York, 1956.

Leech, Margaret, *In the Days of McKinley*, New York, 1959.

LeFevour, Edward, "Western Enterprise and the Ch'ing Bureaucracy in the late 19th Century," Conference Paper for Study Group on the Economic History of East and South-East Asia, London School of Oriental and African Studies.

—— *Western Enterprise in Late Ch'ing China: A Selective Survey of Jardine, Matheson and Company's Operations, 1842–1895*, Cambridge, Mass., 1968.

Leuchtenberg, William E., "Progressivism and Imperialism," *Mississippi Valley Historical Review*, XXIX (1952), 483–504.

Levenson, Joseph R., *Confucian China and its Modern Fate*, London, 1958.

—— *Liang Ch'i-ch'ao and the Mind of Modern China*, Cambridge, Mass., 1953.

Li Chien-nung, *Political History of China, 1840–1928*, Ssu-yü Teng and Jeremy Ingalls, translators, Princeton, 1956.

Li Kuo-ch'i, *Chung-kuo tsao-ch'i te t'ieh-lu ching-ying* (The initial development of railroads in China), Nan-kang, Taiwan, 1961.

Lindbeck, John M. H., *China Missionaries and American Foreign Policy: The Boxer Period*, unpublished manuscript.

McCormick, Thomas, "Insular Imperialism and the Open Door: the China Market and the Spanish-American War," *Pacific Historical Review*, XXXII (1963), 155–169.

—— *China Market, America's Quest for Informal Empire, 1893–1901*, Chicago, 1967.

Malozemoff, Andrew, *Russian Far Eastern Policy, 1881–1904*, Berkeley, Calif., 1958.

May, Ernest R., *Imperial Democracy: The Emergence of America as a Great Power*, New York, 1961.

————— "The Nature of Foreign Policy: the Calculated vs. the Axiomatic," *Daedalus,* XCI (1962), 653–667.

Meng, S. M., *The Tsungli Yamen: Its Origins and Functions,* Cambridge, Mass., 1962.

Morgan, Wayne, *William McKinley and His America,* Syracuse, 1963.

Morse, H. B., *The International Relations of the Chinese Empire,* 3 volumes, Shanghai, 1918.

Munro, Dana C., *American Commercial Interests in Manchuria,* Publication No. 654, American Academy of Political and Social Science, Reprinted from the *Annals,* January, 1912.

Neumann, William N., "Ambiguity and Ambivalence in Ideas of National Interest in Asia," in *Isolation and Security,* ed. Alexander De Conde, Durham, N.C., 1957.

Nevins, Allan, *Henry White and Thirty Years of American Diplomacy,* New York, 1930.

Olcott, Charles S., *The Life of William McKinley,* 2 volumes, Boston and New York, 1916.

Paine, Albert Bigelow, *Mark Twain: A Biography. The Personal and Literary Life of Samuel Langhorne Clemens,* 3 volumes, New York, 1912.

Pelcovits, Nathan, *Old China Hands and the Foreign Office,* New York, 1948.

Pratt, Julius W., *Expansionists of 1898: The Acquisition of Hawaii and the Spanish Islands,* New York, 1951.

Pringle, Henry F., *Theodore Roosevelt, A Biography,* Revised edition, New York, 1956.

Pressman, Harvey, "Hay, Rockhill, and China's Integrity: A Reappraisal," *Papers on China,* XIII (1959), 61–79.

Purcell, Vincent, *The Boxer Uprising, A Background Study,* Cambridge, 1963.

Rankin, Mary B., "The Ku-t'ien Incident (1895): Christians vs. the Ts'ai-hui," *Papers on China,* XV (1961), 30–62.

Remer, C. F., *Foreign Investments in China,* New York, 1933.

Schumpeter, Joseph, *Imperialism and Social Classes,* Heinz Norden, translator, 3rd printing, New York, 1958.

Schwartz, Benjamin, *In Search of Wealth and Power: Yen Fu and the West,* Cambridge, Mass., 1964.

Semmel, Bernard, *Imperialism and Social Reform: English Social-Imperial Thought, 1895–1914,* Cambridge, Mass., 1960.

293

Sprout, Harold and Margaret, *Rise of American Naval Power, 1776–1918,* Princeton, N.J., 1946.

Sun, E-tu Zen, *Chinese Railways and British Interests, 1898–1911,* New York, 1954.

Stoecker, Helmuth, *Deutschland und China im 19. Jahrhundert,* Berlin, 1958.

Strachey, John, *The End of Empire,* New York, 1960.

Tan, Chester C., *The Boxer Catastrophe,* New York, 1955.

Tsou Tang, *America's Failure in China, 1941–1950,* Chicago, 1963.

Varg, Paul A., *Open Door Diplomat: The Life of W. W. Rockhill,* Urbana, Ill., 1952.

Volpicelli, Venone (Vladimir, *pseud.*), *The China-Japan War,* London, 1896.

Williams, William A., *American Russian Relations, 1781–1947,* New York, 1952.

———— "Brooks Adams and American Expansion," *New England Quarterly,* XXV (1952), 217–232.

———— "The Frontier Thesis and American Foreign Policy," *Pacific Historical Review,* XXIV (1955), 379–395.

———— *The Tragedy of American Diplomacy,* Cleveland, Ohio, 1959.

Winters, Yvor, "Henry Adams, or the Creation of Confusion," *In Defense of Reason,* 3rd edition, Denver, Colo., 374–430.

Wright, Mary C., "The Adaptability of Ch'ing Diplomacy: The Case of Korea," *Journal of Asian Studies,* XVII (1958), 363–381.

Wright, Stanley F., *Hart and the Chinese Customs,* Belfast, 1950.

Zabriskie, Edward, *American Russian Rivalry in the Far East, 1895–1914,* Philadelphia, 1946.

Index

Adams, Alva, 97
Adams, Brooks, 6–7, 110, 235 n11, 236 n16; and Theodore Roosevelt, 8; on Hay's China diplomacy, 174; post-*1898* theories, 221–226, 285 n9; on the nineteenth century, 270 n28; anti-Russia, 281 n24
Adams, C. K., 110
Adams, Henry, 156; anti-Russia, 157; on Hay's Boxer diplomacy, 168–170; on depression of *1893*, 235 n2; on the nineteenth century, 236 n18; on suppression of Filipino insurgency, 270 n28
Adee, Alvey A., 80, 127, 172, 183, 184
Allen, Charles H., Asst. Secretary of Navy, 104
Allen, Horace N., 18–19
Alexeieff, Kyril, 207
Ament, Rev. William, 191–196, 278 n46
American Asiatic Association, 109, 258 n43; and Beresford, 118; pressure for active policy, 119–120; and Philadelphia Commercial Convention, 121; role in new China policy, 123; on American relief expedition, 155
American China Development Company, 56; and Peking-Hankow contract, 65–67, 251 n32; and Charles Denby, 66; and Canton-Hankow contract, 90–91; new negotiations, 110ff; final contract, 112; post-*1900* difficulties, 215–216, 283 n45; and Russia, 252 n33; and U.S. base in China, 261 n21
American Review of Reviews, 23, 239 n30
American Trading Company, 57, 58
Aoki Shūzō, 276 n16
Atlanta Constitution, 97–98; on siege of legations, 169; on troop withdrawal, 277 n32

Baldwin Locomotive Company, 68, 71

Barker, Wharton, 38; and telephone concession, 39ff; Sino-American Bank scheme, 41ff; reasons for failure, 51–52, 244 n31, 245 n43; post-*1895* efforts, 62–64, 250 n27
Barrett, John, 110, 120–121; on post-Boxer U.S. policy, 174; on Rockhill, 275 n2
Bash, A. W., 57; and Wilson, 59; appeal to State Department for aid, 90
Bayard, Thomas F., 46, 47
Belgium, 65–68
Beresford, Charles, 114, 118ff; compares U.S. and Japan, 122–123. *See also* Open Door, Rockhill
Bliss, Cornelius N., 121
Boston Herald, 21; anti-Russia, 98, 261 n17; on Anglo-American alliance, 120; on Open Door note, 135; poll on expansion, 143
Boulger, Demetrius C., 174
Boxer rebellion, 11, 138; development and causes, 143–145; action at Taku, 147–148, 150–152; "declaration of war," 148, 158; U.S. and Allied expedition, 152, 154; efforts of south and central viceroys, 159ff; siege of the legations, 149, 160–161, 173–174, 273 n56; murder of Baron von Ketteler, 161, 162; Hay's "modus vivendi," 163–164; court efforts to halt Allied expedition, 172–173; fall of Peking, 174; dangers of post-Boxer situation, 175ff; arrival of von Waldersee, 180
Boxer Settlement, 199ff, 279 n11
Bradford, R. B., 104–105; post-*1900* efforts to acquire base in China, 204, 205
Breckenbridge, Clifton R., 70
Brice, Calvin, 59, 244 n11
Bryan, Charles Page, 98
Burnham, Williams, and Company, 58

295

Campbell, Charles, Jr., 251 n32, 265 n16

Carnegie, Andrew, 61

Cary, Clarence, 59, 60; critic of U.S. policy, 88; negotiates new Canton-Hankow contract, 111, 112

Cassini, Count Arturo Pavlovich, 132–135, 281 n33

Chaffee, General Adna, 154, 157

Chamberlain, Joseph, 116, 117

Chamberlin, Wilbur J., 54, 191

Chamot, A. F., 161

Chandler, Senator William E., 53

Chang Chih-tung, 43; and Boxers, 144–145; response to von Ketteler's murder, 161; urges conciliation of foreigners, 168; Protocol negotiations, 199, 280 n14; Manchurian policy, 208ff; effort to reform missionaries, 214; and Chinese Open Door, 217–218

Chang Ju-mei, 144

Chang Ping-lin, 10

Chang Yin-huan, 243 n18; and Barker concession, 38–40; and Sino-American Bank scheme, 41, 48

Chicago Record, 53

China, 8–12; non-alienation agreements, 75; reform movement of *1898,* 106–107, 263 n41; failure of reform movement, 108–109; Manchurian negotiations, 207–212; renewal of commercial treaty, 214

China Gazette, 87

China market, 54, 248 n71, 282 n36

Ch'ing, Prince (I-k'uang), 199

Choate, Joseph, 132, 155, 164–165

Christian Advocate, 78

Ch'un, Prince (I-huan), 35

Cleveland, Grover, 15, 38

Coleman, Bishop Leighton, 69

Conant, Charles, 226–227

Concord Monitor, 53

Conger, Edwin, 98; on concessions, 98–99; on U.S. base, 99–100, 204, 261 n21; on reform movement, 107; efforts on behalf of American China Development Co., 111; on status leased areas, 137–138; early protest against Boxers, 138; and Boxer rebellion, 149; first message to U.S. during siege, 166–167; post-siege, 179–180; on troop withdrawal, 185; negotiates joint note, 203; and Tientsin concession, 216; on commercial treaty revision, 283 n43

Conger, Sarah, 160, 173

Contemporary Review, 53

Cramp, Charles, 71

Dalny (Talienwan, Darien), 132, 133. *See also* Russia

Davis, Senator Cushman K., 26; on U.S. interests in China, 109; on annexation of Philippines, 113; on U.S. relief expedition, 153–154

Dawes, Charles, 169

Day, William, 89, 90, 93, 95

Delcassé, Théophile, 164

Denby, Charles, 20–21, 238 n20; and spy case, 25, 26; and anti-Manchu plot, 28–29; and Treaty of Shimonoseki, 31–33, 241 n59, n60, 242 n72; and Wilson, 35; and Barker, 43, 46; seeks instructions post Sino-Japanese war, 57; and Russia, 58; and Peking-Hankow concession, 65–66; and anti-missionary riots, 79ff; response to German seizure of Kiaochow, 87, 88–89; on role of U.S. consuls, 100; as publicist, 110

Denby, Charles, Jr., 24–26; business dealings, 58, 248 n8

Department of the Navy, 104, 204ff; instructs Kempff, 152

Dewey, Admiral George, 91; and base in China, 205, 206, 280 n23

De Young, John, 68

Disston, Hamilton, 39

Dolph, Senator, 57

Dunne, Finley Peter, 167

Evans, R. D., 205

Fairbank, John K., 115–116

Ferguson, J. C., 272 n29

Flagler, Henry M., 61

Fling, H. D., 39

Foord, John, 120, 122

Foster, John W., 28, 29; and Treaty of Shimonoseki, 32; and Wilson, 35, 56–57, 69; and U.S. loan, 240 n56; and Bash-Brice group, 249 n12

Fowler, John W., 103–104, 262 n43

France, 33, 54–55; and scramble for concessions, 74, 254 n1; non-alienation agreement, 75; and Cheng-tu anti-missionary riot, 80–81; and Boxer settlement, 201–202

Frazar, Everett, 118

Garland, James, 63

Germany, 20; and Dreibund intervention, 33; seizure of Kiaochow, 74, 94, 254 n2, 257 n41; post-Boxer policy, 175, 187; Anglo-German agreement, 198, 279 n3; in Protocol negotiations, 200, 201

Goodnow, J. F., 111; during Boxer rebellion, 165, 272 n49, 273 n56; and Amoy, 178

Gorelik, C. B., 252 n33, 268 n43

Gotō Shimpei, 175, 275 n10, 276 n16

Gould, Jay, 38

Gracey, J. T., 189

Grand Council, 47

Gray, Senator George, 26

Great Britain, 19–20, 239 n23; demands concession, 55, 254 n3; takes Wei-hai-wei, 74; non-alienation agreement, 75; and Cheng-tu anti-missionary riot, 79–81; and German railroad policy, 89–90, 258 n47; seeks American cooperation against "spheres of influence," 93; supports Italian concession demand, 108; and opening of China, 115; modifies concept of Open Door, 116–117; Anglo-Russian agreement, 118; response to first Open Door note, 131–132, 266 n37; response to July 3 note, 163; lands troops in Shanghai, 176, 272 n49, 281 n25; and Amoy, 177–178; response to August 28 note, 187; Anglo-German agreement, 198, 279 n3; general Protocol policy, 198, 201; commercial treaty revision, 214, 283 n43; on issue of punishments, 279 n11; and Chusan Islands, 281 n23

Gresham, Walter Q., 15; mediation during Sino-Japanese war, 22; and spy case, 23–26; and Treaty of Shimonoseki, 30–31, 32

Griswold, A. W., 260 n5

Hackett, Frank, Asst. Secretary of Navy, 152

Hanna, Mark, 60

Hart, Sir Robert, 54, 115, 116, 194

Hartford, Mabel C., 82

Hartford Times, 169

Hay, John, 7, 93; on Amoy and the "ideal" China policy, 102; on base in China, 102, 204–205; on acquisition territory in China, 105–106; on American China Development Co., 110, 283 n45; and first Open Door note, 123ff; on negotiating with the Russians, 134–135; and early Boxer policy, 149–150; and Russia, 155, 207, 215; desire for Anglo-American alliance, 155–156, 157; policy toward south and central viceroys, 160, 165, 272 n49; and murder of von Ketteler, 161; and July 3 note, 162ff; accepts authenticity Conger message, 167; assesses his Boxer diplomacy, 170; on troop withdrawal, 184–186; on Anglo-German agreement, 198–199; on joint note negotiations, 201, 202; protests Sino-Russian negotiations on Manchuria, 209–210, 281 n30, n33; uses gunboat in Manchuria, 212; on Protocol negotiations, 213–214; on commercial treaty revision, 214, 283 n43, n44; on Tientsin concessions, 284 n48

Heard, Augustine, 21

Hewitt, Abram S., 118

Higham, John, 4

Hilkoff, Prince, 61, 70

Hippisley, Alfred E., 116; correspondence with Rockhill, 123ff; on Russian danger, 125; on integrity of China, 126–127, 130; on domestic uses of Open Door, 265 n23; on China's debt to the U.S., 269 n6

Hitchcock, Ethan Allen, 70–72, 260 n6

Hixson, W. C., 82

Holstrem, Vladimir, 133

Hoover, Herbert, 150

Independent, 96; on Anglo-Russian rivalry, 98; on reform movement, 107; on Beresford, 119; on first Open Door note, 135–136; on mission societies, 142; on missionaries and expansion, 143; on U.S. Boxer policy, 155; on siege, 169

Italy, 108

Itō Hirobumi, 29, 276 n16

I-tsung, 45

Jackson, Henry, 198
Japan, 33; non-alienation agreement, 75;
    Amoy policy, 175–179, 275 n10, 276
    n16, 281 n25; protests Sino-Russian
    negotiations on Manchuria, 207, 208,
    211. *See also* Sino-Japanese war
Jardine, Matheson and Company, 45,
    51
Jernigan, Thomas R., 24, 240 n39; and
    missionaries, 255 n18
Johnson, Alba, 68
Johnson, Anson Burlingame, 100–101;
    on Amoy and the Philippines, 101,
    262 n26; conflict with Japan, 101–
    102; buys property for U.S. mer-
    chants, 102; and Japanese threat dur-
    ing Boxer rebellion, 175–179, 275
    n13
Johnson, Carl, 205–206
Jones, A. C., 83, 84
*Journal of the American Asiatic Asso-
    ciation,* 196–197
Journal of Commerce, 53; on American
    Asiatic Association, 109; on Open
    Door in Philippines, 117–118; re-
    sponse to first Open Door note, 135;
    on southern interests and China mar-
    ket, 260 n8
Jung-lu, 107, 166, 173

Kang-i, 147
K'ang Yu-wei, 10, 106
Katsura Tarō, 176, 178, 275 n10
Kempff, Rear-Admiral Louis, 150–152;
    desires more troops, 153; dangers of
    U.S. presence in China, 157
Kent, Percy H., 112
Keswick, James, 51
Ketteler, Baron von, murder of, 161;
    effects of death on policy, 161ff, 273
    n58
Kiaochow, 133. *See also* Germany
Kinder, C. W., 37
Kodama Gentarō, 175, 176, 178, 275
    n10
Korea, 17–19. *See also* Sino-Japanese
    war
Kosaka Masataka, 217
Kowloon extension, 132
kuan-tu shang-pan (official supervision,
    merchant operation), 36, 44
Kuang-hsu Emperor, 106, 168
Kuhn, Loeb and Company, 60

Kung, Prince (I-hsin), 65, 251 n29
Kurino Shinichiro, 21, 29
Kuropatkin, General Aleksei N., 276
    n20

Lamsdorff, Nicholas, 73, 209, 211, 276
    n20
Langer, William, 117, 198, 254 n1
Leech, Margaret, 273 n61
Li Hung-chang, 17; position in China,
    28; and Treaty of Shimonoseki, 32–
    33; and Wilson, 35; early railroad
    efforts, 35–38; special interest in U.S.,
    41–42, 51; Sino-American Bank
    scheme, 41–47; continued efforts with
    Barker, 49ff, 62–64; *1896* visit to
    U.S., 53; and Boxers, 158–159; and
    post-Boxer negotiations, 175, 199,
    203, 280 n14; indemnification for
    Christians, 192; and Manchurian pol-
    icy, 208ff
Li Kuo-ch'i, 37, 44
Liang Ch'i-ch'ao, 10, 11, 106
Lindbeck, John, 155
Literary Digest, 53; on expansionism,
    95–96; on Anglo-Russian rivalry, 97;
    survey on troop withdrawal, 174, 277
    n32
Liu Hsiang-hsing, 84
Liu K'un-yi, 158; during Boxer rebel-
    lion, 159, 161, 162, 272 n49; and
    Protocol negotiations, 199; on em-
    press dowager, 200; on Manchurian
    policy, 208ff
Liu Ping-chang, 79, 80, 81, 85
Lodge, Henry Cabot, 7, 68; on expan-
    sionism, 97; anti-Russia, 271 n43
Long, Secretary of Navy John D., 105,
    153, 204

Ma Chien-chang, 40, 41, 44, 47, 48, 49,
    50, 62–63
Ma Chien-chung, 40, 62
MacArthur, General Arthur, 152
MacDonald, Sir Claude, 89, 90
MacDonald, William, 96
McCook, General A. W., 61
McCook, John J., 54; and Wilson, 60;
    visit to Russia, 61; ministerial scheme,
    68–69
McKinley, William, 69; growing anti-
    Russian policy, 72–73; interest in
    concessions, 90; response to British

appeal for cooperation, 93–95; message to Congress on China situation, 94; trade ambitions, 112–114; external limits on Boxer policy, 157; troop requirements in China, 165; instructions to Chaffee, 166; accepts Conger message as genuine, 167, 273 n61; responds to Kuang-hsu message, 168–169; business community and his Boxer policy, 169; aspects of his Boxer diplomacy, 170–171; rejects Chinese effort to negotiate prior to relief, 172–173; policy toward Li Hung-chang, 175; response to Russian move for withdrawal, 180–182; on troop withdrawal, 183, 185; influences on Boxer settlement, 196–197; on punishment issue, 200–202; efforts to switch negotiation site, 203; on Open Door in Philippines, 264 n5; press reaction to troop withdrawal, 277 n32

Memphis Commercial Appeal, 277 n32
Miller, Henry, 212
Minneapolis Tribune, 78
Missionaries, 76–77; finances, 77, 254 n7; press reaction to anti-missionary riots, 78; anti-missionary riots (Cheng-tu), 78–81, 82, 256 n24, (Ku-t'ien) 82, 84, 86, 257 n35, (Kiangyin), 83–84, 256 n33; and scramble for concessions, 87; change in U.S. policy toward, 91; on reform movement of *1898,* 108, 263 n44; Rockhill's policy toward, 139–140; financial improvement, 142–143; on expansion, 142–143, 257 n38; and U.S. Boxer policy, 155, 188ff; attitude toward Conger, 188; anti-Li Hung-chang, 188–189; public response to missionaries, post Boxer, 189; policy of home boards, 189–190, 196; on indemnities, 192–193; reject missionary reform, 213–214; opposition to Rockhill, 275 n2; on German behavior during Boxer rebellion, 277 n38; on U.S. troop behavior, 278 n46

Missionary Review of the World, 22; on mission finances, 77; on scramble for concessions, 87; on reform movement of *1898,* 108; on causes of Boxer rebellion, 189

Mitkiewicz, Count Eugène Stanislaw Kostka de, 38ff, 64
Montgomery, Colonel Benjamin F., 169
Morgan, J. P., 58, 61
Morgan, Senator John T., 184
Morrow, T. G., 45
Mortan, Levi P., 118
Muraviev, Count Mikhail N., 132–134, 137, 260 n6, 267 n41
Mutsu Munemitsu, 29

Newell, J. W., 82
New Haven Register, 277 n32
New Orleans Picayune, 137, 277 n32
New York Evening Post, 135, 186, 277 n32
New York Herald, 247 n62
New York Press, 23, 136, 277 n32
New York Sun, 25–26, 53, 191, 193
New York Times, 97–98, 196
New York Tribune, 21, 27, 53, 153, 271 n38
Nieh Shih-ch'eng, 150
North China Daily News, 43
North China Herald, 42–43, 45
Novoe Vremya, 72–73

Olney, Richard, 58, 64; response to anti-missionary riots, 81, 82; change in missionary policy, 86, 91–92; and railroads, 252 n36
Open Door, 115; threatened by spheres of influence, 116; Reid on, 109–110, 118; and Philippines, 117–118, 137, 264 n5; Beresford on, 118–119, 122–123; Barrett on, 120–121, 122; drafting of, 123ff; basic Hippisley memo on, 126; Rockhill memo on, 128–130; phrasing of note to England, 131; Russian acceptance, 132–135, 267 n40, n41, 268 n45; U.S. press reaction to, 135–136; expanding the meaning of, 140–141; July 3 note, 162ff; attempt to include in joint note, 202; China's use of, 210, 217–218; compared to Monroe Doctrine, 217; terms used in, 259 n4; and business interests, 265, n12, n16, n19; domestic use of, 265 n23
Outlook, 27

Paine, Albert B., 278, n49
Paine, William, 38ff

Pangborn, Major J. G., 60–61, 70
Pauncefote, Sir Julian, 93, 95
Peirce, Herbert, 61, 71, 72
Pennsylvania Railroad Company, 54, 61
Pennsylvania Steel Company, 71–72
Perkins, George, 169
Pethick, William, 21; and anti-Manchu plot, 27; and Treaty of Shimonoseki, 32; and Wilson, 35, 52; aid to Bash-Brice group, 59; on railroads, 251 n29, 252 n33
Philadelphia Ledger, 174
Philadelphia North American, 26
Philadelphia Press, 135, 169
Philadelphia Times, 169
Philippines, 113; Open Door in, 117–118, 137, 264 n5; value of during Boxer rebellion, 152, 158; suppression of insurgency, 270 n28
Presbyterian Banner, 189
Porter, Rev. Henry, 188, 195–196
Porter, Horace, 113
Potter, Thomas, 39
Public Opinion, 154, 277 n32
Purdon, John, 48, 50

Railroads, 36, 50; Wilson and, 35; Li Hung-chang and, 35–38, 45; Chinese Railroad Company, 36; Chang Chih-tung and, 37; "Peking-Canton" line, 57; Peking-Hankow line, 65–68, 90, 98, 251 n32; Canton-Hankow line, 68, 90–91, 111–112, 215–216; Tientsin-Chinkiang line, 89, 90. *See also* American China Development Company, Sheng Hsuan-huai Yung Wing
Ralph, Julian, 25
Rankin, Mary B., 84
Reid, Rev. Gilbert, 109–110, 118
Reid, Whitelaw, 72, 118; on duty of U.S., 112; on relief expedition, 153–154; response to Conger's siege message, 167; on missionaries, 187
Remey, Rear-Admiral George C., 151, 152, 154, 175, 212
Review of Reviews (British), 21
Rice, Cecil Spring, 7
Riesman, David, 219
Rockhill, William W., 12; on Sino-Japanese war, 22; and Wilson, 68–69; missionary opposition to, 69, 275 n2;

missionary policy, 83, 84–85, 139–140; rejected as minister to China, 98; and Open Door, 123ff; plans campaign for Open Door, 127; on Barrett, 127; on Beresford, 128–129, 266 n31; on basic aim of Open Door, 129–130, 137, 140–141; on U.S. as balancer of powers, 130–131; on integrity of China, 131; new instructions to Conger, 138–139; underestimates anti-foreign feeling, 141–142; to China as special commissioner, 172; on necessity of backing south and central viceroys, 200; on joint note negotiations, 203; on Russia, 206–207; on Protocol negotiations, 213ff; on missionary reform, 214; on commercial treaty revision, 214, 283 n43; on Tientsin concession, 216–217; on China and Chinese, 227–228; on post-*1898* U.S. position, 228–229; on Russian acceptance of Open Door note, 268 n45; and Yuan Shih-k'ai, 269, n8
Roosevelt, Theodore, 7–9; on Brooks Adams, 8; on expansionism, 96–97; on Russia, 267 n42; on American China Development Company, 283 n45
Root, Elihu, 162, 172; on troop requirements in Philippines, 165; drafting of August 28, 1900, note, 181–182; defends the note, 183; on troop withdrawal, 184
Russell and Company, 45, 244 n41, 245 n43
Russia, 20; and Sino-Japanese war, 33, 55; as focus for U.S. concession hunters, 56, 57, 59, 61, 252 n33; Russo-Chinese treaty of *1896,* 65, 251 n30; Trans-Siberian Railroad policy, 70; pre-*1898* attitude to U.S., 70, 72–73; U.S. trade with, 71; and Dalny, 74, 94; rivalry with Great Britain, 117; czar's ukase, 125–126, 259 n4; response to Open Door note, 132–133, 267 n40; desire for U.S. friendship, 133; fear Anglo-American alliance, 134, 267 n41; independent action during Boxer rebellion, 176; troop withdrawal, 180, 183, 185; Anglo-German alliance, 198; on punishments issue, 201; policy in Manchuria post Boxer,

207ff, 281 n25, 282 n36; and Tientsin concession, 216; on the Philippines, 261 n12; effort to retain China's good will, 276 n20; and conflict with U.S., 281 n24, 282 n36

St. Petersburg Exchange Gazette, 72
St. Petersburg Journal, 72
Saigo Tsugumichi, 276 n16
Salisbury, Marquis of, 131, 155, 259 n4, 279 n3
Schiff, Jacob, 60
Schurman, J. G., 125
Semmel, Bernard, 285 n13
Seymour, Admiral Edward H., 146, 148, 150, 272 n49
Sharretts, General, 283 n43
Sheffield, Rev. D. Z., 188, 195
Sheng Hsuan-huai, 41; railroad neutralization efforts, 65, 251 n29; signs Peking-Hankow with Belgian group, 68, 251 n32; and Boxers, 159, 160; and Protocol negotiations, 200; on negotiations with Russia, 209
Sherman, John, 66, 251 n32; and missionaries, 86; on scramble for concessions, 88, 94, 258 n43; requests clarification from Russians, 260 n6
Shipley, Samuel, R., 39
Sino-Japanese war, 14, 19; Dreibund intervention and treaty, 33, 241 n65; effect of on China, 106; U.S. role in peace negotiations, 242 n75. *See also* Denby, Korea, Japan
Smith, Rev. Arthur, 190, 196
Smith, Charles Emory, 169
Smith, Rev. Judson, 190; inquires into post Boxer missionary behavior, 191, 193; responds to Twain's criticism, 194; cautions Ament, 195
Smith, Polly Condit, 173
Social Darwinism, 3, 5; in China, 10, 11
Spanish-American war, 4; influence on U.S. China policy, 94, 103; effect on U.S. world position, 113
Springfield Republican, 136
Stern, Simon, 40, 41
Stevens, D. W., 28, 29

T'an Ssu-t'ung, 106
Tewksbury, Rev. E. G., 191–193
Thomas, Frank, 61

Tientsin, 148; American concession in, 216–227, 284 n48
Tientsin Convention of *1885,* 17
Times (London), 72
Ting Ju-ch'ang, 19
Tower, Charlemagne, 73, 134
Tratman, J. W., 79
Tributary system, 14, 16, 17
Tseng Ch'i, 207
Tsungli yamen (office for general management), 31; opposition to Barker, 46–47; and missionaries, 85–86; new spirit of resistance, 108; support for Sheng Hsuan-huai, 111–112; effort to negotiate truce during Boxer rebellion, 173; suffers reformation, 213, 214
Tuan, Prince (Tsai-i), 146
Tung Fu-hsiang, 203
Twain, Mark, 193–195, 278 n49
Tz'u-hsi, empress dowager, 107; and Boxers, 144–145, 146–147, 148, 158; flees Peking, 174; accepts joint note, 280 n14

Ukhtomskii, Prince Esper Egorovich, 133–134, 267 n41

Vegetarians (Ts'ai-hui), 84

Waldersee, Count Alfred von, 180, 187
Washburn, W. D., 61, 62, 249 n18
Washington Post, 78
Westinghouse Corporation, 71
Whitridge, F. W., 215–216
Williams, William A., 281 n24
Wilson, James H., 27, 29–30; early railroad efforts, 35; interest in "Peking-Canton" line, 57; effort to coordinate with Russians, 59; outlines proposed syndicate, 60; attacks Bash-Brice, 61–62, 249 n18; ministerial scheme, 68–69
Wise, Capt. Frederick, 151–152. *See also* Kempff
Witte, Count Sergei, 133, 180, 276 n20
Wo Jen, 11
Woodford, General, 118
Wu T'ing-fang, 106; and Boxers, 159, 160, 162, 166; Finley Peter Dunne parody of, 167; transmits Conger's message, 168; and punishment issue,

200; challenges American China Development Company, 215

Yamamoto Gombei, 175–176
Yang Ju (minister to U.S.), 20, 80–81; (minister to Russia, Austria and Holland) 207, 208–211
Yen Fu, 10
Young, John Russell, 17, 46, 47–48

Yu-hsien, 144, 145
Yu Lien-yuan, 160
Yuan Shih-k'ai, 17; and defeat reform movement of *1898*, 106–107; and Boxers, 144; indemnification of Christians, 192; Russian negotiations, 209; and Rockhill, 269 n8
Yung Wing, 89–90, 246 n55. *See also* Railroads, Tientsin-Chinkiang line

HARVARD EAST ASIAN SERIES

1. *China's Early Industrialization: Sheng Hsuan-huai (1844–1916) and Mandarin Enterprise.* By Albert Feuerwerker.
2. *Intellectual Trends in the Ch'ing Period.* By Liang Ch'i-ch'ao. Translated by Immanuel C. Y. Hsü.
3. *Reform in Sung China: Wang An-shih (1021–1086) and His New Policies.* By James T. C. Liu.
4. *Studies on the Population of China, 1368–1953.* By Ping-ti Ho.
5. *China's Entrance into the Family of Nations: The Diplomatic Phase, 1858–1880.* By Immanuel C. Y. Hsü.
6. *The May Fourth Movement: Intellectual Revolution in Modern China.* By Chow Tse-tsung.
7. *Ch'ing Administrative Terms: A Translation of the Terminology of the Six Boards with Explanatory Notes.* Translated and edited by E-tu Zen Sun.
8. *Anglo-American Steamship Rivalry in China, 1862–1876.* By Kwang-Ching Liu.
9. *Local Government in China under the Ch'ing.* By T'ung-tsu Ch'ü.
10. *Communist China, 1955–1959: Policy Documents with Analysis.* With a foreword by Robert R. Bowie and John K. Fairbank. (Prepared at Harvard University under the joint auspices of the Center for International Affairs and the East Asian Research Center.)
11. *China and Christianity: The Missionary Movement and the Growth of Chinese Antiforeignism, 1860–1870.* By Paul A. Cohen.
12. *China and the Helping Hand, 1937–1945.* By Arthur N. Young.
13. *Research Guide to the May Fourth Movement: Intellectual Revolution in Modern China, 1915–1924.* By Chow Tse-tsung.
14. *The United States and the Far Eastern Crises of 1933–1938: From the Manchurian Incident through the Initial Stage of the Undeclared Sino-Japanese War.* By Dorothy Borg.
15. *China and the West, 1858–1861: The Origins of the Tsungli Yamen.* By Masataka Banno.
16. *In Search of Wealth and Power: Yen Fu and the West.* By Benjamin Schwartz.
17. *The Origins of Entrepreneurship in Meiji Japan.* By Johannes Hirschmeier, S.V.D.
18. *Commissioner Lin and the Opium War.* By Hsin-pao Chang.
19. *Money and Monetary Policy in China, 1845–1895.* By Frank H. H. King.
20. *China's Wartime Finance and Inflation, 1937–1945.* By Arthur N. Young.
21. *Foreign Investment and Economic Development in China, 1840–1937.* By Chi-ming Hou.
22. *After Imperialism: The Search for a New Order in the Far East, 1921–1931.* By Akira Iriye.
23. *Foundations of Constitutional Government in Modern Japan, 1868–1900.* By George Ikita.
24. *Political Thought in Early Meiji Japan, 1868–1889.* By Joseph Pittau, S.J.
25. *China's Struggle for Naval Development, 1839–1895.* By John L. Rawlinson.
26. *The Practice of Buddhism in China, 1900–1950.* By Holmes Welch.
27. *Li Ta-chao and the Origins of Chinese Marxism.* By Maurice Meisner.
28. *Pa Chin and His Writings: Chinese Youth Between the Two Revolutions.* By Olga Lang.
29. *Literary Dissent in Communist China.* By Merle Goldman.
30. *Politics in the Tokugawa Bakufu, 1600–1843.* By Conrad Totman.
31. *Hara Kei in the Politics of Compromise, 1905–1915.* By Tetsuo Najita.
32. *The Chinese World Order: Traditional China's Foreign Relations.* Edited by John K. Fairbank.
33. *The Buddhist Revival in China.* By Holmes Welch.
34. *Traditional Medicine in Modern China: Science, Nationalism, and the Tensions of Cultural Change.* By Ralph C. Croizier.
35. *Party Rivalry and Political Change in Taishō Japan.* By Peter Duus.
36. *The Rhetoric of Empire: American China Policy, 1895–1901.* By Marilyn B. Young.